Oracle JDeveloper 11gR2 Cookbook

Over 85 simple but incredibly effective recipes for using
Oracle JDeveloper 11gR2 to build ADF applications

Nick Haralabidis

PACKT PUBLISHING

BIRMINGHAM - MUMBAI

Oracle JDeveloper 11gR2 Cookbook

First published: January 2012

Production Reference: 1170112

Published by Packt Publishing Ltd.
Livery Place
35 Livery Street
Birmingham B3 2PB, UK.

ISBN 978-1-84968-476-7

www.packtpub.com

Cover Image by Artie Ng (artherng@yahoo.com.au)

Credits

Author
Nick Haralabidis

Reviewers
Edwin Biemond
Spyros Doulgeridis
Frank Nimphius

Acquisition Editor
Stephanie Moss

Lead Technical Editor
Meeta Rajani

Technical Editors
Sonali Tharwani
Vishal D'souza

Copy Editor
Laxmi Subramanian

Project Coordinator
Leena Purkait

Proofreader
Dan McMahon

Indexers
Hemangini Bari
Monica Ajmera Mehta
Tejal Daruwale

Production Coordinator
Arvindkumar Gupta

Cover Work
Arvindkumar Gupta

Foreword

Oracle has a long and successful history of building enterprise application development tools, including some that have outlived their competition. As a former Oracle Forms Product Manager and current Oracle JDeveloper and Oracle Application Development Framework (ADF) Product Manager, this part of the Oracle history has been mine for the last 15 years, and I'm very grateful that there's currently no end in sight!

Building enterprise applications based on Java EE standards is a well-accepted and understood concept for building Rich Internet Applications (RIA) and service-oriented user interfaces. While Java language skills are standard knowledge for college graduates, broader topics, such as service-enablement, persistence, application security, customization, portalization, and so on are not always so well understood. Adding to this, the "framework-of-the-day" problem—in which framework solutions quickly wax and wane in popularity—makes it difficult for enterprises to adopt software. What most enterprise businesses require is the benefit of standards, but with an end-to-end framework that provides a stable and consistent interface, which can abstract away future technology shifts.

Proven by Oracle Fusion Applications and customer success, Oracle ADF fulfills that need: a rapid application development environment that reduces the skills required for building modern rich enterprise applications to a single learning curve.

Technically, Oracle ADF is an end-to-end Java EE framework for building rich enterprise web and mobile applications based on Java EE services and SOA. Oracle ADF integrates existing Java frameworks into a single architecture and a fully integrated declarative development environment that shields developers from low-level API programming.

Besides being used by Oracle Fusion Applications and Oracle customers, Oracle ADF is at the heart of Oracle Middleware and is the technology of choice for building Fusion Middleware (FMW) products, such as Enterprise Manager, WebCenter, UCM, BPM, BI, and so on, showing Oracle's commitment to ADF.

Technology alone, however, is no guarantee for success. Community acceptance and contribution is also an important backbone and measurement of software frameworks and products, including Oracle ADF.

Oracle ADF is supported by a very active and growing community of bloggers, forum posters, and speakers, as well as book and article authors. The *Oracle JDeveloper 11gR2 Cookbook* you hold in your hands is another example of the ongoing contribution from the ADF community by author Nick Haralabidis.

The book is a practical guide to learning Oracle ADF, providing code solutions, and technical explanations to common Oracle ADF questions and developer challenges. Being one of the technical reviewers for this book and having written other titles as an author myself, I appreciate the time, effort, and dedication Nick Haralabidis has put into writing this book, as well as the Oracle ADF expertise and practices he shares with you, the reader. This book is not a beginner's guide, but a useful reference for all developers starting enterprise application development with Oracle ADF.

Frank Nimphius
Senior Principal Product Manager, Oracle Application Development Tools

About the Author

Nick Haralabidis has over 20 years experience in the Information Technology industry and a multifaceted career in positions such as Senior IT Consultant, Senior Software Engineer, and Project Manager for a number of U.S. and Greek corporations (Compuware, Chemical Abstracts Service, NewsBank, CheckFree, Intrasoft International, Unisystems, MedNet International, and others). His many years of experience have exposed him to a wide range of technologies, such as Java, J2EE, C++, C, Tuxedo, and a number of other database technologies.

For the last four years, Nick is actively involved in large implementations of next generation enterprise applications utilizing Oracle's JDeveloper, Application Development Framework (ADF), and SOA technologies.

He holds a B.S. in Computer Engineering and a M.S. in Computer Science from the University of Bridgeport.

When he is not pursuing ADF professionally, he writes on his blogs *JDeveloper Frequently Asked Questions* (http://jdeveloperfaq.blogspot.com) and *ADF Code Bits* (http://adfcodebits.blogspot.com). He is active at the *Oracle Technology Network (OTN) JDeveloper and ADF* forum where he both learns and helps.

To Aphrodite, Konstantina and Margaritta, my true inspirations.

To the Packt team and especially to Stephanie Moss for her trust, encouragement, and direction.

To the book reviewers, Frank Nimphius, Edwin Biemond, and Spyros Doulgeridis for their time, expertise, and invaluable insight.

About the Reviewers

Edwin Biemond is an Oracle ACE and Solution Architect at Amis, specializing in messaging with Oracle SOA Suite and Oracle Service Bus. He is an expert in ADF development, WebLogic Administration, high availability, and security. His Oracle career began in 1997, where he was developing an ERP, CRM system with Oracle tools. Since 2001, Edwin has changed his focus to integration, security, and Java development. Edwin was awarded with Java Developer of the year 2009 by Oracle Magazine, won the EMEA Oracle Partner Community Award in 2010, and contributed some content to the Oracle SOA Handbook of Luces Jellema. He is an international speaker at Oracle OpenWorld & ODTUG and has a popular blog called Java/ Oracle SOA blog at `http://biemond.blogspot.com`.

Spyros Doulgeridis holds two M.Sc. degrees, one in Telecommunication from Brunel University in the U.K. and one in Software Engineering from N.T.U.A. in Greece. With proven experience using major Java frameworks in JEE applications, he has been working with Oracle technologies, and especially ADF 11g, since 2008 in a major Form to ADF migration project—one of Oracle's Success Stories. During this project, he had many roles including ADF developer, designer of Forms to ADF migration, ADF/Java reviewer, and was responsible for the application's build process and deployment on Weblogic Server. He likes to share his experiences by blogging on `adfhowto.blogspot.com`.

I would like to thank Packt Publishing and especially Mrs. Stephanie Moss for giving me the opportunity to work on this book. Also, I would like to thank the author for this interesting journey into Oracle ADF through his helpful and practical recipes. Finally and above all, I would like to thank all of those close to me, who missed me while working on this book.

Frank Nimphius is a Senior Principal Product Manager in the Oracle Application Development Tools group at Oracle Corporation, where he specializes in Oracle JDeveloper and the Oracle Application Development Framework (ADF).

As a speaker, Frank represents the Oracle ADF and Oracle JDeveloper development team at user conferences world-wide. Frank owns the ADF Code Corner website (`http://www.oracle.com/technetwork/developer-tools/adf/learnmore/index-101235.html`), and the "OTN Forum Harvest" blog (`http://blogs.oracle.com/jdevotnharvest/`).

As an author, Frank frequently writes for Oracle Magazine and co-authored the "Oracle Fusion Developer Guide" book published in 2009 by McGraw Hill.

www.PacktPub.com

Support files, eBooks, discount offers and more

You might want to visit www.PacktPub.com for support files and downloads related to your book.

Did you know that Packt offers eBook versions of every book published, with PDF and ePub files available? You can upgrade to the eBook version at www.PacktPub.com and as a print book customer, you are entitled to a discount on the eBook copy. Get in touch with us at service@packtpub.com for more details.

At www.PacktPub.com, you can also read a collection of free technical articles, sign up for a range of free newsletters and receive exclusive discounts and offers on Packt books and eBooks.

http://PacktLib.PacktPub.com

Do you need instant solutions to your IT questions? PacktLib is Packt's online digital book library. Here, you can access, read and search across Packt's entire library of books.

Why Subscribe?

- ▶ Fully searchable across every book published by Packt
- ▶ Copy and paste, print and bookmark content
- ▶ On demand and accessible via web browser

Free Access for Packt account holders

If you have an account with Packt at www.PacktPub.com, you can use this to access PacktLib today and view nine entirely free books. Simply use your login credentials for immediate access.

Instant Updates on New Packt Books

Get notified! Find out when new books are published by following @PacktEnterprise on Twitter, or the *Packt Enterprise* Facebook page.

Table of Contents

Preface

This book contains a wealth of resources covering Oracle's JDeveloper 11g release and the Application Development Framework (ADF) and how these technologies can be used for the design, construction, testing, and optimizing of Fusion web applications. Being vast and complex technologies, an attempt has been made to cover a wide range of topics related specifically to Fusion web applications development with ADF, utilizing the complete ADF stack. These topics are presented in the form of recipes, many of them derived from the author's working experience covering real world use cases. The topics include, but are not limited to, foundational recipes related to laying out the project groundwork, recipes related to the ADF business components, recipes related to ViewController, recipes related to security, optimization and so on.

In the maze of information related to Fusion web applications development with ADF, it is the author's hope that aspiring ADF developers will find in this book some of the information they are looking for. So lift up your sleeves, put on your ADF chef's hat, pick up a recipe or two, and let's start cooking!

What this book covers

Chapter 1, Pre-requisites to Success: ADF Project Setup and Foundations, covers a number of recipes related to foundational concepts of Fusion web application development with ADF. By applying and expanding these recipes during the early architectural and design phases as needed, subsequent application development takes on a form, a structure, and the necessary uniformity. Many if not most of the recipes in the following chapters rely on these recipes.

Chapter 2, Dealing with Basics: Entity Objects, starts our journey into the world of ADF business components. First stop: entity objects. The recipes in this chapter deal with some of the most common framework functionality that is overridden in real world applications to provide customized business functionality.

Chapter 3, A Different Point of View: View Objects Techniques, covers a number of recipes related to view objects. This chapter explains how to control attribute updatability, how to set attribute default values, how to iterate view object row sets, and many more.

Chapter 4, Important Contributors: List of Values, Bind Variables, View Criteria, covers additional topics related to view objects. These topics include recipes related to list of values (LOVs), bind variables and view criteria. The reader will learn, among other things, how to setup multiple LOVs using a switcher attribute, cascading and static LOVs, and how to create view criteria programmatically.

Chapter 5, Putting them all together: Application Modules, includes a number of recipes related to application modules. You will learn, among others, how to create and use generic extension interfaces, expose a custom application module method as a web service and access a service interface from another application module. Additional recipes cover topics such as a passivation/activation framework, using shared application modules for static lookup data and custom database transactions.

Chapter 6, Go with the flow: Task Flows, delves into the world of ADF task flows. Among others, you will learn how to use an application module function as a method call to initialize a page, how to use a task flow initializer, how to retrieve the task flow definition programmatically and how to create a train.

Chapter 7, Face Value: ADF Faces, JSPX Pages and Components, includes recipes detailing the use of a variety of ADF Faces components, such as the query component, the popup window component, the tree component, the select many shuttle component, the carousel component, and others.

Chapter 8, Backing not Baking: Bean Recipes, introduces topics related to backing beans. A number of topics are covered including the use of custom table selection listeners, custom query and query operation listeners, session beans to preserve session-wide information, popup windows to handle long running tasks.

Chapter 9, Handling Security, Session Timeouts, Exceptions and Errors, covers topics related to handling security, session timeouts, exceptions and errors for an ADF Fusion web application. The recipes in this chapter will show the reader how to enable ADF security, how to use a custom login page, how to access the application's security information, how to detect and handle session timeouts, and how to use a custom error handler.

Chapter 10, Deploying ADF Applications, includes recipes related to the deployment of ADF Fusion web applications. These recipes include the configuration and use of the standalone WebLogic server, the deployment of applications on the standalone WebLogic server, the use of the ojdeploy tool and the use of Hudson as a continuous integration framework.

Chapter 11, Refactoring, Debugging, Profiling, Testing, deals with topics related to refactoring, debugging, profiling, and testing ADF Fusion web applications. The recipes in this chapter cover topics such as the synchronization of business components to changes in the database, refactoring of ADF components, configuring and using remote debugging, configuring logging in the WebLogic server, CPU profiling and the configuration, and usage of JUnit for unit testing.

Chapter 12, Optimizing, Fine-tuning and Monitoring, covers topics related to optimizing, fine-tuning, and monitoring ADF Fusion web applications. The recipes in this chapter demonstrate how to limit the rows fetched by view objects, how to limit large view object queries, how to use work managers for processing long-running tasks and how to monitor your application using the JRockit Mission Control.

Chapter 13, Miscellaneous Recipes, the additional content recipes cover topics related among others to using JasperReports, uploading images to the server, and handling and customizing database-related errors. This chapter is not present in the book but is available as a free download from the following link: `http://www.packtpub.com/sites/default/files/downloads/4767EN_Chapter 13_Miscellaneous Recipes.pdf`.

What you need for this book

The recipes in this book utilize the latest release of JDeveloper at the time of writing, namely JDeveloper 11*g* R2 11.1.2.1.0. This release of JDeveloper comes bundled with the necessary ADF libraries and a standalone installation of the WebLogic server. Ensure that the WebLogic server is installed as part of the JDeveloper installation.

In addition, you will need a database connection to Oracle's HR schema. This schema is provided along with the Oracle XE database.

A number of recipes cover topics that will require you to download and install the following additional software: Hudson continuous integration, JRockit Mission Control, Jasper Reports, and iReport.

Who this book is for

This book is targeted to intermediate or advanced developers, designers and architects already utilizing JDeveloper, the ADF framework, and Oracle's Fusion technologies. Developers utilizing the complete ADF stack for building ADF Fusion web applications will benefit most from the book. The book uses ADF business components as its model layer technology, ADF binding, ADF task flows and the ADF model for its controller layer technologies, and ADF Faces as its view layer technology.

The introductory concepts in the first chapter, along with the chapters related to handling exceptions, session timeouts, optimizing, and fine tuning may appeal more to application designers and architects.

Conventions

In this book, you will find a number of styles of text that distinguish between different kinds of information. Here are some examples of these styles, and an explanation of their meaning.

Code words in text are shown as follows: "In addition to the `session-timeout` configuration setting in `web.xml`, you can configure a session timeout warning interval by defining the context parameter"

A block of code is set as follows:

```
public class SessionTimeoutFilter implements Filter {
  private FilterConfig filterConfig = null;
  public SessionTimeoutFilter() {
  super();
}
```

When we wish to draw your attention to a particular part of a code block, the relevant lines or items are set in bold:

```
new ExportEmployeesWork(getEmployees().createRowSetIterator(null))
```

Any command-line input or output is written as follows:

```
$ chmod u+x ./jdevstudio11121install.bin

$ ./jdevstudio11121install.bin
```

New terms and **important words** are shown in bold. Words that you see on the screen, in menus or dialog boxes for example, appear in the text like this: "Using the **Property Inspector** change the **URL Invoke** property to **url-invoke-allowed**."

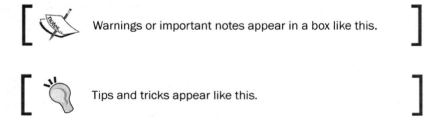

Warnings or important notes appear in a box like this.

Tips and tricks appear like this.

Reader feedback

Feedback from our readers is always welcome. Let us know what you think about this book—what you liked or may have disliked. Reader feedback is important for us to develop titles that you really get the most out of.

To send us general feedback, simply send an e-mail to `feedback@packtpub.com`, and mention the book title through the subject of your message.

If there is a topic that you have expertise in and you are interested in either writing or contributing to a book, see our author guide on www.packtpub.com/authors.

Customer support

Now that you are the proud owner of a Packt book, we have a number of things to help you to get the most from your purchase.

Downloading the example code

You can download the example code files for all Packt books you have purchased from your account at http://www.packtpub.com. If you purchased this book elsewhere, you can visit http://www.packtpub.com/support and register to have the files e-mailed directly to you.

Errata

Although we have taken every care to ensure the accuracy of our content, mistakes do happen. If you find a mistake in one of our books—maybe a mistake in the text or the code— we would be grateful if you would report this to us. By doing so, you can save other readers from frustration and help us improve subsequent versions of this book. If you find any errata, please report them by visiting http://www.packtpub.com/support, selecting your book, clicking on the **errata submission form** link, and entering the details of your errata. Once your errata are verified, your submission will be accepted and the errata will be uploaded to our website, or added to any list of existing errata, under the Errata section of that title.

Piracy

Piracy of copyright material on the Internet is an ongoing problem across all media. At Packt, we take the protection of our copyright and licenses very seriously. If you come across any illegal copies of our works, in any form, on the Internet, please provide us with the location address or website name immediately so that we can pursue a remedy.

Please contact us at copyright@packtpub.com with a link to the suspected pirated material.

We appreciate your help in protecting our authors, and our ability to bring you valuable content.

Questions

You can contact us at questions@packtpub.com if you are having a problem with any aspect of the book, and we will do our best to address it.

1
Prerequisites to Success: ADF Project Setup and Foundations

In this chapter, we will cover:

- ▸ Installation of JDeveloper on Linux
- ▸ Breaking up the application in multiple workspaces
- ▸ Setting up BC base classes
- ▸ Setting up logging
- ▸ Using a custom exception class
- ▸ Using ADFUtils/JSFUtils
- ▸ Using page templates
- ▸ Using a generic backing bean actions framework

Introduction

JDeveloper and **ADF (Application Development Framework)** are amazing technologies. What makes them even more incredible is their sheer complexity and the amount of knowledge and effort that lies covered underneath the declarative, almost magical frontend. What amazes me is that once you scratch the surface, you never stop realizing how much you really don't know. Given this complexity, it becomes obvious that certain development guidelines and practices must be established and followed early in the architectural and design phases of an ADF project.

This chapter presents a number of recipes that are geared towards establishing some of these development practices. In particular, you will see content that serves as a starting point in making your own application modular when using the underlying technologies. You will also learn the importance of extending the Business Components framework (ADF-BC) base classes early in the development cycle. We will talk about the importance of laying out other application foundational components, such as logging and exceptions, again early in the development process, and continue with addressing reusability and consistency at the **ViewController** layer.

The chapter starts with a recipe about installing and configuring JDeveloper on Linux. So, let's get started and don't forget, have fun as you go along. If you get in trouble at any point, take a look at the accompanying source code and feel free to contact me anytime at nharalabidis@gmail.com.

Installation of JDeveloper on Linux

Installation of JDeveloper is, in general, a straightforward task. So, "why have a recipe for this?" you might ask. Did you notice the title? It says "on Linux". You will be amazed at the number of questions asked about this topic on a regular basis on the *JDeveloper and ADF OTN Forum*. Besides, in this recipe, we will also talk about configuration options and the usage of 64-bit JDK along with JDeveloper.

Getting ready

You will need a Linux installation of JDeveloper to use this recipe. For the 64-bit configuration, you will need a 64-bit Linux distribution and a 64-bit version of the Java SDK. We will install the latest version of JDeveloper, which is version 11.1.2.1.0 at the time of this writing.

How to do it...

1. Download JDeveloper from the Oracle JDeveloper Software download page: `http://www.oracle.com/technetwork/developer-tools/jdev/downloads/index.html`.

2. Accept the license agreement, select **Linux Install**, and click on **Download File** to begin with the download.

3. Once the file is downloaded, open a console window and start the installation, by typing the following commands:

   ```
   $ chmod u+x ./jdevstudio11121install.bin
   $ ./jdevstudio11121install.bin
   ```

4. On the **Choose Middleware Home Directory** page, select **Create a new Middleware Home** and enter the Middleware home directory.

5. On the **Choose Install Type** page, select **Complete** to ensure that JDeveloper, ADF and WebLogic Server are installed.

6. Once you confirm your selections, proceed with the installation.

7. Upon a successful installation, you will see the **Installation Complete** page. Uncheck the **Run Quickstart** checkbox and click **Done**.

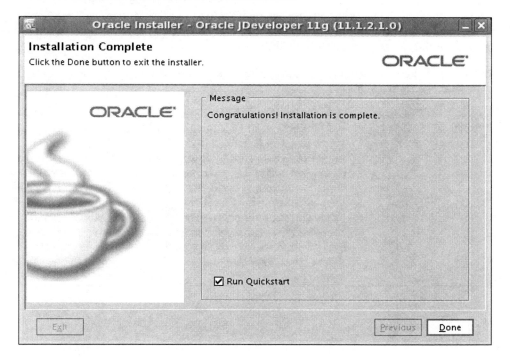

8. To start JDeveloper, go to the `/jdeveloper/jdev/bin` directory under the Middleware home directory you specified during the installation and type the following:

    `$ ./jdev`

9. To make things easier, create an application launcher on your Linux desktop for the specific path indicated in the previous step.

How it works...

As noted earlier, installing JDeveloper on Linux is a straightforward task. You simply have to download the binary executable archive and run it. Ensure that you give execute permissions to the installation archive file and run it as noted. If you are having trouble seeing the **Welcome** page in graphical mode, ensure that the `$DISPLAY` environment variable is set correctly. The important thing to know here is the name of the file to execute in order to start JDeveloper. As mentioned, it is called `jdev` and it is located in the `/jdeveloper/jdev/bin` directory under the Middleware home directory.

There's more...

Now that you have successfully installed JDeveloper, let's spend some time configuring it for optimal performance. Configuration parameters are added to any of the `jdev.conf` or `ide.conf` files located in the `/jdeveloper/jdev/bin` and `/jdeveloper/ide/bin` directories respectively, under the Middleware home directory.

The following is a list of the important tuning configuration parameters with some recommendations for their values:

Parameter	Description
AddVMOption -Xmx	This parameter is defined in the `ide.conf` file and indicates the maximum limit that you will allow the JVM heap size to grow to. In plain words, it is the maximum memory that JDeveloper will consume on your system. When setting this parameter, consider the available memory on your system, the memory needed by the OS, the memory needed by other applications running concurrently with JDeveloper, and so on. On a machine used exclusively for development with JDeveloper, as a general rule of thumb consider setting it to around 50 percent of the available memory.

Parameter	Description
AddVMOption -Xms	This parameter is also defined in the `ide.conf` and indicates the initial JVM heap size. This is the amount that will be allocated initially by JDeveloper and it can grow up to the amount specified by the previous -Xmx parameter. When setting this parameter, consider whether you want to give JDeveloper a larger amount in order to minimize frequent adjustments to the JVM heap. Setting this parameter to the same value as the one indicated by the -Xmx parameter will supply a fixed amount of memory to JDeveloper.
AddVMOption -XX:MaxPermSize	This parameter indicates the size of the JVM permanent generation used to store class definitions and associated metadata. Increase this value if needed in order to avoid `java.lang.OutOfMemoryError: PermGen space` errors. A 256MB setting should suffice.
AddVMOption -DVFS_ENABLE	Set it to `true` in `jdev.conf` if your JDeveloper projects consist of a large number of files, especially if you will be enabling a version control system from within JDeveloper.

Configuring JDeveloper with a 64-bit JDK

The JDeveloper installation is bundled by default with a 32-bit version of the Java JDK, which is installed along with JDeveloper. On a 64-bit system, consider running JDeveloper with a 64-bit version of the JDK. First download and install the 64-bit JDK. Then configure JDeveloper via the `SetJavaHome` configuration parameter in the `jdev.conf`. This parameter should be changed to point to the location of the 64-bit JDK. Note that the 64-bit JDK is supported by JDeveloper versions 11.1.1.4.0 and higher.

Configuring the JDeveloper user directory

This is the directory used by JDeveloper to identify a default location where files will be stored. JDeveloper also uses this location to create the integrated WebLogic domain and to deploy your web applications when running them or debugging them inside JDeveloper. It is configured via the `SetUserHomeVariable` parameter in the `jdev.conf` file. It can be set to a specific directory or to an environment variable usually named `JDEV_USER_DIR`. Note that when JDeveloper is started with the `-singleuser` command-line argument, the user directory is created inside the `/jdeveloper` directory under the Middleware home directory.

Before starting your development in JDeveloper, consider setting the XML file encoding for the XML files that you will be creating in JDeveloper. These files among others include, the JSF pages, the business component metadata files, application configuration files, and so on. You set the encoding via the **Tools | Preferences...** menu. Select the **Environment** node on the left of the **Preferences** dialog and the encoding from the **Encoding** drop-down. The recommended setting is **UTF-8** to support multi-lingual applications.

The minimum recommended open file descriptors limit for JDeveloper on a Linux system is 4096. Use the command `ulimit -n` to determine the open file descriptors limit for your installation and change it if needed in the `limits.conf` file located in `/etc/security/` directory.

Breaking up the application in multiple workspaces

When dealing with large enterprise scale applications, the organization and structure of the overall application in terms of JDeveloper workspaces, projects, and libraries is essential. Organizing and packaging ADF application artifacts, such as business components, task flows, templates, Java code, and so on, into libraries will promote and ensure modularity, and the reuse of these artifacts throughout the application. In this recipe, we will create an application that comprises reusable components. We will construct reusable libraries for shared components, business domain specific components, and a main application for consuming these components.

How to do it...

1. To create the `SharedComponents` library, start by selecting **New Application...** in the **Application Navigator**. This will start the application creation wizard.

2. In the **New Gallery** dialog, click on the **Applications** node (under the **General** category) and select **Fusion Web Application (ADF)** from the list of **Items**.

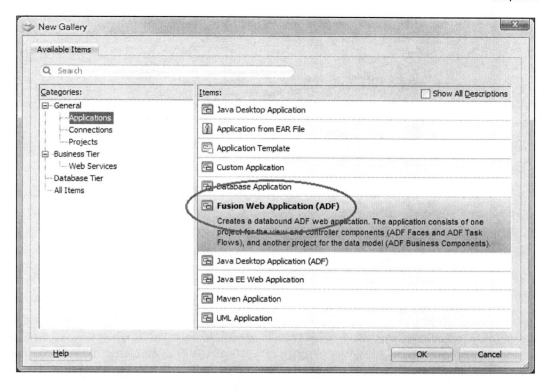

3. In the **Name your application** page, enter the **Application Name**, **Directory** and the **Application Package Prefix**.

4. In the **Name your project** page, enter the business component's **Project Name** and **Directory**. For this recipe, we have called it SharedBC.

5. In the **Configure Java settings** page for the business components project, accept the defaults for **Default Package**, **Java Source Path**, and **Output Directory**.

6. Similarly, in the **Name your project** page for the ViewController project, enter the **Project Name** and **Directory**. For this recipe, we have called the project SharedViewController. Ensuring that you enter a unique package structure for both projects is the best guarantee for avoiding naming conflicts when these projects are deployed as ADF Library JARs.

7. Accept the defaults in the **Configure Java settings** and click **Finish** to proceed with the creation of the workspace.

8. Now, in the **Application Navigator**, you should see the two projects comprising the `SharedComponents` workspace, one for the business components and another for the ViewController.

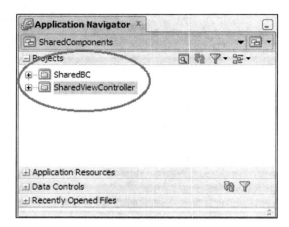

9. You will be using this workspace to add reusable business and ViewController components. For now, we will package the workspace into an ADF library JAR, without any components in it yet. In order to do this, you will need to first setup the project dependencies. Double-click on the `SharedViewController` project to bring up the **Project Properties** dialog and select **Dependencies**.

10. Click on **Edit Dependencies** (the small pen icon) to bring up the **Edit Dependencies** dialog and then click on the **Build Output** checkbox under the business components project.

11. Click **OK** to close the dialog and return to the **Project Properties** dialog.

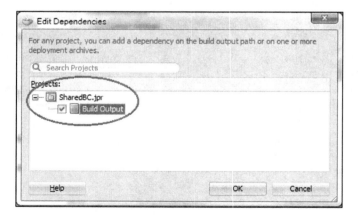

12. The next step is to set up the deployment profile. While at the ViewController **Project Properties** dialog, click on the **Deployment** node.

13. Since we will not be deploying this application as a WAR, select the default WAR deployment profile generated automatically by JDeveloper and delete it.

14. Then, click **New...** to create a new deployment profile.

15. On the **Create Deployment Profile** dialog, select **ADF Library JAR File** for the **Profile Type** and enter the name of the deployment profile. For this recipe, we have called the deployment profile SharedComponents. Click **OK** to proceed with its creation.

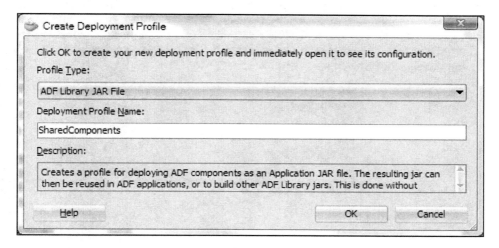

16. In the **Edit ADF Library JAR Deployment Profile Properties** dialog that is opened, select **JAR Options** and specify a location where you will be placing all the reusable JAR libraries. For this recipe, we will place all reusable libraries in a directory called ReUsableJARs.

17. When done, completely exit from the **Project Properties** dialog, saving your changes by clicking **OK**.

18. The last step involves the creation of the **ADF Library JAR**. You do this by right-clicking on the ViewController project in the **Application Navigator** selecting **Deploy** and then the name of the deployment profile name (SharedComponents in this case).

19. Select **Deploy to ADF Library JAR file** in the **Deployment Action** page and click **Finish** to initiate the deployment process. The deployment progress will begin. Its status is shown in the **Deployment** tab of the **Log** window.

20. To create the HRDepartments components library, similarly create a new Fusion web application for the HRDepartment components. Follow the previous steps to setup the project dependencies. No database connection to the HR schema is needed at this stage.

21. Create the deployment profile and deploy the ADF Library JAR. We will not be placing any components yet in this library.

22. To create the `HREmployees` components library, repeat the previous steps once more in order to create another ADF Library JAR for the `HR Employee` related reusable components.

23. Now create another Fusion web application, which will be used as the main application. This application will consume any of the components that reside in the ADF Library JARs created in the previous steps.

24. This can easily be done via the **Resource Palette** by creating a file system connection to the directory where we saved the reusable ADF Library JARs, that is, the directory called `ReUsableJARs`. If the **Resource Palette** is not visible, select **View | Resource Palette** to show it. In the **Resource Palette**, click on the **New** icon and select **New Connection | File System....**

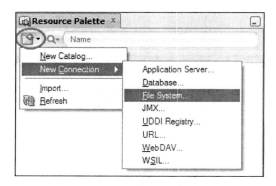

25. In the **Create File System Connection** dialog that is displayed, enter the name of the connection and the directory where you have deployed the reusable components in the previous steps.

26. Click **OK** to continue. You should be able to see the new **File System Connection** in the **Resource Palette**.

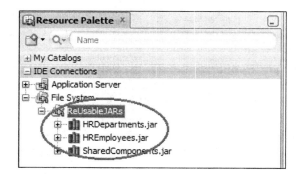

27. To consume reusable components, first select the appropriate project on the **Application Navigator**, then right-click on the ADF Library JAR on the **Resource Palette** and select **Add to Project...**.

28. On the **Confirm Add ADF Library** dialog, click on the **Add Library** button to proceed.

29. Alternatively, expand the ADF Library JAR and drag-and-drop the reusable component onto its appropriate place in the workspace.

How it works...

When you deploy a project as an ADF Library JAR, all ADF reusable components and code are packaged in it and they become available to other consuming applications and libraries. Reusable components include business components, database connections, data controls, task flows, task flow templates, page templates, declarative components, and of course Java code. By setting up the dependencies among the business components and ViewController projects in the way that we have—that is, including the build output of the business components project during the deployment of the ViewController project—you will be producing a single ADF Library JAR file with all the components from all the projects in the workspace. When you add an ADF Library JAR to your project, the library is added to the project's class path. The consuming project can then use any of the components in library. The same happens when you drag-and-drop a reusable component into your project.

There's more...

For this recipe, we packaged both of the business components and ViewController projects in the same ADF Library JAR. If this strategy is not working for you, you have other options, such as adjusting the dependencies among the two and packaging each project in a separate ADF Library JAR. In this case, you will need an additional deployment profile and a separate deployment for the business components project.

Adding the ADF Library JAR manually

You can add an ADF Library JAR into your project manually using the **Project Properties** dialog. Select the **Libraries and Classpath** node and click on the **Add Library...** button. This will display the **Add Library** dialog. On it, click the **New...** button to display the **Create Library** dialog. Enter a name for the library, select **Project** for the library location, and click on the **Deployed by Default** check button. Finally, click on the **Add Entry...** button to locate the ADF Library JAR. The **Deployed by Default** checkbox when checked indicates that the library will be copied to the application's destination archive during deployment of the consuming application. If you leave it unchecked, then the library will not be copied and it must be located in some other way (for example, deployed separately as a shared library on the application server).

Defining the application module granularity

One related topic that also needs to be addressed in the early architectural stages of the ADF project is the granularity for the application modules, that is, how the data model will be divided into application modules. As a general rule of thumb, each application module should satisfy a particular use case. Related use cases and, therefore, application modules can then be packaged into the same reusable ADF Library JAR. In general, avoid creating monolithic application modules that satisfy multiple use cases each.

Entity objects, list of values (LOVs), validation queries

Entity objects, list of values (LOVs) and validation queries should be defined only once for each business components project. To avoid duplication of entity objects, LOVs and validation queries among multiple business components projects, consider defining them only once in a separate business components project.

Structuring of the overall ADF application in reusable components should be well thought and incorporated in the early design and architectural phases of the project.

As your application grows, it is important to watch out for and eliminate circular dependencies among the reusable components that you develop. When they occur, this could indicate a flaw in your design. Use available dependency analyzer tools, such as Dependency Finder (available from `http://depfind.sourceforge.net`) during the development process, to detect and eliminate any circular dependencies that may occur.

Setting up BC base classes

One of the first things to consider when developing large-scale enterprise applications with ADF-BC is to allow for the ability to extend the framework's base classes early on in the development process. It is imperative that you do this before creating any of your business objects, even though you have no practical use of the extended framework classes at that moment. This will guarantee that all of your business objects are correctly derived from your framework classes. In this recipe, you will expand on the previous recipe and add business components framework extension classes to the `SharedComponents` workspace.

Getting ready

You will be adding the business components framework extension classes to the `SharedComponents` workspace. See the previous recipe for information on how to create one.

How to do it...

1. To create framework extension classes for the commonly used business components, start with the creation of an extension class for the entity objects. Open the `SharedComponents` workspace in JDeveloper and right-click on the `SharedBC` business components project.

2. From the context menu, select **New...** to bring up the **New Gallery** dialog. Select **Class** from the **Java** category (under the **General** category) and click **OK**.

3. On the **Create Java Class** dialog that is displayed, enter the name of the custom entity object class, the package where it will be created, and for **Extends** enter the base framework class, which in this case is `oracle.jbo.server.EntityImpl`.

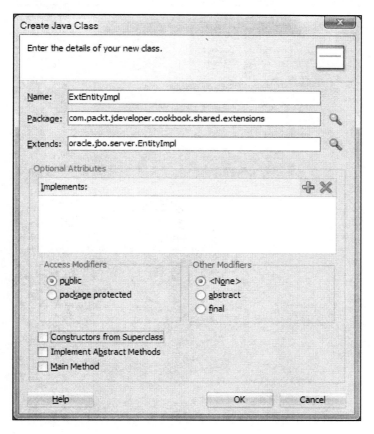

4. Now, repeat the same steps to create framework extension classes for the following components:

Business Component	Framework Class Extended
Entity Definition	`oracle.jbo.server.EntityDefImpl`
View Object	`oracle.jbo.server.ViewObjectImpl`
View Row	`oracle.jbo.server.ViewRowImpl`
Application Module	`oracle.jbo.server.ApplicationModuleImpl`
Database Transaction Factory	`oracle.jbo.server.` `DatabaseTransactionFactory`
Database Transaction	`oracle.jbo.server.DBTransactionImpl2`

5. Once you are done, your project should look similar to the following:

6. The next step is to configure JDeveloper so that all new business components that you create from this point forward will be inherited from the framework extension classes you've just defined. Open the **Preferences** dialog from the **Tools** menu, expand the **ADF Business Components** node, and select **Base Classes**.

7. Then enter the framework extension classes that you created previously, each one in its corresponding category.

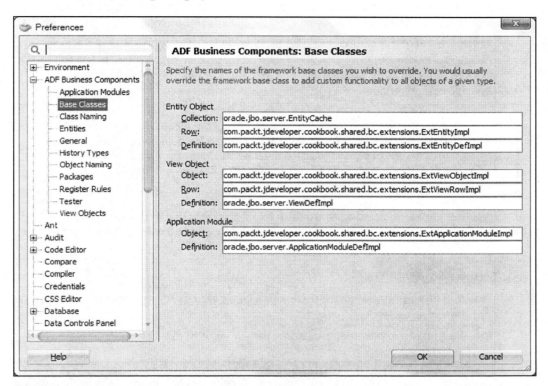

How it works...

Defining and globally configuring business components framework extension classes via the **ADF Business Components Base Classes** settings on the **Preferences** dialog causes all subsequent business components for all projects to be inherited from these classes. This is true for both XML-only components and for components with custom Java implementation classes. For XML-only components observe that the ComponentClass attribute in the object's XML definition file points to your framework extension class.

There's more...

You can configure your business components framework extension classes at two additional levels: the project level and the individual component level.

- ▶ Configuration at the project level is done via the **Project Properties Base Classes** selection under the **ADF Business Components** node. These configuration changes will affect only the components created for the specific project.

- ▶ Configuration at the component level is done via the component's **Java Options** dialog, in the component's definition **Java** page, by clicking on the **Classes Extend...** button and overriding the default settings. The changes will only affect the specific component.

 Do not attempt to directly change or remove the extends Java keyword in your component's implementation class. This would only be half the change, because the component's XML definition will still point to the original class. Instead, use the **Classes Extend...** button on the component's **Java Options** dialog.

Finally, note that the default package structure for all business components can also be specified in the **ADF Business Components | Packages** page of the **Preferences** dialog.

See also

- ▶ *Creating and using generic extension interfaces, Chapter 5, Putting them all together: Application Modules*
- ▶ *Breaking up the application in multiple workspaces, in this chapter*

Setting up logging

Logging is one of those areas that is often neglected during the initial phases of application design. There are a number of logging framework choices to use in your application, such as log4j by Apache. In this recipe, we will demonstrate the usage of the ADFLogger and Oracle Diagnostics Logging (ODL). The main advantage of using ODL when compared to other logging frameworks is its tight integration with WebLogic and JDeveloper. In WebLogic, the logs produced conform to and integrate with the diagnostics logging facility. Diagnostic logs include, in addition to the message logged, additional information such as the session and user that produced the log entry at run-time. This is essential when analyzing the application logs. In JDeveloper, the log configuration and analysis is integrated via the **Oracle Diagnostics Logging Configuration** and **Oracle Diagnostics Log Analyzer** respectively.

Getting ready

We will be adding logging to the application module framework extension class that we developed in the previous recipe.

How to do it...

1. ODL logs can be generated programmatically from within your code by using the `ADFLogger` class. Instantiate an `ADFLogger` via the static `createADFLogger()` method and use its `log()` method. Go ahead and add logging support to the application module framework extension class we developed in the previous recipe, as shown in the following code snippet:

```
import oracle.adf.share.logging.ADFLogger;
public class ExtApplicationModuleImpl extends
  ApplicationModuleImpl {
  // create an ADFLogger
  private static final ADFLogger LOGGER =
    ADFLogger.createADFLogger(ExtApplicationModuleImpl.class);
  public ExtApplicationModuleImpl() {
    super();
    // log a trace
    LOGGER.log(ADFLogger.TRACE,
      "ExtApplicationModuleImpl was constructed");
  }
}
```

Downloading the example code

You can download the example code files for all Packt books you have purchased from your account at `http://www.packtpub.com`. If you purchased this book elsewhere, you can visit `http://www.packtpub.com/support` and register to have the files e-mailed directly to you.

2. The next step involves the configuration of the logger in the `logging.xml` file. The file is located in the `config\fmwconfig\servers` directory under the WebLogic domain for the server you are configuring. For the integrated WebLogic server, this file is located in the `%JDEV_USER_DIR%\system11.1.2.1.38.60.81\DefaultDomain\config\fmwconfig\servers\DefaultServer` directory. The exact location can vary slightly depending on the version of JDeveloper that you use.

Open the file in JDeveloper and create a custom logger called `com.packt` by clicking on the **Add Persistent Logger** icon, as shown in the following screenshot:

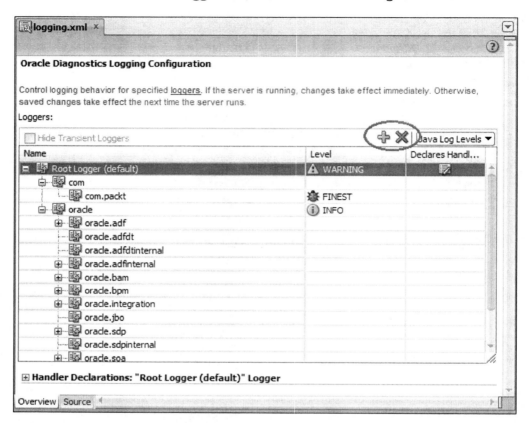

3. This will display the **Add Persistent Logger** dialog to add your logger. Enter `com.packt` for the **Logger Name** and choose `FINEST` for the **Logger Level**.

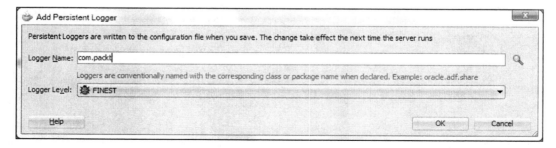

4. Repeat this step and add another logger named com if one does not already exist for it. The final result should look similar to the following screenshot:

5. One more step that is required to complete the configuration is to use the -Djbo. debugoutput=adflogger and -Djbo.adflogger.level=FINEST options when starting the JVM. You can do this in JDeveloper by double-clicking on the main application's ViewController project to bring up the **Project Properties** dialog and selecting the **Run/Debug/Profile** node.

6. Then select the appropriate **Run Configuration** on the right and click on the **Edit...** button.

7. On the **Edit Run Configuration** dialog that is displayed, enter these Java options in the **Java Options**.

How it works...

In this example, we have declared a static ADFLogger and associated it with the class ExtApplicationModuleImpl by passing ExtApplicationModuleImpl.class as a parameter during its construction. We have declared the ADFLogger as static so we don't have to worry about passivating it. We then use its log() method to do our logging. The log() method accepts a java.util.logging.Level parameter indicating the log level of the message and it can be any of the following values: ADFLogger.INTERNAL_ERROR, ADFLogger.ERROR, ADFLogger.WARNING, ADFLogger.NOTIFICATION, or ADFLogger. TRACE.

ADFLogger leverages the Java Logging API to provide logging functionality. Because standard Java logging is used, it can be configured through the logging.xml configuration file. This file is located under the WebLogic domain directory config\fmwconfig\servers for the specific server that you are configuring. The file is opened and a logger is added.

Logging is controlled at the package level; we have added a logger for the `com.packt` package but we can fine-tune it for the additional levels: `com.packt.jdeveloper`, `com.packt.jdeveloper.cookbook`, `com.packt.jdeveloper.cookbook.shared`, and so on. The class name that we passed as an argument to the `ADFLogger` during its instantiation—that is, `ExtApplicationModuleImpl.class`—represents a logger that is defined in the logging configuration file. The logger that is added is a persistent logger, which means that it will remain permanently in the `logging.xml` configuration file. Transient loggers are also available; these persist only for the duration of the user session.

Each logger configured in the `logging.xml` is associated with a log handler. There are a number of handlers defined in the `logging.xml` namely a `console-handler` to handle logging to the console, an `odl_handler` to handle logging for ODL and others.

There's more...

You can also use the `ADFLogger` methods `severe()`, `warning()`, `info()`, `config()`, `fine()`, `finer()`, and `finest()` to do your logging.

When you configure logging, ensure that you make the changes to the appropriate `logging.xml` file for the WebLogic server you are configuring.

See also

- ▶ *Breaking up the application in multiple workspaces*, in this chapter
- ▶ *Configuring diagnostics logging, Chapter 11, Refactoring, Debugging, Profiling, Testing*
- ▶ *Dynamically configure ADF trace logs on WebLogic, Chapter 11, Refactoring, Debugging, Profiling, Testing*

Using a custom exception class

In this recipe, we will go over the steps necessary to set up a custom application exception class derived from the JboException base exception class. Some Reasons why you might want to do this include:

► Customize the exception error message

► Use error codes to locate the error messages in the resource bundle

► Use a single resource bundle per locale for the error messages and their parameters

Getting ready

We will add the custom application exception class to the SharedComponents workspace we created in the *Breaking up the application in multiple workspaces* recipe in this chapter.

How to do it...

1. Start by opening the SharedComponents workspace.

2. Create a new class called ExtJboException by right-clicking on the business components project and selecting **New...**.

3. Then select **Java** under the **General** category and **Java Class** from list of **Items** on the right.

4. Click **OK** to display the **Create Java Class** dialog. Enter ExtJboException for the **Name**, com.packt.jdeveloper.cookbook.shared.bc.exceptions for the **Package** and oracle.jbo.JboException for the **Extends**.

5. Click **OK** to proceed with the creation of the custom exception class.

6. The next step is to add two additional constructors, to allow for the instantiation of the custom application exception using a standard error message code with optional error message parameters. The additional constructors look similar to the following code sample:

```
public ExtJboException(final String errorCode,
  final Object[] errorParameters) {
  super(ResourceBundle.class, errorCode, errorParameters);
}
public ExtJboException(final String errorCode) {
  super(ResourceBundle.class, errorCode, null);
}
```

7. Now, click on the **Override Methods...** icon on the top of the editor window and override the `getMessage()` method, as shown in the following screenshot:

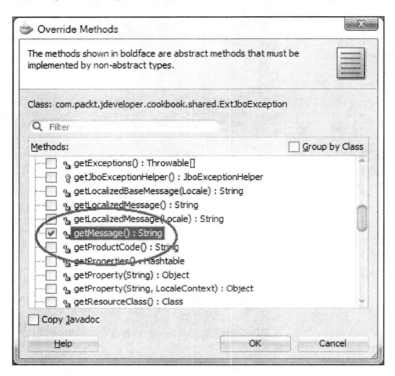

8. Enter the following code for the `getMessage()` method:

```java
public String getMessage() {
  // default message
  String errorMessage = "";
  try {
    // get access to the error messages bundle
    final ResourceBundle messagesBundle = ResourceBundle.getBundle
      (ERRORS_BUNDLE, Locale.getDefault());
    // construct the error message
    errorMessage =this.getErrorCode() + " - " + messages
      Bundle.getString(MESSAGE_PREFIX + this.getErrorCode());
    // get access to the error message parameters bundle
    final ResourceBundle parametersBundle = ResourceBundle
      .getBundle(PARAMETERS_BUNDLE, Locale.getDefault());
    // loop for all parameters
    for (int i = 0; i < this.getErrorParameters().length; i++) {
      // get parameter value
      final String parameterValue =
```

```
      parametersBundle.getString(PARAMETER_PREFIX +
      (String)this.getErrorParameters()[i]);
    // replace parameter placeholder in the error message string
    errorMessage = errorMessage.replaceAll
      ("\\{" + (i + 1) + "}", parameterValue);
  }
} catch (Exception e) {
  // log the exception
  LOGGER.warning(e);
}
return errorMessage;
}
```

9. Make sure that you also add the following constants:

```
private static final String ERRORS_BUNDLE = "com.packt.jdeveloper.
  cookbook.shared.bc.exceptions.messages.ErrorMessages";
private static final String PARAMETERS_BUNDLE = "com.packt.
  jdeveloper.cookbook.shared.bc.exceptions.messages.ErrorParams";
private static final String MESSAGE_PREFIX = "message.";
private static final String PARAMETER_PREFIX = "parameter.";
private static final ADFLogger LOGGER =ADFLogger
  .createADFLogger(ExtJboException.class);
```

10. For testing purposes add the following `main()` method:

```
// for testing purposes; remove or comment if not needed
  public static void main(String[] args) {
  // throw a custom exception with error code "00001" and two
    parameters
  throw new ExtJboException("00001",
    new String[] { "FirstParameter", "SecondParameter" });
}
```

How it works...

We have created a custom exception at the ADF-BC level by overriding the `JboException` class. In order to use application-specific error codes, we have introduced two new constructors. Both of them accept the error code as a parameter. One of them also accepts the message error parameters.

```
public ExtJboException(final String errorCode,
  final Object[] errorParameters) {
  super(ResourceBundle.class, errorCode, errorParameters);
}
```

In our constructor, we call the base class' constructor and pass the message error code and parameters to it.

Then we override the getMessage() method in order to construct the exception message. In getMessage(), we first get access to the error messages resource bundle by calling ResourceBundle.getBundle() as shown in the following code snippet:

```
final ResourceBundle messagesBundle = ResourceBundle.getBundle(ERRORS_
BUNDLE, Locale.getDefault());
```

This method accepts the name of the resource bundle and the locale. For the name of the resource bundle, we pass the constant ERRORS_BUNDLE, which we define as com.packt. jdeveloper.cookbook.shared.bc.exceptions.messages.ErrorMessages. This is the ErrorMessages.properties file in the com/packt/jdeveloper/cookbook/ shared/bc/exceptions/messages directory where we have added all of our messages. For the locale, we use the default locale by calling Locale.getDefault().

Then we proceed by loading the error message from the bundle:

```
errorMessage = this.getErrorCode() + " - " + messagesBundle.
getString(MESSAGE_PREFIX + this.getErrorCode());
```

An error message definition in the messages resource bundle looks similar to the following:

```
message.00001=This is an error message that accepts two parameters.
The first parameter is '{1}'. The second parameter is '{2}'.
```

As you can see, we have added the string prefix message. to the actual error message code. How you form the error message identifiers in the resource bundle is up to you. You could, for example, use a module identifier for each message and change the code in getMessage() appropriately. Also, we have used braces, that is, {1}, {2} as placeholders for the actual message parameter values. Based on all these, we constructed the message identifier by adding the message prefix to the message error code as: MESSAGE_PREFIX + this. getErrorCode() and called getString() on the messagesBundle to load it.

Then we proceed with iterating the message parameters. In a similar fashion, we call getString() on the parameters bundle to load the parameter values.

The parameter definitions in the parameters resource bundle look similar to the following:

```
parameter.FirstParameter=Hello
parameter.SecondParameter=World
```

So we add the prefix parameter to the actual parameter identifier before loading it from the bundle.

The last step is to replace the parameter placeholders in the error message with the actual parameter values. We do this by calling `replaceAll()` on the raw error message, as shown in the following code snippet:

```
errorMessage = errorMessage.replaceAll("\\{" + (i + 1) + "}",
parameterValue);
```

For testing purposes, we have added a `main()` method to test our custom exception. You will similarly `throw` the exception in your business components code, as follows:

```
throw new ExtJboException("00001", // message code
    new String[] { "FirstParameter", "SecondParameter" }
    // message parameters);
```

There's more...

You can combine the error message and the error message parameters bundles into a single resource bundle, if you want, and change the `getMessage()` method as needed to load both from the same resource bundle.

Bundled Exceptions

By default, exceptions are bundled at the transaction level for ADF-BC-based web applications. This means that all exceptions thrown during attribute and entity validations are saved and reported once the validation process is complete. In other words, the validation will not stop on the first error, rather it will continue until the validation process completes and then report all exceptions in a single error message. Bundled validation exceptions are implemented by wrapping exceptions as details of a new parent exception that contains them. For instance, if multiple attributes in a single entity object fail attribute validation, these multiple `ValidationException` objects are wrapped in a `RowValException`. This wrapping exception contains the row key of the row that has failed validation. At transaction commit time, if multiple rows do not successfully pass the validation performed during commit, then all of the `RowValException` objects will get wrapped in an enclosing `TxnValException` object. Then you can use the `getDetails()` method of the `JboException` base exception class to recursively process the bundled exceptions contained inside it.

Exception bundling can be configured at the transaction level by calling `setBundledExceptionMode()` on the `oracle.jbo.Transaction`. This method accepts a Boolean value indicating that bundled transactions will be used or not, respectively.

Note that in the *Using a generic backing bean actions framework* recipe in this chapter, we refactored the code in `getMessage()` to a reusable `BundleUtils.loadMessage()` method. Consequently, we changed the `ExtJboException getMessage()` in that recipe to the following:

```
public String getMessage() {
    return BundleUtils.loadMessage(this.getErrorCode(),
    this.getErrorParameters());
}
```

See also

▶ *Handling security, session timeouts, exceptions and errors*, Chapter 9, *Handling Security, Session Timeouts, Exceptions and Errors*

▶ *Breaking up the application in multiple workspaces*, in this chapter

Using ADFUtils/JSFUtils

In this recipe, we will talk about how to incorporate and use the `ADFUtils` and `JSFUtils` utility classes in your ADF application. These are utility classes used at the ViewController level that encapsulate a number of lower level ADF and JSF calls into higher level methods. Integrating these classes in your ADF application early in the development process, and subsequently using them, will be of great help to you as a developer and contribute to the overall project's clarity and consistency. The `ADFUtils` and `JSFUtils` utility classes, at the time of writing, are not part of any official JDeveloper release. You will have to locate them, configure them, and expand them as needed in your project.

Getting ready

We will be adding the `ADFUtils` and `JSFUtils` classes to the `SharedComponents` ViewController project that we developed in the *Breaking up the application in multiple workspaces* recipe in this chapter.

How to do it...

1. To get the latest version of these classes, download and extract the latest version of the **Fusion Order Demo** application in your PC. This sample application can be found currently in the **Fusion Order Demo (FOD) - Sample ADF Application** page at the following address: `http://www.oracle.com/technetwork/developer-tools/jdev/index-095536.html`.

2. The latest version of the Fusion Order Demo application is 11.1.2.1 R2 at the time of this writing and is bundled in a zipped file. So go ahead download and extract the Fusion Order Demo application in your PC.

3. You should be able to locate the `ADFUtils` and `JSFUtils` classes in the location where you have extracted the Fusion Order Demo application. If multiple versions of the same class are found, compare them and use the ones that are most up-to-date. For this recipe, we have included in the source code the `ADFUtils` and `JSFUtils` found in the `SupplierModule\ViewController\src\oracle\fodemo\supplier\view\utils` directory.

4. Copy these classes to a specific location in your shared ViewController components project. For this recipe, we have copied them into the `SharedComponents\SharedViewController\src\com\packt\jdeveloper\cookbook\shared\view\util` directory.

5. Once copied, open both files with JDeveloper and change their `package` to reflect their new location, in this case to `com.packt.jdeveloper.cookbook.shared.view.util`.

How it works...

The public interfaces of both `ADFUtils` and `JSFUtils` define `static` methods, so you can call them directly without any class instantiations. The following are some of the methods that are commonly used.

Locating an iterator binding

To locate an iterator in the bindings, use the `ADFUtils.findIterator()` method. The method accepts the bound iterator's identifier and returns an `oracle.adf.model.binding.DCIteratorBinding`. The following is an example:

```
DCIteratorBinding it = ADFUtils.findIterator("IteratorID");
```

Locating an operation binding

To locate an operation in the bindings, use the `ADFUtils.findOperation()` method. This method accepts the bound operation's identifier and returns an `oracle.binding.OperationBinding`.

```
OperationBinding oper = ADFUtils.findOperation("OperationID");
```

Locating an attribute binding

Use `ADFUtils.findControlBinding()` to retrieve an attribute from the bindings. This method accepts the bound attribute's identifier and returns an `oracle.binding.AttributeBinding`.

```
AttributeBinding  attrib =
  ADFUtils.findControlBinding("AttributeId");
```

Getting and setting an attribute binding value

To get or set a bound attribute's value, use the `ADFUtils.getBoundAttributeValue()` and `ADFUtils.setBoundAttributeValue()` methods respectively. Both of these methods accept the identifier of the attribute binding as an argument. The `getBoundAttributeValue()` method returns the bound attribute's data value as a `java.lang.Object`. The `setBoundAttributeValue()` method accepts a `java.lang.Object` and uses it to set the bound attribute's value.

```
// get some bound attribute data
String someData =
  (String)ADFUtils.getBoundAttributeValue("AttributeId");
// set some bound attribute data
ADFUtils.setBoundAttributeValue("AttributeId", someData);
```

Getting the binding container

You can get the `oracle.adf.model.binding.DCBindingContainer` binding container by calling the `ADFUtils.getDCBindingContainer()` method.

```
DCBindingContainer bindings = ADFUtils.getDCBindingContainer();
```

Adding Faces messages

Use the `JSFUtils.addFacesInformationMessage()` and `JSFUtils.addFacesErrorMessage()` methods to display Faces information and error messages respectively. These methods accept the message to display as a `String` argument.

```
JSFUtils.addFacesInformationMessage("Information message");
JSFUtils.addFacesErrorMessage ("Error message");
```

Finding a component in the root view

To locate a UI component in the root view based on the component's identifier, use the `JSFUtils.findComponentInRoot()` method. This method returns a `javax.faces.component.UIComponent` matching the specified component identifier.

```
UIComponent component = JSFUtils.findComponentInRoot("ComponentID");
```

Getting and setting managed bean values

Use the `JSFUtils.getManagedBeanValue()` and `JSFUtils.setManagedBeanValue()` methods to get and set a managed bean value respectively. These methods both accept the managed bean name. The `JSFUtils.getManagedBeanValue()` method returns the managed bean value as a `java.lang.Object`. The `JSFUtils.setManagedBeanValue()` method accepts a `java.lang.Object` and uses it to set the managed bean value.

```
Object filePath = JSFUtils.getManagedBeanValue
    ("bindings.FilePath.inputValue");
JSFUtils.setManagedBeanValue("bindings.FilePath.inputValue", null);
```

Using page templates

In this recipe, we will go over the steps required to create a JSF page template that you can use to create JSF pages throughout your application. It is very likely that for a large enterprise-scale application you will need to construct and use a number of different templates, each serving a specific purpose. Using templates to construct the actual application JSF pages will ensure that pages throughout the application are consistent, and provide a familiar look and feel to the end user. You can follow the steps presented in this recipe to construct your page templates and adapt them as needed to fit your own requirements.

Getting ready

We will be adding the JSF template to the `SharedComponents` ViewController project that we developed in the *Breaking up the application in multiple workspaces* recipe in this chapter.

How to do it...

1. Start by right-clicking on the ViewController project in the `SharedComponents` workspace and selecting **New...**.

2. On the **New Gallery** dialog select **JSF/Facelets** from the list of **Categories** and **ADF Page Template** from the **Items** on the right.

3. Click **OK** to proceed. This will display the **Create ADF Page Template** dialog.

4. Enter the name of the template on the **Page Template Name**. Note that as you change the template name, the template **File Name** also changes to reflect the template name. For this recipe, we will simply call the template `TemplateDef1`.

5. Now, click on the **Browse...** button and select the directory where the template will be stored.

6. On the **Choose Directory** dialog navigate to the `public_html/WEB-INF` directory and click on the **Create new subdirectory** icon to create a new directory called `templates`.

7. For the **Document Type**, select **JSP XML**.

8. We will not be using any of the pre-defined templates, so uncheck the **Use a Quick Start Layout** checkbox.

9. Also, since we will not be associating any data bindings to the template, uncheck the **Create Associated ADFm Page Definition** checkbox.

10. Next, you will be adding the template facets. You do this by selecting the **Facet Definitions** tab and clicking on the **New** icon button. Enter the following facets:

Facet	Description
mainContent	This facet will be used for the page's main content.
menuBar	This facet will be used to define a menu at the top of the page.
topBar	This facet will be used to define a toolbar under the page's menu.
popupContent	This facet will be used to define the page's pop-ups.

11. Now click **OK** to proceed with the creation of the ADF page template.

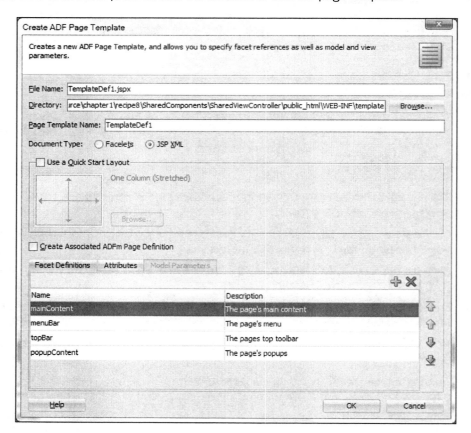

12. Once the template is created, it is opened in the JDeveloper editor. If you followed the previous steps, the template should look similar to the following code snippet:

```
<af:pageTemplateDef var="attrs">
  <af:xmlContent>
    <component xmlns
      ="http://xmlns.oracle.com/adf/faces/rich/component">
      <display-name>TemplateDef1</display-name>
      <facet>
        <description>The page's main content</description>
        <facet-name>mainContent</facet-name>
      </facet>
      <facet>
        <description>The page's menu</description>
        <facet-name>menuBar</facet-name>
      </facet>
      <facet>
        <description>The page's top toolbar</description>
        <facet-name>topBar</facet-name>
      </facet>
      <facet>
        <description>The page's popups</description>
        <facet-name>popupContent</facet-name>
      </facet>
    </component>
  </af:xmlContent>
</af:pageTemplateDef>
```

As you can see, at this point, the template contains only its definition in an `af:xmlContent` tag with no layout information whatsoever. We will proceed by adding the template's layout content.

13. From the **Layout** components in the **Component Palette**, grab a `Form` component and drop it into the template.

14. From the **Layout** container, grab a `Panel Stretch Layout` and drop it into the `Form` component. Remove the `top`, `bottom`, `start`, and `end` facets.

15. From the **Layout** container, grab a `Panel Splitter` component and drop it on the `center` facet of the `Panel Stretch Layout`. Using the **Property Inspector** change the `Panel Splitter Orientation` to `vertical`. Also adjust the `SplitterPosition` to around 100.

16. Add your application logo by dragging and dropping an `Image` component from the **General Controls** onto the `first` facet of the `Panel Splitter`. For this recipe, we have created a `public_html\images` directory and we copied a `logo.jpg` logo image there. We then specified `/images/logo.jpg` as image `Source` for the `Image` component.

17. Let's proceed by adding the main page's layout content. Drop a `Decorative Box` from the **Layout** components onto the second facet of the `Panel Splitter`. We will not be using the top facet of `Decorative Box`, so remove it.

18. OK, we are almost there! Drag a `Panel Stretch Layout` from the **Layout** components and drop it onto the `center` facet of the `Decorative Box`. Remove the `start` and `end` facets, since we will not be using them.

19. Drag a `Facet Ref` component from the **Layout components** and drop it onto the `center` facet of the `Panel Stretch Layout`. On the **Insert Facet** dialog, select the `mainContent` facet that you added during the template creation.

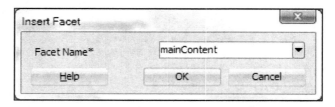

20. Finally, add the following code to the `Panel Stretch Layout topBar` facet:

```
<f:facet name="top">
  <af:panelGroupLayout id="pt_pgl5" layout="vertical">
    <af:facetRef facetName="popupContent"/>
    <af:menuBar id="pt_mb1">
      <af:facetRef facetName="menuBar"/>
    </af:menuBar>
    <af:panelGroupLayout id="pt_pgl2" layout="horizontal">
      <af:toolbar id="pt_t2">
        <af:facetRef facetName="topBar"/>
      </af:toolbar>
    </af:panelGroupLayout>
  </af:panelGroupLayout>
</f:facet>
```

How it works...

When the template is created, there is no layout information in it, so we have to add it ourselves. We do this by using a variety of layout components to arrange the contained UI. Also, notice the usage of the `af:facetRef` component. It is being used to reference a template facet in the specific place within the layout content. The facet is then available to you when you create a JSF page from the template. This will become obvious when we generate a JSF page from the template. Note that each `Facet` can only be added once to the template.

So, how do you use the JSF page template? Since we have created the template in a `SharedComponents` project, we will first need to deploy the project to an ADF Library JAR. Then we will be able to use it from other consuming projects. This was explained in the *Breaking up the application in multiple workspaces* recipe, earlier in this chapter. When you do so, the template will be visible to all consuming projects, as shown in the following screenshot:

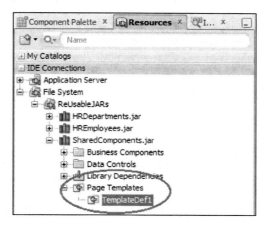

Once the ADF Library JAR containing the template is added to the consuming project, you can see and select the template when you create a new JSF page in the **Create JSF Page** dialog. The template introduced in this recipe is shown in the following screenshot:

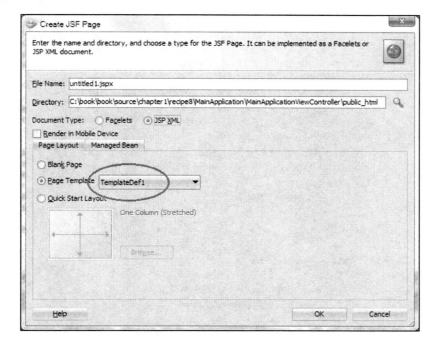

The XML source code that is generated for a JSF page created from this template will look similar to the following code snippet:

```
<f:view>
  <af:document id="d1" title="Test">
    <af:pageTemplate viewId="/WEB-INF/templates/TemplateDef1.jspx"
      id="pt1">
      <f:facet name="mainContent"/>
      <f:facet name="menuBar"/>
      <f:facet name="topBar"/>
      <f:facet name="bottomBar"/>
      <f:facet name="popupContent"/>
    </af:pageTemplate>
  </af:document>
</f:view>
```

You can see in the listing that the page references the template via the af:pageTemplate tag. The template facets that you have defined are available so you can enter the page-specific UI content. After adding an af:menuBar to the menuBar facet and some af:commandToolbarButton components to the topBar facet, the JSF page could look similar to the following code:

```
<f:view>
  <af:document id="d1" title="Test">
    <af:pageTemplate viewId="/WEB-INF/templates/TemplateDef1.jspx"
      id="pt1">
      <f:facet name="mainContent"/>
      <f:facet name="menuBar">
        <af:menuBar id="mb1">
          <af:menu text="File" id="m1">
            <af:commandMenuItem text="Save" id="cmi1"
              icon="/images/filesave.png"/>
            <af:commandMenuItem text="Action" id="cmi2"
              icon="/images/action.png"/>
            <af:commandMenuItem text="Mail" id="cmi3"
              icon="/images/envelope.png"/>
            <af:commandMenuItem text="Print" id="cmi4"
              icon="/images/print.png"/>
          </af:menu>
        </af:menuBar>
      </f:facet>
      <f:facet name="topBar">
        <af:group id="g1">
          <af:commandToolbarButton id="ctb1" shortDesc="Save"
            icon="/images/filesave.png"/>
```

```
        <af:commandToolbarButton id="ctb2" shortDesc="Action"
          icon="/images/action.png"/>
        <af:commandToolbarButton id="ctb3" shortDesc="Mail"
          icon="/images/envelope.png"/>
        <af:commandToolbarButton id="ctb4" shortDesc="Print"
          icon="/images/print.png"/>
      </af:group>
    </f:facet>
    <f:facet name="popupContent"/>
  </af:pageTemplate>
 </af:document>
</f:view>
```

Running the page in JDeveloper will produce the following:

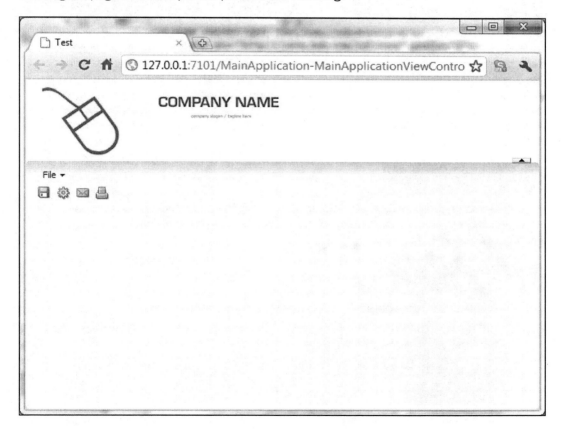

There's more...

Although adding a `Form` component to a template is not recommended practice, this is not a problem for the template created in this recipe, since we will not be using it for the creation of page fragments. Using a template that contains a `Form` component to create page fragments will result in a problem when a consuming page already contains a `Form` component itself. The template developed in this recipe will not be used for page fragments. It was developed specifically to be used along with the generic backing bean actions framework explained in the *Using a generic backing bean actions framework* recipe in this chapter.

Using a generic backing bean actions framework

In this recipe we will create a base backing bean class that we will use to encapsulate common functionality for common JSF page actions, such as committing and rolling back data, creating new records, deleting records and so on. Creating and using such a generic backing bean actions framework will guarantee that you provide consistent functionality throughout the application and encapsulate common functionality at a base class level. This class is not intended to be used as a utility class. Any new helper methods that were developed to demonstrate the recipe were added to the `ADFUtils` utility class discussed earlier in this chapter.

Getting ready

We will be adding the generic backing bean actions framework to the `SharedComponents` ViewController project that we developed in the *Breaking up the application in multiple workspaces* recipe in this chapter.

How to do it...

1. Right-click on the shared ViewController project and select **New...**.
2. On the **New Gallery** dialog, select **Java** under the **General** category and **Java Class** from the list of items on the right.
3. On the **Create Java Class** dialog, enter `CommonActions` for the class name and `com.packt.jdeveloper.cookbook.shared.view.actions` for the class package.
4. Let's go ahead and add methods to provide consistent commit functionality:

```
public void commit(ActionEvent actionEvent) {
  if (ADFUtils.hasChanges()) {
    // allow derived beans to handle before commit actions
    onBeforeCommit(actionEvent);
```

```
      // allow derived beans to handle commit actions
      onCommit(actionEvent);
      // allow derived beans to handle after commit actions
      onAfterCommit(actionEvent);
    } else {
      // display "No changes to commit" message
      JSFUtils.addFacesInformationMessage(BundleUtils.
        loadMessage("00002"));
    }
  }
  protected void onBeforeCommit(ActionEvent actionEvent) {
  }
  /**
  protected void onCommit(ActionEvent actionEvent) {
    // execute commit
    ADFUtils.execOperation(Operations.COMMIT);
  }
  protected void onAfterCommit(ActionEvent actionEvent) {
    // display "Changes were committed successfully" message
    JSFUtils.addFacesInformationMessage(BundleUtils.
      loadMessage("00003"));
  }
```

5. We have also added similar methods for consistent rollback behaviour. To provide uniform record creation/insertion functionality, let's add these methods:

```
  public void create(ActionEvent actionEvent) {
    if (hasChanges()) {
      onCreatePendingChanges(actionEvent);
    } else {
      onContinueCreate(actionEvent);
    }
  }
  protected void onBeforeCreate(ActionEvent actionEvent) {
    // commit before creating a new record
    ADFUtils.execOperation(Operations.COMMIT);
  }
  public void onCreate(ActionEvent actionEvent) {
    execOperation(Operations.INSERT);
  }
  protected void onAfterCreate(ActionEvent actionEvent) {
  }
  public void onCreatePendingChanges(ActionEvent actionEvent) {
    ADFUtils.showPopup("CreatePendingChanges");
  }
  public void onContinueCreate(ActionEvent actionEvent) {
    onBeforeCreate(actionEvent);
    onCreate(actionEvent);
    onAfterCreate(actionEvent);
  }
```

6. Similar methods were added for consistent record deletion behaviour. In this case, we have added functionality to show a delete confirmation pop-up.

How it works...

To provide consistent functionality at the JSF page actions level, we have implemented the `commit()`, `rollback()`, `create()`, and `remove()` methods. Derived backing beans should handle these actions by simply delegating to this base class via calls to `super.commit()`, `super.rollback()`, and so on. The base class `commit()` implementation first calls the helper `ADFUtils.hasChanges()` to determine whether there are transaction changes. If there are, then the `onBeforeCommit()` is called to allow derived backing beans to perform any pre-commit processing. Commit processing continues by calling `onCommit()`. Again, derived backing beans can override this method to provide specialized commit processing. The base class implementation of `onCommit()` calls the helper `ADFUtils.execOperation()` to execute the `Operations.COMMIT` bound operation. The commit processing finishes by calling the `onAfterCommit()`. Derived backing beans can override this method to perform post-commit processing. The default base class implementation displays a **Changes were committed successfully** message on the screen.

The generic functionality for a new record creation is implemented in the `create()` method. Derived backing beans should delegate to this method for default record creation processing by calling `super.create()`. In `create()`, we first check to see if we have any changes to the existing transaction. If we do, we will inform the user by displaying a message dialog. We do this in the `onCreatePendingChanges()` method. The default implementation of this method displays the `CreatePendingChanges` confirmation pop-up. The derived backing bean can override this method to handle this event in a different manner. If the user chooses to go ahead with the record creation, the `onContinueCreate()` is called. This method calls `onBeforeCreate()` to handle precreate functionality. The default implementation commits the current record by calling `ADFUtils.execOperation(Operations.COMMIT)`. Record creation continues with calling `onCreate()`. The default implementation of this method creates and inserts the new record by calling `ADFUtils.execOperation(Operations.INSERT)`. Finally, `onAfterCreate()` is called to handle any creation post processing.

The generic rollback and record deletion functionality is similar. For the default delete processing, a pop-up is displayed asking the user to confirm whether the record should be deleted or not. The record is deleted only after the user's confirmation.

There's more...

Note that this framework uses a number of pop-ups in order to confirm certain user choices. Rather than adding these pop-ups to all JSF pages, these pop-ups are added once to your JSF page template, providing reusable pop-ups for all of your JSF pages. In order to support this generic functionality, additional plumbing code will need to be added to the actions framework. We will talk at length about it in the *Using page templates for pop-up reuse* recipe in *Chapter 7, Face Value: ADF Faces, JSPX Pages and Components*.

See also

▶ *Using page templates for pop-up reuse, Chapter 7, Face Value: ADF Faces, JSPX Pages and Components*

▶ *Breaking up the application in multiple workspaces*, in this chapter

2

Dealing with Basics: Entity Objects

In this chapter, we will cover:

- ▶ Using a custom property to populate a sequence attribute
- ▶ Overriding doDML() to populate an attribute with a gapless sequence
- ▶ Creating and applying property sets
- ▶ Using getPostedAttribute() to determine the posted attribute's value
- ▶ Overriding remove() to delete associated child entities
- ▶ Overriding remove() to delete a parent entity in an association
- ▶ Using a method validator based on a view object accessor
- ▶ Using Groovy expressions to resolve validation error message tokens
- ▶ Using doDML() to enforce a detail record for a new master record

Introduction

Entity objects are the basic building blocks in the chain of business components. They represent a single row of data and they encapsulate the business model, data, rules, and persistence behavior. Usually, they map to database objects, most commonly to database tables, and views. Entity object definitions are stored in XML metadata files. These files are maintained automatically by JDeveloper and the ADF framework, and they should not be edited by hand. The default entity object implementation is provided by the ADF framework class `oracle.jbo.server.EnityImpl`. For large-scale projects you should create your own custom entity framework class, as demonstrated in the *Setting up BC base classes* recipe in *Chapter 1, Pre-requisites to Success: ADF Project Setup and Foundations*.

Likewise, it is not uncommon in large-scale projects to provide custom implementations for the entity object methods doDML(), create(), and remove(). The recipes in this chapter demonstrate, among other things, some of the custom functionality that can be implemented in these methods. Furthermore, other topics such as generic programming using custom properties and property sets, custom validators, entity associations, populating sequence attributes, and more, are covered throughout the chapter.

Using a custom property to populate a sequence attribute

In this recipe, we will go over a generic programming technique that you can use to assign database sequence values to specific entity object attributes. Generic functionality is achieved by using custom properties. Custom properties allow you to define custom metadata that can be accessed by the ADF business components at runtime.

Getting ready

We will add this generic functionality to the custom entity framework class. This class was created back in the *Setting up BC base classes* recipe in *Chapter 1, Pre-requisites to Success: ADF Project Setup and Foundations*. The custom framework classes in this case reside in the SharedComponets workspace. This workspace was created in the recipe *Breaking up the application in multiple workspaces, Chapter1, Pre-requisites to Success: ADF Project Setup and Foundations*. You will need to create a database connection to the HR schema, if you are planning to run the recipe's test case. You can do this either by creating the database connection in the **Resource Palette** and dragging-and-dropping it to **Application Resources | Connections,** or by creating it directly in **Application Resources | Connections**.

How to do it...

1. Start by opening the SharedComponets workspace in JDeveloper. If needed, follow the steps in the referenced recipe to create it.

2. Locate the custom entity framework class in the SharedBC project and open it in the editor.

3. Click on the **Override Methods...** icon on the toolbar (the green left arrow) to bring up the **Override Methods** dialog.

4. From the list of methods that are presented, select the **create()** method and click **OK**. JDeveloper will insert a create() method in to the body of your custom entity class.

5. Add the following code to the `create()` method immediately after the call to `super.create()`:

```
// iterate all entity attributes
for (AttributeDef atrbDef :
  this.getEntityDef().getAttributeDefs()) {
  // check for a custom property called CREATESEQ_PROPERTY
  String sequenceName =
    (String)atrbDef.getProperty(CREATESEQ_PROPERTY);
  if (sequenceName != null) {
    // create the sequence based on the custom property sequence
      name
    SequenceImpl sequence = new SequenceImpl(sequenceName,
      this.getDBTransaction());
    // populate the attribute with the next sequence number
    this.populateAttributeAsChanged(atrbDef.getIndex(),
      sequence.getSequenceNumber());
  }
}
```

How it works...

In the previous code, we have overridden the `create()` method for the custom entity framework class. This method is called by the ADF framework each time a new entity object is constructed. We call `super.create()` to allow the framework processing, and then we retrieve the entity's attribute definitions by calling `getEntityDef()`. `getAttributeDefs()`. We then iterate over them, calling `getProperty()` for each attribute definition. `getProperty()` accepts the name of a custom property defined for the specific attribute. In our case, the custom property is called `CreateSequence` and it is indicated by the constant definition `CREATESEQ_PROPERTY`, representing the name of the database sequence used to assign values to the particular attribute. Next, we instantiate a `SequenceImpl` object using the database sequence name retrieved from the custom property. Note that this does not create the database sequence, rather an `oracle.jbo.server.SequenceImpl` object representing a database sequence.

Finally, the attribute is populated with the value returned from the sequence—via the `getSequenceNumber()` call—by calling `populateAttributeAsChanged()`. This method will populate the attribute without marking the entity as changed. By calling `populateAttributeAsChanged()`, we will avoid any programmatic or declarative validations on the attribute while marking the attribute as changed, so that its value is posted during the entity object DML. Since all of the entity objects are derived from the custom entity framework class, all object creations will go through this `create()` implementation.

There's more...

So how do you use this technique to populate your sequence attributes? First you must deploy the `SharedComponets` workspace into an **ADF Library JAR** and add the library to the project where it will be used. Then, you must add the `CreateSequence` custom property to the specific attributes of your entity objects that need to be populated by a database sequence. To add a custom property to an entity object attribute, select the specific attribute in the entity **Attributes** tab and click on the arrow next to the **Add Custom Property** icon (the green plus sign) in the **Custom Properties** tab. From the context menu, select **Non-translatable Property**.

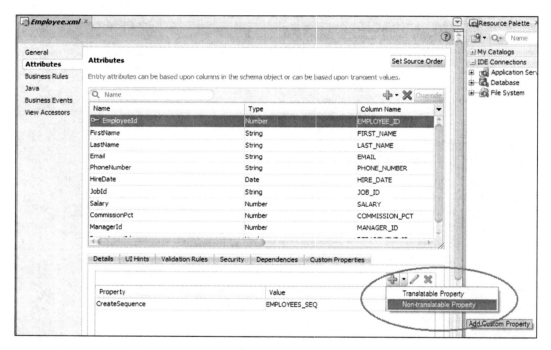

Click on the **Property** field and enter `CreateSequence`. For the **Value** enter the database sequence name that will be used to assign values to the specific attribute. For the **Employee** entity object example mentioned earlier, we will use the **EMPLOYEES_SEQ** database sequence to assign values to the **EmployeeId** attribute.

> Note that for testing purposes, we have created in the HREmployees workspace an `Employee` entity object and added the `CreateSequence` custom property to its `EmployeeId` attribute. To test the recipe, you can run the `EmployeeAppModule` application module.

▸ *Breaking up the application in multiple workspaces, Chapter 1, Pre-requisites to Success: ADF Project Setup and Foundations*

▸ *Setting up BC base classes, Chapter 1, Pre-requisites to Success: ADF Project Setup and Foundations*

▸ *Overriding doDML() to populate an attribute with a gapless sequence*, in this chapter

▸ *Creating and applying property sets*, in this chapter

Overriding doDML() to populate an attribute with a gapless sequence

In this recipe, we will go over a generic programming technique that you can use to assign gapless database sequence values to entity object attributes. A gapless sequence will produce values with no gaps in between them. The difference between this technique and the one presented in the *Using a custom property to populate a sequence attribute* recipe, is that the sequence values are assigned during the transaction commit cycle instead of during component creation.

Getting ready

We will add this generic functionality to the custom entity framework class that we created in the *Setting up BC base classes* recipe in *Chapter 1, Pre-requisites to Success: ADF Project Setup and Foundations*. The custom framework classes in this case reside in the `SharedComponets` workspace. You will need access to the HR database schema to run the recipe's test case.

How to do it...

1. Start by opening the `SharedComponets` workspace in JDeveloper. If needed, follow the steps in the referenced recipe to create it.

2. Locate the custom entity framework class in the `SharedBC` project and open it in the editor.

3. Click on the **Override Methods...** icon on the toolbar (the green left arrow) to bring up the **Override Methods** dialog.

4. From the list of methods that are presented, select the **doDML()** method and click **OK**. JDeveloper will go ahead and insert a `doDML()` method into the body of your custom entity class.

5. Add the following code to the `doDML()` before the call to `super.doDML()`:

```
// check for insert operation
if (DML_INSERT == operation) {
  // iterate all entity attributes
  for (AttributeDef atrbDef :this.getEntityDef().
    getAttributeDefs()) {
    // check for a custom property called COMMITSEQ_PROPERTY
    String sequenceName=(String)atrbDef.getProperty
      (COMMITSEQ_PROPERTY);
    if (sequenceName != null) {
      // create the sequence based on the custom property sequence
        name
      SequenceImpl sequence = new SequenceImpl(sequenceName,
        this.getDBTransaction());
      // populate the attribute with the next sequence number
      this.populateAttributeAsChanged(atrbDef.getIndex(),
      sequence.getSequenceNumber());
    }
  }
}
```

How it works...

If you examine the code presented in this recipe, you will see that it looks similar to the code presented in the *Using a custom property to populate a sequence attribute* recipe in this chapter. The difference is that this code executes during the transaction commit phase. During this phase, the ADF framework calls the entity's `doDML()` method. In our overridden `doDML()`, we first check for a `DML_INSERT` operation flag. This would be the case when inserting a new record into the database. We then iterate the entity's attribute definitions looking for a custom property identified by the constant `COMMITSEQ_PROPERTY`. Based on the property's value, we create a sequence object and get the next sequence value by calling `getSequenceNumber()`. Finally, we assign the sequence value to the specific attribute by calling `populateAttributeAsChanged()`. Assigning a sequence value during the commit phase does not allow the user to intervene. This will produce gapless sequence values. Of course to guarantee that there are no final gaps in the sequence values, deletion should not be allowed. That is, if rows are deleted, gaps in the sequence values will appear. Gaps will also appear in case of validation failures, if you do not subsequently rollback the transaction. Since all of the entity objects are derived from the custom entity framework class, all object commits will go through this `doDML()` implementation.

To use this technique, first you will need to re-deploy the shared components project. Then add the `CommitSequence` custom property as needed to the specific attributes of your entity objects. We explained how to do this in the *Using a custom property to populate a sequence attribute* recipe.

There's more...

`doDML()` is called by the ADF framework during a transaction commit operation. It is called for every entity object in the transaction's pending changes list. This is true even when entity **Update Batching** optimization is used. For an entity-based view object, this means that it will be called for every row in the row set that is in the pending changes list. The method accepts an operation flag; `DML_INSERT`, `DML_UPDATE`, or `DML_DELETE` to indicate an insert, update, or delete operation on the specific entity.

Data is posted to the database once `super.doDML()` is called, so any exceptions thrown before calling `super.doDML()` will result in no posted data. Once the data is posted to the database, queries or stored procedures that rely upon the posted data should be coded in the overridden application module's `beforeCommit()` method. This method is also available at the entity object level, where it is called by the framework for each entity in the transaction's pending changes list. Note that the framework calls `beforeCommit()` for each entity object in the *transaction pending changes list* prior to calling the application module `beforeCommit()`.

For additional information on `doDML()`, consult the sections *Methods You Typically Override in Your Custom EntityImpl Subclass* and *Transaction "Post" Processing (Record Cache)* in the *Fusion Developer's Guide for Oracle Application Development Framework*,which can be found at `http://docs.oracle.com/cd/E24382_01/web.1112/e16182/toc.htm`.

> Note that for testing purposes, we have created a `Department` entity object in the `HRDepartments` workspace and added the `CommitSequence` custom property to its `DepartmentId` attribute. The value of the `CommitSequence` property was set to `DEPARTMENTS_SEQ`, the database sequence that is used to assign values to the `DepartmentId` attribute. To test the recipe, run the `DepartmentAppModule` application module on the **ADF Model Tester**.

See also

- ▸ *Breaking up the application in multiple workspaces, Chapter 1, Pre-requisites to Success: ADF Project Setup and Foundations*
- ▸ *Setting up BC base classes, Chapter 1, Pre-requisites to Success: ADF Project Setup and Foundations*
- ▸ *Using a custom property to populate a sequence attribute*, in this chapter
- ▸ *Creating and applying property sets*, in this chapter

Creating and applying property sets

In the *Using a custom property to populate a sequence attribute* and *Overriding doDML() to populate an attribute with a gapless sequence* recipes of this chapter, we introduced custom properties for generic ADF business component programming. In this recipe, we will present a technique to organize your custom properties in reusable **property sets**. By organizing application-wide properties in a property set and exporting them as part of an ADF Library JAR, you can then reference them from any other ADF-BC project. This in turn will allow you to centralize the custom properties used throughout your ADF application in a single property set.

getting ready

We will create a property set in the `SharedComponets` workspace. I suggest that you go over the *Using a custom property to populate a sequence attribute* and *Overriding doDML() to populate an attribute with a gapless sequence* recipes in this chapter before continuing with this recipe. To run the recipe's test cases, you will need access to the `HR` schema in the database.

How to do it...

1. Start by opening the `SharedComponets` workspace. If needed, follow the steps in the referenced recipe to create it.

2. Right-click on the `SharedBC` project and select **New...**.

3. On the **New Gallery** dialog select **ADF Business Components** under the **Business Tier** node and **Property Set** from the **Items** on the right.

4. Click **OK** to proceed. This will open the **Create Property Set** dialog.

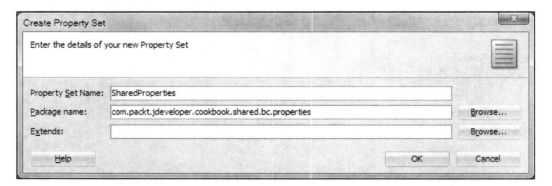

5. Enter the property set name and package in the appropriate fields. For this recipe, we will call it `SharedProperties` and use the `com.packt.jdeveloper.cookbook.shared.bc.properties` package. Click **OK** to continue.

6. JDeveloper will create and open the `SharedProperties` property set.

7. To add a custom property to the property set, click on the **Add Custom Property** button (the green plus sign icon).

8. Go ahead and add two non-translatable properties called **CommitSequenceDepartmentDepartmentId** and **CreateSequenceEmployeeEmployeeId**. Set their values to **DEPARTMENTS_SEQ** and **EMPLOYEES_SEQ** respectively. Your property set should look similar to the following screenshot:

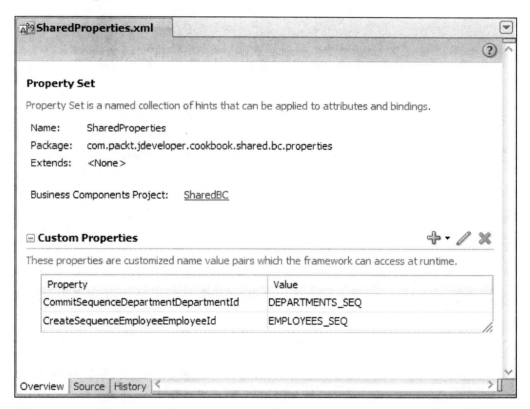

9. Next you need to change the `create()` method in the custom entity framework class so that the custom property is now similar to the following block of code:

```
// construct the custom property name from the entity name and
attribute
String propertyName = CREATESEQ_PROPERTY +
  getEntityDef().getName() + atrbDef.getName();
// check for a custom property called CREATESEQ_PROPERTY
String sequenceName = (String)atrbDef.getProperty(propertyName);
```

10. Similarly change the `doDML()` method in the custom entity framework class so that the custom property is also constructed, as shown in the following block of code:

```
// construct the custom property name from the entity name and
  attribute
String propertyName = COMMITSEQ_PROPERTY +
  getEntityDef().getName() + atrbDef.getName();
// check for a custom property called COMMITSEQ_PROPERTY
String sequenceName =(String)atrbDef.getProperty(propertyName);
```

11. Redeploy the `SharedComponets` workspace into an ADF Library JAR.

12. Open the `HREmployees` workspace and double-click on the `HREmployeesBC` business components project to bring up the **Project Properties** dialog.

13. Select **Imports** under the **ADF Business Components** node and click on the **Import...** button on the right.

14. On the **Import Business Components XML File** dialog browse for the shared components ADF Library JAR file in the `ReUsableJARs` directory. Select it and click **Open**.

15. You should see the imported `SharedBC` project under the **Imported Business Component Projects** along with the imported packages and package contents. Click **OK** to continue with importing the business components.

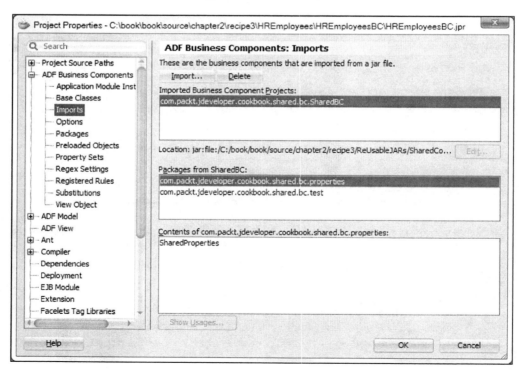

16. Double-click on the **Employee** entity object and go to the **Attributes** tab.

17. Click on the **Details** tab, and from the **Property Set** choice list select the imported property set.

18. Repeat steps 12-17 for the `HRDepartments` workspace and apply the property set to the `DepartmentId` attribute of the `Department` entity object.

How it works...

Property sets are a way to gather all of your custom properties together into logical collections. Instead of applying each custom property separately to a business components object or to any of its attributes, custom properties defined in these collections can be applied at once on them. Property sets can be applied to entity objects and their attributes, view objects and their attributes, and application modules. You access custom properties programmatically as indicated earlier, by calling `AttributeDef.getProperty()` for properties applied to attributes, `EntityDefImpl.getProperty()` for properties applied to entity objects, `ViewDefImpl.getProperty()` for properties applied to view objects, and so on.

How you organize your custom properties into property sets is up to you. In this recipe, for example, we use a single property set called `SharedProperties`, which we define in the shared components ADF library. In this way, we kept all custom properties used by the application in a single container. For this to work, we had to devise a way to differentiate among them. The algorithm that we used was to combine the property name with the business components object name and the attribute name that the property applies to. So we have properties called `CommitSequenceDepartmentDepartmentId` and `CreateSequenceEmployeeEmployeeId`.

Finally, we import the property set from the `SharedComponets` workspace into the relevant business components projects using the **Import Business Components** facility of the business components **Project Properties** dialog.

There's more...

To test the recipe, you can run the `EmployeeAppModule` and `DepartmentAppModule` application modules in the `HREmployees` and `HRDepartments` workspaces respectively.

Note that you can override any of the properties defined in a property set by explicitly adding the same property to the business component object or to any of its attributes.

Also note that property sets can be applied onto entity objects, view objects, and application modules by clicking on the **Edit property set selection** button (the pen icon) on the business component object definition **General** tab. On the same tab, you can add custom properties to the business component object by clicking on the **Add Custom Property** button (the green plus sign icon).

See also

> ▸ *Breaking up the application in multiple workspaces, Chapter 1, Pre-requisites to Success: ADF Project Setup and Foundations*

> ▸ *Setting up BC base classes, Chapter 1, Pre-requisites to Success: ADF Project Setup and Foundations*

> ▸ *Using a custom property to populate a sequence attribute,* in this chapter

> ▸ *Overriding doDML() to populate an attribute with a gapless sequence,* in this chapter

Using getPostedAttribute() to determine the posted attribute's value

There are times when you need to get the original database value of an entity object atttribute, such as when you want to compare the attribute's current value to the original database value. In this recipe, we will illustrate how to do this by utilizing the getPostedAttribute() method.

Getting ready

We will be working on the SharedComponets workspace. We will add a helper method to the custom entity framework class.

How to do it...

1. Start by opening the SharedComponets workspace. If needed, follow the steps in the referenced recipe to create it.

2. Locate the custom entity framework class and open it into the source editor.

3. Add the following code to the custom entity framework class:

```
/**
 * Check if attribute's value differs from its posted value
 * @param attrIdx the attribute index
 * @return
 */
public boolean isAttrValueChanged(int attrIdx) {
  // get the attribute's posted value
  Object postedValue = getPostedAttribute(attrIdx);
  // get the attribute's current value
  Object newValue = getAttributeInternal(attrIdx);
  // return true if attribute value differs from its posted value
  return isAttributeChanged(attrIdx) &&
    ((postedValue == null && newValue != null) ||
    (postedValue != null && newValue == null) ||
    (postedValue != null && newValue != null &&
    !newValue.equals(postedValue)));
}
```

How it works...

We added a helper method called isAttrValueChanged() to the our custom entity framework class. This method accepts the attribute's index. The attribute index is generated and maintained by JDeveloper itself. The method first calls getPostedAttribute() specifying the attribute index to retrieve the attribute value that was posted to the database. This is the attribute's database value. Then it calls getAttributeInternal() using the same attribute index to determine the current attribute value. The two values are then compared. The method isAttributeChanged() returns true if the attribute value was changed in the current transaction.

The following is an example of calling isAttrValueChanged() from an entity implementation class to determine whether the current value of the employee's last name differs from the value that was posted to the database:

```
super.isAttrValueChanged(this.LASTNAME);
```

See also

▶ *Breaking up the application in multiple workspaces, Chapter 1, Pre-requisites to Success: ADF Project Setup and Foundations*

▶ *Setting up BC base classes, Chapter 1, Pre-requisites to Success: ADF Project Setup and Foundations*

Overriding remove() to delete associated children entities

When deleting a parent entity, there are times you will want to delete all of the child entity rows in an entity assocation relation. In this recipe, we will see how to accomplish this task.

Getting ready

You will need access to the HR database schema.

How to do it...

1. Start by creating a new **Fusion Web Application (ADF)** workspace called **HRComponents**.

2. Create a **Database Connection** for the HR schema in the **Application Resource** section of the **Application Navigator**.

3. Use the **Business Components from Tables** selection on the **New Gallery** dialog to create business components objects for the DEPARTMENTS and EMPLOYEES tables. The components in the **Application Navigator** should look similar to the following:

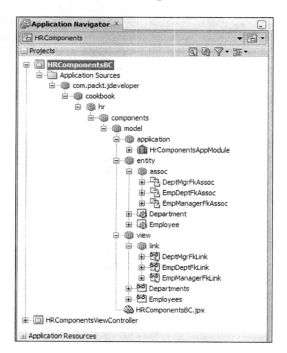

4. Double-click on the **EmpDeptFkAssoc** association on the **Application Navigator** to open the association definition, then click on the **Relationship** tab.

5. Click on the **Edit accessors** button (the pen icon) in the **Accessors** section to bring up the **Association Properties** dialog.

6. Change the **Accessor Name** in the **Destination Accessor** section to **DepartmentEmployees** and click **OK** to continue.

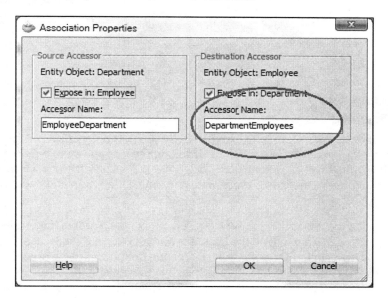

7. Double-click on the **Department** entity object in the **Application Navigator** to open its definition and go to the **Java** tab.

8. Click on the **Edit Java Options** button (the pen icon on the top right of the tab) to bring up the **Select Java Options** dialog.

9. On the **Select Java Options** dialog, select **Generate Entity Object Class**.

10. Ensure that both the **Accessors** and **Remove Method** checkboxes are selected. Click **OK** to continue.

11. Repeat steps 7-10 to create a Java implementation class for the Employee entity object. You do not have to click on the **Remove Method** checkbox in this case.

12. Open the DepartmentImpl Java implementation class for the Department entity object in the JDeveloper Java editor and locate the remove() method.

13. Add the following code before the call to `super.remove()`:

```
// get the department employeess accessor
RowIterator departmentEmployees = this.getDepartmentEmployees();
// iterate over all department employees
while (departmentEmployees.hasNext()) {
  // get the department employee
  EmployeeImpl departmentEmployee =
    (EmployeeImpl)departmentEmployees.next();
  // remove employee
  departmentEmployee.remove();
}
```

How it works...

During the creation of the `Department` and `Employee` entity objects, JDeveloper automatically creates the entity associations based on the foreign key constraints that exist among the `DEPARTMENTS` and `EMPLOYEES` database tables. The specific association that relates a department to its employees was automatically created and it was called `EmpDeptFkAssoc`.

Jdeveloper exposes the association to both the source and destination entity objects via accessors. In step 6, we changed the accessor name to make it more meaningful. We called the the association accessor that returns the department employees `DepartmentEmployees`. Using Java, this accessor is available in the `DepartmentImpl` class by calling `getDepartmentEmployees()`. This method returns an `oracle.jbo.RowIterator` object that can be iterated over.

Now, let's take a closer look at the code added to the `remove()` method. This method is called by the ADF framework each time we delete a record. In it, first we access the current department's employees by calling `getDepartmentEmployees()`. Then we iterate over the department employees, by calling `hasNext()` on the employees `RowIterator`. Then for each employee, we get the `Employee` entity object by calling `next()`, and call `remove()` on it to delete it. The call to `super.remove()` finally deletes the `Department` entity itself. The net result is to delete all employees associated with the specific department before deleting the department itself.

There's more...

A specific type of association called composition association can be enabled in those cases where an object composition behavior is observed, that is, where the child entity cannot exist on its own without the associated "parent" entity. In these cases, there are special provisions by the ADF framework and JDeveloper itself to fine-tune the delete behavior of child entities when the parent entity is removed. These options are available in the association editor **Relationship** tab, under the **Behavior** section.

Once you indicate a **Composition Association** for the association, two options are presented relating to cascading deletion:

  ▸ **Optimize for Database Cascade Delete**: This option prevents the framework from issuing a DELETE DML statement for each composed entity object destination row. You do this if ON DELETE CASCADE is implemented in the database.

  ▸ **Implement Cascade Delete**: This option implements the cascade delete in the middle layer, that is if the source composing entity object contains any composed children, its deletion is prevented.

This recipe shows how to remove children entity objects for which composition association is not enabled. This may be the case when a requirement exists to allow in some cases composed children entities to exist without associated composing parent entities. For example, when a new employee is not yet assigned to a particular department.

Overriding remove() to delete a parent entity in an association

In this recipe, we will present a technique that you can use in cases that you want to delete the parent entity in an association when the last child entity is deleted. An example of such a case would be to delete a department when the last department employee is deleted.

Getting ready

You will need access to the HR schema in your database.

How to do it...

1. Start by creating a new **Fusion Web Application (ADF)** workspace called `HRComponents`.

2. Create a database connection for the `HR` schema in the **Application Resource** section of the **Application Navigator**.

3. Use the **Business Components from Tables** selection on the **New Gallery** dialog to create `Business Components` objects for the `DEPARTMENTS` and `EMPLOYEES` tables.

4. Double-click on the **EmpDeptFkAssoc** association on the **Application Navigator** to bring up the Association editor, then click on the **Relationship** tab.

5. Click on the **Edit accessors** button (the pen icon) in the **Accessors** section to bring up the **Association Properties** dialog.

6. Change the **Accessor Name** in the **Source Accessor** section to **EmployeeDepartment** and click **OK** to continue.

7. Generate custom Java implementation classes for both the `Employee` and `Department` entity objects.

8. Open the `EmployeeImpl` custom Java implementation class for the `Employee` entity object and locate the `remove()` method.

9. Replace the call to `super.remove()` with the following code:

```
// get the associated department
DepartmentImpl department = this.getEmployeeDepartment();
// get number of employees in the department
int numberOfEmployees =
  department.getDepartmentEmployees().getRowCount();
// check whether last employee in the department
if (numberOfEmployees == 1) {
  // delete the last employee
  super.remove();
  // delete the department as well
  department.remove();
}
else {
  // just delete the employee
  super.remove();
}
```

How it works...

If you followed the *Overriding remove() to delete associated children entities* recipe in this chapter, then steps 1 through 8 should look familiar. These are the basic steps to create the `HRComponents` workspace, along with the business components associated with the `EMPLOYEES` and `DEPARTMENTS` tables in the `HR` schema. These steps also create custom Java implementation classes for the `Employee` and `Department` entity objects and setup the `EmpDeptFkAssoc` association.

The code in `remove()` first gets the `Department` entity row by calling the accessor `getEmployeeDepartment()` method. Remember, this was the name of accessor—`EmployeeDepartment`—that we setup in step 6. `getEmployeeDepartment()` returns the custom `DepartmentImpl` that we setup in step 7. In order to determine the number of employees in the associated `Department`, we first get the `Employee RowIterator` by calling `getDepartmentEmployees()` on it, and then `getRowCount()` on the `RowIterator`. All that is done in the following statement:

```
int numberOfEmployees =
department.getDepartmentEmployees().getRowCount();
```

Remember that we setup the name of the `DepartmentEmployees` accessor in step 6. Next, we checked for the number of employees in the associated department, and if there was only one employee—the one we are about to delete—we first deleted it by calling `super.remove()`. Then we deleted the department itself by calling `department.remove()`. If more than one employee was found for the specific department, we just delete the employee by calling `super.remove()`. This was done in the `else` part of the `if` statement.

There's more...

Note the implications of using `getRowCount()` versus `getEstimatedRowCount()` in your code when dealing with large result sets: `getRowCount()` will perform a database count query each time it is called to return the exact number of rows in the view object. On the other hand, `getEstimatedRowCount()` executes a database count query only once to fetch the view object row count to the middle layer. Then, it fetches the row count from the middle layer. The row count in the middle layer is adjusted as view object rows are added or deleted. This may not produce an accurate row count when multiple user sessions are manipulating the same view object at the same time. For more information on this topic, consult the section *How to Count the Number of Rows in a Row Set* in the *Fusion Developer's Guide for Oracle Application Development Framework*.

See also

- *Overriding remove() to delete associated children entities*, in this chapter

Using a method validator based on a view object accessor

In this recipe, we will show how to validate an entity object against a **view accessor** using a custom entity method validator. The use case that we will cover—based on the HR schema—will not allow the user to enter more than a specified number of employees per department.

Getting ready

We will be using the HRComponents workspace that we created in the previous recipes in this chapter so that we don't repeat these steps again. You will need access to the HR database schema.

How to do it...

1. Right-click on the com.packt.jdeveloper.cookbook.hr.components. model.view package of the HRComponentsBC business components project of the HRComponents workspace, and select **New View Object...**.

2. Use the **Create View Object** wizard to create a **SQL query** view object called **EmployeeCount** based on the following query:

   ```
   SELECT COUNT(*) AS EMPLOYEE_COUNT FROM EMPLOYEES WHERE DEPARTMENT_
   ID = :DepartmentId
   ```

3. While on the **Create View Object** wizard, also do the following:

   ❑ Create a **Bind Variable** called **DepartmentId** of type **Number**

   ❑ On the **Attribute Settings** page, ensure that you select **Key Attribute** for the **EmployeeCount** attribute

   ❑ On the **Java** page make sure that both the **Generate View Row Class** and **Include accessors** checkboxes are checked

   ❑ Do not add the view object to an application module

4. Now, double-click on the **Employee** entity object to open its definition and go to the **View Accessors** page.

5. Click on the **Create new view accessors** button (the green plus sign icon) to bring up the **View Accessors** dialog.

6. On the **View Accessors** dialog locate the **EmployeeCount** view object and click the **Add instance** button—the blue right arrow button. Click **OK** to dismiss the dialog.

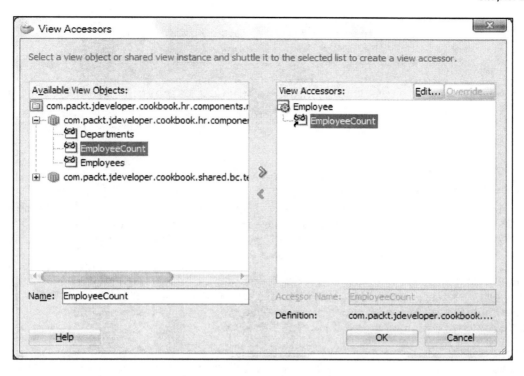

7. On the entity object definition **Business Rules** tab, select the **Employee** entity and click on the **Create new validator** button (the green plus sign icon).

8. On the **Add Validation Rule** dialog, select **Method** for the **Rule Type** and enter `validateDepartmentEmployeeCount` for the **Method Name**.

9. Click on the **Failure Handling** tab and in the **Message Text** enter the message `Department has reached maximum employee limit`. Click **OK**.

10. Open the `EmployeeImpl` custom implementation Java class, locate the `validateDepartmentEmployeeCount()` method and add the following code to it before the `return true` statement:

```
// get the EmployeeCount view accessor
RowSet employeeCount = this.getEmployeeCount();
// setup the DepartmentId bind variable
employeeCount.setNamedWhereClauseParam("DepartmentId",
  this.getDepartmentId());
// run the View Object query
employeeCount.executeQuery();
// check results
if (employeeCount.hasNext()) {
  // get the EmployeeCount row
```

```
EmployeeCountRowImpl employeeCountRow =
   (EmployeeCountRowImpl)employeeCount.next();
// get the deparment employee count
Number departmentEmployees =
   employeeCountRow.getEmployeeCount();
if (departmentEmployees.compareTo(MAX_DEPARTMENT_EMPLOYEES)>0) {
   return false;
}
}
```

How it works...

We have created a separate query-based view object called `EmployeeCount` for validation purposes. If you look closely at the `EmployeeCount` query, you will see that it determines the number of employees in a department. Which department is determined by the bind variable `DepartmentId` used in the `WHERE` clause of the query.

We then add the `EmployeeCount` view object as a view accessor to the `Employee` object. We call the accessor instance `EmployeeCount` as well. Once you have generated a custom Java implementation class for the `Employee` entity object, the `EmployeeCount` view accessor is available by calling `getEmployeeCount()`.

We proceed by adding a method validator to the entity object. We call the method to use for the validator `validateDepartmentEmployeeCount`. JDeveloper created this method for us in the entity custom implementation Java class.

The code that we add to the `validateDepartmentEmployeeCount()` method first gets the `EmployeeCount` accessor, and calls `setNamedWhereClauseParam()` on it to set the value of the `DepartmentId` bind variable to the value of the department identifier from the current `Employee`. This value is accessible via the `getDepartmentId()` method. We then execute the `EmployeeCount` view object query by calling its `executeQuery()` method. We check for the results of the query by calling `hasNext()` on the view object. If the query yields results, we get the next result row by calling `next()`. We have casted the `oracle.job.Row` returned by `next()` to an `EmployeeCountRowImpl` so we can directly call its `getEmployeeCount()` accessor. This returns the number of employees for the specific department. We then compare it to a predefined maximum number of employees per department identified by the constant `MAX_DEPARTMENT_EMPLOYEES`.

The method validator returns a `false` to indicate that the validation will fail. Otherwise it returns `true`.

Observe what happens when you run the application module with the ADF Model Tester. When you try to add a new employee to a department that has more than a predefined number of employees (identified by the constant `MAX_DEPARTMENT_EMPLOYEES`), a validation message is raised. This is the message that we defined for our method validator.

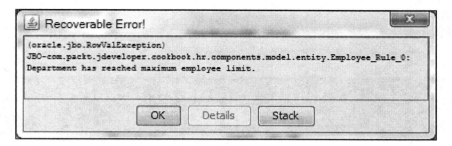

There's more...

Note that in the previous code we called `setNamedWhereClauseParam()` on the `EmployeeCount` view object to set the value of the `DepartmentId` bind variable to the current employee's department ID. This could have been done declaratively as well using the **Edit View Accessor** dialog, which is available on the **View Accessors** page of the `Employee` entity definition page by clicking on the **Edit selected View Accessor** button (the pen icon). On the **Edit View Accessor** dialog, locate the `DepartmentId` bind variable in the **Bind Parameter Values** section, and on the **Value** field enter `DepartmentId`. This will set the value of the `DepartmentId` bind variable to the value of the `DepartmentId` attribute of the `Employee` entity object.

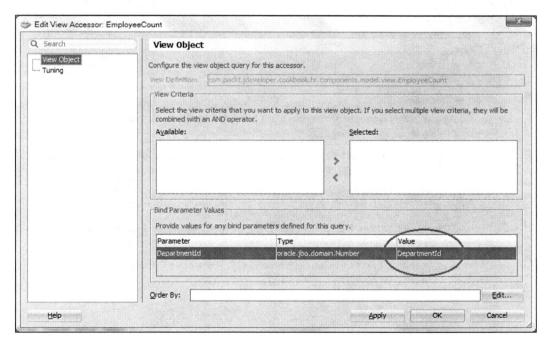

See also

▸ *Overriding remove() to delete associated children entities*, in this chapter

Using Groovy expressions to resolve validation error message tokens

In this recipe, we will expand on the *Using a custom validator based on a View Object accessor* recipe to demonstrate how to use validation message parameter values based on Groovy expressions. Moreover, we will show how to retrieve the parameter values from a specific parameter bundle.

Groovy is a dynamic language that runs inside the Java Virtual Machine. In the context of the ADF Business Components framework, it can be used to provide declarative expressions that are interpreted at runtime. Groovy expressions can be used in validation rules, validation messages, and parameters, attribute initializations, bind variable initializations, and more.

Getting ready

This recipe builds on the *Using a custom validator based on a View Object accessor* recipe. It also relies on the recipes *Breaking up the application in multiple workspaces* and *Setting up BC base classes* presented in *Chapter 1, Pre-requisites to Success: ADF Project Setup and Foundations*.

How to do it...

1. In the **Application Navigator** double-click on the **Employee** entity object definition and go to its **Business Rules** tab.

2. Double-click on the **validateDepartmentEmpoyeeCount Method Validator** to bring up the **Edit Validation Rule** dialog and go to the **Failure Handling** tab.

3. Change the **Error Message** to *Department has reached maximum employee limit of {1}*.

4. For the **Message Token 1 Expression** in the **Token Message Expressions** section, enter the following expression:

```
source.getBundleParameter('DepartmentEmployeeLimit')
```

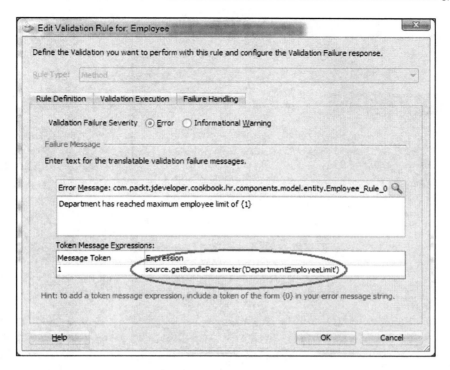

5. Now, open the `SharedComponets` workspace and locate the entity framework extension class `ExtEntityImpl`. Add the following `getBundleParameter()` method to it:

```
public String getBundleParameter(String parameterKey) {
  // use BundleUtils to load the parameter
  return BundleUtils.loadParameter(parameterKey);
}
```

6. Locate the `BundleUtils` helper class in the `com.packt.jdeveloper.cookbook.shared.bc.exceptions.messages` package and add the following `loadParameter()` method:

```
public static String loadParameter(final String parameterKey) {
  // get access to the error message parameters bundle
  final ResourceBundle parametersBundle =
  ResourceBundle.getBundle(PARAMETERS_BUNDLE,
    Locale.getDefault());
  // get and return the the parameter value
  return parametersBundle.getString(PARAMETER_PREFIX +
    parameterKey);
}
```

7. Finally, locate the `ErrorParams.properties` property file and add the following text to it:

    ```
    parameter.DepartmentEmployeeLimit=2
    ```

How it works...

For this recipe, first we added a parameter to the method validator message. The parameter is indicated by adding parameter placeholders to the message using braces { }. The parameter name is indicated by the value within the braces. In our case, we defined a parameter called 1 by entering {1}. We then had to supply the parameter value. Instead of hardcoding the parameter value, we used the following Groovy expression:

```
source.getBundleParameter('DepartmentEmployeeLimit').
```

The `source` prefix allows us to reference an entity object method from the validator. In this case, the method is called `getBundleParameter()`. This method accepts a parameter key which is used to load the actual parameter value from the parameters bundle. In this case, we have used the `DepartmentEmployeeLimit` parameter key.

Then we implemented the `getBundleParameter()` method. We implemented this method in the base entity custom framework class so that it is available to all entity objects. If you look at the code in `getBundleParameter()`, you will see that it loads and returns the parameter value using the helper `BundleUtils.loadParameter()`.

 We introduced the helper class `BundleUtils` while we worked on the *Using a generic backing bean actions framework* recipe in *Chapter 1, Pre-requisites to Success: ADF Project Setup and Foundations*.

The `BundleUtils.loadParameter()` method pre-pends the parameter with the prefix `parameter`.

Finally, we defined the `parameter.DepartmentEmployeeLimit` parameter in the `ErrorParams.properties` parameters bundle. For further information on this bundle, refer to the *Using a custom exception class* recipe in *Chapter 1, Pre-requisites to Success: ADF Project Setup and Foundations*. When the validation is raised at runtime, the message parameter placeholder {1}, which was originally defined in the message, will be substituted with the actual parameter value (in this case, the number 2).

See also

▶   *Breaking up the application in multiple workspaces, Chapter 1, Pre-requisites to Success: ADF Project Setup and Foundations*

▶   *Setting up BC base classes, Chapter 1, Pre-requisites to Success: ADF Project Setup and Foundations*

▶ *Using a custom exception class, Chapter 1, Pre-requisites to Success: ADF Project Setup and Foundations*

▶ *Using a generic backing bean actions framework, Chapter 1, Pre-requisites to Success: ADF Project Setup and Foundations*

Using doDML() to enforce a detail record for a new master record

In this recipe, we will consider a simple technique that we can use to enforce having detailed records when inserting a new master record in an entity association relationship. The use case demonstrates how to enforce creating at least one employee at the time when a new department is created.

Getting ready

We will use the HR database schema and the HRComponents workspace that we have created in previous recipes in this chapter.

How to do it...

1. Open the DepartmentImpl custom entity implementation class and override the doDML() method using the **Override Methods** dialog.

2. Add the following code to the doDML() method before the call to super.doDML():

```
// check for insert
if (DML_INSERT == operation) {
  // get the department employees accessor
  RowIterator departmentEmployees = this.getDepartmentEmployees();
  // check for any employees
  if (!departmentEmployees.hasNext()) {
    // avoid inserting the department if there are no employees
      for it
    throw new ExtJboException("00006");
  }
}
```

How it works...

In the overridden doDML(), we only check for insert operations. This is indicated by comparing the DML operation flag which is passed as a parameter to doDML() to the DML_INSERT flag. Then we get the department employees from the DepartmentEmployees accessor by calling getDepartmentEmployees(). The DepartmentEmployees accessor was set up during the creation of the HRComponents workspace earlier in this chapter. We check whether the RowIterator returned has any rows by calling hasNext() on it. If this is not the case, that is, there are no employees associated with the specific department that we are about to insert, we alert the user by throwing an ExtJboException exception. The ExtJboException exception is part of the SharedComponets workspace and it was developed in the *Using a custom exception class* recipe back in *Chapter 1, Pre-requisites to Success: ADF Project Setup and Foundations*.

When testing the application module with the ADF Model Tester, we get the following error message when we try to insert a new department without any associated employees:

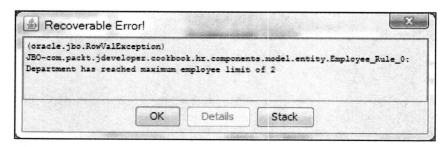

 Note that in case that an exception is thrown during DML, which could result in partial data being posted to the database.

See also

▶ *Using a custom exception class, Chapter 1, Pre-requisites to Success: ADF Project Setup and Foundations*

▶ *Overriding remove() to delete associated children entities, Chapter 1, Pre-requisites to Success: ADF Project Setup and Foundations*

3

A Different Point of View: View Object Techniques

In this chapter, we will cover:

- ▸ Iterating a view object using a secondary rowset iterator
- ▸ Setting default values for view row attributes
- ▸ Controlling the updatability of view object attributes programmatically
- ▸ Setting the Queryable property of a view object attribute programmatically
- ▸ Using a transient attribute to indicate a new view object row
- ▸ Conditionally inserting new rows at the end of a rowset
- ▸ Using findAndSetCurrentRowByKey() to set the view object currency
- ▸ Restoring the current row after a transaction rollback
- ▸ Dynamically changing the WHERE clause of the view object query
- ▸ Removing a row from a rowset without deleting it from the database

Introduction

View objects are an essential part of the ADF business components. They work in conjunction with entity objects, making entity-based view objects, to support querying the database, retrieving data from the database, and building rowsets of data. The underlying entities enable an updatable data model that supports the addition, deletion, and modification of data. They also support the enforcement of business rules and the permanent storage of the data to the database.

In cases where an updatable data model is not required, the framework supports a read-only view object, one that is not based on entity objects but on a SQL query supplied by the developer. Read-only view objects should be used in cases where UNION and GROUP BY clauses appear in the view object queries. In other cases, even though an updatable data model is not required, the recommended practice is to base the view objects on entity objects and allow the JDeveloper framework-supporting wizards to build the SQL query automatically instead.

This chapter presents several techniques covering a wide area of expertise related to view objects.

Iterating a view object using a secondary rowset iterator

There are times when you need to iterate through a view object rowset programmatically. In this recipe, we will see how to do this using a secondary rowset iterator. We will iterate over the Employees rowset and increase the employee's commission by a certain percentage for each employee that belongs to the Sales department.

Getting ready

This recipe was developed using the HRComponents workspace, which was created in the *Overriding remove() to delete associated children entities* recipe in *Chapter 2, Dealing with Basics: Entity Objects*. The HRComponents workspace requires a database connection to the HR schema.

How to do it...

1. Open the Employees view object definition and go to the **Java** page.
2. Click on the **Edit java options** button (the pen icon) to open the **Select Java Options** dialog.
3. Click on the **Generate View Object Class** and **Generate View Row Class** checkboxes. Ensure that the **Include accessors** checkbox is also selected.
4. Click **OK** to proceed with the creation of the custom implementation classes.

5. Add the following helper method to `EmployeesImpl.java`. If the import dialog is shown for the `Number` class, make sure that you choose the `oracle.jbo.domain.Number` class.

```
public void adjustCommission(Number commissionPctAdjustment) {
   // check for valid commission adjustment
   if (commissionPctAdjustment != null) {
     // create an employee secondary rowset iterator
     rowsetIterator employees = this.createrowsetIterator(null);
     // reset the iterator
     employees.reset();
     // iterate the employees
     while (employees.hasNext()) {
       // get the employee
       EmployeesRowImpl employee =
         (EmployeesRowImpl)employees.next();
       // check for employee belonging to the sales department
       if (employee.getDepartmentId() != null &&
         SALES_DEPARTMENT_ID ==
           employee.getDepartmentId().intValue()) {
         // calculate adjusted commission
         Number commissionPct = employee.getCommissionPct();
         Number adjustedCommissionPct = commissionPct != null) ?
           commissionPct.add(commissionPctAdjustment) :
           commissionPctAdjustment;
         // set the employee's new commission
         employee.setCommissionPct(adjustedCommissionPct);
       }
     }
     // done with the rowset iterator
     employees.closerowsetIterator();
   }
}
```

6. On the **Employees Java** page click on the **Edit view object client interface** button (the pen icon).

7. On the **Edit Client Interface** dialog, shuttle the `adjustCommission()` method to the **Selected** list and click **OK**.

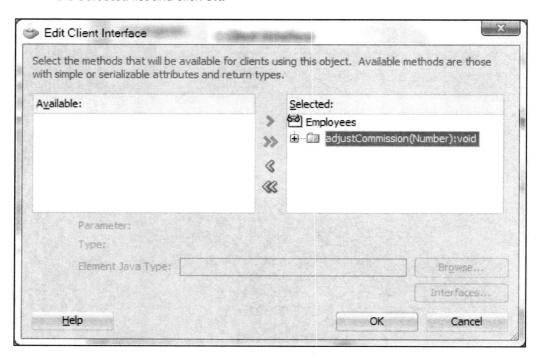

8. Open the `HRComponentsAppModule` application module definition and go to the **Java** page.

9. Click on the **Edit java options** button.

10. On the **Select Java Options** dialog, click on the **Generate Application Module Class** checkbox. Then click **OK** to close the dialog.

11. Open the `HrComponentsAppModuleImpl` class and add the following method:

```
public void adjustCommission(Number commissionPctAdjustment) {
    // execute the Employees view object query to create
      a rowset
    this.getEmployees().executeQuery();
    // adjust the employees commission
    this.getEmployees().adjustCommission(commissionPctAdjustment);
}
```

12. Return to the application module definition **Java** page, then use the **Edit application module client interface** button to add the `adjustCommission()` method to the application module's client interface.

How it works...

We created a view object custom Java implementation class for the `Employees` view object and add a method called `adjustCommission()`. The method is then exposed to the view object's client interface so that it can be accessible and called using the `Employees` interface.

The `adjustCommission()` method adjusts the commission for all employees belonging to the Sales department. The method accepts the commission adjustment percentage as an argument. We call the `createrowsetIterator()` method to create a secondary iterator, which we then use to iterate over the `Employees` rowset. This is the recommended practice to perform programmatic iteration over a rowset. The reason is that the view object instance that is being iterated may be bound to UI components and that iterating it directly will interfere with the UI. In this case, you will see the current row changing by itself.

We then call the `reset()` method to initialize the rowset iterator. This places the iterator in the slot before the first row in the rowset. We iterate the rowset by checking whether a next row exists. This is done by calling `hasNext()` on the iterator. If a next row exists, we retrieve it by calling `next()`, which returns an `oracle.jbo.Row`. We cast the default `Row` object that is returned to an `EmployeesRowImpl`, so we can use the custom setter and getter methods to manipulate the `Employee` row.

For testing purposes, we create a custom application module implementation class and add a method called `adjustCommission()` to it. We expose this method to the application module client interface so that we can call it from the **ADF Model Tester**. Note that methods can also be added to the view object client interface. Then these methods are shown under the view object collection in the **Data Control** panel and can be bound to the JSF page simply by dropping them on the page. Inside the `adjustCommission()`, we execute the `Employees` view object query by calling `executeQuery()` on it. We get the `Employees` view object instance via the `getEmployees()` getter method. Finally, we call the `adjustCommission()` method that we implemented in `EmployeesImpl` to adjust the employees' commission.

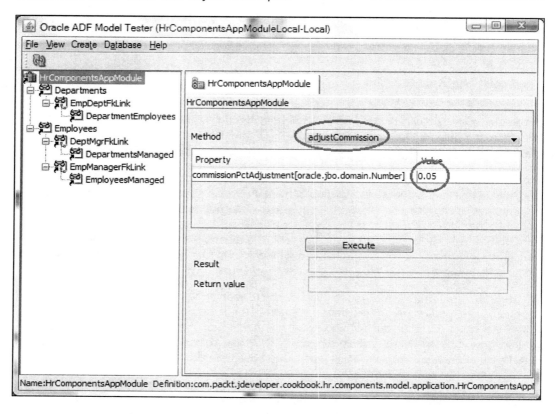

There's more...

In order to be able to iterate a view object rowset using a secondary iterator, the view object access mode in the **General | Tuning** section must set to `Scrollable`. Any other access mode setting will result in a **JBO-25083: Cannot create a secondary iterator on row set {0} because the access mode is forward-only or range-paging** error when attempting to create a secondary iterator. To iterate view objects configured with range paging, use the range paging view object API methods. Specifically, call `getEstimatedRangePageCount()` to determine the number of pages and for each page call `scrollToRangePage()`. Then determine the range page size by calling `getRangeSize()` and iterate through the page calling `getRowAtRangeIndex()`.

Pitfalls when iterating over large rowsets

Before iterating a view object rowset, consider that iterating the rowset may result in fetching a large number of records from the database to the middle layer. In this case, other alternatives should be considered, such as running the iteration asynchronously on a separate **Work Manager,** for instance (see recipe *Using a Work Manager for processing of long running tasks* in *Chapter 12, Optimizing, Fine-tuning and Monitoring*). In certain cases, such as when iterating in order to compute a total amount, consider using any of the following techniques. These methods are far more optimized in determining the total amount for an attribute than iterating the view object using Java code.

- ▶ **Groovy expressions** such as `object.getRowSet().sum('SomeAttribute')`
- ▶ **Analytic functions**, such as `COUNT(args) OVER ([PARTITION BY <...>] ...)`, in the view object's SQL query

For instance, consider the following view object query that calculates the department's total salaries using an analytic function. This would have been much more costly if it had to be done programmatically by iterating the underlying view objects.

```
SELECT DISTINCT DEPARTMENTS.DEPARTMENT_NAME,
SUM (EMPLOYEES.SALARY) OVER (PARTITION BY EMPLOYEES.DEPARTMENT_ID)
AS DEPARTMT_SALARIES
FROM EMPLOYEES
INNER JOIN DEPARTMENTS
ON DEPARTMENTS.DEPARTMENT_ID = EMPLOYEES.DEPARTMENT_ID
ORDER BY DEPARTMENTS.DEPARTMENT_NAME
```

See also

- ▶ *Overriding remove() to delete associated children entities, Chapter 2, Dealing with Basics: Entity Objects*

Setting default values for view row attributes

In this recipe, we will see how to set default values for view object attributes. There are a number of places where you can do this, namely:

- ▶ In the overridden `create()` method of the view object row implementation class
- ▶ Declaratively using a Groovy expression
- ▶ In the attribute getter method

For example, for a newly created employee, we will set the employee's hire date to the current date.

Getting ready

This recipe was developed using the HRComponents workspace, which was created in the *Overriding remove() to delete associated children entities* recipe in *Chapter 2, Dealing with Basics: Entity Objects*. The HRComponents workspace requires a database connection to the HR schema.

How to do it...

1. Create a view row Java implementation class for the Employees view object.

2. Open the EmployeesRowImpl.java custom view row Java implementation class and override the create() method using the **Override Methods...** button (the green left arrow on the editor toolbar).

3. To set the default employee's hire date to today's date, add the following code to create() immediately after the call to super.create():

   ```
   // set the default hire date to today
   this.setHireDate((Date)Date.getCurrentDate());
   ```

4. Open the Employees view object definition and go to the **Attributes** page.

5. Select the attribute that you want to initialize, **HireDate** in this case.

6. Select the **Details** tab.

7. In the **Default Value** section, select **Expression** and enter the following Groovy expression: adf.currentDate

8. Locate the view object attribute getter in the view object row implementation class. In this example, this is the `getHireDate()` method in `EmployeesRowImpl.java`.

9. Replace the existing code in `getHireDate()` with the following:

```
// get the HireDate attribute value
Date hireDate = (Date)getAttributeInternal(HIREDATE);
// check for null and return today's date if needed
return (hireDate == null) ? (Date)Date.getCurrentDate() :
   hireDate;
```

How it works...

This recipe presents three different techniques to set default values to view object attributes. The first technique (steps 1-3) overrides the view row `create()` method. This method is called by the ADF Business Components framework when a view object row is being created. In the previous code sample, we first call the parent `ViewRowImpl create()` to allow the framework processing. Then we initialize the attribute by calling its setter method— `setHireDate()` in this case—supplying `Date.getCurrentDate()` for the attribute value.

The second technique (steps 4-7) initializes the view object attribute declaratively using a Groovy expression. The Groovy expression used to initialize the `HireDate` attribute is `adf.currentDate`. Note that we change the attribute's **Value Type** field to **Expression**, so that it can be interpreted as an expression instead of a literal value. This expression when evaluated at runtime by the framework retrieves the current date.

Finally, the last technique (steps 8-9) uses the attribute getter—`getHireDate()` for this example—to return a default value. Using this technique, we don't actually set the attribute value; instead we return a default value, which can be subsequently applied to the attribute. Also notice that this is done only if the attribute does not already have a value (the check for `null`).

There's more...

A common use case related to this topic is setting an attribute's value based on the value of another related attribute. Consider, for instance, the use case where the employee's commission should be set to a certain default value if the employee is part of the Sales department. Also, consider the case where the employee's commission should be cleared if the employee is not part of the sales department. In addition to accomplishing this task with Groovy as stated earlier, it can also be implemented in the employee's `DepartmentId` setter, that is, in the `setDepartmentId()` method as follows:

```
public void setDepartmentId(Number value) {
   // set the department identifier
   setAttributeInternal(DEPARTMENTID, value);
   // set employee's commission based on employee's department
```

```
    try {
      // check for Sales department
      if (value != null && SALES_DEPARTMENT_ID == value.intValue()) {
        // if the commission has not been set yet
        if (this.getCommissionPct() == null) {
          // set commission to default
          this.setCommissionPct(new Number(DEFAULT_COMMISSION));
        }
      } else {
        // clear commission for non Sales department
        this.setCommissionPct(null);
      }
    } catch (SQLException e) {
      // log the exception
      LOGGER.severe(e);
    }
}
```

Specifying default values at the entity object level

Note that default values can be supplied at the entity object level as well. In this case, all view objects based on the particular entity object will inherit the specific behavior. You can provide variations for this behavior by implementing the techniques outlined in this recipe for specific view objects. To ensure consistent behavior throughout the application, it is recommended that you specify attribute defaults at the entity object level.

See also

> ▶ *Overriding remove() to delete associated children entities, Chapter 2, Dealing with Basics: Entity Objects*

Controlling the updatability of view object attributes programmatically

In ADF, there are a number of ways to control whether a view object attribute can be updated or not. It can be done declaratively in the **Attributes** tab via the **Updatable** combo, or on the frontend **ViewController** layer by setting the `disabled` or `readOnly` attributes of the **JSF** page component. Programmatically, it can be done either on a backing bean, or if you are utilizing ADF business components, on a custom view object row implementation class. This recipe demonstrates the latter case. For our example, we will disable updating any of the `Department` attributes specifically for departments that have more than a specified number of employees.

Getting ready

This recipe was developed using the HRComponents workspace, which was created in the *Overriding remove() to delete associated children entities* recipe in *Chapter 2, Dealing with Basics: Entity Objects*. The HRComponents workspace requires a database connection to the HR schema.

How to do it...

1. Create view row implementation classes for the Department and Employee view objects. Ensure that in both cases you have selected **Include accessors** on the **Java Options** dialog.

2. Open the DepartmentsRowImpl class in the Java editor.

3. Use the **Override Methods...** button to override the isAttributeUpdateable() method.

4. Replace the call to super.isAttributeUpdateable(i) with the following code:

```
// get the number of employees for the specific department
int departmentEmployeeCount = this.getEmployees() != null
  ? this.getEmployees().getRowCount() : 0;
// set all attributes to non-updatable if the department
// has more than a specified number of employees
return (departmentEmployeeCount > 5)? false :
  super.isAttributeUpdateable(i);
```

How it works...

The isAttributeUpdateable() method is called by the framework in order to determine whether a specific attribute is updateable or not. The framework supplies the attribute in question to the isAttributeUpdateable() method as an attribute index parameter. Inside the method, we add the necessary code to conditionally enable or disable the specific attribute. We do this by returning a Boolean indicator: a true return value indicates that the attribute can be updated.

There's more...

Because the isAttributeUpdateable() method could potentially be called several times for each of the view object attributes (when bound to page components for instance), avoid writing code in it that will hinder the performance of the application. For instance, avoid calling database procedures or executing expensive queries in it.

Controlling attribute updatability at the entity object level

Note that we can conditionally control attribute updatability at the entity object level as well, by overriding the `isAttributeUpdateable()` method of `EntityImpl`. In this case, all view objects based on the particular entity object will exhibit the same attribute updatability behavior. You can provide different behavior for specific view objects in this case by overriding `isAttributeUpdateable()` for those objects. To ensure consistent behavior throughout the application, it is recommended that you control attribute updatability defaults at the entity object level.

See also

> ▶   *Overriding remove() to delete associated children entities, Chapter 2, Dealing with Basics: Entity Objects*

Setting the Queryable property of a view object attribute programmatically

The `Queryable` property, when set for a view object attribute, indicates that the specific attribute can appear on the view object's WHERE clause. This has the effect of making the attribute available in all search forms and allows the user to search for it. In an `af:query` ADF Faces component, for instance, a queryable attribute will appear in the list of fields shown when you click on the **Add Fields** button in the **Advanced** search mode. Declaratively you can control whether an attribute is queryable or not by checking or un-checking the **Queryable** checkbox in the view object **Attributes | Details** tab. But how do you accomplish this task programmatically and for specific conditions?

This recipe will show how to determine the `Queryable` status of an attribute and change it if needed based on a particular condition.

Getting ready

You will need to have access to the shared components workspace that was developed in the *Breaking up the application in multiple workspaces* recipe in *Chapter 1, Pre-requisites to Success: ADF Project Setup and Foundations*. The functionality will be added to the `ExtViewObjectImpl` custom framework class that was developed in the *Setting up BC base classes* recipe in *Chapter 1, Pre-requisites to Success: ADF Project Setup and Foundations*.

How to do it...

1.   Open the `ExtViewObjectImpl` view object custom framework class in the Java editor.

2. Add the following method to it:

```
protected void setQueriable(int attribute, boolean condition) {
  // get the attribute definition
  AttributeDef def = getAttributeDef(attribute);
  // set/unset only if needed
  if (def != null && def.isQueriable() != condition) {
    // set/unset queriable
    ViewAttributeDefImpl attributeDef = ViewAttributeDefImpl)def;
    attributeDef.setQueriable(condition);
  }
}
```

How it works...

We have added the `setQueriable()` method to the `ExtViewObjectImpl` view object custom framework class. This makes the method available to all view objects. The method accepts the specific attribute index (`attribute`) and a Boolean indicator whether to set or unset the `Queryable` flag (`condition`) for the specific attribute.

In `setQueriable()`, we first call `getAttributeDef()` to retrieve the `oracle.jbo.AttributeDef` attribute definition. Then we call `isQueriable()` on the attribute definition to retrieve the `Queryable` condition. If the attribute's current `Queryable` condition differs from the one we have passed to `setQueriable()`, we call `setQueriable()` on the attribute definition to set the new value.

Here is an example of calling `setQueriable()` from an application module method based on some attribute values:

```
public void prepare(boolean someCondition) {
  // make the EmployeeId queryable based on some condition
  this.getEmployees().setQueriable(EmployeesRowImpl.EMPLOYEEID,
  someCondition);
}
```

There's more...

Note that you can control the `Queryable` attribute at the entity object level as well. In this case, all view objects based on the specific entity object will inherit this behavior. This behavior can be overridden declaratively or programmatically for the view object, as long as the new value is more restrictive than the inherited value.

See also

▶ *Breaking up the application in multiple workspaces, Chapter 1, Pre-requisites to Success: ADF Project Setup and Foundations*

▶ *Setting up BC base classes, Chapter 1, Pre-requisites to Success: ADF Project Setup and Foundations*

Using a transient attribute to indicate a new view object row

For entity-based view objects, there is a simple technique you can use to determine whether a particular row has a new status. The status of a row is new when the row is first created. The row remains in the new state until it is successfully committed to the database. It then goes to an unmodified state. Knowledge of the status of the row can be used to set up enable/disable conditions on the frontend user interface.

In this recipe, we will see how to utilize a transient view object attribute to indicate the new status of the view object row.

Getting ready

This recipe was developed using the HRComponents workspace, which was created in the *Overriding remove() to delete associated children entities* recipe in *Chapter 2, Dealing with Basics: Entity Objects*. The HRComponents workspace requires a database connection to the HR schema.

How to do it...

1. Open the Departments view object definition.

2. Go to the **Attributes** tab and click on the **Create new attribute** button (the green plus sign icon).

3. Select **New Attribute...** from the context menu.

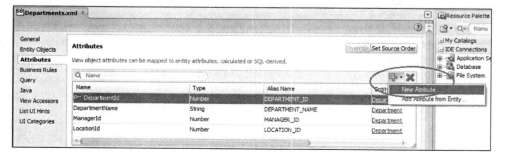

4. On the **New View Object Attribute** dialog, enter `IsNewRow` and click **OK**.

5. By default the new attribute is of type `String`, so change it to a `Boolean` using the **Type** choice list in the **Details** tab.

6. If you don't already have a custom view row implementation class created, use the **Java** tab to create one. In any case, make sure that you have selected the **Include accessors** checkbox.

7. Open the `DepartmentsRowImpl.java` view row implementation class and locate the `getIsNewRow()` method.

8. Replace the code inside the `getIsNewRow()` method with the following:

```
// return true if the row status is New
return Row.STATUS_NEW == this.getDepartment().getEntityState();
```

How it works...

First we create a new transient attribute called `IsNewRow`. This attribute will be used to indicate whether the status of the view object row is new or not. A transient attribute is one that does not correspond to a database table column; it can be used as placeholder for intermediate data. Then we generate a custom view row implementation class. On the transient attribute getter, `getIsNewRow()` in this case, we get access to the entity object. For this recipe, the `Department` entity is returned by calling the `getDepartment()` getter. We get the entity object state by calling `getEntityState()` on the `Department` entity object and compare it to the constant `Row.STATUS_NEW`.

Once the `IsNewRow` attribute is bound to a JSF page, it can be used in **Expression Language (EL)** expressions. For instance, the following EL expression indicates a certain disabled condition based on the row status not being New:

```
disabled="#{bindings.IsNewRow.inputValue ne true}"
```

There's more...

The following table summarizes all the available entity object states:

Entity Object State	Description	Transition to this State
New	Indicates a new entity object. An entity object in this state is in the transaction pending changes list (see Initialized state).	When a new entity object is first created. When `setAttribute()` is called on an *Initialized* entity object.
Initialized	Indicates that a new entity object is initialized and thus it is removed from the transaction's pending changes list.	When `setNewRowState()` is explicitly called on a New entity object.

Entity Object State	Description	Transition to this State
Unmodified	Indicates an unmodified entity object.	When the entity object is retrieved from the database. After successfully committing a New or Modified entity object.
Modified	Indicates the state of a modified entity object.	When `setattribute()` is called on an Unmodified entity object.
Deleted	Indicates a deleted entity object.	When `remove()` is called on an Unmodified or Modified entity object.
Dead	Indicates a dead entity object.	When `remove()` is called on a New or Initialized entity object. After successfully committing a Deleted entity object.

See also

▶ *Overriding remove() to delete associated children entities*, Chapter 2, *Dealing with Basics: Entity Objects*

Conditionally inserting new rows at the end of the rowset

When you insert a new row into a rowset, by default the new row is inserted at the current slot within that rowset. There are times, however, that you want to override this default behavior for the application that you are developing.

In this recipe, we will see how to conditionally insert new rows at the end of the rowset by implementing generic programming functionality at the base view object framework implementation class.

Getting ready

You will need to have access to the shared components workspace that was developed in the *Breaking up the application in multiple workspaces* recipe in Chapter 1, *Pre-requisites to Success: ADF Project Setup and Foundations*. The functionality will be added to the `ExtViewObjectImpl` custom framework class that was developed in the *Setting up BC base classes* recipe in Chapter 1, *Pre-requisites to Success: ADF Project Setup and Foundations*.

How to do it...

1. Open the `ExtViewObjectImpl.java` custom view object framework class in the Java editor.

2. Override the `insertRow()` method.

3. Replace the call to `super.insertRow()` in the generated `insertRow()` method with the following code:

```
// check for overriden behavior based on custom property
if ("true".equalsIgnoreCase((String)this.getProperty(
    NEW_ROW_AT_END))) {
  // get the last row in the rowset
  Row lastRow = this.last();
  if (lastRow != null) {
    // get index of last row
    int lastRowIdx = this.getRangeIndexOf(lastRow);
    // insert row after the last row
    this.insertRowAtRangeIndex(lastRowIdx + 1, row);
    // set inserted row as the current row
    this.setCurrentRow(row);
  } else {
    super.insertRow(row);
  }
} else {
  // default behavior: insert at current rowset slot
  super.insertRow(row);
}
```

How it works...

We have overridden the ADF Business Components framework `insertRow()` method in order to implement custom row insertion behavior. Moreover, we conditionally override the default framework behavior based on the existence of the **custom property** `NewRowAtEnd` identified by the constant `NEW_ROW_AT_END`. So, if this custom property is defined for specific view objects, we determine the index of the last row in the rowset by calling `getRangeIndexOf()` and then call `insertRowAtRangeIndex()` to insert the new row at the specific last row index. Finally, we set the rowset currency to the row just inserted.

If the `NewRowAtEnd` custom property is not defined in the view object, then the row is inserted by default at the current slot in the rowset.

There's more...

To add a custom property to a view object, use the drop-down menu next to the **Add Custom Property** button (the green plus sign icon) and select **Non-translatable Property**. The **Add Custom Property** button is located in the **Attributes | Custom Properties** tab.

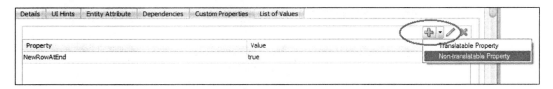

In addition, note that if you have configured range paging access mode for the view object, calling `last()` will produce a **JBO-25084: Cannot call last() on row set {0} because the access mode uses range-paging** error. In this case, call `getEstimatedRangePageCount()` to determine the number of pages and `setRangeStart()` to set the range to the last page instead.

Inserting new rows at the beginning of the rowset

The use case presented in this recipe can be easily adapted to insert a row at the beginning of the rowset. In this case, you will need to call `this.first()` to get the first row. The functionality of getting the row index and inserting the row at the specified index should work as is.

See also

> ▸ *Breaking up the application in multiple workspaces, Chapter 1, Pre-requisites to Success: ADF Project Setup and Foundations*

> ▸ *Setting up BC base classes, Chapter 1, Pre-requisites to Success: ADF Project Setup and Foundations*

Using findAndSetCurrentRowByKey() to set the view object currency

You can set the currency on a view object by calling its `findAndSetCurrentRowByKey()` method. The method accepts two arguments: a `Key` object that is used to locate the row in the view object, and an integer indicating the range position of the row (for view objects configured with range paging access mode).

This recipe demonstrates how to set the view object row currency by implementing a helper method called `refreshView()`. In it we first save the view object currency, re-query the view object and finally restore its currency to the original row before the re-query. This has the effect of refreshing the view object while keeping the current row.

Getting ready

You will need to have access to the shared components workspace that was developed in the *Breaking up the application in multiple workspaces* recipe in *Chapter 1, Pre-requisites to Success: ADF Project Setup and Foundations*. The functionality will be added to the `ExtViewObjectImpl` custom framework class that was developed in the *Setting up BC base classes* recipe in *Chapter 1, Pre-requisites to Success: ADF Project Setup and Foundations*.

How to do it...

1. Open the `ExtViewObjectImpl.java` view object framework extension class in the Java editor.

2. Override the `create()` method.

3. Add the following code after the call to `super.create()`:

   ```
   // allow read-only view objects to use findByKey() methods
   this.setManageRowsByKey(true);
   ```

4. While at the `ExtViewObjectImpl.java` add the following `refreshView()` method:

   ```
   public void refreshView() {
     Key curRowKey = null;
     int rangePosOfCurRow = -1;
     int rangeStart = -1;
     // get and save the current row
     Row currentRow = getCurrentRow();
     // do this only if we have a current row
     if (currentRow != null) {
       // get the row information
       curRowKey = currentRow.getKey();
       rangePosOfCurRow = getRangeIndexOf(currentRow);
       rangeStart = getRangeStart();
     }
     // execute the view object query
     executeQuery();
     // if we have a current row, restore it
     if (currentRow != null) {
       setRangeStart(rangeStart);
       findAndSetCurrentRowByKey(curRowKey, rangePosOfCurRow);
     }
   }
   ```

How it works...

First we override the `create()` method in the view object framework extension class. We do this so we can call the `setManageRowsByKey()` method. This method will allow us to use framework find methods utilizing key objects on read-only view objects as well. By default this is not the case for read-only view objects.

Then we implement the `refreshView()` method. We made `refreshView()` public so that it could be called explicitly for all view objects. Once bound to a page definition as an operation binding, `refreshView()` can be called from the UI. You can, for instance, include a refresh button on your UI page, which when pressed refreshes the data presented in a table. In it, we first determine the current row in the rowset by calling `getCurrentRow()`. This method returns an `oracle.jbo.Row` object indicating the current row, or `null` if there is no current row in the rowset. If there is a current row, we get all the necessary information in order to be able to restore it after we re-query the view object. This information includes the current row's key (`getKey()`), the index of the current row in range (`getRangeIndexOf()`), and the row's range (`getRangeStart()`).

Once the current row information is saved, we re-execute the view object's query by calling `executeQuery()`.

Finally, we restore the current row by setting the range and the row within the range by calling `setRangeStart()` and `findAndSetCurrentRowByKey()` respectively.

There's more...

The methods `getRangeIndexOf()`, `getRangeStart()`, and `setRangeStart()` used in this recipe indicate that range paging optimization is utilized.

Range paging optimization

Range paging is an optimization technique that can be utilized by view objects returning large result sets. The effect of using it is to limit the result set to a specific number of rows, as determined by the **range size** option setting. So instead of retrieving hundreds or even thousands of rows over the network and caching them in the middle layer memory, only the ranges of rows utilized are retrieved.

 The methods used in this recipe to retrieve the row information will work regardless of whether we use range paging or not.

For more information on this recipe consult Steve Muench's original post *Refreshing a View Object's Query, Keeping Current Row and Page* in the URL address: `http://radio-weblogs.com/0118231/2004/11/22.html`.

See also

▶ *Breaking up the application in multiple workspaces, Chapter 1, Pre-requisites to Success: ADF Project Setup and Foundations*

▶ *Setting up BC base classes, Chapter 1, Pre-requisites to Success: ADF Project Setup and Foundations*

▶ *Restoring the current row after a transaction rollback, Chapter 2, Dealing with Basics: Entity Objects*

Restoring the current row after a transaction rollback

On a transaction rollback, the default behavior of the ADF framework is to set the current row to the first row in the rowset. This is certainly not the behavior you expect to see when you rollback while editing a record.

This recipe shows how to accomplish the task of restoring the current row after a transaction rollback.

Getting ready

You will need to have access to the shared components workspace that was developed in the *Breaking up the application in multiple workspaces* recipe in *Chapter 1, Pre-requisites to Success: ADF Project Setup and Foundations*. The functionality will be added to the `ExtApplicationModuleImpl` and `ExtViewObjectImpl` custom framework classes that were developed in the *Setting up BC base classes* recipe in *Chapter 1, Pre-requisites to Success: ADF Project Setup and Foundations*.

How to do it...

1. Open the `ExtApplicationModuleImpl.java` application module framework extension class into the Java editor.

2. Click on the **Override Methods...** button (the green left arrow button) and choose to override the `prepareSession(Session)` method.

3. Add the following code after the call to `super.prepareSession()`:

   ```
   // do not clear the cache after a rollback
   getDBTransaction().setClearCacheOnRollback(false);
   ```

4. Open the `ExtViewObjectImpl.java` view object framework extension class into the Java editor.

5. Override the `create()` method.

6. Add the following code after the call to `super.create()`:

```
// allow read-only view objects to use findByKey() methods
this.setManageRowsByKey(true);
```

7. Override the `beforeRollback()` method.

8. Add the following code before the call to `super.beforeRollback()`:

```
// check for query execution
if (isExecuted()) {
  // get the current row
  ViewRowImpl currentRow = (ViewRowImpl)getCurrentRow();
  if (currentRow != null) {
    // save the current row's key
    currentRowKeyBeforeRollback = currentRow.getKey();
    // save range start
    rangeStartBeforeRollback = getRangeStart();
    // get index of current row in range
    rangePosOfCurrentRowBeforeRollback =
      getRangeIndexOf(currentRow);
  }
}
```

9. Override the `afterRollback()` method and add the following code after the call to `super.afterRollback()`:

```
// check for current row key to restore
if (currentRowKeyBeforeRollback != null) {
  // execute view object's query
  executeQuery();
  // set start range
  setRangeStart(rangeStartBeforeRollback);
  // set current row in range
  findAndSetCurrentRowByKey(currentRowKeyBeforeRollback,
    rangePosOfCurrentRowBeforeRollback);
}
// reset
currentRowKeyBeforeRollback = null;
```

How it works...

We override the application module `prepareSesssion()` method so we can call `setClearCacheOnRollback()` on the `Transaction` object. `prepareSession()` is called by the ADF Business Components framework the first time that an application module is accessed. The call to `setClearCacheOnRollback()` in `prepareSession()` tells the framework whether the entity cache will be cleared when a rollback operation occurs. Since the framework by default clears the cache, we call `setClearCacheOnRollback()` with a `false` argument to prevent this from happening. We need to avoid clearing the cache because we will be getting information about the current row during the rollback operation.

Whether to clear the entity cache on transaction rollback or not is a decision that needs to be taken at the early design stages, as this would affect the overall behavior of your ADF application. For the specific technique in this recipe to work, that is, to be able to maintain the current row after a transaction rollback, the entity cache must not be cleared after a transaction rollback operation. If this happens, fresh entity rows for the specific entity type will be retrieved from the database, which prevents this recipe from working properly.

Next, we override the `create()` method in the view object framework extension class. We do this so we can call the `setManageRowsByKey()` method. This method will allow us to use framework find methods utilizing key objects on read-only view objects, which is not the default behavior.

Then we override the `beforeRollback()` and `afterRollback()` methods in the view object framework extension class. As their names indicate, they are called by the framework before and after the actual rollback operation. Let's take a look at the code in `beforeRollback()` first. In it, we first get the current row by calling `getCurrentRow()`. Then, for the current row we determine the row's key, range, and position of the current row within the range. This will work whether range paging is used for the view object or not. Range paging should be enabled for optimization purposes for view objects that may return large rowsets. We save these values into corresponding member variables. We will be using them in `afterRollback()` to restore the current row after the rollback operation.

 Notice that we do all that after checking whether the view object query has been executed (`isExecuted()`). We do this because `beforeRollback()` may be called multiple times by the framework, and we need to ensure that we retrieve the current row information only if the view object's rowset has been updated, which is the case after the query has been executed.

In afterRollback() we use the information obtained about the current row in beforeRollback() to restore the rowset currency to it. We do this by first executing the view object query, the call to executeQuery(), and then calling setRangeStart() and findAndSetCurrentRowByKey() to restore the range page and the row within the range to the values obtained for the current row earlier. We do all that only if we have a current row key to restore to – the check for currentRowKeyBeforeRollback not being null.

There's more...

Note that for this technique to work properly on the frontend ViewController, you will need to call setExecuteOnRollback() on the oracle.adf.model.binding. DCBindingContainer object before executing the Rollback operation binding. By calling setExecuteOnRollback() on the binding container, we prevent the view objects associated with the page's bindings being executed after the rollback operation. This means that in order to call setExecuteOnRollback() you can't just execute the rollback action binding directly. Rather, you will have to associate the Rollback button with a backing bean action method, similar to the one shown in the following instance:

```
public void rollback() {
  // get the binding container
  DCBindingContainer bindings = ADFUtils.getDCBindingContainer();
  // prevent view objects from executing after rollback
  bindings.setExecuteOnRollback(false);
  // execute rollback operation
  ADFUtils.findOperation("Rollback").execute();
}
```

Such a method could be added to the CommonActions generic backing bean actions framework class introduced in the recipe *Using a generic backing bean actions framework* in *Chapter 1, Pre-requisites to Success: ADF Project Setup and Foundations*. By doing so, we will make it available to all managed beans derived from the CommonActions base class.

 For testing purposes, a ViewController project page called recipe3_8.jspx has been provided that demonstrates this technique. To run it, just right-click on the **recipe3_8.jspx** page and select **Run** from the context menu.

For more information on this technique, consult Steve Muench's original post *Example of Restoring Current Row On Rollback* (example number 68) on the URL address: http://radio-weblogs.com/0118231/2006/06/15.html.

▶ *Breaking up the application in multiple workspaces, Chapter 1, Pre-requisites to Success: ADF Project Setup and Foundations*

▶ *Setting up BC base classes, Chapter 1, Pre-requisites to Success: ADF Project Setup and Foundations*

▶ *Using findAndSetCurrentRowByKey() to set the view object currency, Chapter 2, Dealing with Basics: Entity Objects.*

▶ *Overriding prepareSession() to do session-specific initializations, Chapter 5, Putting them all together: Application Modules*

Dynamically changing the WHERE clause of the view object query

During the execution of the view object's query, the ADF Business Components framework calls a series of methods to accomplish its task. You can intervene during this process by overriding any of the methods called by the framework, in order to change the query about to be executed by the view object. You can also explicitly call methods in the public view object interface to accomplish this task prior to the view object's query execution. Depending on what exactly you need to change in the view object's query, the framework allows you to do the following:

▶ Change the query's SELECT clause by overriding `buildSelectClause()` or calling `setSelectClause()`

▶ Change the query's FROM clause by overriding `buildFromClause()` or calling `setFromClause()`

▶ Change the query's WHERE clause via `buildWhereClause()`, `setWhereClause()`, `addWhereClause()`, `setWhereClauseParams()`, and other methods

▶ Change the query's ORDER BY clause via the `buildOrderByClause()`, `setOrderByClause()`, and `addOrderByClause()` methods

Even the complete query can be changed by overriding the `buildQuery()` method or directly calling `setQuery()`. Moreover, adding named view criteria will alter the view object query.

This recipe shows how to override `buildWhereClause()` to alter the view object's WHERE clause. The use case implemented in this recipe is to limit the result set of the `Employee` view object by a pre-defined number of rows indicated by a custom property.

Getting ready

You will need to have access to the shared components workspace that was developed in the *Breaking up the application in multiple workspaces* recipe in *Chapter 1, Pre-requisites to Success: ADF Project Setup and Foundations*. The functionality will be added to the ExtViewObjectImpl custom framework class that was developed in the *Setting up BC base classes* recipe in *Chapter 1, Pre-requisites to Success: ADF Project Setup and Foundations*.

How to do it...

1. Open the ExtViewObjectImpl.java view object framework extension class in the Java editor.
2. Override the buildWhereClause() method.
3. Replace the code inside the buildWhereClause() with the following:

```
// framework processing
boolean appended = super.buildWhereClause(sqlBuffer,noUserParams);
// check for a row count limit
String rowCountLimit = (String)this.getProperty(ROW_COUNT_LIMIT);
// if a row count limit exists, limit the query
if (rowCountLimit != null) {
  // check to see if a WHERE clause was appended;
  // if not, we will append it
  if (!appended) {
    // append WHERE clause
    sqlBuffer.append(" WHERE ");
    // indicate that a where clause was added
    appended = true;
  }
  // a WHERE clause was appended by the framework;
  // just amend it
  else {
    sqlBuffer.append(" AND ");
  }
  // add ROWNUM limit based on the pre-defined
  // custom property
  sqlBuffer.append("(ROWNUM <= " + rowCountLimit + ")");
}
// a true/false indicator whether a WHERE clause was appended
// is returned to the framework
return appended;
```

How it works...

We override `buildWhereClause()` in order to alter the the `WHERE` clause of the view object's query. Specifically, we limit the result set produced by the view object's query. We do this only if the custom property called `RowCountLimit` (indicated by the constant `ROW_COUNT_LIMIT`) is defined by a view object. The value of the `RowCountLimit` indicates the number of rows that the view object's result set should be limited to.

First we call `super.buildWhereClause()` to allow the framework processing. This call will return a Boolean indicator of whether a `WHERE` clause was appended to the query, indicated by the Boolean `appended` local variable. Then we check for the existence of the `RowCountLimit` custom property. If it is defined by the specific view object, we alter or we add to the `WHERE` clause depending on whether one was added or not by the framework. We make sure that we set the `appended` flag to `true` if we actually have appended the `WHERE` clause. Finally, the `appended` flag is returned back to the framework.

There's more...

The use case implemented in this recipe shows one of the possible ways of limiting the view object result set. You can explore additional techniques in *Chapter 12, Optimizing, Fine-tuning and Monitoring*.

See also

▸   *Breaking up the application in multiple workspaces, Chapter 1, Pre-requisites to Success: ADF Project Setup and Foundations*

▸   *Setting up BC base classes, Chapter 1, Pre-requisites to Success: ADF Project Setup and Foundations*

Removing a row from a rowset without deleting it from the database

There are times when you want to remove a row from the view object's query collection (the query result set) without actually removing it from the database. The query collection, `oracle.jbo.server.QueryCollection`, gets populated each time the view object is executed—when the view object's associated query is run—and represents the query result. While the `Row.remove()` method will remove a row from the query collection, it will also remove the underlying entity object for an entity-based view object, and post a deletion to the database. If your programming task requires the row to be removed from the query collection itself, that is, removing a table row in the UI without actually posting a delete to the database, use the `Row` method `removeFromCollection()` instead.

Note, however, that each time the view object query is re-executed the row will show up, since it is not actually deleted from the database.

This recipe will demonstrate how to use removeFromCollection() by implementing a helper method in the application module to remove rows from the Employees collection.

Getting ready

This recipe was developed using the HRComponents workspace, which was created in the *Overriding remove() to delete associated children entities* recipe in *Chapter 2, Dealing with Basics: Entity Objects*. The HRComponents workspace requires a database connection to the HR schema.

How to do it...

1. Open the HrComponentsAppModuleImpl.java application module custom implementation class in the Java editor.

2. Add the following removeEmployeeFromCollection() method to it:

```
public void removeEmployeeFromCollection() {
  // get the current employee
  EmployeesRowImpl employee =
    (EmployeesRowImpl)(this.getEmployees().getCurrentRow());
  // remove employee from collection
  if (employee != null) {
    employee.removeFromCollection();
  }
}
```

3. Expose the removeEmployeeFromCollection() method to the application module's client interface using the **Edit application module client interface** button (the pen icon) in the **Client Interface** section of the application module's **Java** page.

How it works...

We implemented removeEmployeeFromCollection() and exposed it to the application module's client interface. By doing so, we will be able to call this method using the **Oracle ADF Model Tester** for testing purposes.

First, we get the current employee by calling `getCurrentRow()` on the `Employees` view object instance. We retrieve the `Employees` view object instance by calling the `getEmployees()` getter method. Then we call `removeFromCollection()` on the current employee view row to remove it from the `Employees` view object rowset. This has the effect of removing the employee from the rowset without removing the employee from the database. A subsequent re-query of the `Employees` view object will retrieve those `Employee` rows that were removed earlier.

There's more...

Note that there is a quick and easy way to remove all rows from the view object's rowset by calling the view object `executeEmptyrowset()` method. This method re-executes the view object's query ensuring that the query will return no rows; however, it achieves this in an efficient programmatic way without actually sending the query to the database for execution. Calling `executeEmptyrowset()` marks the query's `isExecuted` flag to `true`, which means that it will not be re-executed upon referencing a view object attribute.

See also

▶ *Overriding remove() to delete associated children entities, Chapter 2, Dealing with Basics: Entity Objects*

4
Important Contributors: List of Values, Bind Variables, View Criteria

In this chapter, we will cover:

- Setting up multiple LOVs using a switcher attribute
- Setting up cascading LOVs
- Creating static LOVs
- Overriding bindParametersForCollection() to set a view object bind variable
- Creating view criteria programmatically
- Clearing the values of bind variables associated with the view criteria
- Searching case-insensitively using view criteria

Introduction

List of values (LOV), **bind variables** and **view criteria** are essential elements related to view objects. They allow further refinements to the view object's query (bind variables and view criteria) and make the development of the frontend user interface easier when dealing with list controls (LOVs) and query-by-example (view criteria) components.

Many of the user interface aspects that deal with list controls and query-by-example components can be pre-defined in a set of default values via the **UI Hints** sections and pages in JDeveloper, thus providing a standard UI behavior. By using LOVs, for instance, we can pre-define a number of attributes for UI list components, such as the default UI list component, the attributes to be displayed, whether "No Selection" items will be included in the list, and others. These defaults can be overridden as needed for specific LOVs.

Bind variables and view criteria, usable in conjunction or separately, allow you to dynamically alter the view object query based on certain conditions. Furthermore, using bind variables as placeholders in the query allows the database to effectively reuse the same parsed query for multiple executions, without the need to re-parse it.

In this chapter, we will examine how these components are supported, both programmatically and declaratively, by the ADF-BC framework and by JDeveloper.

Setting up multiple LOVs using a switcher attribute

Enabling LOVs for view object attributes greatly simplifies the effort involved in utilizing list controls in the frontend user interface. LOV-enabling a view object attribute is a straightforward task, done declaratively in JDeveloper. Moreover, the ADF-BC framework allows you to define multiple LOVs for the same attribute. In this case, in order to differentiate among the LOVs, a separate attribute called a LOV switcher is used. The differentiation is usually done based on some data value. The advantage of using this technique is that you can define a single LOV component in your UI page and then vary its contents based on a certain condition, such as the value of the switcher attribute.

This recipe shows how to enable multiple LOVs for a view object attribute and how to use an LOV switcher to switch among the LOVs. For example, depending on the employee's job we will associate a different LOV to an `Employees view object` transient attribute.

Getting ready

This recipe was developed using the `HRComponents` workspace, which was created in the *Overriding remove() to delete associated children entities* recipe in *Chapter 2, Dealing with Basics: Entity Objects*. The `HRComponents` workspace requires a database connection to the HR schema.

How to do it...

1. Create a new read-only view object called `DepartmentsLov` by right-clicking on a package of the `HRComponents` business components project in the **Application Navigator** and selecting **New View Object...**.

2. Base the view object on the following SQL query:

   ```
   SELECT DEPARTMENT_ID, DEPARTMENT_NAME FROM DEPARTMENTS
   ```

   In addition, set the `DepartmentId` attribute as the a **Key attribute**. Do not add the `DepartmentsLov` view object to the application module.

3. Repeat the previous steps to create another read-only view object called `JobsLov` based on this SQL query:

   ```
   SELECT JOB_ID, JOB_TITLE FROM JOBS
   ```

4. In this case, set the `JobId` attribute as the key attribute.

5. Create yet another read-only view object called `CountriesLov` based on the following SQL query:

   ```
   SELECT COUNTRY_ID, COUNTRY_NAME FROM COUNTRIES
   ```

   Define `CountryId` as the key attribute.

6. Now, open the `Employees` view object definition and go to the **Attributes** tab. Create a new attribute called `LovAttrib` by selecting **New Attribute...** from the context menu.

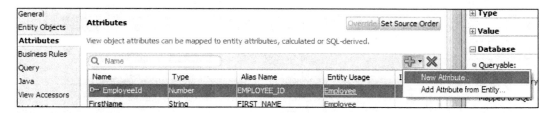

7. In the **Details** tab, change the attribute **Updatable** value to **Always**.

8. Switch to the **List of Values** tab and click on the **Add list of values** button (the green plus sign icon).

9. On the **Create List of Values** dialog, enter `LOV_Departments` for the **List of Values Name**.

10. Click on the **Create new view accessor** button (the green plus sign icon next to the **List Data Source**) to create a new **List Data Source**. This will bring up the **View Accessors** dialog.

11. On the **View Accessors** dialog, locate the `DepartmentsLov`, shuttle it to the **View Accessors** list on the right and click **OK**.

12. Select the `DepartmentName` for the **List Attribute**. In the **List Return Values** section, the `DepartmentName` view accessor attribute should be associated with the `LovAttrib`. Click **OK** when done.

13. Repeat the previous steps to add another LOV, called `LOV_Jobs`. Add the `JobsLov` as a view accessor, as you did in the previous steps, and select it as the **List Data Source**. Use the `JobTitle` attribute as the **List Attribute**.

14. Add one more LOV called `LOV_Countries` by repeating the previous steps. Add `CountriesLov` as a view accessor and select it as the **List Data Source**. For the **List Attribute**, use the `CountryName` attribute.

15. While at the **List of Values** tab, click on the **Create new attribute** button (the green plus sign icon) next to the **List of Values Switcher** field to create a switcher attribute. Call the attribute `LovSwitcher`. Now, the **List of Values** tab should look similar to the following:

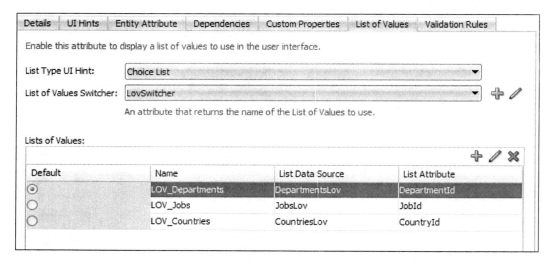

16. Select the `LovSwitcher` attribute and go to the **Details** tab. Click on the **Expression** radio button in the **Default Value** section, and then on the **Edit value** button (the pen icon). Enter the following expression:

```
if(JobId == 'SA_REP'){
  return 'LOV_Countries'
} else if(JobId == 'ST_CLERK'){
  return 'LOV_Jobs'
} else if(JobId == 'ST_MAN'){
  return 'LOV_Departments'
} else {
  return null;
}
```

17. Optionally click on the **UI Hints** tab and change the **Display Hint** from **Display** to **Hide**.

How it works...

In steps 1 through 4 we created three read-only view objects, one for each LOV. We did not add any of these read-only view objects to the application module's data model as they are used internally by the business service. We then created a new transient attribute, called `LovAttrib`, for the `Employees` view object (step 5). This is the attribute that we will use to add the three LOVs. We added the LOVs by switching to the **List of Values** tab. In steps 6 through 13, we added the appropriate view objects as accessors to the `Employees` view object and associated the accessors with the LOV **List Data Source**. This indicates the view accessor that provides the list data at runtime. In each case, we also specified a view accessor attribute as the list attribute. This is the view accessor attribute that supplies the data value to the `LovAttrib` attribute. You can specify additional view accessor attributes to supply data for other `Employees` view object attributes in the **List Return Values** section of the **Create/Edit List of Values** dialog. In step 14, we created a new transient attribute, called `LovSwitcher`, to act as the LOV switcher. In step 15, we supplied the default value to the LOV switcher `LovSwitcher` attribute in the form of a Groovy expression. In the Groovy expression, we examine the value of the `JobId` attribute and based on its value we assign (by returning the LOV name) the appropriate LOV to the `LovSwitcher` attribute. Since the `LovSwicher` attribute is used as an LOV switcher, the result is that the appropriate LOV is associated with the `LovAttrib` attribute. Finally, note that in step 16 you can optionally set the **Display Hint** to **Hide** for the `LovAttrib` attribute. This will ensure that the specific attribute is not visible in the presentation layer UI.

There's more...

For entity-based view objects, you can LOV-enable an attribute using a list data source that is based on an entity object view accessor. This way a single entity-based view accessor is used for all view objects based on the entity object, and is applied to each instance of the LOV. Note, however, that while this will work fine on create and edit forms, it will not work for search forms. In this case, the LOV must be based on a view accessor defined at the view object level. For a use case where two LOVs are defined on an attribute—one based on an entity object accessor and another on a view object accessor—you can use a switcher attribute that differentiates among the two LOVs based on the following expression:

```
adf.isCriteriaRow ?  "LOV_ViewObject_accessor" :
"LOV_EntityObject_accessor"
```

For more information on this consult the section *How to Specify Multiple LOVs for an LOV-Enabled View Object Attribute* in the *Fusion Developer's Guide for Oracle Application Development Framework* which can be found at `http://docs.oracle.com/cd/E24382_01/web.1112/e16182/toc.htm`.

▶ *Overriding remove() to delete associated children entities, Chapter 2, Dealing with Basics: Entity Objects*

Setting up cascading LOVs

Cascading LOVs refer to two or more LOVs where the possible values of one LOV depend on specific attribute values defined in another LOV. These controlling attributes are used in order to filter the result set produced by the controlled LOVs. The filtering is usually accomplished by adding named view criteria, based on bind variables, to the controlled LOV list data source (the view accessor). This allows you to filter the view object result set by adding query conditions that augment the view object query WHERE clause. Furthermore, the filtering can be done by directly modifying the controlled LOV view accessor query, adding the controlling attributes as bind variable placeholders in its query. This technique comes handy when you want to set up interrelated LOV components in your UI pages, where the contents of one LOV are filtered based on the value selected in the other LOV.

For this recipe, we will create two LOVs, one for the DEPARTMENTS table and another for the EMPLOYEES table, so that when a department is selected only the employees of that particular department are shown.

Getting ready

This recipe was developed using the HRComponents workspace, which was created in the *Overriding remove() to delete associated children entities* recipe in *Chapter 2, Dealing with Basics: Entity Objects*. The HRComponents workspace requires a database connection to the HR schema. You will also need an additional table added to the HR schema called CASCADING_LOVS. You can create it by running the following SQL command:

```
CREATE TABLE CASCADING_LOVS (EMPLOYEE_ID NUMBER(6), DEPARTMENT_ID
NUMBER(4));
```

How to do it...

1. Create a new entity object based on the CASCADING_LOVS table.

2. Since the CASCADING_LOVS table does not define a primary key, the **Create Entity Object** wizard will ask you if you want to create an attribute with a primary key property based on the ROWID. Select **OK**.

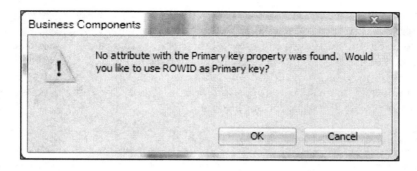

3. Create a view object based on the `CascadingLovs` entity object.

4. Create a read-only view object called `DepartmentsLov` based on the following query:

   ```
   SELECT DEPARTMENT_ID, DEPARTMENT_NAME FROM DEPARTMENTS
   ```

5. Create another read-only view object called `EmployeesLov` based on the following query:

   ```
   SELECT DEPARTMENT_ID, EMPLOYEE_ID, FIRST_NAME, LAST_NAME
      FROM EMPLOYEES
   ```

6. In the **Query** section, use the **Create new bind variable** button (the green plus sign icon) to add a bind variable to `EmployeesLov`. Call the bind variable `inDepartmentId` of **Type** `Number` and ensure that the **Required** checkbox is unchecked.

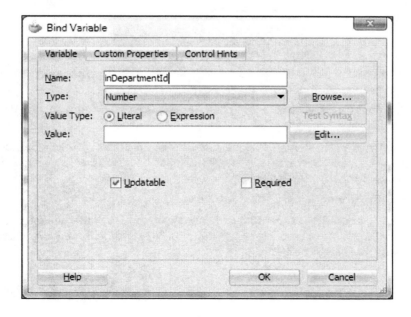

7. While in the **Query** section, click on the **Create new view criteria** button (the green plus sign icon) to add view criteria to the `EmployeesLov` view object. Click the **Add Item** button and select `DepartmentId` for the **Attribute**. For the **Operator** select **Equals** and for the **Operand** select **Bind Variable**. Ensure that you select the `inDepartmentId` bind variable that you created in the previous step from the **Parameter** combo. Make sure the **Ignore Null Values** checkbox is unchecked and that the **Validation** selection is **Optional**.

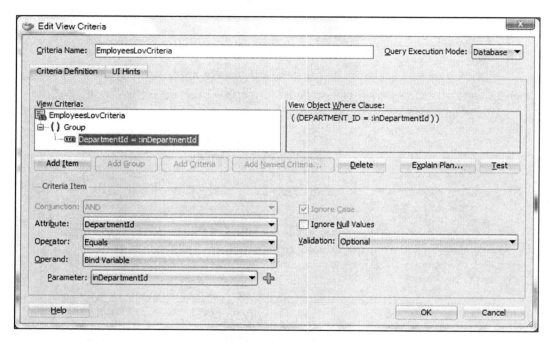

8. Back to the `CascadingLovs` view object, go to the **Attributes** section and select the `DepartmentId` attribute.

9. Click on the **List of Values** tab and then on the **Add list of values** button (the green plus sign icon).

10. On the **Create List of Values** dialog, click on the **Create new view accessor** button (the green plus sign icon) next to the **List Data Source** combo and add the `DepartmentsLov` view accessor.

11. Select **DepartmentId** for the **List Attribute**.

12. While on the **Create List of Values** dialog, click on the **UI Hints** tab and in the **Display Attributes** section shuttle the `DepartmentName` attribute from the **Available** list to the **Selected** list. Click **OK**.

13. Repeat steps 8 through 12 to add an LOV for the `EmployeeId` attribute. Use the `EmployeesLov` as the list data source and `EmployeeId` as the list attribute. For the display attributes in the **UI Hints** tab, use the `FirstName` and `LastName` attributes.

14. In the `CascadingLovs` view object, go to the **View Accessors** section select the `EmployeesLov` view accessor (do not click on the **View Definition** link). Then click on the **Edit selected View Accessor** button (the pen icon).

15. In the **Edit View Accessor** dialog, select the **View Object** section and shuttle the `EmployeesLovCriteria` from the **Available** list to the **Selected** list. Also, for the `inDepartmentId` parameter in the **Bind Parameter Values** section, enter `DepartmentId` in the **Value** field and click **OK**.

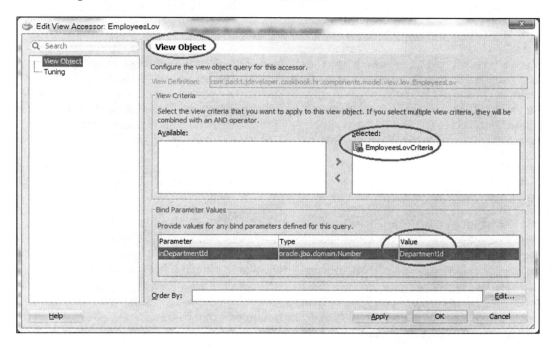

16. Double-click on the `HrComponentsAppModule` application module in the **Application Navigator** to open the application module definition.

17. Go to the **Data Model** section, select the `CascadingLovs` view object and shuttle it from the **Available View Objects** list to the **Data Model**.

How it works...

To demonstrate this recipe, we created a new table in the HR schema called CASCADING_ LOVS. This table has two columns an EMPLOYEE_ID and a DEPARTMENT_ID. The table does not have a primary key constraint, so we will be able to freely add records to it. In a real world development project, a proper database design would require that all of your database tables have a primary key defined. Based on this table, we created an entity object called CascadingLovs (step 1). Since we did not indicate a primary key for the CASCADING_LOVS table, the framework asked us to indicate a primary key attribute (step 2). We did so by creating a key attribute called RowID based on the row's ROWID. Then we proceeded to create a view object called CascadingLovs based on the CascadingLovs entity object (step 3).

In order to setup LOVs for the DepartmentId and EmployeeId attributes, we had to create the LOV accessor view objects, namely the DepartmentsLov and the EmployeesLov view objects (steps 4 and 5). We also added named view criteria to the EmployeesLov (steps 6 and 7) based on the inDepartmentId bind variable. This way we will be able to control the result set produced by the EmployeesLov based on the department ID value. In step 7 when we created the view criteria, we saw that JDeveloper suggested a default name in the **Criteria Name** field. This is the name that is used to programmatically access the view criteria in your Java code. The name of the view criteria can be changed; however, we have chosen to use the default EmployeesLovCriteria provided by JDeveloper.

In steps 8 through 13, we proceeded by LOV-enabling the DepartmentId and EmployeeId attributes.

The important glue work was done in steps 14 and 15. In these steps, we edited the EmployeesLov view accessor and declaratively applied the EmployeesLovCriteria on the accessor. We also provided a value for the inDepartmentId bind variable using the expression DepartmentId, which indicates the value of the DepartmentId attribute at runtime. This is the CascadingLovs department identifier attribute that is updated by the controlling DepartmentsLov LOV. By doing so, we have set the controlling variable's value, the inDepartmentId bind variable, using the value provided by the DepartmentsLov data source, that is, the DepartmentId.

Finally, in steps 16 and 17, we added the CascadingLovs view object to the application module's data model, so that we may be able to test it using the ADF Model Tester. While running the ADF Model Tester, notice how the employees list is controlled by the selected department.

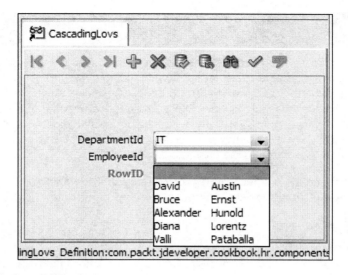

There's more...

For the cascading LOVs to work properly on the frontend Fusion web application user interface, you need to make sure that the autoSubmit property is set to true for the controlling LOV UI component. This will ensure that, upon selection, the controlling attribute's value is submitted to the server. The UI component's autoSubmit property can also be set to a default value by setting the attribute's **Auto Submit** property at the business component level. This can be done in the view object's **Attributes | UI Hints** tab.

Also, note the behavior of the controlled LOV based on the view criteria **Ignore Null Values** setting. When this checkbox is selected, null values for the criteria item will be ignored and the result set will not be filtered yielding all possible employee rows. In this case, the EmployeesLov view object's WHERE clause is amended by adding OR (:inDepartmentId is null) to the query. If the **Ignore Null Values** checkbox is not selected, then null values for the criteria item are not ignored, yielding no employees rows.

See also

 ▶ _Overriding remove() to delete associated children entities, Chapter 2, Dealing with Basics: Entity Objects_

Creating static LOVs

A static LOV is produced by basing its list data source view accessor on a static view object, that is, a view object that uses a static list as its data source. A static list is a list of constant data that you either enter manually or import from a text file using JDeveloper. A static list could also be produced by basing the view object on a query that generates static data. The advantage of using a static LOV is that you can display static read-only data in your application's user interface without having to create a database table for it. In all cases, the amount of static data presented to the user should be small.

In this recipe, we will create a static view object called ColorLov and use it as an LOV list data source to LOV-enable a transient attribute of the Employees view object.

Getting ready

This recipe was developed using the HRComponents workspace, which was created in the *Overriding remove() to delete associated children entities* recipe in *Chapter 2, Dealing with Basics: Entity Objects*. The HRComponents workspace requires a database connection to the HR schema.

How to do it...

1. Create a new view object using the **Create View Object** wizard.
2. In the **Name** page, enter ColorsLov for the name of the view object and select **Static list** for the **Data Source**.
3. In the **Attributes** page, click on the **New...** button. Create an attribute called ColorDesc.
4. In the **Attribute Settings** page, select **Key Attribute** for the ColorDesc attribute.
5. In the **Static List** page, use the **Add Row** button (the green plus sign icon) to add the following data: Black, Blue, Green, Red, White, and Yellow.
6. Click **Finish** to complete the creation of the ColorsLov view object.
7. Add a new transient attribute to the Employees view object called FavoriteColor.
8. In the **Attributes | Details** tab for the FavoriteColor attribute, ensure that the **Updatable** property is set to **Always**.
9. Click on the **List of Values** tab and add an LOV called LOV_FavoriteColor. For the LOV **List Data Source**, use the **Create new view accessor** button (the green plus sign icon) and select the ColorsLov static view object.
10. For the LOV **List Attribute**, select the ColorDesc attribute.

How it works...

In steps 1 through 6, we went through the process of creating a view object, called `ColorsLov`, which uses a static list as its data source. We have indicated that the view object has one attribute called `ColorDesc` (step 3) and we have indicated that attribute as a key attribute (step 4). Notice in step 5 how the **Create View Object** wizard allows you to manually enter the static data. In the same **Static List** page, the wizard allows you to import data from a file in a comma-separated-values (CSV) format.

In order to test the static LOV, we added a transient variable called `FavoriteColor` to the `Employees` view object (step 7-8) and we LOV-enabled the attribute using the `ColorsLov` as the list data source view accessor (steps 9-10).

When we test the application module with the ADF Model Tester, the `FavoriteColor` attribute is indeed populated by the static values we have entered for the `ColorsLov` view object.

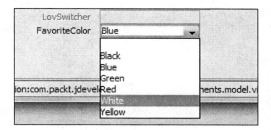

There's more...

Notice that the static data that is entered for the static view object is saved on a resource bundle. This allows you to localize the data as needed.

Also note that in some cases where localization of static data is not needed, a read-only view object that is based on a query producing static data can simulate a static view object. For instance, consider the read-only view object that is based on the following query:

```
SELECT 'Black' AS COLOR_DESC FROM DUAL
UNION
SELECT 'Blue' AS COLOR_DESC FROM DUAL
UNION
SELECT 'Green' AS COLOR_DESC FROM DUAL
UNION
SELECT 'Red' AS COLOR_DESC FROM DUAL
UNION
SELECT 'White' AS COLOR_DESC FROM DUAL
UNION
SELECT 'Yellow' AS COLOR_DESC FROM DUAL;
```

It can be used as a list data source for the `FavoriteColor` LOV producing the same results.

See also

▶ *Overriding remove() to delete associated children entities, Chapter 2, Dealing with Basics: Entity Objects*

Overriding bindParametersForCollection() to set a view object bind variable

There are times when you need to programmatically set the value of a bind variable used in the view object query. One way to accomplish this task is by overriding the view object method `bindParametersForCollection()` and explicitly specifying the value for the particular bind variable. This technique comes handy when the bind variable values cannot be specified in a declarative way, or the bind variable value source changes dynamically at runtime.

This recipe will show how to provide a default value for a bind variable used in the view object query if a value has not already been specified for it.

Getting ready

You will need to have access to the shared components workspace that was developed in the *Breaking up the application in multiple workspaces* recipe in *Chapter 1, Pre-requisites to Success: ADF Project Setup and Foundations*. Additional functionality will be added to the `ExtViewObjectImpl` and `ExtApplicationModuleImpl` custom framework classes that were developed in the *Setting up BC base classes* recipe in *Chapter 1, Pre-requisites to Success: ADF Project Setup and Foundations*.

This recipe is also using the `HRComponents` workspace, which was created in the *Overriding remove() to delete associated children entities* recipe in *Chapter 2, Dealing with Basics: Entity Objects*. The `HRComponents` workspace requires a database connection to the `HR` schema.

Moreover, we will modify the `EmployeeCount` view object, which was introduced in the *Using a method validator based on a view accessor* recipe in *Chapter 2, Dealing with Basics: Entity Objects*.

How to do it...

1. Open the shared components workspace.
2. Open the `ExtViewObjectImpl` view object framework extension class and add the following method to it:

```
protected void setBindVariableValue(Object[] bindVariables,
    String name, Object value) {
    // iterate all bind variables
```

```
    for (Object bindVariable : bindVariables) {
      // check for the specific bind variable name
      if (((Object[])bindVariable)[0].toString().equals(name)) {
        // set the bind variable's new value
        ((Object[])bindVariable)[1] = value;
        return;
      }
    }
  }
```

2. Open the `ExtApplicationModuleImpl` application module framework extension class and add the following method to it:

```
public Object getCustomData(String key) {
  // base class returns no custom data
  return null;
}
```

3. Deploy the shared components workspace into an ADF Library JAR.

4. Open the `HRComponents` workspace.

5. Open the `HrComponentsAppModuleImpl` custom application module implementation class and override the `getCustomData()` method. In it, replace the `return super.getCustomData()` with the following:

```
return DEFAULT_DEPARTMENT_ID_KEY.equals(key)
  ? DEFAULT_DEPARTMENT_ID : null;
```

6. Open the `EmployeeCount` view object, go to the **Java** page and create a custom view object class.

7. Open the `EmployeeCountImpl` custom view object implementation class and override the `bindParametersForCollection()` method. Add the following code to it before the call to `super.bindParametersForCollection()`:

```
// if bind variable value has not been provided,
// provide a default setting
if (this.getDepartmentId() == null) {
  // get default department id
  Number departmentId = ((Number)((ExtApplicationModuleImpl)
    this.getApplicationModule()).getCustomData(
    DEFAULT_DEPARTMENT_ID_KEY));
  // set bind variable right on the query to
  // default variable
  super.setBindVariableValue(object, "DepartmentId",
    departmentId.toString());
  // set bind variable on view object as well,
  //to be available for this time forward
  this.setDepartmentId(departmentId);
}
```

8. Finally, add the `EmployeeCount` view object to the `HrComponentsAppModule` application module data model.

How it works...

In the recipe *Using a method validator based on a view accessor* in *Chapter 2, Dealing with Basics: Entity Objects*, we created a view object called `EmployeeCount`, which we used in order to get the employee count for specific departments. The view object was based on the following query:

```
SELECT COUNT(*) AS EMPLOYEE_COUNT
FROM EMPLOYEES
WHERE DEPARTMENT_ID = :DepartmentId
```

The `EmployeeCount` view object was added as a view accessor to the employee entity object and it was used in a method validator. In that method validator, a value was supplied programmatically for the `DepartmentId` bind variable prior to executing the `EmployeeCount` query.

In this recipe, we have used the same `EmployeeCount` view object to demonstrate how to supply a default value for the `DepartmentId` bind variable. We did this by creating a custom view object implementation class (step 7) and then by overriding its `bindParametersForCollection()` method (step 8). This method is called by the ADF-BC framework to allow you to set values for the view object query's bind variables. When the framework calls `bindParametersForCollection()`, it supplies among the other parameters an `Object[]`, which contains the query's bind variables (the `bindVariables` parameter). We set a default value of the `DepartmentId` bind variable by calling `super.setBindVariableValue()`. This is the helper method that we added to the view object framework extension class in step 2. In the `setBindVariableValue()` method we iterate over the query's bind variables until we find the one we are looking for and once we find it, we set its new value.

Note that in `bindParametersForCollection()` we have called `getApplicationModule()` to get the application module for this `EmployeeCount` view object instance (having added the `EmployeeCount` view object to the `HrComponentsAppModule` data model in step 9). This method returns an `oracle.jbo.ApplicationModule` interface, which we cast to an `ExtApplicationModuleImpl`. As a recommended practice, you should not be accessing specific application modules from within your view objects. In this case, we relaxed the rule a bit by casting the `oracle.jbo.ApplicationModule` interface returned by the `getApplicationModule()` method to our application module framework extension class. We have then called `getCustomData()`, which we overrode in step 6, to get the default `DepartmentId` value. It is this default value (stored in variable `departmentId`) that we supply when calling `super.setBindVariableValue()`.

There's more...

Although the `executeQueryForCollection()` method of `ViewObjectImpl` method can be used to set the view object's query bind variable values, do not use this method because the framework will never invoke it when `getEstimatedRowCount()` is called to identify the result set's row count. If you do, `getEstimatedRowCount()` will not produce the correct row count as you are altering the query by supplying values to the query's bind variables.

Also, note that with the 11.1.1.5.0 (PS4) release, a new `ViewObjectImpl` method called `prepareRowSetForQuery()` was introduced that can be used to set the query's bind parameter values. The following code illustrates how to use it to set a value for the `DepartmentId` bind variable in this recipe:

```
public void prepareRowSetForQuery(ViewRowSetImpl vrsImpl) {
  // get default departmentId value as before
  Number departmentId =
    vrsImpl.ensureVariableManager().setVariableValue(
    "DepartmentId", departmentId);
  super.prepareRowSetForQuery(vrsImpl);
}
```

Both `bindParametersForCollection()` and `prepareRowSetForQuery()` are valid choices for setting the view object's query bind variable values. If for some reason both of them are overridden, note that the framework will first call `prepareRowSetForQuery()` and then `bindParametersForCollection()`.

See also

▸ *Setting up BC base classes, Chapter 1, Pre-requisites to Success: ADF Project Setup and Foundations*

▸ *Overriding remove() to delete associated children entities, Chapter 2, Dealing with Basics: Entity Objects*

▸ *Using a method validator based on a view accessor, Chapter 2, Dealing with Basics: Entity Objects*

Creating view criteria programmatically

View criteria augment the view object's WHERE clause by appending additional query conditions to it. They work in conjunction with the af:query ADF Faces UI component to provide query-by-example support to the frontend user interface. View criteria can be created declaratively in JDeveloper in the **Query** section of the view object definition by clicking on the **Create new view criteria** button (the green plus sign icon) in the **View Criteria** section. Programmatically, the ADF-BC API supports the manipulation of view criteria among others via the ViewCriteria, ViewCriteriaRow, and ViewCriteriaItem classes, and through a number of methods implemented in the ViewObjectImpl class. This technique comes handy when the view criteria cannot be specified during the design stage. One example might be the creation of a custom query-by-example page for your application, in which case the view criteria must be created programmatically at runtime.

In this recipe, we will see how to create view criteria programmatically. The use case will be to dynamically amend the Employees view object query by adding it to the view criteria. The values that we will use for the view criteria items will be obtained from the result set of yet another view object.

Getting ready

You will need to have access to the shared components workspace that was developed in the *Breaking up the application in multiple workspaces* recipe in *Chapter 1, Pre-requisites to Success: ADF Project Setup and Foundations*. The functionality will be added to the ExtViewObjectImpl custom framework class that was developed in the *Setting up BC base classes* recipe in *Chapter 1, Pre-requisites to Success: ADF Project Setup and Foundations*. For testing purposes, we will be using the HRComponents workspace, which was created in the *Overriding remove() to delete associated children entities* recipe in *Chapter 2, Dealing with Basics: Entity Objects*. The HRComponents workspace requires a database connection to the HR schema.

How to do it...

1. Open the shared components workspace.

2. Open the ExtViewObjectImpl.java view object framework extension class in the Java editor and add the following searchUsingAdditionalCriteria() method:

```java
public void searchUsingAdditionalCriteria(
  ViewObject providerViewObject,
  String[] attribNames) {
  // create the criteria
  ViewCriteria vc = this.createViewCriteria();
  // set the view criteria name
    vc.setName("searchUsingAdditionalCriteria");
```

```
   // AND with previous criteria
   vc.setConjunction(ViewCriteriaComponent.VC_CONJ_AND);
   // get criteria item data from the provider
   // view object
   RowSetIterator it =
     providerViewObject.createRowSetIterator(null);
   it.reset();
   while (it.hasNext()) {
     Row providerRow = it.next();
     // add a criteria item for each attribute
     for (String attribName : attribNames) {
       try {
       // create the criteria item
       ViewCriteriaRow vcRow = vc.createViewCriteriaRow();
       // set the criteria item value
       vcRow.setAttribute(attribName,
         providerRow.getAttribute(attribName));
         // add criteria item to the view criteria
         vc.insertRow(vcRow);
       } catch (JboException e) {
         LOGGER.severe(e);
       }
     }
   }
   // done with iterating provider view object
   it.closeRowSetIterator();
   // apply the criteria to this view object
   this.applyViewCriteria(vc);
   // execute the view object's query
   this.executeQuery();
 }
```

3. For logging purposes, add an `ADFLogger` to the same class as shown in the following code:

```
private static ADFLogger LOGGER = ADFLogger.createADFLogger(
  ExtViewObjectImpl.class);
```

4. Deploy the shared components projects into an ADF Library JAR.

5. For testing purposes, open the `HRComponents` workspace and add the
   following `searchEmployeesUsingAdditionalCriteria()` method to the
   `HrComponentsAppModuleImpl` custom application module implementation class:

```
public void searchEmployeesUsingAdditionalCriteria() {
    // invoke searchUsingAdditionalCriteria() to create
    // result set based on View criteria item
    // data obtained from another view object's rowset
    this.getEmployees()
      .searchUsingAdditionalCriteria(this.getCascadingLovs(),
      new String[] { "EmployeeId" });
}
```

How it works...

In step 1, we created a method called `searchUsingAdditionalCriteria()` in the shared
components workspace `ExtViewObjectImpl` view object framework extension class, to
allow view objects to alter their queries by dynamically creating and applying view criteria. The
data for the view criteria items are provided by another view object. The method accepts the
view object that will provide the view criteria item data values (`providerViewObject`) and
an array of attribute names (`attribNames`) that is used to create the view criteria items, and
also retrieve the data from the provider view object. The following lines show how this method
is called from the `searchEmployeesUsingAdditionalCriteria()` method that we
added to the application module implementation class in step 5:

```
((ExtViewObjectImpl)this.getEmployees())
  .searchUsingAdditionalCriteria(this.getCascadingLovs(),
  new String[] { "EmployeeId" });
```

As you can see, we have used the view object returned by `this.getCascadingLovs()` in
order to obtain the view criteria item values. A single criteria item based on the employee ID
was also used.

In the `searchUsingAdditionalCriteria()`, we first called `createViewCriteria()`
to create view criteria for the view object. This returns an `oracle.jbo.ViewCriteria`
object representing the view criteria. This object can be used subsequently to add
criteria items onto it. Then we called `setConjunction()` on the view criteria to set the
conjunction operator (OR, AND, UNION, NOT). The conjunction operator is used to combine
multiple criteria when nested view criteria are used by the view object. This could be
the case if the view object has defined additional view criteria. We have used an AND
conjunction in this example (the `ViewCriteriaComponent.VC_CONJ_AND` constant),
although this can easily be changed by passing the conjunction as another parameter to
`searchUsingAdditionalCriteria()`.

In order to retrieve the view criteria item data, we iterated the provider view object, and for each row of data we called `createViewCriteriaRow()` on the view criteria to create the criteria row. This method returns an `oracle.jbo.ViewCriteriaRow` object representing a criteria row. We added the view criteria row data by calling `setAttribute()` on the newly created criteria row, and we added the criteria row to the view criteria by calling `insertRow()` on the view criteria, passing the criteria row as an argument.

Once all criteria items have been setup, we call `applyViewCriteria()` on the view object, specifying the newly created view criteria. Then we call `executeQuery()` to execute the view object's query based on the applied view criteria. The result set produced matches the applied criteria.

There's more...

Note what happens when the framework executes the view object query after applying the view criteria programmatically. Adding two criteria rows, for example, will append the following to the query's WHERE clause:

```
( ( (Employee.EMPLOYEE_ID = :vc_temp_1 ) ) OR ( (Employee.EMPLOYEE_ID
= :vc_temp_2 ) ) )
```

As you can see, the framework amends the query using temporary bind variables (`vc_temp_1`, `vc_temp_2`, and so on) for each criteria row.

Also note the following:

- Calling `applyViewCriteria()` on the view object erases any previously applied criteria. In order to preserve these, the framework provides another version of `applyViewCriteria()` that accepts an extra bAppend Boolean parameter. Based on the value of bAppend, the newly applied criteria can be appended to the existing criteria, if any. Moreover, to apply multiple criteria at once, the framework provides the `setApplyViewCriteriaNames()` method. This method accepts a `java.lang.String` array of the criteria names to apply, and by default ANDs the criteria applied.

- The way the `setAttribute()` method of `ViewCriteriaRow` was used in this recipe sets up an equality operation for the criterion, that is, `EmployeeId = someValue`. In order to specify a different operation for the criterion item, you must specify the operation as part of the `setAttribute()` method call. For example, `vcRow.setAttribute("EmployeeId","< 150")`, `vcRow.setAttribute("EmployeeId","IN (100,200,201)")` and so on.

▶ Finally, note that you can setup the view criteria item via the `setOperator()` and `setValue()` methods supplied by the `ViewCriteriaItem` class. You will need to call `ensureCriteriaItem()` on the criteria row in order to get access to a `ViewCriteriaItem`. The following is an example:

```
// get the criteria item from the criteria row
ViewCriteriaItem criteriaItem =
  vcRow.ensureCriteriaItem("EmployeeId");
// set the criteria item operator
criteriaItem.setOperator("<");
// set the criteria item value
criteriaItem.getValues().get(0).setValue(new Integer(150));
```

See also

▶ *Setting up BC base classes, Chapter 1, Pre-requisites to Success: ADF Project Setup and Foundations*

▶ *Overriding remove() to delete associated children entities, Chapter 2, Dealing with Basics: Entity Objects*

Clearing the values of bind variables associated with the view criteria

This recipe shows you how to clear the values associated with bind variables used as operands in view criteria items for a specific view object. It implements a method called `clearCriteriaVariableValues()` in the view object framework extension class, which becomes available for all view objects to call. Bind variables are associated as operands for criteria items during the process of creating the view object's view criteria in the **Create View Criteria** dialog. Also, as we have seen in the *Creating view criteria programmatically* recipe, bind variables are generated automatically by the framework when programmatically creating view criteria. You can use this technique when you want to clear the search criteria on a search form based on some user action. A use case might be, for instance, that you want to immediately clear the search criteria after the search button is pressed.

Getting ready

You will need to have access to the shared components workspace that was developed in the *Breaking up the application in multiple workspaces* recipe in *Chapter 1, Pre-requisites to Success: ADF Project Setup and Foundations*. The functionality will be added to the `ExtViewObjectImpl` custom framework class that was developed in the *Setting up BC base classes* recipe in *Chapter 1, Pre-requisites to Success: ADF Project Setup and Foundations*.

How to do it...

1. Open the shared components workspace.

2. Open the `ExtViewObjectImpl.java` view object framework extension class in the Java editor and add the following `clearCriteriaValues()` method:

```
public void clearCriteriaVariableValues(
    String[] criteriaNames) {
  // iterate all view criteria names
  for (String criteriaName : criteriaNames) {
    // get the view criteria
    ViewCriteria vc = this.getViewCriteria(criteriaName);
    if (vc != null) {
      VariableValueManager vvm = vc.ensureVariableManager();
      Variable[] variables = vvm.getVariables();
      for (Variable var: variables) {
        vvm.setVariableValue(var, null);
      }
    }
  }
}
```

How it works...

The `clearCriteriaVariableValues()` is added to the `ExtViewObjectImpl` view object framework extension class, thus making it available for all view objects to call it. The method accepts a `java.lang.String` array of view criteria names (`criteriaNames`) and iterates over them, getting the associated view criteria for each of them. It then calls `ensureVariableManager()` on the view criteria to retrieve the bind variables manager, an `oracle.jbo.VariableValueManager` interface, which is implemented by the framework to manage named variables.

The bind variables are retrieved by calling `getVariables()` on the variable manager. This method returns an array of objects implementing the `oracle.jbo.Variable` interface, the actual bind variables. Finally, we iterate over the bind variables used by the view criteria, setting their values to null by calling `setVariableValue()` for each one of them.

There's more...

Note that the technique used in the recipe does not remove the view criteria associated with the view object, it simply resets the values of the bind variables associated with the view criteria. In order to completely remove the view criteria associated with a particular view object, call the `ViewObjectImpl` method `removeViewCriteria()`. This method first unapplies the specific view criteria and then completely removes them from the view object. If you want to unapply the view criteria without removing them from the view object, use the `removeApplyViewCriteriaName()` method. Furthermore, you can also clear all the view object view criteria in effect by calling `applyViewCriteria()` on the view object and specifying `null` for the view criteria name. Finally, to clear any view criteria in effect, you can also delete all the view criteria rows from it using the `remove()` method. Any of the above calls will alter the view criteria for the lifetime of the specific view object instance until the next time any of these calls are invoked again.

See also

- ▶ *Setting up BC base classes, Chapter 1, Pre-requisites to Success: ADF Project Setup and Foundations*

Searching case insensitively using view criteria

This recipe shows you a technique that you can use to handle case-insensitive (or case sensitive for that matter) searching for strings, when using view criteria for a view object. The framework provides various methods, such as `setUpperColumns()` and `isUpperColumns()`, for instance, at various view criteria levels (`ViewCriteria`, `ViewCriteriaRow` and `ViewCriteriaItem`) that can be used to construct generic helper methods to handle case searching. This technique can be used to allow case-insensitive or case-sensitive searches in your application based on some controlling user interface component or some application configuration option. For instance, a custom search form can be constructed with a checkbox component indicating whether the search will be case sensitive or not.

Getting ready

You will need to have access to the shared components workspace that was developed in the *Breaking up the application in multiple workspaces* recipe in *Chapter 1, Pre-requisites to Success: ADF Project Setup and Foundations*. The functionality will be added to the `ExtViewObjectImpl` custom framework class that was developed in the *Setting up BC base classes* recipe in *Chapter 1, Pre-requisites to Success: ADF Project Setup and Foundations*.

1. Open the shared components workspace.

2. Open the `ExtViewObjectImpl.java` view object framework extension class in the Java editor and add the following `setViewCriteriaCaseInsensitive()` method:

```
public void setViewCriteriaCaseInsensitive(
   boolean bCaseInsensitive) {
   // get all View Criteria managed by this view object
   ViewCriteria[] vcList = getAllViewCriterias();
   if (vcList != null) {
     // iterate over all view criteria
     for (ViewCriteria vc : vcList) {
       // set case-insensitive or case-sensitive as
       // indicated by the bCaseInsensitive parameter
       if (vc.isUpperColumns() != bCaseInsensitive)
       vc.setUpperColumns(bCaseInsensitive);
     }
   }
}
```

How it works...

We have added the `setViewCriteriaCaseInsensitive()` method in the `ExtViewObjectImpl` view object framework extension class to allow all view objects to call it in order to enable or disable case-insensitive search based on view criteria managed by the specific view object. The boolean parameter `bCaseInsensitive` indicates whether case-insensitive search is to be enabled for the view criteria.

The method gets access to all view criteria managed by the specific view object by calling `getAllViewCriterias()`. This framework method returns an `oracle.jbo.ViewCriteria` array containing all view criteria (both applied and unapplied) that are managed by the view object. It then iterates over them, checking in each iteration whether the current case-insensitive setting, obtained by calling `isUpperColumns()`, differs from the desired setting indicated by `bCaseInsensitive`. If this is the case, case-insensitivity is set (or reset) by calling `setUpperColumns()` for the specific view criteria.

When you enable case-insensitive search for the view criteria, the framework—when it adjusts the view object a query, based on the view criteria—calls the `UPPER()` database function in the `WHERE` clause for those criteria items where case-insensitive search has been enabled. This behavior can be seen when you declaratively define view criteria using the **Create View Criteria** dialog. Notice how the **View Object Where Clause** is altered as you check and uncheck the **Ignore Case** checkbox. This behavior is achieved programmatically as explained in this recipe by calling `setUpperColumns()`.

There's more...

As mentioned earlier, the framework allows you to control case-insensitive search at various levels. In this recipe, we have seen how to affect case searching for the view criteria as a whole, by utilizing the `setUpperColumns()` method defined for the `ViewCriteria` object. Individual criteria rows and items can be set separately by calling `setUpperColumns()` for specific `ViewCriteriaRow` and `ViewCriteriaItem` objects respectively.

See also

▶ *Setting up BC base classes, Chapter 1, Pre-requisites to Success: ADF Project Setup and Foundations*

5

Putting them all together: Application Modules

In this chapter, we will cover:

- ▶ Creating and using generic extension interfaces
- ▶ Exposing a custom method as a web service
- ▶ Accessing a service interface method from another application module
- ▶ A passivation/activation framework for custom session-specific data
- ▶ Displaying application module pool statistics
- ▶ Using a shared application module for static lookup data
- ▶ Using a custom database transaction

Introduction

An application module in the ADF Business Components framework represents a basic transactional unit that implements specific business use cases. It encompasses a data model comprising a hierarchy of view objects and optionally other application module instances, along with a number of custom methods that together implement a specific business use case. It allows the creation of **bindings** at the ViewController project layer, through the corresponding application model **data control** and the **ADF model layer** (**ADFm**). Moreover, it allows for the creation of custom functionality that can be exposed through its client interface and subsequently bound as method bindings. Method bindings declaratively *bind* user interface components to back-end data and services providing data access.

Custom application module methods can easily be exposed as web services through the application module service interface. Moreover, application modules and their configured view object instances can be exposed as service data object (SDO) components for consumption in a SOA infrastructure.

Creating and using generic extension interfaces

Back in *Chapter 1, Pre-requisites to Success: ADF Project Setup and Foundations* in the *Setting up BC base classes* recipe, we introduced a number of framework extension classes for various business components. We did this so that we could provide common implementation functionality for all derived business components throughout the application. In this recipe, we will go over how to expose parts of that common functionality as a generic extension interface. By doing so, this generic interface becomes available to all derived business components, which in turn can expose it to their own client interface and make it available to the ViewController layer through the bindings layer.

Getting ready

You will need to have access to the SharedComponents workspace that was developed in the *Breaking up the application in multiple workspaces* recipe in *Chapter 1, Pre-requisites to Success: ADF Project Setup and Foundations*. Additional functionality will be added to the ExtApplicationModuleImpl custom framework class that was developed in the *Setting up BC base classes* recipe in *Chapter 1, Pre-requisites to Success: ADF Project Setup and Foundations*.

This recipe also uses the HRComponents workspace, which was created in the *Overriding remove() to delete associated children entities* recipe in *Chapter 2, Dealing with Basics: Entity Objects*. The HRComponents workspace requires a database connection to the HR schema.

How to do it...

1. Open the shared components workspace in JDeveloper.
2. Create an interface called ExtApplicationModule as follows:

```
public interface ExtApplicationModule {
   // return some user authority level, based on
   // the user's name
   public int getUserAuthorityLevel();
}
```

3. Locate and open the custom application module framework extension class `ExtApplicationModuleImpl`. Modify it so that it implements the `ExtApplicationModule` interface.

4. Then, add the following method to it:

```
public int getUserAuthorityLevel() {
    // return some user authority level, based on the user's name
    return ("anonymous".equalsIgnoreCase(this.
getUserPrincipalName())) ?
        AUTHORITY_LEVEL_MINIMAL : AUTHORITY_LEVEL_NORMAL;
}
```

5. Rebuild the `SharedComponents` workspace and deploy it as an ADF Library JAR.

6. Now, open the `HRComponents` workspace.

7. Locate and open the `HrComponentsAppModule` application module definition.

8. Go to the **Java** section and click on the **Edit application module client interface** button (the pen icon in the **Client Interface** section).

9. On the **Edit Client Interface** dialog, shuttle the **getUserAuthorityLevel()** interface from the **Available** to the **Selected** list.

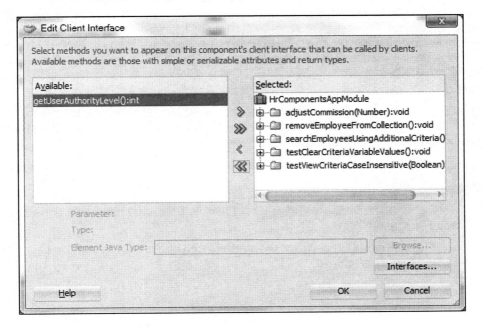

How it works...

In steps 1 and 2, we have opened the `SharedComponents` workspace and created an interface called `HrComponentsAppModule`. This interface contains a single method called `getUserAuthorityLevel()`.

Then, we updated the application module framework extension class `HrComponentsAppModuleImpl` so that it implements the `HrComponentsAppModule` interface (step 3). We also implemented the method `getUserAuthorityLevel()` required by the interface (step 4). For the sake of this recipe, this method returns a user authority level based on the authenticated user's name. We retrieve the authenticated user's name by calling `getUserPrincipal().getName()` on the `SecurityContext`, which we retrieve from the current ADF context (`ADFContext.getCurrent().getSecurityContext()`). If security is not enabled for the ADF application, the user's name defaults to `anonymous`. In this example, we return `AUTHORITY_LEVEL_MINIMAL` for anonymous users, and for all others we return `AUTHORITY_LEVEL_NORMAL`. We rebuilt and redeployed the `SharedComponents` workspace in step 5.

In steps 6 through 9, we opened the `HRComponents` workspace and added the `getUserAuthorityLevel()` method to the `HrComponentsAppModuleImpl` client interface. By doing this, we exposed the `getUserAuthorityLevel()` generic extension interface to a derived application module, while keeping its implementation in the base framework extension class `ExtApplicationModuleImpl`.

There's more...

Note that the steps followed in this recipe to expose an application module framework extension class method to a derived class' client interface can be followed for other business components framework extension classes as well.

See also

▶ *Setting up BC base classes, Chapter 1, Pre-requisites to Success: ADF Project Setup and Foundations*

▶ *Overriding remove() to delete associated children entities, Chapter 2, Dealing with Basics: Entity Objects*

Exposing a custom method as a web service

Service-enabling an application module allows you, among others, to expose custom application module methods as web services. This is one way for service consumers to consume the service-enabled application module. The other possibilities are accessing the application module by another application module, and accessing it through a Service Component Architecture (SCA) composite. Service-enabling an application module allows access to the same application module both through web service clients and interactive web user interfaces. In this recipe, we will go over the steps involved in service-enabling an application module by exposing a custom application module method to its service interface.

Getting ready

This recipe was developed using the HRComponents workspace, which was created in the *Overriding remove() to delete associated children entities* recipe in *Chapter 2, Dealing with Basics: Entity Objects*. The HRComponents workspace requires a database connection to the HR schema.

Furthermore, for this recipe, we will expose the adjustCommission() application module method that was developed back in *Chapter 3, A Different Point of View: View Objects Techniques* for the *Iterating a view object using a secondary rowset iterator* recipe as a web service.

How to do it...

1. Open the HRComponents project in JDeveloper.
2. Double-click on the HRComponentsAppModule application module in the **Application Navigator** to open its definition.
3. Go to the **Service Interface** section and click on the **Enable support for Service Interface** button (the green plus sign icon in the **Service Interface** section). This will start the **Create Service Interface** wizard.
4. In the **Service Interface** page, accept the defaults and click **Next**.

5. In the **Service Custom Methods** page, locate the `adjustCommission()` method and shuttle it from the **Available** list to the **Selected** list. Click on **Finish**.

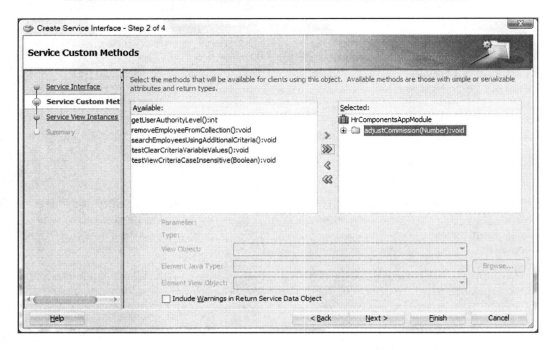

6. Observe that the `adjustCommission()` method is shown in the **Service Interface Custom Methods** section of the application module's **Service Interface**. The service interface files were generated in the `serviceinterface` package under the application module and are shown in the **Application Navigator**.

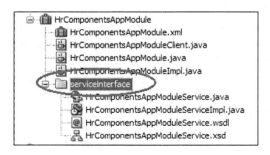

7. Double-click on the `weblogic-ejb-jar.xml` file under the `META-INF` package in the **Application Navigator** to open it.

8. In the **Beans** section, select the `com.packt.jdeveloper.` `cookbook.hr.components.model.application.common.` `HrComponentsAppModuleService Bean` bean and click on the **Performance** tab. For the `Transaction timeout` field, enter `120`.

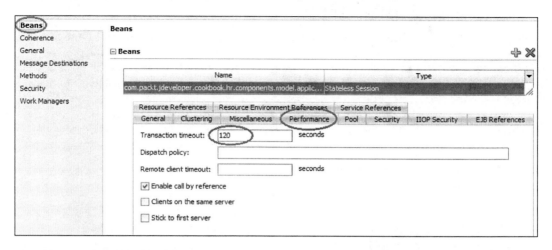

How it works...

In steps 1 through 6, we have exposed the `adjustCommission()` custom application module method to the application module's service interface. This is a custom method that adjusts all the Sales department employees' commissions by the percentage specified. As a result of exposing the `adjustCommission()` method to the application module service interface, JDeveloper generates the following files:

- `HrComponentsAppModuleService.java`: Defines the service interface

- `HrComponentsAppModuleServiceImpl.java`: The service implementation class

- `HrComponentsAppModuleService.xsd`: The service schema file describing the input and output parameters of the service

- `HrComponentsAppModuleService.wsdl`: The Web Service Definition Language (WSDL) file, describing the web service

- `ejb-jar.xml`: The EJB deployment descriptor. It is located in the `src/META-INF` directory

- `weblogic-ejb-jar.xml`: The WebLogic-specific EJB deployment descriptor, located in the `src/META-INF` directory

In steps 7 and 8, we adjust the service Java Transaction API (JTA) transaction timeout to 120 seconds (the default is 30 seconds). This will avoid any exceptions related to transaction timeouts when invoking the service. This is an optional step added specifically for this recipe, as the process of adjusting the commission for all sales employees might take longer than the default 30 seconds, causing the transaction to time out.

To test the service using the JDeveloper integrated WebLogic application server, right-click on the `HrComponentsAppModuleServiceImpl.java` service implementation file in the **Application Navigator** and select **Run** or **Debug** from the context menu. This will build and deploy the `HrComponentsAppModuleService` web service into the integrated WebLogic server. Once the deployment process is completed successfully, you can click on the service URL in the **Log** window to test the service. This will open a test window in JDeveloper and also enable the HTTP Analyzer. Otherwise, copy the target service URL from the **Log** window and paste it into your browser's address field. This will bring up the service's endpoint page.

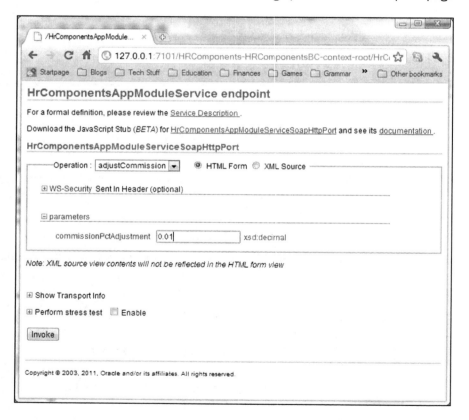

On this page, select the **adjustCommission** method from the **Operation** drop down, specify the **commissionPctAdjustment** parameter amount and click on the **Invoke** button to execute the web service. Observe how the employees' commissions are adjusted in the EMPLOYEES table in the HR schema.

There's more...

For more information on service-enabling application modules consult chapter *Integrating Service-Enabled Application Modules* in the *Fusion Developer's Guide for Oracle Application Development Framework* which can be found at `http://docs.oracle.com/cd/E24382_01/web.1112/e16182/toc.htm`.

See also

▸ *Overriding remove() to delete associated children entities, Chapter 2, Dealing with Basics: Entity Objects*

▸ *Iterating a view object using a secondary rowset iterator, Chapter 3, A Different Point of View: View Objects Techniques*

Accessing a service interface method from another application module

In the recipe *Exposing a custom method as a web service* in this chapter, we went through the steps required to service-enable an application module and expose a custom application module method as a web service. We will continue in this recipe by explaining how to invoke the custom application module method, exposed as a web service, from another application module.

Getting ready

This recipe will call the `adjustCommission()` custom application module method that was exposed as a web service in the *Exposing a custom method as a web service* recipe in this chapter. It requires that the web service is deployed in WebLogic and that it is accessible.

The recipe also requires that both the `SharedComponents` workspace and the `HRComponents` workspace are deployed as ADF Library JARs and that are added to the workspace used by this specific recipe. Additionally, a database connection to the HR schema is required.

How to do it...

1. Ensure that you have built and deployed both the `SharedComponents` and `HRComponents` workspaces as ADF Library JARs.

2. Create a File System connection in the **Resource Palette** to the directory path where the `SharedComponents.jar` and `HRComponents.jar` ADF Library JARs are located. In the book source code, they are located in the `chapter5/recipe3/ReUsableJARs` directory.

3. Create a new **Fusion Web Application (ADF)** called `HRComponentsCaller` using the **Create Fusion Web Application (ADF)** wizard.

4. Create a new application module called `HRComponentsCallerAppModule` using the **Create Application Module** wizard. In the **Java** page, check on the **Generate Application Module Class** checkbox to generate a custom application module implementation class. JDeveloper will ask you for a database connection during this step, so make sure that a new database connection to the `HR` schema is created.

5. Expand the **File System | ReUsableJARs** connection in the **Resource Palette** and add both the `SharedComponents` and `HRComponents` libraries to the project. You do this by right-clicking on the jar file and selecting **Add to Project...** from the context menu.

6. Bring up the business components **Project Properties** dialog and go to the **Libraries and Classpath** section. Click on the **Add Library...** button and add the **BC4J Service Client** and **JAX-WS Client** extensions.

7. Double-click on the `HRComponentsCallerAppModuleImpl.java` custom application module implementation file in the **Application Navigator** to open it in the Java editor.

8. Add the following method to it:

```
public void adjustCommission(
   BigDecimal commissionPctAdjustment) {
   // get the service proxy
   HrComponentsAppModuleService service =
     (HrComponentsAppModuleService)ServiceFactory
     .getServiceProxy(
     HrComponentsAppModuleService.NAME);
   // call the adjustCommission() service
   service.adjustCommission(commissionPctAdjustment);
}
```

9. Expose `adjustCommission()` to the `HRComponentsCallerAppModule` client interface.

10. Finally, in order to be able to test the `HRComponentsCallerAppModule` application module with the ADF Model Tester, locate the `connections.xml` file in the **Application Resources** section of the **Application Navigator** under the **Descriptors | ADF META-INF** node, and add the following configuration to it:

```
<Reference
   name="{/com/packt/jdeveloper/cookbook/hr/components/model/
   application/common/}HrComponentsAppModuleService"
   className="oracle.jbo.client.svc.Service" xmlns="">
<Factory
   className="oracle.jbo.client.svc.ServiceFactory"/>
<RefAddresses>
<StringRefAddr addrType="serviceInterfaceName">
```

```
<Contents>com.packt.jdeveloper.cookbook.hr.components.model.
application.common.serviceinterface.HrComponentsAppModuleService
</Contents>
</StringRefAddr>
<StringRefAddr addrType="serviceEndpointProvider">
<Contents>ADFBC</Contents>
</StringRefAddr>
<StringRefAddr addrType="jndiName">
<Contents>HrComponentsAppModuleServiceBean#com.packt.jdeveloper.
  cookbook.hr.components.model.application.common.
  serviceinterface.HrComponentsAppModuleService</Contents>
</StringRefAddr>
<StringRefAddr addrType="serviceSchemaName">
<Contents>HrComponentsAppModuleService.xsd</Contents>
</StringRefAddr>
<StringRefAddr addrType="serviceSchemaLocation">
<Contents>com/packt/jdeveloper/cookbook/hr/components/model/
application/common/serviceinterface/</Contents>
</StringRefAddr>
<StringRefAddr addrType="jndiFactoryInitial">
<Contents>weblogic.jndi.WLInitialContextFactory</Contents>
</StringRefAddr>
<StringRefAddr addrType="jndiProviderURL">
<Contents>t3://localhost:7101</Contents>
</StringRefAddr>
</RefAddresses>
</Reference>
```

How it works...

In steps 1 and 2, we have made sure that both the SharedComponents and HRComponents ADF Library JARs are deployed and that a file system connection was created, in order that both of these libraries get added to a newly created project (in step 5). Then, in steps 3 and 4, we create a new Fusion web application based on ADF, and an application module called HRComponentsCallerAppModule. It is from this application module that we intend to call the adjustCommission() custom application module method, exposed as a web service by the HrComponentsAppModule service-enabled application module in the HRComponents library JAR. For this reason, in step 4, we have generated a custom application module implementation class. We proceed by adding the necessary libraries to the new project in steps 5 and 6. Specifically, the following libraries were added: SharedComponents.jar, HRComponents.jar, BC4J Service Client, and JAX-WS Client.

In steps 7 through 9, we create a custom application module method called `adjustCommission()`, in which we write the necessary glue code to call our web service. In it, we first retrieve the web service proxy, as a `HrComponentsAppModuleService` interface, by calling `ServiceFactory.getServiceProxy()` and specifying the name of the web service, which is indicated by the constant `HrComponentsAppModuleService.NAME` in the service interface. Then we call the web service through the retrieved interface.

In the last step, we have provided the necessary configuration in the `connections.xml` so that we will be able to call the web service from an RMI client (the ADF Model Tester). This file is used by the web service client to locate the web service. For the most part, the `<Reference>` information that was added to it was generated automatically by JDeveloper in the *Exposing a custom method as a Web service* recipe, so it was copied from there. The extra configuration information that had to be added is the necessary JNDI context properties `jndiFactoryInitial` and `jndiProviderURL` that are needed to resolve the web service on the deployed server. You should change these appropriately for your deployment. Note that these parameters are the same as the initial context parameters used to lookup the service when running in a managed environment.

To test calling the web service, ensure that you have first deployed it and that it is running. You can then use the ADF Model Tester, select the **adjustCommission** method and execute it.

There's more...

For additional information related to such topics as securing the ADF web service, enabling support for binary attachments, deploying to WebLogic, and more, refer to the Integrating Service-Enabled Application Modules section in the Fusion Developer's Guide for Oracle Application Development Framework which can be found at `http://docs.oracle.com/cd/E24382_01/web.1112/e16182/toc.htm`.

See also

- *Setting up BC base classes, Chapter 1, Pre-requisites to Success: ADF Project Setup and Foundations*
- *Overriding remove() to delete associated children entities, Chapter 2, Dealing with Basics: Entity Objects*
- *Exposing a custom method as a web service, Chapter 5, Putting them all together: Application Modules*

A passivation/activation framework for custom session-specific data

In order to improve performance and preserve a stateful notion while utilizing a stateless protocol (that is, HTTP) the ADF Business Components framework implements the concept of **application module pooling**. This is a technique of maintaining a limited number of application modules, the exact number specified by configuration, in a pool, which are preserved across multiple user requests for the same HTTP session. If an application module instance for a session already exists in the application module pool, it gets reused. When all available application modules in the pool have been associated with specific sessions, an application module already linked with a particular session must be freed. This requires that the data associated with the application module is saved.

The process of saving the information associated with the specific application module is called **passivation**. The information is stored in a **passivation store**, usually a database, in XML format. The opposite process of restoring the state of the application module from the passivation store is called **activation**. Custom data is associated with specific application modules, and therefore with specific user sessions, by using a `Hashtable` obtained from an `oracle.jbo.Session` object. The `Hashtable` is obtained by calling `getSession().getUserData()` from the application module implementation class.

If you are using such custom data as part of some algorithm in your application and you expect the custom data to persist from one user request to another, passivation (and subsequent activation) support for these custom data must be implemented programmatically. You can add custom passivation and activation logic to your application module implementation class by overriding the `ApplicationModuleImpl` methods `passivateState()` and `activateState()` respectively. The `passivateState()` method creates the necessary XML elements for the application module's custom data that must be passivated. Conversely, the `activateState()` method detects the specific XML elements that identify the custom data in the passivated XML document and restores them back into the session custom data.

This recipe will show you how to do this, and at the same time build a mini framework to avoid duplication of the basic passivation/activation code that you must write for all the application modules in your project.

Getting ready

You will need to have access to the `SharedComponents` workspace that was developed in the *Breaking up the application in multiple workspaces* recipe in *Chapter 1, Pre-requisites to Success: ADF Project Setup and Foundations*. Additional functionality will be added to the `ExtApplicationModuleImpl` custom framework class that was developed in the *Setting up BC base classes* recipe in *Chapter 1, Pre-requisites to Success: ADF Project Setup and Foundations*.

This recipe is also using the HRComponents workspace, which was created in the *Overriding remove() to delete associated children entities* recipe in Chapter 2, *Dealing with Basics: Entity Objects*. The HRComponents workspace requires a database connection to the HR schema.

How to do it...

1. Open the SharedComponents workspace in JDeveloper and load the ExtApplicationModuleImpl application module framework extension class in the Java editor.

2. Add the following methods to the ExtApplicationModuleImpl application module framework extension class:

```
protected String[] onStartPassivation() {
  // default implementation: no passivation ids
  // are defined
  return new String[] { };
}
protected String onPassivate(String passivationId) {
  // default implementation: passivates nothing
  return null;
}
protected void onEndPassivation() {
  // default implementation: does nothing
}
protected String[] onStartActivation() {
  // default implementation: no activation ids
  // are defined
  return new String[] { };
}
protected void onActivate(String activationId,
  String activationData) {
  // default implementation: activates nothing
}
protected void onEndActivation() {
  // default implementation: does nothing
}
```

3. Override the void passivateState(Document, Element) method. Add the following code after the call to super.passivateState():

```
// begin custom data passivation: returns a
// list of the custom data passivation identifiers
String[] passivationIds = onStartPassivation();
// process all passivation identifiers
for (String passivationId : passivationIds) {
// check for valid identifier
```

```
      if (passivationId != null &&
        passivationId.trim().length() > 0) {
        // passivate custom data: returns
        // the passivation data
        String passivationValue =
           onPassivate(passivationId);
        // check for valid passivation data
        if (passivationValue != null &&
          passivationValue.length() > 0) {
        // create a new text node in the
        // passivation XML
        Node node =
          document.createElement(passivationId);
        Node cNode =
          document.createTextNode(passivationValue);
        node.appendChild(cNode);
        // add the passivation node to the
        // parent element
        element.appendChild(node);
        }
      }
    }
    // inform end of custom data passivation
    onEndPassivation();
```

4. Override the `activateState(Element element)` method. Add the following code
    after the call to `super.activateState()`:

```
// check for element to activate
if (element != null) {
  // begin custom data activation: returns a
  // list of the custom data activation identifiers
  String[] activationIds = onStartActivation();
  // process all activation identifiers
  for (String activationId : activationIds) {
    // check for valid identifier
    if (activationId != null &&
      activationId.trim().length() > 0) {
        // get nodes from XML for the specific
        // activation identifier
        NodeList nl =
          element.getElementsByTagName(activationId);
        // if it was found in the activation data
        if (nl != null) {
          // activate each node
```

```
      for (int n = 0, length =
        nl.getLength(); n < length; n++) {
        Node child =
          nl.item(n).getFirstChild();
        if (child != null) {
          // do the actual custom data
          // activation
          onActivate(activationId,
            child.getNodeValue().toString());
          break;
        }
      }
    }
  }
}
// inform end of custom data activation
onEndActivation();
}
```

5. Rebuild and redeploy the SharedComponents ADF Library JAR.

6. Open the HRComponents workspace and load the HrComponentsAppModuleImpl
    and HrComponentsAppModule application module custom implementation classes
    into the Java editor.

7. Add the following getActivationPassivationIds() helper method. Also, ensure
    that you define a constant called CUSTOM_DATA_PASSIVATION_ID indicating the
    custom data passivation identifier.

```
private static final String CUSTOM_DATA_PASSIVATION_ID =
  "customDataPassivationId";
private String[] getActivationPassivationIds() {
  // return the passivation/activation identifiers
  return new String[] { CUSTOM_DATA_PASSIVATION_ID };
}
```

8. Override the onStartPassivation(), onPassivate(),
    onStartActivation(), and onActivate() methods. Provide the following
    implementation for them:

```
protected String[] onStartPassivation() {
  // return the passivation identifiers
  return getActivationPassivationIds();
}
protected String onPassivate(String passivationId) {
  String passivationData = null;
  // passivate this application module's
  // custom data only
```

```
    if (CUSTOM_DATA_PASSIVATION_ID.equals(
    passivationId)) {
      // return the custom data from the Application
      // Module session user data
      passivationData = (String)getSession()
        .getUserData().get(CUSTOM_DATA_PASSIVATION_ID);
    }
    return passivationData;
  }
  protected String[] onStartActivation() {
    // return the activation identifiers
    return getActivationPassivationIds();
  }
  protected void onActivate(String activationId,
    String activationData) {
    // activate this application module's custom data only
    if (CUSTOM_DATA_PASSIVATION_ID.equals(activationId)) {
      // add custom data to the Application
      // Module's session
      getSession().getUserData().put(
        CUSTOM_DATA_PASSIVATION_ID, activationData);
    }
  }
}
```

9. Finally, for testing purposes, override the `prepareSession()` method and add the following code after the call to `super.prepareSession()`:

```
// add some custom data to the Application
// Module session
getSession().getUserData()
  .put(CUSTOM_DATA_PASSIVATION_ID,
  "Some custom data");
```

How it works...

In the first two steps, we have laid out a basic passivation/activation framework by adding a number of methods to the `ExtApplicationModuleImpl` application module framework extension class dealing specifically with this process. Specifically, these methods are:

▶ `onStartPassivation()`: The framework calls this method to indicate that a passivation process is about to start. Derived application modules that need to passivate custom data will override this method and return a `java.lang.String` array of passivation identifiers, indicating custom data that needs to be passivated.

- ▶ onPassivate(): The framework calls this method to indicate that some specific custom data, identified by the passivationId parameter, needs to be passivated. Derived application modules will override this method to passivate the specific custom data. It returns the passivated data as a java.lang.String.

- ▶ onEndPassivation(): This method is called by the framework to indicate that the passivation process is complete. Derived application modules could override this method to perform post-passivation actions.

- ▶ onStartActivation(): This method is called by the framework to indicate that an activation process is about to begin. Derived application modules in need of activating custom data, should override this method and return a list of activation identifiers.

- ▶ onActivate(): This method is called by the framework when some custom data— that is, the parameter activationData—needs to be activated. The custom data is identified by a unique identifier indicated by the parameter activationId. Derived application modules should override this method and restore the custom data being activated into the application module's user data Hashtable.

- ▶ onEndActivation(): This method indicates the end of the activation process. It can be overriden by derived application modules to do some post-activation actions.

These methods do nothing at the base class level. It is when they are overridden by derived application modules (see step 8) that they come to life.

In step 3, we have overridden the ADF Business Components framework method passivateState() and hooked up our own passivation/activation framework to it. ADF calls this method to indicate that a passivation is taking place. In it, after calling super. passivateState() to allow for the ADF processing, we first call onStartPassivation(). If a derived application module has overridden this method, it should return a list of passivation identifiers. These identifiers should uniquely identify the application module custom data that needs to be passivated at the application module level. We then iterate over the passivation identifiers, calling onPassivate() each time to retrieve the passivation data. We create a new XML node for the passivation identifier, we add the passivation data to it and append it to the parent XML node that is passed as a parameter by the ADF framework (the element parameter) to passivateState(). When all passivation identifiers have been processed, onEndPassivation() is called.

Step 4 is somewhat similar and does the activation. In this case, we have overridden the ADF `activateState()` method, which is called by the framework to indicate that the activation process is taking place. In it, we first call `super.activateState()` to allow for framework processing and then call `onStartActivation()` to get a list of the activation identifiers. We iterate over the activation identifiers, looking for each identifier in the activated XML data for the application module element. This is done by calling `element.getElementsByTagName()`. This method could possibly return multiple nodes, so for each we call `onActivate()` to activate the specific custom data. When we call `onActivate()`, we pass the activation identifier and the activation data to it as arguments. It is then the responsibility of the derived application module to handle the specifics of the activation. Finally, when all activation identifiers have been processed, we call `onEndActivation()` to indicate that the activation process has ended.

After we have added these changes to the `ExtApplicationModuleImpl` application module framework extension class, we make sure that the `SharedComponents` ADF Library JAR was redeployed (in step 5).

In steps 6 through 8, we have added passivation/activation support for custom data to the `HrComponentsAppModule` application module in the `HRComponents` workspace. This is done by overriding the `onStartPassivation()`, `onPassivate()`, `onStartActivation()`, and `onActivate()` methods (in step 8). The list of passivation and activation identifiers comes from the `getActivationPassivationIds()` method that we added in step 7. For this recipe, only a single custom data, identified by the constant `CUSTOM_DATA_PASSIVATION_ID`, is passivated. Custom data is saved at the user data `Hashtable` in the `oracle.jbo.Session` associated with the specific application module. It is retrieved by calling `getSession().getUserData().get(CUSTOM_DATA_PASSIVATION_ID)` in the `onPassivate()` method. Similarly, it is set in `onActivate()` by calling `getSession().getUserData().put(CUSTOM_DATA_PASSIVATION_ID` and `activationData()`.

> In this case, the activation data is passed as an argument (the `activationData` parameter) to the `onActivate()` by the `activateState()` implemented in application module framework extension class, as in step 4.

Finally, note the code in step 9. In the overridden `prepareSession()`, we have initialized the custom data by calling `getSession().getUserData().put(CUSTOM_DATA_PASSIVATION_ID, "Some custom data")`.

To test the custom data passivation/activation framework, run the application module with the ADF Model Tester. The ADF Model Tester provides support for passivation and activation via the **Save Transaction State** and **Restore Transaction State** menu items under the **File** menu. Observe the generated passivation XML data in the JDeveloper Log window when **File | Save Transaction State** is chosen. In particular, observe that the `<customDataPassivationId>Some custom data</customDataPassivationId>` node is added to the `<AM>` node of the passivated XML document. This is the session data added in step 9 for testing purposes to demonstrate this passivation/activation framework.

```
[81] **syncSequenceIncrementSize** altered sequence 'increment by' value to 50
[82] <AM MomVer="0">
   <cd></cd>
   <TXN Def="0" New="0" Lok="2" tsi="0" pcid="1"/>
   <CONN/>
   <VO>
      <VO sig="1310500543716" qf="0" RS="0" Def="com.packt.jdeveloper.cookbook.hr.components.model.view.Employees" Name="Employees"/>
      <VO sig="1310500543836" qf="0" RS="0" Def="com.packt.jdeveloper.cookbook.hr.components.model.view.Departments"
Name="Departments"/>
      <VO sig="1310500543836" qf="1" RS="0" Def="com.packt.jdeveloper.cookbook.hr.components.model.view.Departments"
Name="DepartmentsManaged"/>
      <VO sig="1310500543836" qf="1" RS="0" Def="com.packt.jdeveloper.cookbook.hr.components.model.view.Employees"
Name="EmployeesManaged"/>
      <VO sig="1310500543836" qf="1" RS="0" Def="com.packt.jdeveloper.cookbook.hr.components.model.view.Employees"
Name="DepartmentEmployees"/>
   </VO>
   <customDataPassivationId>Some custom data</customDataPassivationId>
</AM>
```

There's more...

Note that the `activateState()` method is called by the ADF Business Components framework after the view objects instances associated with the application module have been activated by the framework. If you need to activate custom data that would be subsequently accessed by your view objects, then you will need to enhance the custom data passivation/activation framework by overriding `prepareForActivation()` and provide the activation logic there instead.

Also, note that the ADF Business Components framework provides similar `passivateState()` and `activateState()` methods at the view object level for passivating and activating view object custom data. In this case, custom data is stored in the user data `Hashtable` of the `oracle.jbo.Session` associated with the specific application module that contains the particular view object in its data model.

Finally, observe the following points:

- ▸ This framework does not cover the passivation/activation of view object custom data. If needed, you will need to expand this framework to support this extra requirement.

- ▸ It is important that during the development process you test your application modules for being activation-safe. This is done by disabling the application module pooling in the application module configuration. For more information on this topic, consult the *Testing to Ensure Your Application Module is Activation-Safe* section in the *Fusion Developer's Guide for Oracle Application Development Framework*.

- *Setting up BC base classes, Chapter 1, Pre-requisites to Success: ADF Project Setup and Foundations*

- *Overriding remove() to delete associated children entities, Chapter 2, Dealing with Basics: Entity Objects*

Displaying application module pool statistics

In the *A passivation/activation framework for custom session-specific data* recipe in this chapter, we touched upon how application module pools are used by the ADF Business Components framework. In this recipe, we will introduce the `oracle.jbo.common.ampool.PoolMgr` application module pool manager and `oracle.jbo.common.ampool.ApplicationPool` application module pool classes, and explore how they can be utilized to collect statistical pool information. This may come in handy when debugging.

The use case that will be implemented by the recipe is to collect application module statistics and make them available in a generic view object, that can then be used by all application modules to gather and present statistical information to the frontend user interface.

Getting ready

You will need to have access to the `SharedComponents` workspace that was developed in the *Breaking up the application in multiple workspaces* recipe in *Chapter 1, Pre-requisites to Success: ADF Project Setup and Foundations*. Additional functionality will be added to the `ExtApplicationModuleImpl` custom framework class that was developed in the *Setting up BC base classes* recipe in *Chapter 1, Pre-requisites to Success: ADF Project Setup and Foundations*.

This recipe also uses the `HRComponents` workspace, which was created in the *Overriding remove() to delete associated children entities* recipe in *Chapter 2, Dealing with Basics: Entity Objects*. The `HRComponents` workspace requires a database connection to the `HR` schema.

How to do it...

1. Open the `SharedComponents` workspace in JDeveloper.

2. Create a new view object called `ApplicationModulePoolStatistics` using the following SQL query as its data source:

```
SELECT NULL AS POOL_NAME, NULL AS APPLICATION_MODULE_CLASS,  NULL
AS AVAILABLE_INSTANCE_COUNT, NULL AS INIT_POOL_SIZE, NULL AS
INSTANCE_COUNT, NULL AS MAX_POOL_SIZE, NULL AS
```

```
NUM_OF_STATE_ACTIVATIONS, NULL AS NUM_OF_STATE_PASSIVATIONS,
NULL AS NUM_OF_INSTANCES_REUSED, NULL AS REF_INSTANCES_RECYCLED,
NULL AS UNREF_INSTANCES_RECYCLED, NULL AS
REFERENCED_APPLICATION_MODULES, NULL AS NUM_OF_SESSIONS, NULL AS
AVG_NUM_OF_SESSIONS_REF_STATE   FROM DUAL
```

3. With the exception of the `PoolName` and `ApplicationModuleClass` attributes, which should be `String` data types, all other attributes should be `Number` types.

4. Designate the `PoolName` and `ApplicationModuleClass` attributes as key attributes.

5. In the **Java** section, create a custom view row class and ensure that the **Include accessors** checkbox is also checked.

6. Open the `ExtApplicationModuleImpl` application module custom framework class in the Java editor and add the following two methods to it:

```
public ExtViewObjectImpl
  getApplicationModulePoolStatistics() {
  return (ExtViewObjectImpl)findViewObject(
    "ApplicationModulePoolStatistics");
}
public void getAMPoolStatistics() {
  // get the pool manager
  PoolMgr poolMgr = PoolMgr.getInstance();
  // get the pools managed
  Enumeration keys = poolMgr.getResourcePoolKeys();
  // iterate over pools
  while (keys != null && keys.hasMoreElements()) {
    // get pool name
    String poolname = (String)keys.nextElement();
    // get the pool
    ApplicationPool pool =
      (ApplicationPool)poolMgr.getResourcePool(poolname);
    // get the pool statistics
    Statistics statistics = pool.getStatistics();
    // get and populate pool statistics view object
    ExtViewObjectImpl amPoolStatistics =
      getApplicationModulePoolStatistics();
    if (amPoolStatistics != null) {
      // empty the statistics
      amPoolStatistics.executeEmptyRowSet();
      // create and fill a new statistics row
      ApplicationModulePoolStatisticsRowImpl poolInfo
        (ApplicationModulePoolStatisticsRowImpl)
        amPoolStatistics.createRow();
      poolInfo.setPoolName(pool.getName());
```

```
poolInfo.setApplicationModuleClass(
pool.getApplicationModuleClass());
poolInfo.setAvailableInstanceCount(new
  Number(pool.getAvailableInstanceCount()));
poolInfo.setInitPoolSize(new
  Number(pool.getInitPoolSize()));
poolInfo.setInstanceCount(new
  Number(pool.getInstanceCount()));
poolInfo.setMaxPoolSize(new
  Number(pool.getMaxPoolSize()));
poolInfo.setNumOfStateActivations(new
  Number(statistics.mNumOfStateActivations));
poolInfo.setNumOfStatePassivations(new
  Number(statistics.mNumOfStatePassivations));
poolInfo.setNumOfInstancesReused(new
  Number(statistics.mNumOfInstancesReused));
poolInfo.setRefInstancesRecycled(new
  Number(statistics.mNumOfReferencedInstancesRecycled));
poolInfo.setUnrefInstancesRecycled(new
  Number(statistics.mNumOfUnreferencedInstancesRecycled));
poolInfo.setReferencedApplicationModules(new
  Number(statistics.mReferencedApplicationModules));
poolInfo.setNumOfSessions(new
  Number(statistics.mNumOfSessions));
poolInfo.setAvgNumOfSessionsRefState(new
  Number(statistics.mAvgNumOfSessionsReferencingState));
// add the statistics
amPoolStatistics.insertRow(poolInfo);
    }
  }
}
```

7. Open the `ExtApplicationModule` application module custom framework interface and add the following code to it:

```
public void getAMPoolStatistics();
```

8. Redeploy the `SharedComponents` ADF Library JAR.

9. Now, open the `HRComponents` workspace and in the **Resource Palette** create a file system connection for the `ReUsableJARs` directory where the `SharedComponents.jar` is deployed. Add the `SharedComponents.jar` to the `HRComponentsBC` business components project.

10. Double-click on the `HrComponentsAppModule` application module in the **Application Navigator** to open its definition.

11. Go to the **Data Model** section and locate the **ApplicationModulePoolStatistics** view object in the **Available View Objects** list. Shuttle it to the **Data Model** list.

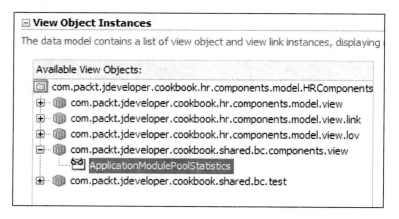

12. Finally, go to the **Java** section, locate and add the `getAMPoolStatistics()` method to the `HRComponents` application module client interface.

How it works...

In steps 1 through 5, we created `ApplicationModulePoolStatistics`, a read-only view object, which we used to collect the application module pool statistics. By adding this view object to the `SharedComponents` workspace, it becomes available to all other projects in all workspaces throughout the ADF application that import the `SharedComponents` ADF Library JAR. In step 6, we have added the necessary functionality to collect the application module statistics and populate the `ApplicationModulePoolStatistics` view object. This is done in the `getAMPoolStatistics()` method. This gets an instance of the `oracle.jbo.common.ampool.PoolMgr` application module pool manager, via the call to the static `getInstance()`, along with an `Enumeration` of the application module pools managed by the pool manager by calling `getResourcePoolKeys()` on the pool manager. We iterate over all the pools managed by the manager and retrieve each pool using `getResourcePool()` on the pool manager. Then for each pool we call `getStatistics()` to get the pool statistics. We create a new `ApplicationModulePoolStatistics` view object row and populate it with the statistics information.

In step 7, we have added the `getAMPoolStatistics()` to the `ExtApplicationModule` application module framework extension interface, so that it becomes available to all application modules throughout the application.

In steps 8 and 9, we redeploy the `SharedComponents` library and created a file system connection in the **Resource Palette**. We use this file system connection to add the shared components `SharedComponents.jar` ADF Library JAR to the `HRComponents` business components project.

In steps 10 and 11, we add the `ApplicationModulePoolStatistics` view object to the `HrComponentsAppModule` application module data model. Notice how the `ApplicationModulePoolStatistics` view object is listed in the available view objects list, although it is implemented in the `SharedComponents` workspace.

Finally, in step 12, we add `getAMPoolStatistics()` to the `HrComponentsAppModule` application module client interface. By doing so, we will be able to call it using the ADF Model Tester.

To test the recipe, run the `HrComponentsAppModule` application module with the ADF Model Tester. In the ADF Model Tester double-click on the `HrComponentsAppModule` application module to open it, select the **getAMPoolStatistics** method from the **Method** combo, and click on the **Execute** button. Then open the **ApplicationModulePoolStatistics** view object to see the results.

Now you can bind both the `getAMPoolStatistics` method and the `ApplicationModulePoolStatistics` view object to any of your ViewController projects in your ADF application, and present a visual of this statistical information for debugging purposes.

There's more...

Note that the `oracle.jbo.common.ampool.ApplicationPool` interface provides a method called `dumpPoolStatistics()` to dump all pool statistics to a `PrintWriter` object. You can use this method to quickly print the application module pool statistics to the JDeveloper **Log** window, as shown in following code:

```
PrintWriter out = new PrintWriter(System.out, true);
pool.dumpPoolStatistics(new PrintWriter(out));
out.flush();
```

See also

- ▶ *Setting up BC base classes, Chapter 1, Pre-requisites to Success: ADF Project Setup and Foundations*
- ▶ *Overriding remove() to delete associated children entities, Chapter 2, Dealing with Basics: Entity Objects*
- ▶ *Creating and using generic extension interfaces, Chapter 5, Putting them all together: Application Modules*

Using a shared application module for static lookup data

Shared application modules allow you to share static read-only data models across multiple user sessions. They are the ideal place to collect all the static read-only view accessors used throughout your ADF application for validation purposes or as data sources for your list of values (LOVs). This is because a single shared application module is constructed and used throughout the ADF application for all user sessions, thus minimizing the system resources used by it. In this case, a single database connection is used. In addition, by collecting all of your static read-only view objects in a shared application module, you avoid possible duplication and redefinition of read-only view objects throughout your ADF application.

Internally, the ADF Business Components framework manages a pool of query collections for each view object as it is accessed by multiple sessions by utilizing a query collection pool, something comparable to application module pools used for session-specific application modules. The framework offers a number of configuration options to allow for better management of this pool. Moreover, as multiple threads will access the data, the framework partitions the iterator space by supporting multiple iterators for the same rowset, preventing race conditions among iterators on different sessions.

In this recipe, we will define a shared application module called `HrSharedAppModule`, and we will migrate to it all of the static read-only view objects defined for the `HrComponents` project. Furthermore, we will update all the view objects that currently reference these static read-only view objects, so that they are now referencing the view objects in the shared application module.

Getting ready

This recipe was developed using the `HRComponents` workspace, which was created in the *Overriding remove() to delete associated children entities* recipe in *Chapter 2, Dealing with Basics: Entity Objects*. The `HRComponents` workspace requires a database connection to the `HR` schema.

How to do it...

1. Right-click on the `com.packt.jdeveloper.cookbook.hr.components.model.application` package on the **Application Navigator** and select **New Application Module...**.

2. Follow the steps in the **Create Application Module** wizard to create an application module called `HrSharedComponentsAppModule`.

3. In the **Data Model** page, expand the `com.packt.jdeveloper.cookbook.`
   `hr.components.model.view.lov` package and shuttle all of the view objects
   currently under this package from the **Available View Objects** list to the **Data Model**
   list. Click on **Finish** when done.

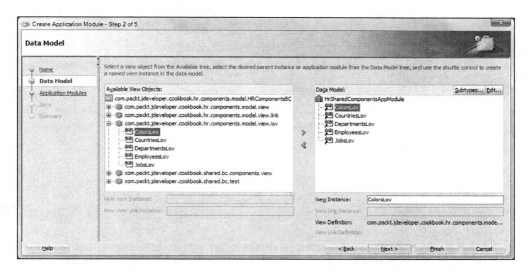

4. Now, double-click on the `HRComponentsBC` in the **Application Navigator** to bring up
   the **Project Properties** dialog.

5. Locate the **Application Module Instances** page by selecting **ADF Business
   Components | Application Module Instances** in the selection tree.

6. Click on the **Application** tab and shuttle the **HrSharedComponentsAppModule**
   application module from the **Available Application Modules** list to the **Application
   Module Instances** list. Click **OK** to dismiss the **Project Properties** dialog.

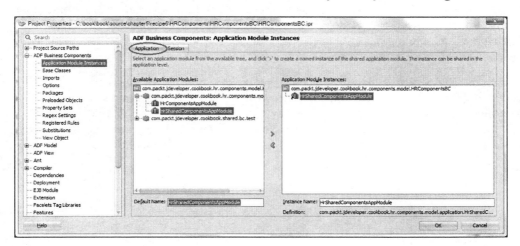

7. For each view object that was added to the **HrSharedComponentsAppModule** shared application module, locate (through **Find Usages**) where it is used as a view accessor, and change its usage so that it is referenced from inside the HrSharedComponentsAppModule shared application module. The following screenshot shows the view accessors that were added to the Employees view object.

8. Also for each view accessor used as a data source for an LOV, ensure that you are now using the view accessor included in HrSharedComponentsAppModule.

How it works...

In steps 1 through 6, we have defined a new application module called HrSharedComponentsAppModule and added all static read-only view objects developed so far—throughout the HRComponents business components project—in its data model. We have indicated that HrSharedComponentsAppModule will be a shared application module through the **Application Module Instances** page in the **Project Properties**, when we indicate that HrSharedComponentsAppModule will be an instance at application-level rather than an instance at session-level (in steps 4 through 6). By defining an application module at application-level, we allow all user sessions to access the same view instances contained in the application module data model.

In steps 7 and 8, we have identified all read-only view objects used as view accessors throughout the HRComponents business components project and updated each one at a time, so that the view object instance residing within the shared HrSharedComponentsAppModule application module is used. We have also ensured that for each LOV, we redefined its data source by using the updated view accessor.

There's more...

Ideally, the shared application module should contain a static read-only data model. If you expect that the data returned by any of the view objects might be updated, ensure that it will always return the latest data from the database by setting the view object **Auto Refresh** property to **true** in the **Tuning** section of the **Property Inspector**. This property is accessible while in the **General** section of the view object definition.

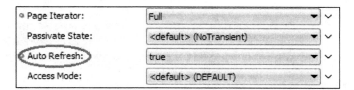

The auto-refresh feature relies on the database change notification feature, so ensure that the data source database user has database notification privileges. This can be achieved by issuing the following `grant` command for the database connection user:

```
grant change notification to <ds_user_name>
```

For more information on shared application modules, consult the *Sharing Application Module View Instances* chapter in the *Fusion Developer's Guide for Oracle Application Development Framework* which can be found at `http://docs.oracle.com/cd/E24382_01/web.1112/e16181/toc.htm`.

See also

▶ *Overriding remove() to delete associated children entities, Chapter 2, Dealing with Basics: Entity Objects*

Using a custom database transaction

In the *Setting up BC base classes* recipe in *Chapter 1, Pre-requisites to Success: ADF Project Setup and Foundations*, we introduced a number of custom framework extension classes for most of the ADF business components. Among these are classes that can be used to extend the global ADF framework transaction implementation, in particular the `ExtDatabaseTransactionFactory` and `ExtDBTransactionImpl2` classes. In this recipe, we will cover how to use these classes, so that we can implement our own custom transaction implementation. The use case for this recipe will be to provide logging support for all transaction commit and rollback operations.

Getting ready

You will need to have access to the `SharedComponents` workspace that was developed in the *Breaking up the application in multiple workspaces* recipe in *Chapter 1, Pre-requisites to Success: ADF Project Setup and Foundations*. Additional functionality will be added to the `ExtDatabaseTransactionFactory` and `ExtDBTransactionImpl2` custom framework classes that were developed in the *Setting up BC base classes* recipe in *Chapter 1, Pre-requisites to Success: ADF Project Setup and Foundations*.

This recipe also uses the `HRComponents` workspace, which was created in the *Overriding remove() to delete associated children entities* recipe in *Chapter 2, Dealing with Basics: Entity Objects*. The `HRComponents` workspace requires a database connection to the `HR` schema.

How to do it...

1. Open the `SharedComponents` workspace and open the `ExtDatabaseTransactionFactory.java` file in the Java editor.

2. Override the `DatabaseTransactionFactory` `create()` method and replace the `return super.create()` method with the following code:

    ```
    // return custom transaction framework
    // extension implementation
    return new ExtDBTransactionImpl2();
    ```

3. Load the `ExtDBTransactionImpl2.java` file in the Java editor, add an `ADFLogger` to it and override the `commit()` and `rollback()` `DBTransactionImpl2` methods. The code should look similar to the following:

    ```
    // create an ADFLogger
    private static final ADFLogger LOGGER =
      ADFLogger.createADFLogger(ExtDBTransactionImpl2.class);
    public void commit() {
      // log a trace
      LOGGER.info("Commit was called on the transaction");
      super.commit();
    }
    public void rollback() {
      // log a trace
      LOGGER.info("Rollback was called on the transaction");
      super.rollback();
    }
    ```

4. Rebuild and redeploy the `SharedComponents` workspace into an ADF Library JAR.

5. Open the `HRComponents` workspace and open the `HrComponentsAppModule` application module definition by double-clicking on it in the **Application Navigator**.

6. Go to the **Configurations** section.

7. Select the **HrComponentsAppModuleLocal** configuration and click the **Edit selected configuration object** button (the pen icon).

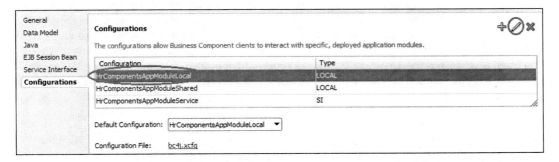

8. In the **Edit Configuration** dialog, click on the **Properties** tab and locate the **TransactionFactory** property. For the property value, enter the custom transaction framework extension class com.packt.jdeveloper.cookbook.shared. bc.extensions.ExtDatabaseTransactionFactory.

How it works...

In steps 1 and 2, we have overridden the DatabaseTransactionFactory create() method for the custom transaction factory framework class ExtDatabaseTransactionFactory that we created in the recipe *Setting up BC base classes* recipe in *Chapter 1, Pre-requisites to Success: ADF Project Setup and Foundations*. Now it will return our custom transaction implementation class ExtDBTransactionImpl2. This informs the ADF Business Components framework that a custom oracle.jbo. server.DBTransaction implementation will be used. Then, in step 3, we provide custom implementations for our ExtDBTransactionImpl2 transaction commit and rollback operations. In this case, we have provided a global transaction logging facility for all commit and roll back operations throughout the ADF application for application modules utilizing our custom DBTransaction implementation. We then rebuild and redeploy the shared components workspace (step 4).

In steps 5 through 8, we have explicitly indicated in the HrComponentsAppModule local configuration, the one used to configure session-specific application modules, that a custom transaction factory will be used. We did this by setting the TransactionFactory configuration property to our custom transaction factory implementation class com.packt.jdeveloper.cookbook.shared.bc.extensions. ExtDatabaseTransactionFactory.

There's more...

In order to change application module configuration parameters for all application modules throughout your ADF application, adopt the practice of using Java system-defined properties via the -D switch at JVM startup. In this case, ensure that no specific configuration parameters are defined for individual application modules, unless needed, as they would override the values specified globally with the -D Java switch. You can determine the specific parameter names that you must specify with the D switch, from the **Property** field in the **Edit Configuration** dialog. For example, for this recipe you will specify DTransactionFactory="com.packt.jdeveloper. cookbook.shared.bc.extensions.ExtDatabaseTransactionFactory" at JVM startup, to indicate that the custom transaction factory will be used. For WebLogic, these startup parameters can be specified via the JAVA_OPTIONS environment variable or in any of the WebLogic startup scripts (setDomainEnv.*, startWebLogic.*, startManagedWebLogic.*). These scripts can be found in the bin directory under the WebLogic domain directory. Furthermore, the WebLogic server Java startup parameters can be specified using the administrator console in the server **Configuration | Server Start** tab.

See also

▶ *Setting up BC base classes, Chapter 1, Pre-requisites to Success: ADF Project Setup and Foundations*

▶ *Overriding remove() to delete associated children entities, Chapter 2, Dealing with Basics: Entity Objects*

6

Go with the Flow: Task Flows

In this chapter, we will cover:

- ▶ Using an application module function to initialize a page
- ▶ Using a task flow initializer to initialize a task flow
- ▶ Calling a task flow as a URL programmatically
- ▶ Retrieving the task flow definition programmatically using MetadataService
- ▶ Creating a train

Introduction

Task flows are used for designing the ADF Fusion web application's control flow. They were introduced with the advent of the JDeveloper 11g R1 release as an alternative to standard JSF navigation flows. As such, they allow for the decomposition of monolithic application navigation flows (as in the case of JSF navigation flows) into modular, transaction, and memory scope aware controller flow components. The ADF Fusion web application is now composed of numerous task flows, called bounded task flows, usually residing in various ADF Library JARs, calling each other in order to construct the application's overall navigation flow.

In the traditional JSF navigation flow, navigation occurs between pages. Task flows introduce navigation between activities. A task flow activity is not necessarily a visual page component (view activity) as in the case of JSF navigation flows. It can be a call to Java code (method call activity), the invocation of another task flow (task flow call activity), a control flow decision (router activity), or something else. This approach provides a high degree of flexibility, modularity, and reusability when designing the application's control flow.

Using an application module function to initialize a page

A common use case when developing an ADF Fusion web application is to perform some sort of initialization before a particular page of the application is shown. Such an initialization could be: the creation of a new view object row, which will in effect place the view object in insert mode; the execution of a view object query, which could populate a table on the page; the execution of a database stored procedure; or something similar. This can easily be accomplished by utilizing a method call activity.

In this recipe, we will demonstrate the usage of the method call task flow activity by implementing the familiar use case of placing a web page in insert mode. Before the page is presented, a custom application module method (implemented in another workspace) will be called to place the view object in insert mode.

Getting ready

You will need a skeleton **Fusion Web Application (ADF)** workspace created before you proceed with this recipe. For this, we have used the `MainApplication` workspace that was developed in the *Breaking up the application in multiple workspaces* recipe in *Chapter 1, Pre-requisites to Success: ADF Project Setup and Foundations*.

The recipe also uses the `HRComponents` workspace, which was created in the *Overriding remove() to delete associated children entities* recipe in *Chapter 2, Dealing with Basics: Entity Objects*.

Both the `HRComponents` and `MainApplication` workspaces require database connections to the `HR` schema.

How to do it...

1. Open the `HRComponents` workspace in JDeveloper.

2. Load the `HrComponentsAppModuleImpl` custom application module implementation class into the Java editor and add the following `prepare()` method to it:

```
public void prepare() {
  // get the Employees view object instance
  EmployeesImpl employees = this.getEmployees();
  // remove all rows from rowset
  employees.executeEmptyRowSet();
  // create a new employee row
```

```
      Row employee = employees.createRow();
      // add the new employee to the rowset
      employees.insertRow(employee);
}
```

3. Open the `HrComponentsAppModule` application module definition and go to the **Java** section. Click on the **Edit application module client interface** button (the pen icon) and shuttle the `prepare()` method from the **Available** methods list to the **Selected** list.

4. Rebuild and redeploy the `HRComponents` workspace into an ADF Library JAR.

5. Now, open the `MainApplication` workspace and using the **Resource Palette** create a new **File System** connection to the `ReUsableJARs` directory where the `HRComponents.jar` ADF Library JAR is placed. Select the ViewController project in the **Application Navigator** and then right-click on the `HRComponents.jar` ADF Library JAR in the **Resource Palette**. From the context menu, select **Add to Project...**.

6. Right-click on the ViewController project in the **Application Navigator** and select **New...**. Select **ADF Task Flow** from the **Web Tier | JSF/Facelets** category.

7. In the **Create Task Flow** dialog, enter `methodInitializer.xml` for the task flow name and ensure that you have selected the **Create as Bounded Task Flow** checkbox. Also, make sure that the **Create with Page Fragments** checkbox is not selected. Then click **OK**.

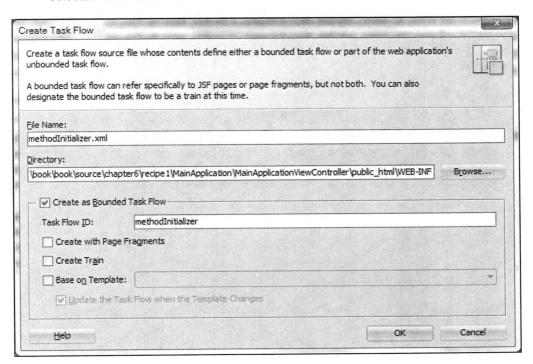

8. The `methodInitializer` task flow should open automatically in **Diagram** mode. If not, double-click on it in the **Application Navigator** to open it. Click anywhere in the task flow and in the **Property Inspector** change the **URL Invoke** property to **url-invoke-allowed**.

9. Expand the **Data Controls** section in the **Application Navigator**; locate and expand the `HrComponentsAppModuleDataControl` data control. Find the `prepare()` method and drag-and-drop it onto the `methodInitializer` task flow. JDeveloper will create a method call activity called prepare.

10. Drag-and-drop a **View** activity from the **Component Palette** onto the `methodInitializer` task flow.

11. Using the **Component Palette**, create a **Control Flow Case** from the prepare method call activity to the view activity.

12. Ensure that the prepare method call activity is marked as the default task flow activity by clicking on the **Mark Default Activity** button in the toolbar. The task flow should look similar to the following screenshot:

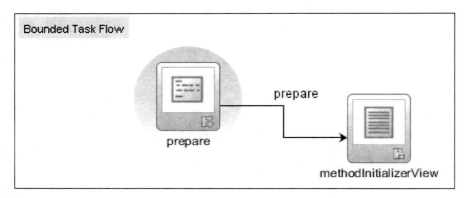

13. Double-click on the view activity to bring up the **Create JSF Page** dialog. In it, select **JSP XML** for the **Document Type**. For the **Page Layout**, you may select any of the **Quick Start Layout** options. Click **OK**. The page should open automatically in **Design** mode. If not, double-click on it in the **Application Navigator** to open it.

14. Expand the **Data Controls** section in the **Application Navigator** and locate the `Employees` view object under the `HrComponentsAppModuleDataControl`. Drag-and-drop the `Employees` view object onto the page.

15. From the **Create** context menu, select **Form | ADF Form...**. This will present the **Edit Form Fields** dialog. Click **OK** to accept the defaults and proceed with the creation of the ADF form.

How it works...

In steps 1 through 4, we have added a method called `prepare()` to the `HrComponentsAppModule` application module residing in the `HRComponents` workspace. In this method, we retrieved the `Employees` view object instance by calling the `getEmployees()` method, and called `executeEmptyRowSet()` on the view object to empty its rowset. We then created an employee row by calling `createRow()` on the `Employees` view object, and added the new row to the `Employees` view object rowset by calling `insertRow()` and passing the newly created employee row as an argument to it. This will, in effect, place the `Employees` view object in insert mode. We exposed the `prepare()` method to the application module client interface (in step 3), so that we will be able to call this method via the bindings layer using a task flow method call activity. Then (in step 4), we rebuild and redeployed the `HRComponents` workspace to an ADF Library JAR. This will allow us to import the ADF components implemented in the ADF Library JAR to other projects throughout the ADF application.

In order to be able to reuse the components defined and implemented in the `HRComponents` ADF Library JAR, we created a file system connection using the **Resource Palette** in JDeveloper and added the library to our main project (in step 5).

In steps 6 through 8, we created a bounded task flow called `methodInitializer` and ensured (in step 8) that its **URL Invoke** property was set to `url-invoke-allowed`. We needed to do this because the method call activity that is added in step 9 to call the `prepare()` method in the `HrComponentsAppModule` application module is indicated as the default task flow activity (in step 12). In this case, leaving the default setting of `calculated` for the **URL Invoke** property will produce an *HTTP 403 Forbidden* error. This is a security precaution to disallow URL-invoking a task flow that does not have a view activity as its default activity. In our case, as we have indicated a method call activity as the default activity, we need to ensure that the **URL Invoke** property is set to `url-invoke-allowed`.

In step 9, we dragged-and-dropped the `prepare()` method, under the `HrComponentsAppModuleDataControl` data control (in the **Data Controls** section of the **Application Navigator**), onto the task flow. This creates the method call activity and the necessary bindings to bind the method call activity to the `prepare()` method in the `HrComponentsAppModule` application module. By default, the page definition is placed in the `pageDefs` package under the default package defined for the ViewController project (`com.packt.jdeveloper.cookbook.hr.main.view` in this case). Note that the `HrComponentsAppModuleDataControl` data control becomes available once the `HRComponents` ADF Library JAR is added to the project.

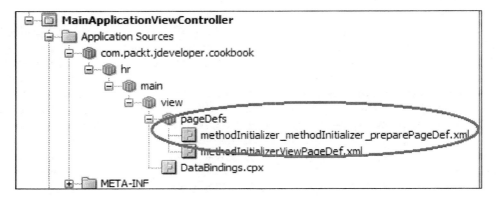

In steps 10 and 11, we placed a view activity onto the task flow and added a control flow case (called `prepare` by default) to allow the transition from the `prepare()` method call activity to the view activity.

The definition of the task flow is completed by ensuring that the `prepare()` method call activity is marked as the default task flow activity (step 12). This indicates that it will be the first activity to be executed in the task flow.

Finally, in steps 13 through 15, we create a JSF page for the task flow view activity and add an ADF form to it for the `Employees` view object. We did this by dragging-and-dropping the `Employees` view object from the `HrComponentsAppModuleDataControl` data control onto the JSPX page.

To test the recipe, right-click on the `methodInitializer` task flow in the **Application Navigator** and select **Run** or **Debug** from the context menu. This will build, deploy, and run the workspace into the integrated WebLogic application server. As you can see, the `prepare()` method call activity is called prior to transitioning to the view activity. The effect of calling the `prepare()` method is to place the `Employees` view object in insert mode.

There's more...

Using a task flow method call activity is one of the possible ways to perform an initialization before displaying a page. Another approach, explained in more detail in the *Using a task flow initializer for task flow initialization* recipe in this chapter, is to use a task flow initializer. The difference between the two is that the task flow initializer is called once during the instantiation of the task flow, while multiple method call activities may be placed anywhere in the task flow. Also, consider the definition of an `invokeAction` in the page definition to perform page-specific initialization. As best practice, consider using either a method call task flow activity or a task flow initializer as they are highly abstracted and loosely coupled. Using an `invokeAction` on the other hand would be more appropriate if you want the initialization method to be executed for multiple phases of the page's lifecycle.

Furthermore, note that the `prepare()` method we use for initializing the page, does not accept any parameters and it returns nothing. If your initialization method requires parameters to be specified, they can be specified either in the **Parameters** section of the **Edit Action Binding** dialog (for a data control bound method) or otherwise, using the **Parameters** section in the method call **Property Inspector**. In either case, the parameter values are usually communicated via the `pageFlowScope`. Finally, based on the return type of your initialization method, you could set the value of the `toString()` outcome in the **Outcome** section of the **Property Inspector** and allow further processing of the return value, using a router activity for instance. When returning `void`, the outcome must be fixed and `toString()` cannot be used (must be set to `false`).

See also

▶ *Breaking up the application in multiple workspaces, Chapter 1, Pre-requisites to Success: ADF Project Setup and Foundations*

▶ *Overriding remove() to delete associated children entities, Chapter 2, Dealing with Basics: Entity Objects*

▶ *Using a task flow initializer to initialize a task flow*, in this chapter

Using a task flow initializer to initialize a task flow

In the *Using an application module function to initialize a page* recipe in this chapter, we demonstrated how to use a method residing in the application module to perform page initialization, by bounding the method as a method call activity in the task flow. This recipe shows a different way to accomplish the same task by using a task flow initializer method instead. Unlike the method call activity, which once bound to the task flow may be called multiple times in the task flow, the initializer method is called only once during the task flow initialization.

Getting ready

You will need a skeleton **Fusion Web Application (ADF)** workspace created before you proceed with this recipe. For this, we have used the `MainApplication` workspace that was developed in the *Breaking up the application in multiple workspaces* recipe in *Chapter 1, Pre-requisites to Success: ADF Project Setup and Foundations*.

The recipe also uses the HRComponents workspace, which was created in the *Overriding remove() to delete associated children entities* recipe in *Chapter 2, Dealing with Basics: Entity Objects*.

Both the HRComponents and MainApplication workspaces require database connections to the HR schema.

How to do it...

1. Open the HRComponents workspace in JDeveloper.

2. Load the HrComponentsAppModuleImpl custom application module implementation class into the Java editor and add the following method to it:

```java
public void prepare() {
    // get the Employees view object instance
    EmployeesImpl employees = this.getEmployees();
    // remove all rows from rowset
    employees.executeEmptyRowSet();
    // create a new employee row
    Row employee = employees.createRow();
    // add the new employee to the rowset
    employees.insertRow(employee);
}
```

3. Open the HrComponentsAppModule application module definition and go to the **Java** section. Click on the **Edit application module client interface** button (the pen icon) and shuttle the prepare() method from the **Available** methods list to the **Selected** list.

4. Rebuild and redeploy the HRComponents workspace into an ADF Library JAR.

5. Now, open the MainApplication workspace and using the **Resource Palette** create a new **File System** connection to ReUsableJARs directory where the HRComponents.jar ADF Library JAR is placed. Select the ViewController project in the **Application Navigator** and then right-click on the HRComponents.jar ADF Library JAR in the **Resource Palette**. From the context menu, select **Add to Project...**.

6. Right-click on the ViewController project in the **Application Navigator** and select **New...**. Select **ADF Task Flow** from the **Web Tier | JSF/Facelets** category.

7. In the **Create Task Flow** dialog, enter taskflowInitializer.xml for the task flow **File Name** and ensure that you have selected the **Create as Bounded Task Flow** checkbox. Also make sure that the **Create with Page Fragments** checkbox is not selected. Then click **OK**.

8. The `taskflowInitializer` task flow should open automatically in **Diagram** mode. If not, double-click on it in the **Application Navigator** to open it. Click anywhere in the task flow, then in the **Property Inspector** change the **URL Invoke** property to **url-invoke-allowed**.

9. Go to the task flow **Overview | Managed Beans** section and add a managed bean called `InitializerBean`. Enter `com.packt.jdeveloper.cookbook.hr.main.view.beans.Initializer` for the managed bean **Class** and select **pageFlow** for the bean **Scope**.

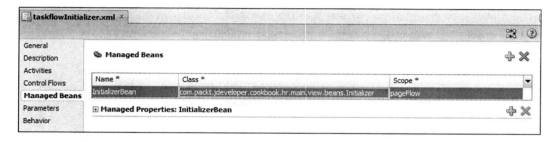

10. While at the **Managed Beans** section, select **Generate Class** from the **Property Menu** next to the **Managed Bean Class** in the **Property Inspector**.

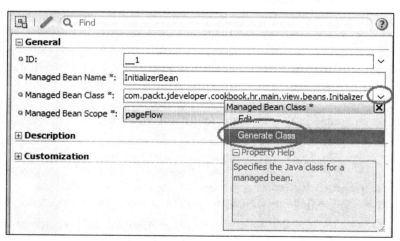

11. Locate the `Initializer.java` bean in the **Application Navigator** and open it in the Java editor. Add the following `initialize` method to it:

```
public void initialize() {
    // get the application module
    HrComponentsAppModule hrComponentsAppModule =
        (HrComponentsAppModule)ADFUtils
        .getApplicationModuleForDataControl(
        "HrComponentsAppModuleDataControl");
    if (hrComponentsAppModule != null) {
        // call the initializer method
        hrComponentsAppModule.prepare();
    }
}
```

12. Return to the task flow, diagram and add a task flow initializer by clicking on the **Property Menu** next to the **Initializer** property in the **Property Inspector** and selecting **Method Expression Builder...**.

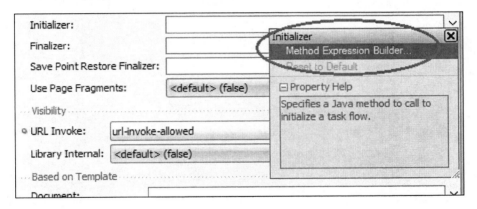

In the **Expression Builder** dialog that opens, locate and select the **initialize** method of the **InitilizerBean** under the **ADF Managed Beans** node. The click **OK** to dismiss the dialog. The initializer expression #{pageFlowScope.InitializerBean. initialize} should be reflected in the **Initializer** property of the task flow in the **Property Inspector**.

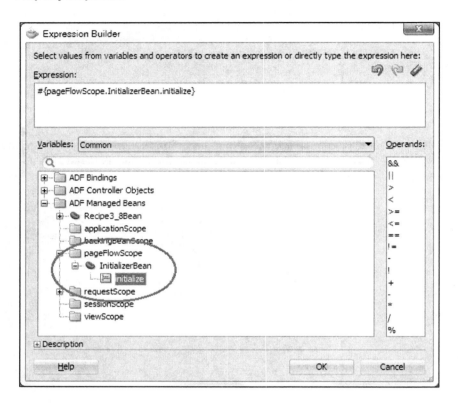

13. Drag-and-drop a **View** activity from the **Component Palette** onto the taskflowInitializer task flow.

14. Double-click on the view activity to bring up the **Create JSF Page** dialog. In it, select **JSP XML** for the **Document Type**. For the **Page Layout**, you may select any of the **Quick Start Layout** options. Click **OK**. The page should open automatically in **Design** mode. If not, double-click on it in the **Application Navigator** to open it.

15. Expand the **Data Controls** section in the **Application Navigator** and locate the Employees view object under the HrComponentsAppModuleDataControl. Drag-and-drop the Employees view object onto the page.

16. From the **Create** context menu, select **Form | ADF Form…**. This will present the **Edit Form Fields** dialog. Click **OK** to accept the defaults and proceed with the creation of the ADF form.

How it works...

Steps 1 through 8 have been thoroughly explained in the *Using an application module function to initialize a page* recipe in this chapter, so we won't get into the specific details here.

In steps 9 and 10, we defined a managed bean called `InitializerBean` and generated a Java class for it. We used `pageFlow` for the bean's memory scope. This ensures that the `InitializerBean` bean persists throughout the task flow's execution.

In step 11, we added an `initialize()` method to the `InitializerBean` bean. This is the method indicated as the task flow initializer in steps 12 and 13. Inside the `initialize()` method, we get hold of the `HrComponentsAppModule` by utilizing the `ADFUtils.getApplicationModuleForDataControl()` helper method. We introduced the `ADFUtils` helper class back in *Chapter 1, Pre-requisites to Success: ADF Project Setup and Foundations* in the *Using ADFUtils/JSFUtils* recipe. We have packaged the `ADFUtils` helper class inside the `SharedComponents` ADF Library JAR (`SharedComponents.jar`), which is imported into the project in step 5. The `getApplicationModuleForDataControl()` method returns an `oracle.jbo.ApplicationModule` interface, which we then cast to our specific `HrComponentsAppModule` custom application module interface. Through the `HrComponentsAppModule` interface, we call the `prepare()` method to do the necessary initializations. We explained the logic in `prepare()` in the *Using an application module function to initialize a page* recipe in this chapter.

In steps 12 and 13, we declaratively setup the task flow initializer property using the Expression Language expression `#{pageFlowScope.InitializerBean.initialize}`. This expression indicates that the `initialize()` method of the `InitializerBean` is called during the instantiation of the task flow.

Finally, in steps 14 through 17, we defined a view activity and the corresponding JSF page. Again, we explained these steps in more detail in the *Using an application module function to initialize a page* recipe in this chapter.

To test the recipe, right-click on the `taskFlowInitializer` task flow in the **Application Navigator** and select **Run** from the context menu. This will build, deploy and run the workspace into the integrated WebLogic application server. The page displayed in the browser will be presented in insert mode, as the task flow initializer method calls the application module `prepare()` method to set the `Employees` view object in insert mode.

There's more...

Both this technique and the one presented in the *Using an application module function to initialize a page* recipe in this chapter may be used to run task flow initialization code. However, note one difference pertaining to their handling of the Web browser's back button. While the task flow initializer approach calls the initializer method upon reentry via the browser's back button, no task flow initialization code is called when reentering the task flow via the browser's back button in the method call activity approach. However, this behaviour seems to be inconsistent among browsers, depending on how they handle page caching. For more information about this, refer to section *About Creating Complex Task Flows* in the *Fusion Developer's Guide for Oracle Application Framework* which can be found at `http://docs.oracle.com/cd/E24382_01/web.1112/e16182/toc.htm`.

See also

▶ *Breaking up the application in multiple workspaces*, Chapter 1, Pre-requisites to Success: ADF Project Setup and Foundations

▶ *Overriding remove() to delete associated children entities*, Chapter 2, Dealing with Basics: Entity Objects

▶ *Using an application module function to initialize a page*, in this chapter

Calling a task flow as a URL programmatically

A task flow that is indicated as URL invokable (by setting its `visibility` attribute `url-invoke-allowed` to `true`) may be accessed directly by constructing and invoking its URL. This allows you to dynamically invoke task flows from within your Java code depending on some condition that is satisfied at runtime. Programmatically, this can be done using the `oracle.adf.controller.ControllerContext.getTaskFlowURL()` method and specifying the task flow identifier and parameters.

For this recipe, to demonstrate calling a task flow via its URL, we will create a task flow that is URL invokable and call it from a JSF page programmatically. The task flow accepts a parameter and based on the parameter's value, determines whether to call any of the `methodInitializer` or `taskflowInitializer` task flows. These task flows were developed in the *Using an application module function to initialize a page* and *Using a task flow initializer to initialize a task flow* recipes respectively in this chapter.

Getting ready

You need to have access to the `methodInitializer` and `taskflowInitializer` task flows that were developed in the _Using an application module function to initialize a page_ and _Using a task flow initializer to initialize a task flow_ recipes in this chapter. Also, note the additional prerequisites stated for those recipes, that is, the usage of the `HRComponents` and `MainApplication` workspaces and the database connection to the `HR` schema.

How to do it...

1. Start by creating a new task flow called `programmaticallyInvokeTaskFlow`. Ensure that you create it as a bounded task flow, and that it is not created with page fragments.

2. In the **Visibility** section in the task flow **Property Inspector**, make sure that the **URL Invoke** attribute is set to **url-invoke-allowed**.

3. While in the task flow **Property Inspector**, in the **Parameters** section add a parameter called `taskFlowToCall` of type `java.lang.String`. For the parameter **Value** enter `#{pageFlowScope.taskFlowToCall}`.

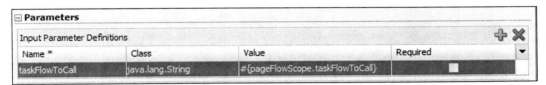

4. From the **Component Palette**, drop a **Router** activity on the task flow.

5. Locate the `methodInitializer` and `taskflowInitializer` task flows in the **Application Navigator** and drop them on the task flow.

6. Using the **Component Palette**, create control flow cases from the router activity to `methodInitializer` and `taskflowInitializer` task flow calls. Call these control flow cases `callMethodInitializer` and `callTaskFlowInitializer` respectively.

7. Next select the router activity, and in the **Property Inspector** set its **Default Outcome** property to `callMethodInitializer`. Also, add the following expression `#{pageFlowScope.taskFlowToCall eq 'calTaskFlowInitializer'}` in the **Cases** section and `callTaskFlowInitializer` as the expression's **Outcome** value. The router's properties in the Property Inspector should look similar to the following screenshot:

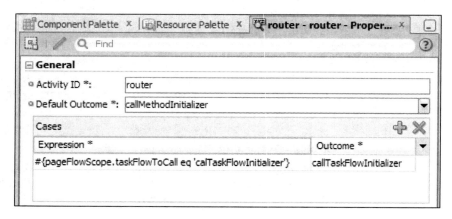

8. The complete `programmaticallyInvokeTaskFlow` task flow should look similar to the following screenshot:

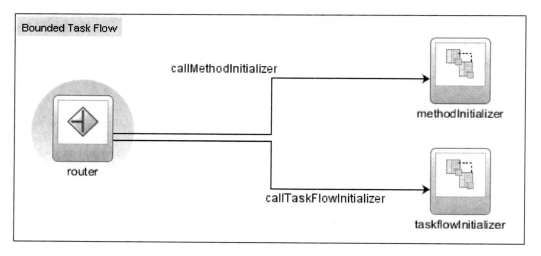

9. Now, locate the `adfc-config.xml` unbounded task flow in the **Application Navigator** and double-click on it to open it. Go to the **Overview | Managed Beans** section and add a `TaskFlowURLCallerBean` managed bean. Specify `com.packt.jdeveloper.cookbook.hr.main.view.beans.TaskFlowURLCaller` for the bean **Class** and leave the default **request** for the bean's **Scope**.

10. Create the managed bean by selecting **Generate Class** from the **Property Menu** in the **Property Inspector**, next to the **Managed Bean Class** attribute.

11. Locate the `TaskFlowURLCallerBean` bean in the **Application Navigator** and double-click on it to open it in the Java editor. Add the following methods to it:

```java
public String getProgrammaticallyInvokeTaskFlow() {
    // setup task flow parameters
    Map<String, Object> parameters =
        new java.util.HashMap<String, Object>();
    parameters.put("taskFlowToCall", "calTaskFlowInitializer");
    // construct and return the task flow's URL
    return getTaskFlowURL("/WEB-
        INF/programmaticallyInvokeTaskFlow.xml
        #programmaticallyInvokeTaskFlow", parameters);
}
private String getTaskFlowURL(String taskFlowSpecs, Map<String,
Object> parameters) {
    // create a TaskFlowId from the task flow specification
    TaskFlowId tfid = TaskFlowId.parse(taskFlowSpecs);
    // construct the task flow URL
    String taskFlowURL =
        ControllerContext.getInstance().getTaskFlowURL(
        false, tfid, parameters);
    // remove the application context path from the URL
    FacesContext fc = FacesContext.getCurrentInstance();
    String taskFlowContextPath =
        fc.getExternalContext().getRequestContextPath();
    return taskFlowURL.replaceFirst(taskFlowContextPath, "");
}
```

12. Finally, create a JSPX page called `taskFlowURLCaller.jspx` and drop a **Link (Go)** component on it from the **Component Palette**. Specify the link's text, destination, and targetFrame properties as follows:

```xml
<af:goLink text="Call programmaticallyInvokeTaskFlow as a URL"
    id="gl1"
destination="#{TaskFlowURLCallerBean.
    programmaticallyInvokeTaskFlow}"
targetFrame="_blank"/>
```

How it works...

In steps 1 through 3, we created a task flow called `programmaticallyInvokeTaskFlow` and set its visibility to `url-invoke-allowed`. This allows us to call the task flow via a URL. If we don't do this, a security exception will be thrown when trying to access the task flow via a URL. This was discussed in greater detail in recipe *Using an application module function to initialize a page* in this chapter. We also added (in step 3), a single task flow parameter called `taskFlowToCall` to indicate which task flow to call once our `programmaticallyInvokeTaskFlow` is executed. We stored the value of this parameter to a pageFlow scope variable called `taskFlowToCall`. This parameter is accessible via the EL expression `#{pageFlowScope.taskFlowToCall}`. We will see in step 7 how this pageFlow scope variable is accessed to determine the subsequent task flow to call.

In steps 4 through 8, we completed the task flow definition by adding a router activity and two task flow call activities, one for each of the `callMethodInitializer` and `callTaskFlowInitializer` task flows. Note, in step 5, how we just dropped the `callMethodInitializer` and `callTaskFlowInitializer` task flows from the **Application Navigator**, to create the task flow calls. Also, observe in step 6, how we have created the control flow cases to connect the router activity with each of the task flow call activities. Finally, note how in step 7, we configured the router activity outcomes based on the value of the input task flow parameter `taskFlowToCall`. Specifically, we checked the parameter's value using the EL expression `#{pageFlowScope.taskFlowToCall eq 'calTaskFlowInitializer'}`. In this case, the router's outcome was set to `callTaskFlowInitializer`, which calls the `taskflowInitializer` task flow. In any other case, we configured the default router outcome to be `callMethodInitializer`, which calls the `methodInitializer` task flow.

In steps 9 through 11, we configured a globally accessible managed bean called `TaskFlowURLCallerBean`, by adding it to the application's unbounded task flow `adfc-config.xml`. We generated the bean class in step 10 and 11, where we added the necessary code to be able to call our `programmaticallyInvokeTaskFlow` task flow programmatically. The specific details about this code follow.

We introduced two methods in the `TaskFlowURLCallerBean`. One called `getProgrammaticallyInvokeTaskFlow()`, which will be called from a page component to return the task flow's URL (see step 12) and another one called `getTaskFlowURL()`, a helper method to do the actual work of determining and returning the task flow's URL. We call `getTaskFlowURL()` indicating the task flow specification and its parameters.

Observe in `getProgrammaticallyInvokeTaskFlow()`, how we specify the parameter value and the task flow specifications. In `getTaskFlowURL()`, we obtain an `oracle. adf.controller.TaskFlowId` from the task flow identifier, and then call the `oracle. adf.controller.ControllerContext.getTaskFlowURL()` method to retrieve the task flow URL. Once the URL is returned, we strip the application's context path from it before returning it. This is something that we need to do before calling the task flow via a URL because the application context path should not be part of the task flow URL when invoking the task flow. The final format of the task flow URL returned by `getTaskFlowURL()` looks something similar to `/faces/adf.task-flow?adf.tfDoc=/WEB-INF/ programmaticallyInvokeTaskFlow.xml&adf.tfId=programmaticallyInvokeTas kFlow&taskFlowToCall=calTaskFlowInitializer`.

The final part of the implementation is done in step 12. In this step, we created a new JSF page, called `taskFlowURLCaller.jspx`, and added an `af:golink` ADF Faces UI component to it. We use the go link to programmatically call our `programmaticallyInvokeTaskFlow` task flow, via the URL returned by the `getProgrammaticallyInvokeTaskFlow()` method defined in the `TaskFlowURLCallerBean`. We do this by setting the destination attribute of the `af:golink` component to `#{TaskFlowURLCallerBean. programmaticallyInvokeTaskFlow}`. We also indicate `_blank` for the go link `targetFrame` attribute, so that the called task flow opens in a new browser frame.

To test the recipe, right-click on the `taskFlowURLCaller.jspx` page in the **Application Navigator** and select **Run** or **Debug** from the context menu.

There's more...

When calling a task flow programmatically via its URL, always use the ADF Controller API indicated in this recipe to obtain the task flow's URL. Do not hardcode the task flow's URL in your application or in database tables, as the specifications of the task flow URL in the ADF framework (the task flow URL format) may change in the future.

See also

- ▸ *Using an application module function to initialize a page*, in this chapter
- ▸ *Using a task flow initializer to initialize a task flow*, in this chapter

Retrieving the task flow definition programmatically using MetadataService

Task flow definition in JDeveloper is done through the declarative support provided by the IDE. This includes defining the task flow activities and their relevant control flow cases by dragging-and-dropping task flow components from the **Component Palette** to the **Diagram** tab and adjusting their properties through the **Property Inspector**, defining managed beans in the **Overview** tab, and so on. JDeveloper saves the task flow definition metadata in an XML document, which is accessible in JDeveloper anytime you click on the **Source** tab. The task flow definition metadata is available programmatically at runtime through the `oracle.adf.controller.metadata.MetadataService` object by calling `getTaskFlowDefinition()`. This API is public since the release of JDeveloper version 11.1.2.

In this recipe, we will show how to get the task flow definition metadata by implementing the following use case. For each task flow in our ADF application, this will provide a generic technique for logging the task flow input parameters upon task flow entry and the task flow return values upon task flow exit.

Getting ready

You will need to have access to the `SharedComponents` workspace that was developed in the *Breaking up the application in multiple workspaces* recipe in *Chapter 1, Pre-requisites to Success: ADF Project Setup and Foundations*. New functionality will be added to the ViewController project that is part of the `SharedComponents` workspace.

Moreover, this recipe enhances the `taskflowInitializer` task flow developed in the *Using a task flow initializer to initialize a task flow* recipe in this chapter. Note the additional prerequisites stated for those recipes, that is, the usage of the `HRComponents` and `MainApplication` workspaces and the database connection to the HR schema.

How to do it...

1. Open the `SharedComponents` workspace and create a new Java class called `TaskFlowBaseBean`. Add the following methods to it:

```
public void initialize() {
  // get task flow parameters
  Map<String, TaskFlowInputParameter> taskFlowParameters =
    getTaskFlowParameters();
  // log parameters
  logParameters(taskFlowParameters);
}
public void finalize() {
  // get task flow return values
```

```
    Map<String, NamedParameter> taskFlowReturnValues =
      getReturnValues();
    // log return values
    logParameters(taskFlowReturnValues);
  }
  protected TaskFlowId getTaskFlowId() {
    // get task flow context from the current view port
    TaskFlowContext taskFlowContext =
      ControllerContext.getInstance().getCurrentViewPort()
      .getTaskFlowContext();
    // return the task flow id
    return taskFlowContext.getTaskFlowId();
  }
  protected TaskFlowDefinition getTaskFlowDefinition() {
    // use MetadataService to return the task flow
    // definition based on the task flow id
    return MetadataService.getInstance()
      .getTaskFlowDefinition(getTaskFlowId());
  }
  protected Map<String, TaskFlowInputParameter>
    getTaskFlowParameters() {
    // get task flow definition
    TaskFlowDefinition taskFlowDefinition =
      getTaskFlowDefinition();
    // return the task flow input parameters
    return taskFlowDefinition.getInputParameters();
  }
  protected Map<String, NamedParameter> getReturnValues() {
    // get task flow definition
    TaskFlowDefinition taskFlowDefinition =
      getTaskFlowDefinition();
    // return the task flow return values
    return taskFlowDefinition.getReturnValues();
  }
  public void logParameters(Map taskFlowParameters) {
    // implement parameter logging here
  }
```

2. Rebuild and redeploy the `SharedComponents` ADF Library JAR.

3. Open the `MainApplication` workspace and add the `SharedComponents` ADF Library JAR—deployed in the previous step—to its ViewController project.

4. Load the `InitializerBean` managed bean implementation class `com.packt.jdeveloper.cookbook.hr.main.view.beans.Initializer` into the Java editor, and change it so that it extends the `TaskFlowBaseBean` class:

```
public class Initializer extends TaskFlowBaseBean
```

5. Also, update its `initialize()` method by adding a call to `super.initialize()` and add the following `finalize()` method:

```
public void finalize() {
    // allow base class processing
    super.finalize();
}
```

6. Finally, add a finalizer to the `taskflowInitializer` task flow using the following EL expression:

```
#{pageFlowScope.InitializerBean.finalize}
```

How it works...

In step 1, we create a class called `TaskFlowBaseBean` that we can use throughout our ADF application as the base class from which beans providing task flow initializer and finalizer methods can be derived (as we did in step 3 in this recipe). This class consists of initializer and finalizer methods that retrieve and log the task flow input parameters and return values respectively. These methods are implemented by `initialize()` and `finalize()` and they are publicly accessible, which means that they can be directly used from within JDeveloper when defining task flow initializers and/or finalizers. This is useful if you don't want to provide any specific implementations of the task flow initializer and/or finalizer method. The `initialize()` method calls the helper `getTaskFlowParameters()` to retrieve the input task flow parameters and then calls `logParameters()` to log these parameters. Similarly, `finalize()` calls `getReturnValues()` to retrieve the returned values and `logParameters()` to log them. The `getTaskFlowParameters()` and `getReturnValues()` helper methods rely on getting the task flow definition `oracle.adf.controller.metadata.model.TaskFlowDefinition` object and calling `getInputParameters()` and `getReturnValues()` on it, respectively. The task flow definition is returned by the helper `getTaskFlowDefinition()`, which retrieves it by calling the `oracle.adf.controller.metadata.MetadataService` method `getTaskFlowDefinition()`. This method accepts an `oracle.adf.controller.TaskFlowId`, indicating the task flow identifier for which we are inquiring the task flow definition. We retrieve the current task flow identifier by calling the helper `getTaskFlowId()`, which retrieves the current task flow from the task flow context obtained from the current view port, as shown in the following lines of code:

```
// get task flow context from the current view port
TaskFlowContext taskFlowContext =
    ControllerContext.getInstance()
    .getCurrentViewPort().getTaskFlowContext();
// return the task flow id
return taskFlowContext.getTaskFlowId();
```

In step 2, we re-deployed the `SharedComponents` workspace as an ADF Library JAR. Then, in step 3, we added it to the `MainApplication` ViewController project. One way to do this is through the **Resource Palette**.

To demonstrate the usage of the `TaskFlowBaseBean` class, we have updated the `InitializerBean` managed bean class `Initializer` that was developed in an earlier recipe, so that `TaskFlowBaseBean` class is derived from it (in step 4). Then (in step 5), we updated the `Initializer` class `initialize()` method to call `TaskFlowBaseBean`'s `initialize()` to do the base class processing, that is, to log any input parameters.

In steps 5 and 6, to complete the recipe, we added a task flow finalizer, which simply calls the base class' `super.finalize()` to log the returned task flow parameters.

There's more...

The implementation of `logParameters()`, not included in the book's source, is left as an exercise. This method should basically iterate over the task flow parameters and for each one obtain its value expression by calling the `oracle.adf.controller.metadata.model.Parameter.getValueExpression()` method. The parameter's value expression can be evaluated by calling the `javax.faces.application.Application.evaluateExpressionGet()` method.

Also, note that task flow metadata is loaded from ADF Controller metadata resources using the following search rules. Firstly, resources named `META-INF/adfc-config.xml` in the classpath are loaded and then the existence of the web application configuration resource named `/WEB-INF/adfc-config.xml` is checked and loaded if it exists. Once these resources are loaded, they may reference other metadata objects that reside in other resources. These ADF Controller metadata resources are used to construct a model for the unbounded task flow. Metadata for bounded task flows is loaded on demand.

For a complete reference to all the methods available by the `MetaDataService` and `TaskFlowDefinition` classes, consult the *Oracle Fusion Middleware Documentation Library 11g Release 2 Java API Reference for Oracle ADF Controller*. It can be found at the URL `http://download.oracle.com/docs/cd/E16162_01/apirefs.1112/e17480/toc.htm`.

Furthermore, consult the article *Programmatically capturing task flow parameters* by Chris Muir where he describes the topic in greater detail. It can be found at the URL `http://one-size-doesnt-fit-all.blogspot.com/2010/10/jdev-programmatically-capturing-task.html`.

> ▶ *Breaking up the application in multiple workspaces, Chapter 1, Pre-requisites to Success: ADF Project Setup and Foundations*
>
> ▶ *Using a task flow initializer to initialize a task flow*, in this chapter

Creating a train

Wizard-like user interfaces can be created in ADF using task flows created as trains and ADF Faces user interface components, such as the `af:train` (Train) and `af:trainButtonBar` (Train Button Bar) components. Using such an interface, you are presented with individual steps, called train stops, in a multi-step process, each step being a task flow activity or a combination of activities. Options exist that allow for the configuration of the train stops, controlling the sequential execution of the train stops, whether a train stop can be skipped, and others. Furthermore, a train stop can incorporate other task flow activities, such as method calls. Other task flows themselves can be added as train stops in the train (as task flow call activities).

In this recipe, we will go over the creation of a train consisting of view, method call, and task flow call activities.

Getting ready

You will need a skeleton **Fusion Web Application (ADF)** workspace created before you proceed with this recipe. For this, we have used the `MainApplication` workspace that was developed in the *Breaking up the application in multiple workspaces* recipe in *Chapter 1, Pre-requisites to Success: ADF Project Setup and Foundations*.

To demonstrate a method call activity as part of the train stop, the recipe uses the `HRComponents` workspace, which was created in the *Overriding remove() to delete associated children entities* recipe in *Chapter 2, Dealing with Basics: Entity Objects*. Moreover, to demonstrate a task flow call as a train stop, the recipe uses the `taskflowInitializer` task flow created in the *Using a task flow initializer to initialize task flow* recipe in this chapter.

Both the `HRComponents` and `MainApplication` workspaces require database connections to the `HR` schema.

How to do it...

1. Create a bounded task flow called `trainTaskFlow`. Ensure that the **Create Train** checkbox in the **Create Task Flow** dialog is selected. We will not be using page fragments, so ensure that the **Create with Page Fragments** checkbox is not selected.

2. From the **Component Palette** drop four view activities on the task flow. Call the view activities `trainStop1`, `trainStop2`, `trainStop3`, and `trainStop4`.

3. Expand the **Data Controls** node in the **Application Navigator** and the `HrComponentsAppModuleDataControl`. Locate and drop the `prepare()` method on the task flow.

4. Create a **Control Flow Case** from the `prepare()` method call to the `trainStop3` view activity.

5. Drop a **Wildcard Control Flow Rule** from the **Component Palette** to the task flow and create a **Control Flow Case** called `callPrepareBeforeStop3` from the **Wildcard Control** to the `prepare()` method call.

6. Select the `trainStop3` view activity and in the **Property Inspector** enter `callPrepareBeforeStop3` for its **Outcome** attribute.

7. Locate the `taskflowInitializer` task flow in the **Application Navigator** and double-click on it to open it. From the **Component Palette**, drop two **Task Flow Return** components to it, called `previousStop` and `nextStop`.

8. From the **Component Palette** add two **Control Flow Cases** and connect them from the `taskFlowInitializerView` view activity to the `previousStop` and `nextStop` task flow return activities. Call them `previous` and `next` respectively. The modified `taskflowInitializer` task flow should look similar to the following screenshot:

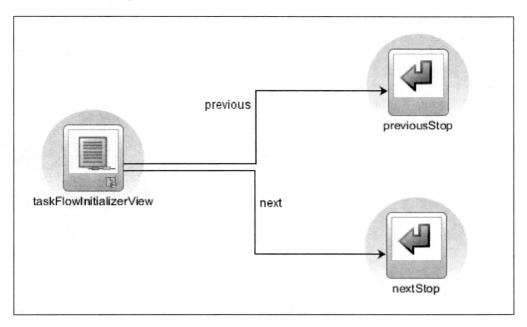

9. Return to the `trainTaskFlow` task flow. In the **Application Navigator**, locate the `taskflowInitializer` task flow and drop it in the `trainTaskFlow` task flow.

10. Right-click on the `trainStop4` view activity and select **Train | Move Backward** from the context menu.

11. Create two **Control Flow Cases** called `previousStop` and `nextStop` from the `taskflowInitializer` task flow call activity to the `trainStop3` and `trainStop4` view activities. This complete `taskflowInitializer` task flow should look similar to the following screenshot:

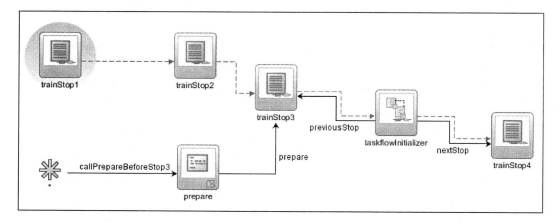

12. Now, double-click on each of the `trainStop1`, `trainStop2`, `trainStop3`, and `trainStop4` view activities in the `taskflowInitializer` task flow to create the JSF pages. In the **Create JSF** page dialog, select **JSP XML** for the **Document Type**.

13. For each of the pages created, select a **Train** component from the **ADF Faces Component Palette** and drop them on the pages. On the **Bind train** dialog that is displayed, accept the default binding and click **OK**.

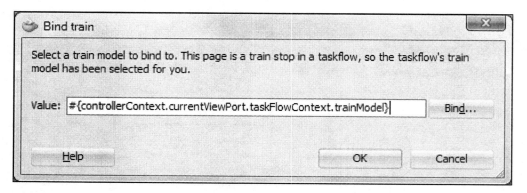

Each page should look similar to the following one:

14. Finally, modify the `taskFlowInitializerView.jspx` JSF page by adding two extra buttons called **Previous** and **Next**. Using the **Property Inspector**, set their **Action** attributes to **previous** and **next** respectively. To ensure that validation will not be raised on the page, ensure that for both buttons the `Immediate` attribute is set to `true`. The `taskFlowInitializerView.jspx` page should look similar to the following screenshot:

taskFlowInitializer		Previous	Next

EmployeeId	#{...EmployeeId.inputValue}
FirstName	#{...FirstName.inputValue}
LastName	#{...LastName.inputValue}
Email	#{...Email.inputValue}
PhoneNumber	#{...PhoneNumber.inputValue}
HireDate	#{...HireDate.inputValue}
JobId	#{...JobId.inputValue}
Salary	#{...Salary.inputValue}
CommissionPct	#{...CommissionPct.inputValue}
ManagerId	#{...ManagerId.inputValue}
DepartmentId	#{...DepartmentId.inputValue}
LovAttrib	
FavoriteColor	

First | Previous | Next | Last
Submit

How it works...

In step 1, we created a bounded task flow called `trainTaskFlow`. We indicated that the task flow will implement a train by ensuring that the **Create Train** checkbox in the **Create Task Flow** dialog was selected. Then, in step 2, we dropped four view activities to the task flow, called train stops in train terminology, each one being part of the train. Notice how JDeveloper connects these train stops with a dotted line indicating that they are part of the train.

In steps 3 through 6, we combined a method call activity, called `prepare`, with the `trainStop3` view activity in a single train stop. The way we did this was by wiring the `prepare()` method call activity via a control flow rule to the `trainStop3` view activity (step 4). The `prepare()` method call activity is wired to a wildcard control flow rule called `callPrepareBeforeStop3` (in step 5). In order to ensure that the `prepare()` method call activity and the `trainStop3` view activity are combined in a single train step, we have set the outcome of the `trainStop3` train stop to `callPrepareBeforeStop3` (step 6). This ensures that at runtime the `prepare()` method call activity is executed before the `trainStop3` view activity together in a single train stop.

In steps 7 and 8, we have modified the `taskflowInitializer` task flow, which was originally developed in the *Using a task flow initializer to initialize task flow* recipe in this chapter, so that it can be used as part of the train. In particular, we added two task flow return activities, one for navigating backwards on the train and another one for navigating forward. We wired the task flow return activities to the existing `taskFlowInitializerView` view activity. Based on the specific outcomes (`previous` or `next`) originating from the `taskFlowInitializerView` view activity (see step 14), navigation on the train can be accomplished.

Once these changes were made to the `taskflowInitializer` task flow, we are able to complete the `trainTaskFlow` train, by first adding it to the train as a task flow call activity (in step 9) and then wiring it to the train by adding the relevant control flow cases (step 11). In step 10, we just adjusted the task flow call train stop position in the train.

The rest of the recipe steps (12 through 14) deal with the creation and modification of the JSF pages related to the view activities participating in the train task flow. In steps 12 and 13, we created the JSF pages corresponding to the four view activity train stops. In each page, we added an `af:train` ADF Faces component to allow for the navigation over the train. Finally, in step 14, we made the necessary changes to the existing `taskFlowInitializerView.jspx` page to be able to hook it to the train. Specifically, we added two buttons, called `Previous` and `Next`, and we set their actions appropriately (to `previous` and `next` respectively), to allow for the `taskflowInitializer` task flow to return to the calling `trainTaskFlow` task flow (see step 8).

To run the train, right-click on the `trainTaskFlow` task flow in the **Application Navigator** and select **Run** or **Debug**.

There's more...

Each train stop can be dynamically configured at runtime using EL expressions to allow for a number of options. These options are available in the **Property Inspector** for each train stop selected in the train task flow during development. They are briefly explained as follows:

- Outcome: Used in order to combine multiple activities preceding the view or task flow call activity in a single train stop. This was demonstrated in step 6 where we combined a method call activity with a view activity in a single train stop.

- Sequential: When set to false, the train stop can be selected even though a previous train stop has not been visited yet.

- Skip: When set to true, the train stop will be skipped. At runtime a skipped train stop will be shown as disabled and you will not be able to select it.

- Ignore: When set to true, the train stop will not be shown.

By dynamically setting these attributes at runtime, you can effectively create multiple trains out of a single train definition.

For more information about train task flows, check out the section _Using Train Components in Bounded Task Flows_ in the _Fusion Developer's Guide for Oracle Application Framework_ which can be found at http://docs.oracle.com/cd/E24382_01/web.1112/e16182/toc.htm.

See also

- _Breaking up the application in multiple workspaces, Chapter 1, Pre-requisites to Success: ADF Project Setup and Foundations_

- _Overriding remove() to delete associated children entities, Chapter 2, Dealing with Basics: Entity Objects_

- _Using a task flow initializer to initialize task flow, in this chapter_

7
Face Value: ADF Faces, JSF Pages, and User Interface Components

In this chapter, we will cover:

- ▶ Using an af:query component to construct a search page
- ▶ Using an af:pop-up component to edit a table row
- ▶ Using an af:tree component
- ▶ Using an af:selectManyShuttle component
- ▶ Using an af:carousel component
- ▶ Using an af:poll component to periodically refresh a table
- ▶ Using page templates for pop-up reuse
- ▶ Exporting data to a client file

Introduction

ADF Faces Rich Client Framework (ADF RC) contains a plethora (more than 150) of AJAX-enabled JSF components that can be used in your JSF pages to realize **Rich Internet Applications (RIA)**. ADF RC hides the complexities of using JavaScript, and declarative partial page rendering allows you to develop complex pages using a declarative process. Moreover, these components integrate with the **ADF Model layer (ADFm)** to support data bindings and model-driven capabilities, provide support for page templates, and reusable page regions. In JDeveloper, ADF Faces components are made available through the **Component Palette**. For each component, the available attributes can be manipulated via the **Property Inspector**.

Using an af:query component to construct a search page

The `af:query` (or query search form) ADF Faces user interface component allows for the creation of search forms in your ADF Fusion web application. It is a model-driven component, which means that it relies on the model definition of named view criteria. This implies that changes made to the view criteria are automatically reflected by the `af:query` component without any additional work. This fact, along with the JDeveloper's declarative support for displaying query results in a table (or tree table) component, makes constructing a search form a straightforward task.

In this recipe, we will cover the creation of a query search form and the display of search results in a table component.

Getting ready

You will need to create a skeleton **Fusion Web Application (ADF)** workspace before you proceed with this recipe. We will be using the `MainApplication` workspace that was developed in the *Breaking up the application in multiple workspace, Chapter 1, Pre-requisites to Success: ADF Project Setup and Foundation*s.

The recipe also uses the `HRComponents` workspace, which was created in the *Overriding remove() to delete associated children entities, Chapter 2, Dealing with Basics: Entity Objects*.

Both the `HRComponents` and `MainApplication` workspaces require database connections to the HR schema.

How to do it...

1. Open the HRComponents workspace and locate the Employees view object in the **Application Navigator**. Double-click on it to open its definition.

2. Go to the **Query** section and add two bind variables of type **String**, named varFirstName and varLastName. Ensure that the **Required** checkbox in the **Bind Variable** dialog is unchecked for both these variables. Also, in the **Control Hints** tab of the **Bind Variable** dialog, ensure that the **Display Hint** is set to **Hide**.

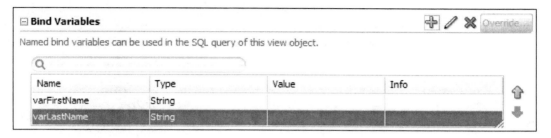

3. While in the **Query** section, add named view criteria for the FirstName and LastName attributes using the bind variables varFirstName and varLastName respectively. For both criteria items, ensure that the **Ignore Case** and **Ignore Null Values** checkboxes are checked and that the **Validation** is set to **Optional**.

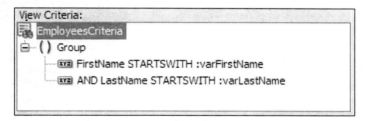

4. Rebuild and redeploy the HRComponents workspace as an ADF Library JAR.

5. Open the MainApplication workspace and ensure that the HRComponents and SharedComponents ADF Library JARs are added to the ViewController project.

6. Create a bounded task flow called queryTaskFlow and add a view activity called queryView. Ensure that the task flow is not created with page fragments.

7. Double-click on the queryView activity in the task flow to bring up the **Create JSF Page** dialog. Proceed with creating a **JSP XML** page called queryView.jspx using any one of the pre-defined layouts.

8. In the **Application Navigator**, expand the **Data Controls** section and locate the EmployeesCriteria view criteria under the **HrComponentsAppModuleDataControl | Employees | Named Criteria** node. Drag-and-drop the EmployeesCriteria view criteria onto the page.

9. From the **Create** context menu, select **Query | ADF Query Panel with Table...**.

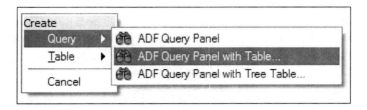

10. JDeveloper will bring up the **Edit Table Columns** dialog. Click **OK** to accept the default settings for now. When previewing the page in the browser, you should see something similar to the following screenshot:

11. In the **Structure** window, locate and select the **af:table** component. Then, in the **Table Property Inspector**, click on the **Edit Component Definition** button (the pen icon). In the **Edit Table Components** dialog, adjust the table definition by removing any columns indicating row selection and enabling sorting or filtering. Adjust the table's width by specifying the width in pixels in the **Style** section of the **Table Property Inspector**.

How it works...

In steps 1 through 3, we have updated the `Employees` view object, which is part of the `HRComponents` workspace, by adding named view criteria to it. Based on the earlier mentioned criteria, we subsequently (in steps 8 and 9) associate an `af:query` component to create the search page. The view criteria comprises two criteria items, one for the employee's first name and another for their last name. We have based the criteria items on corresponding bind variables created in step 2. Note the view criteria item settings that are used in step 3. For both name criteria the search is case-insensitive; null values are ignored, which means that the search will yield results when no data is specified; and that both are optional. Also note that we have based both of the criteria items on the **Starts with** operation and that the `AND` conjunction is used for the criteria items.

In steps 4 and 5, we redeployed the `HRComponents` workspace to an ADF Library JAR, which we then add to the `MainApplication` ViewController project. The `HRComponents` library has dependencies to the `SharedComponents` workspace, so we make sure that the `SharedComponents` ADF Library JAR is also added to the project.

In step 6, we created a bounded task flow called `queryTaskFlow` and added a single view activity. Then (in step 7), we created a JSF page for the view activity.

To add search capability to the page, we have located the view criteria added earlier to the `Employees` view object. We have done this by expanding the **Named Criteria** node under the `Employees` view object node of the `HrComponentsAppModuleDataControl` data control. This data control is added to the list of available data controls once we add the `HRComponents` ADF Library JAR to our workspace in step 5. JDeveloper supports the creation of databound search pages declaratively by presenting a context menu of choices when dropping view criteria onto the page, as in step 9. From the context menu that is presented, we had chosen **ADF Query Panel with Table...**, which created a query panel with an associated results table. If you take a look at the page's source, you will see a code snippet similar to the following:

```
<af:panelGroupLayout layout="vertical" ...
  <af:panelHeader ...
    <af:query value="#{bindings.EmployeesCriteriaQuery.
      queryDescriptor}"
    queryListener="#{bindings.EmployeesCriteriaQuery.processQuery}"
    queryOperationListener="#{bindings.EmployeesCriteriaQuery
      .processQueryOperation}"
    resultComponentId="::resId1" ...
  </af:panelHeader>
  <af:table id="resId1" value="#{bindings.Employees.collectionModel}"
    var="row" ....
  <af:column ...
  </af:table>
</af:panelGroupLayout>
```

As you can see, JDeveloper wraps the `af:query` and `af:table` components in an `af:panelGroupLayout`, arranged vertically. Also, note that this simple drag-and-drop of the view criteria onto the page in the background creates the corresponding search region and iterator executables, along with the tree binding used by the `af:table` component and the necessary glue code to associate the search region executable and tree binding to the iterator. It also associates the `af:query` component with the table component that will be used to display the search results. This is done by specifying the table component's identifier (`resId1` in the previous sample code) in the `af:query resultComponentId` attribute.

Finally, notice in steps 10 and 11 some of the possibilities that are available in JDeveloper to declaratively manipulate the table, either through the **Edit Table Columns** dialog or the **Property Inspector**.

There's more...

In addition to the `af:query` component, ADF Faces supports the creation of model-driven search pages using the `af:quickQuery` (Quick Query) component. You can create a search page using an `af:quickQuery` by dragging the **All Queriable Attributes** item under the view object **Named Criteria** node in the **Data Controls** window and dropping it on the page and selecting any of the **Quick Query** options in the **Create** context menu. The **All Queriable Attributes** node represents the implicit view object criteria that are created for each `Queryable` view object attribute.

For information about creating databound search pages, refer to the *Creating ADF Databound Search Forms* chapter in the *Fusion Developer's Guide for Oracle Application Framework*, which can be found at `http://docs.oracle.com/cd/E24382_01/web.1112/e16182/toc.htm`.

See also

▶ *Breaking up the application in multiple workspaces, Chapter 1, Pre-requisites to Success: ADF Project Setup and Foundations*

▶ *Overriding remove() to delete associated children entities, Chapter 2, Dealing with Basics: Entity Objects*

Using an af:pop-up component to edit a table row

An `af:popup` component can be used in conjunction with an `af:dialog` to display and edit data within a page on a separate pop-up dialog. The pop-up is added to the corresponding JSF page, and can be raised either declaratively using an `af:showPopupBehavior` or programmatically by adding dynamic JavaScript code to the page.

In this recipe, we will expand the functionality introduced in the previous recipe, to allow for the editing of a table row. The use case that we will demonstrate is to raise an edit form inside a pop-up dialog by double-clicking on the table row. The changes made to the data inside the dialog are carried over to the table.

Getting ready

This recipe relies on having completed the *Using an af:query component to construct a search page* recipe in this chapter.

How to do it...

1. Open the `MainApplication` workspace. Locate the `queryTaskFlow` in the **Application Navigator** and double-click on it to open it.

2. Go to the task flow **Overview | Managed Beans** section and add a managed bean called `QueryBean`. Specify a class for the managed bean, then use the **Generate Class** selection in the **Property Menu**—located next to the **Managed Bean Class** property in the **Property Inspector** to create the managed bean class.

3. Double-click on the managed bean Java class in the **Application Navigator** to open it in the Java editor. Add the following method to it:

```
public void onEmployeeEdit(ClientEvent clientEvent) {
    FacesContext facesContext = FacesContext.getCurrentInstance();
    ExtendedRenderKitService service =
      Service.getRenderKitService(facesContext,
      ExtendedRenderKitService.class);
    service.addScript(facesContext,
      "AdfPage.PAGE. findComponentByAbsoluteId(
      'editEmployee').show();");
}
```

4. Locate the `queryView.jspx` JSF page in the **Application Navigator** and double-click on it to open it.

5. Locate and select the **af:table** component in the **Structure** window. Right-click on it and select **Insert Inside af:table | ADF Faces | Client Listener**.

6. In the **Insert Client Listener** dialog, enter onEmployeeEdit for the **Method** and select **dblClick** for the **Type**.

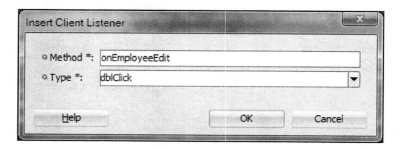

7. Right-click on the af:table component in the Structure window and this time select **Insert Inside af:table | ADF Faces | Server Listener**. For the **Type** field in the **Insert Server Listener** dialog type onEmployeeEdit.

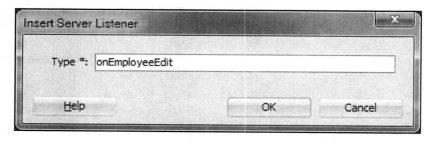

8. Use the **Property Inspector** to set the af:serverListener **Method** property to the **onEmployeeEdit** method of the **QueryBean**.

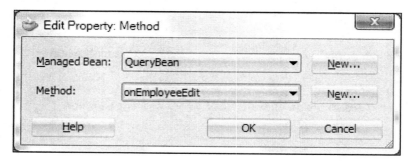

9. Right-click on the `af:document` in the **Structure** window and select **Insert Inside af:document | ADF Faces....** Then select **Resource** from the **Insert ADF Faces Item** dialog.

10. In the **Insert Resource** dialog, specify **javascript** for the **Type** and click **OK**.

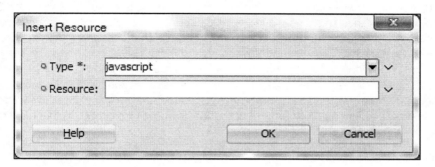

11. Locate the `af:resource` in the `queryView` page and add the following JavaScript code to it:

```
function onEmployeeEdit(event){
    var table = event.getSource();
    AdfCustomEvent.queue(table, "onEmployeeEdit",{}, true);
    event.cancel();
}
```

12. Locate a **Popup** component in the **Component Palette** and drop it on the page, inside the `af:form` tag.

13. Right-click on the `af:popup` component in the **Structure** window and select **Insert Inside af:popup | Dialog** from the context menu.

14. Locate the `Employees` collection under `HrComponentsAppModuleDataControl` in the **Data Controls** window and drop it on the `af:dialog` component in the page. From the **Create** menu, select **Form | ADF Form....** Adjust the fields you want to display in the **Edit Form Fields** dialog and click **OK**.

15. Using the **Property Inspector** for the `af:popup` component, change the **Id** property to `editEmployee` and the **ContentDelivery** to **lazyUncached**.

16. Finally, adjust the results table **PartialTriggers** by adding the `af:dialog` identifier to it.

How it works...

In steps 1 and 2, we have updated the `queryTaskFlow` task flow definition, which was introduced in the *Using an af:query component to construct a search page* recipe in this chapter, by adding a managed bean definition and generating the bean class. In step 3, we have added a method to the managed bean called `onEmployeeEdit()`. This method is used as an event listener for the `af:serverListener` that is added to the `af:table` component in step 8. It is used to programmatically show the `editEmployee af:popup`. The `editEmployee` pop-up is added to the page in step 13. The pop-up is shown programmatically by infusing the page with dynamic JavaScript code using the `addScript()` method implemented by the `ExtendedRenderKitService` interface. The JavaScript code that is added is specified as an argument to the `addScript()` method. In this case the code is as follows:

```
AdfPage.PAGE.findComponentByAbsoluteId('editEmployee').show();
```

This piece of JavaScript code locates the `editEmployee` component in the page and displays it.

The pop-up is invoked by double-clicking on a table row. In order to accomplish this behavior, a combination of an `af:clientListener` and an `af:serverListener` tag is used. We add these components in steps 6 and 7 respectively.

When we added the `af:clientListener` tag in step 6, we indicated that a JavaScript method called `onEmployeeEdit()` will be executed when we double-click on a table row. This JavaScript method is added directly to the page in steps 9 through 12. The JavaScript `onEmployeeEdit()` method is shown as follows:.

```
function onEmployeeEdit(event){
   var table = event.getSource();
   AdfCustomEvent.queue(table, "onEmployeeEdit",{}, true);
   event.cancel();
}
```

The method retrieves the table component from the event and queues a custom event to the table component called `onEmployeeEdit`. This indicates the `af:serverListener` that was added in step 7.

Back in step 7, when we added the af:serverListener to the af:table, we identified the serverListener of type onEmployeeEdit and indicated that the backing bean QueryBeanonEmployeeEdit method will be executed upon its activation. This is the method implemented in step 3 that programmatically raises the pop-up.

We mentioned earlier that the JavaScript code for the af:clientListener onEmployeeEdit method was added in steps 9 through 11. JavaScript is added directly on the page by adding an af:resource component of type javascript to the af:document. The actual page code looks similar to the following:

```
<af:document ...
  <af:resource type="javascript">
  function onEmployeeEdit(event){
    var table = event.getSource();
    AdfCustomEvent.queue(table, "onEmployeeEdit",{}, true);
    event.cancel();
  }
  </af:resource>
</af:document>
```

The pop-up is added to the page in steps 12 through 14 using a combination of the af:popup and af:dialog components. In step 14, we dropped the Employees collection from the **Data Controls** right on the af:dialog as an editable form. Since the collection is bound to the page's table, we will be editing the same data.

Finally, note the adjustments that we have made to the pop-up and table components in steps 15 and 16. First we changed the pop-up identifier to editEmployee. This is necessary since we specify pop-up in step 3 by name: AdfPage.PAGE.findComponentByAbsolut eId('editEmployee').show(). Then we set the pop-up's contentDelivery attribute to lazyUncached. This attribute indicates how the pop-up content is delivered to the client. The lazyUncached content delivery setting is used because the data delivered to the pop-up component from the server will change as we double-click in different rows on the table. The PartialTriggers settings indicate how the related page components are refreshed. In this case, we want changes made to the data in the pop-up, to be mirrored in the table. We can accomplish this by adding the dialog's identifier to the table's list of partial triggers.

To run the recipe, right-click on the `queryTaskFLow` in the **Application Navigator** and select **Run** or **Debug**. When the page is displayed, click **Search** to perform a search. Double-click on a row in the results table to show the **Edit Employee** dialog. Any changes you make are saved by clicking **OK** on the **Edit Employee** dialog. If you click **Cancel**, the changes are dismissed. The table is updated to match the adjusted data.

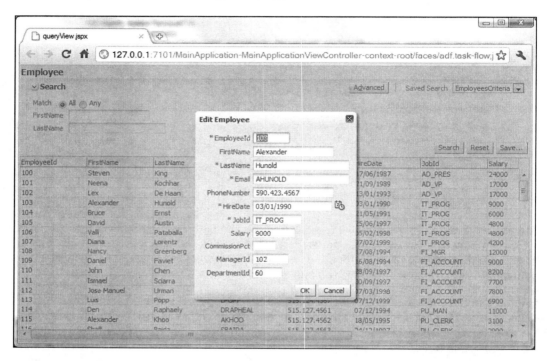

There's more...

Note that the page does not implement a commit or rollback functionality, so changes done to the table's data are not committed to the database. To rollback the changes for now, just refresh the browser; this will re-fetch the data from the database and re-populate the results table. Also, note the functionality of the **Search** and **Reset** buttons. The **Search** button populates the results table by searching the database, while at the same time preserving any changed records in the entity cache. This means that your changes still show in the table after a new search. The behavior of the **Reset** button does not refresh by default in the results table. We will cover how to accomplish this in the recipe *Using a custom af:query operation listener to clear both the query criteria and results* in Chapter 8, *Backing not Baking: Bean Recipes*.

Moreover, note that this recipe shows how to launch a pop-up component programmatically using the `ExtendedRenderKitService` class by infusing dynamic JavaScript code into the page. It is this infused JavaScript code that actually shows the pop-up. Another approach to programmatically launching a pop-up is to bind the `af:popup` component to a backing bean as an `oracle.adf.view.rich.component.rich.RichPopup` object, then use its `show()` method to display the pop-up. For more information about this technique, take a look at the section *Programmatically invoking a Pop-up* in the *Web User Interface Developer's Guide for Oracle Application Development Framework* which can be found at `http://docs.oracle.com/cd/E24382_01/web.1112/e16181/toc.htm`.

See also

▸ *Using an af:query component to construct a search page*, in this chapter

Using an af:tree component

The ADF Faces Tree component (`af:tree`) can be used to display model-driven master-detail data relationships in a hierarchical manner. In this case, the parent node of the tree indicates the master object, while the child nodes of the tree are the detail objects.

In this recipe, we will demonstrate the usage of the `af:tree` component to implement the following use case: Using the HR schema, we will create a JSF page that presents a hierarchical list of the departments and their employees in a tree. As you navigate the tree, the detailed department or employee information will be displayed in an editable form. The recipe makes use of a custom selection listener to determine the type of the tree node (department or employee) being clicked. Based on the type of node, it then displays the department or the employee information.

Getting ready

You will need to create a skeleton **Fusion Web Application (ADF)** workspace before you proceed with this recipe. For this, we will use the `MainApplication` workspace that was developed in *Breaking up the application in multiple workspaces* recipe, *Chapter 1, Pre-requisites to Success: ADF Project Setup and Foundations*.

The recipe also uses the `HRComponents` workspace, which was created in *Overriding remove() to delete associated children entities, Chapter 2, Dealing with Basics: Entity Objects*.

Both the `HRComponents` and `MainApplication` workspaces require database connections to the HR schema.

How to do it...

1. Ensure that the HRComponents and the SharedComponents ADF Library JARs are added to the ViewController project of your workspace.

2. Using the **Create JSF Page** wizard, create a **JSP XML** page called treeView.jspx. Use any of the predefined quick start layouts.

3. Expand the **Data Controls** section in the **Application Navigator** and locate the Departments collection under the HrComponentsAppModuleDataControl data control. Drag-and-drop it on the treeView.jspx page.

4. From the **Create** menu, select **Tree | ADF Tree...**.

5. In the **Tree Level Rules** section of the **Edit Tree Binding** dialog, click on the **Add Rule** button (the green plus sign icon) and add the Employees collection. Also adjust the attributes in the **Display Attributes** list so that the DepartmentName is listed for the Departments rule and the LastName and FirstName are listed for the Employees rule. Click **OK** to proceed.

6. Right-click on the af:tree component in the **Structure** window and select **Surround With...**. From the **Surround With** dialog, select the **Panel Group Layout** and click **OK**. Using the **Properties Inspector**, set the **Valign** and **Layout** attributes to **top** and **horizontal** respectively.

7. In the **Data Controls** section, locate the Departments and Employees collections under the HrComponentsAppModuleDataControl data control and drop them inside the **panelGroupLayout**. In both cases, select **Form | ADF Form...** from the **Create** menu.

8. For each of the af:panelFormLayout components created previously for the Departments and Employees collections, set their **Visible** property to **false** and bind them to a backing bean called TreeBean. If needed, create the TreeBean backing bean as well.

9. Surround both of the af:panelFormLayout components created previously for the Departments and Employees collections with the same af:panelGroupLayout. Using the **Property Inspector**, set the **Layout** attribute of the new af:panelGroupLayout to **vertical**. Also, ensure that you specify the tree's identifier in the **PartialTriggers** attribute of the af:panelGroupLayout. Your components in the Structure window should look similar to the following screenshot:

10. With `af:tree` selected in the **Structure** window, click on the **Edit Component Definition** button (the pen icon) in the **Property Inspector** to open the **Edit Tree Binding** dialog. With the `Employees` rule selected in the **Tree Level Rules**, expand the **Target Data Source** section at the bottom of the dialog. Use the **EL Picker** button and select the `EmployeesIterator` under **the ADF Bindings | bindings** node. The **EL Expression** `${bindings.EmployeesIterator}` should be added, as shown in the following screenshot:

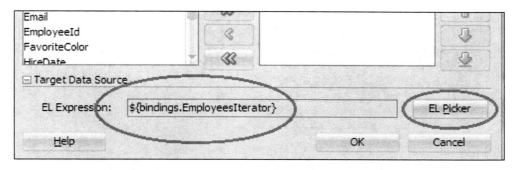

11. While at the `af:tree` **Property Inspector**, change the **SelectionListener** to a newly created selection listener in the `TreeBean` backing bean.

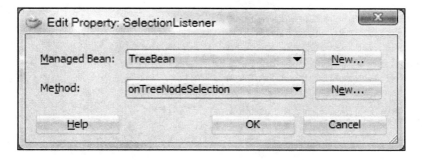

12. Locate the `TreeBean.java` in the **Application Navigator** and double-click on it to open it in the Java editor. Add the following code to the `onTreeNodeSelection()` selection listener:

```
// invoke default selection listener via bindings
invokeMethodExpression(
  "#{bindings.Departments.treeModel.makeCurrent}",
  Object.class, new Class[] { SelectionEvent.class},
  new Object[] { selectionEvent});
// get the tree component from the event
RichTree richTree = (RichTree)selectionEvent.getSource();
// make the selected row current
RowKeySet rowKeySet = richTree.getSelectedRowKeys();
Object key = rowKeySet.iterator().next();
richTree.setRowKey(key);
// get the tree node selected
JUCtrlHierNodeBinding currentNode =
    (JUCtrlHierNodeBinding)richTree.getRowData();
// show or hide the department and employee information
// panels depending the type of node selected
this.departmentInfoPanel.setVisible(
  currentNode.getCurrentRow() instanceof DepartmentsRowImpl);
this.employeeInfoPanel.setVisible(
  currentNode.getCurrentRow() instanceof EmployeesRowImpl);
```

13. Add the following `invokeMethodExpression()` helper method to the `TreeBean.java`:

```
private Object invokeMethodExpression(String expression,
  Class returnType, Class[] argTypes, Object[] args) {
  FacesContext fc = FacesContext.getCurrentInstance();
  ELContext elContext = fc.getELContext();
  ExpressionFactory elFactory =
    fc.getApplication().getExpressionFactory();
  MethodExpression methodExpression =
    elFactory.createMethodExpression(elContext,
    expression, returnType, argTypes);
  return methodExpression.invoke(elContext, args);
}
```

How it works...

Since we will be using business components from the `HRComponents` workspace, in step 1 we have ensured that the `HRComponents` ADF Library JAR is added to the workspace's ViewController project. This can be done either through the **Resource Palette** or using the **Project Properties | Libraries and Classpath** dialog. The `HRComponents` library has dependencies to the `SharedComponents` workspace, so we make sure that the `SharedComponents` ADF Library JAR is also added to the project. Then, we proceed with the creation of the JSF page (step 2).

In steps 3 through 5, we added the Tree component to the page. The tree is comprised of two nodes or level rules: the parent node represents the departments, and is set up by dragging and dropping the `Departments` collection of the `HrComponentsAppModuleDataControl` data control onto the page as an ADF Tree component. The child nodes represent the department employees and are set up in step 5 by adding a rule for the `Employees` collection. The rules control the display order of the tree. The tree binding populates the component starting at the top of the tree level rules list and continues until it reaches the last rule.

In steps 6 through 9, we dropped the `Departments` and `Employees` collections on the page as editable forms (`af:panelFormLayout` components) and rearranged the page in such a way that the tree will be displayed on the left-hand side of the page, while the department or employee information will be displayed on the right-hand side. We also bound the department and employee `af:panelFormLayout` components in a backing (in step 8), so that we will be able to dynamically show and hide them depending on the currently selected node (see step 12). For this to work, we also need to do a couple more things:

- Set the `af:panelGroupLayout` component's (used to vertically group the department and employee `af:panelFormLayout` components) `partialTriggers` attribute to the tree's identifier (in step 9)
- Setup the tree's target data source for the `Employees` rule, so that the `Employees` iterator is updated based on the selected node in the tree hierarchy (in step 10)

Finally, in steps 11 through 13, we created a custom selection listener for the tree component, so that we are able to dynamically show and hide the department and employee forms depending on the tree node type that is selected. The custom selection listener is implemented by the backing bean method called `onTreeNodeSelection()`. If we look closer at this method, we will see that first we invoke the default tree selection listener with the expression `#{bindings.Departments.treeModel.makeCurrent}`. In order to do this, we use a helper method called `invokeMethodExpression()`. Then, we obtain the currently selected node from the tree by calling `getRowData()` on the `oracle.adf.view.rich.component.rich.data.RichTree` component (obtained earlier from the selection event). Finally, we dynamically change the visible property of the department and employee `af:panelFormLayout` components, depending on the type of the selected node. We do this by calling `setVisible()` on the bound department and employee `af:panelFormLayout` components.

There's more...

Note that when adding an `af:tree` component to the page, a single iterator binding is added to the page definition for populating the root nodes of the tree. The accessors specified in the tree level rules, which return the detailed data for each child node, are indicated by the `nodeDefinition` XML nodes of the `tree` binding in the page definition.

See also

► *Breaking up the application in multiple workspaces, Chapter 1, Pre-requisites to Success: ADF Project Setup and Foundations*

► *Overriding remove() to delete associated children entities, Chapter 2, Dealing with Basics: Entity Objects*

Using an af:selectManyShuttle component

The `af:selectManyShuttle` ADF Faces component is a databound model-driven component that can be used to select multiple items from a given list. Using a set of pre-defined buttons, you move the selected items from an available items list to a selected items list. Upon completion of the selection process, you can programmatically retrieve and process the selected items.

In this recipe, we will go over the steps to declaratively create an `af:selectManyShuttle` component in a pop-up dialog and programmatically retrieve the selected items.

Getting ready

You will need to create a skeleton **Fusion Web Application (ADF)** workspace before you proceed with this recipe. For this, we will use the `MainApplication` workspace that was developed in the *Breaking up the application in multiple workspaces, Chapter 1, Pre-requisites to Success: ADF Project Setup and Foundations*.

The recipe also uses the `HRComponents` workspace, which was created in the *Overriding remove() to delete associated children entities, Chapter 2, Dealing with Basics: Entity Objects*.

Both the `HRComponents` and `MainApplication` workspaces require database connections to the `HR` schema.

How to do it...

1. Ensure that the HRComponents and the SharedComponents ADF Library JARs are added to the ViewController project of your workspace.

2. Using the **Create JSF Page** wizard, create a **JSP XML** page called selectManyShuttleView.jspx. Use any of the predefined quick start layouts.

3. Using the **Component Palette**, add a **Popup** component (af:popup) to the page. Also add a **Dialog** component (af:dialog) inside the pop-up.

4. Expand the **Data Controls** section in the **Application Navigator** and locate the Employees collection under the HrComponentsAppModuleDataControl data control. Drag-and-drop it on the selectManyShuttleView.jspx page inside the dialog.

5. From the **Create** menu, select **Multiple Selection | ADF Select Many Shuttle...**.

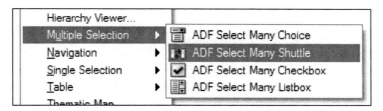

6. In the **Edit List Binding** dialog, use the **Select Multiple...** selection from the **Multi Select Display Attribute** dropdown and select the LastName and FirstName attributes.

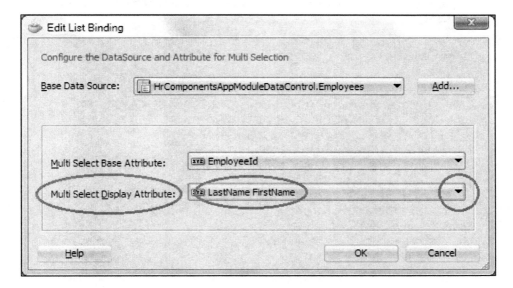

7. Select af:popup in the **Structure** window. Using the **Property Menu** next to the **PopupFetchListener** attribute in the **Property Inspector**, select **Edit...** to add a pop-up fetch listener. When presented with the **Edit Property: PopupFetchListener** dialog, create a new managed bean called SelectManyShuttleBean and a method called onEmployeesShuttleInit. While in the **Property Inspector**, also change the **ContentDelivery** attribute to **lazyUncached**.

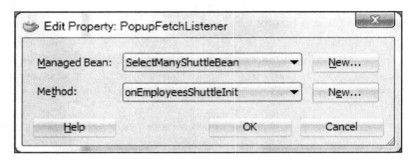

8. Open the SelectManyShuttleBean bean in the Java editor and add the following code to the onEmployeesShuttleInit() method:

```
JUCtrlListBinding employeesList =
   (JUCtrlListBinding)ADFUtils.findCtrlBinding("Employees");
employeesList.clearSelectedIndices();
```

9. Select af:dialog in the **Structure** window. Using the **Property Menu** next to the **DialogListener** attribute in the **Property Inspector**, select **Edit...** and add a dialog listener. In the **Edit Property: DialogListener** dialog, use the SelectManyShuttleBean and add a new method called onSelectManyShuttleDialogListener.

10. Add the following code to the onSelectManyShuttleDialogListener() method of the SelectManyShuttleBean managed bean:

```
if (DialogEvent.Outcome.ok.equals(dialogEvent.getOutcome())) {
   JUCtrlListBinding employeesList =
     (JUCtrlListBinding)ADFUtils.findCtrlBinding("Employees");
   Object[] employeeIds = employeesList.getSelectedValues();
   for (Object employeeId : employeeIds) {
     // handle selection
   }
}
```

11. Finally, add a **Button** component (af:commandButton) to the page and a **Show Popup Behavior** component (af:showPopupBehavior) in it. For the Show Pop-up Behavior component setup its PopupId attribute to point to the pop-up created previously.

How it works...

Since we will be importing business components from the HRComponents workspace, in step 1 we ensured that the corresponding ADF Library JAR was added to our ViewController project. This can be done either through the **Project Properties | Libraries and Classpath** dialog or via the **Resource Palette**. The HRComponents library has dependencies to the SharedComponents workspace, so we make sure that the SharedComponents ADF Library JAR is also added to the project.

In steps 2 and 3, we have created a new JSF page called selectManyShuttleView.jspx and added a pop-up to it with a dialog component in it. We will display this pop-up via the command button added in step 11.

In steps 4 through 6, we declaratively added a model-driven af:selectManyShuttle component. We did this by dragging and dropping the Employees collection available under the HrComponentsAppModuleDataControl data control in the **Data Controls** section of the **Application Navigator**. This was added to the list of the available data controls in step 1 when the HRComponents ADF Library JAR was added to our project. Note in step 6 how we have modified the Employees collection attributes that will be displayed by the ADF Select Many Shuttle. In this case, we have indicated that the employee's last name and first name will be displayed. In the same step, we have left the **Multi Select Base Attribute** to the default EmployeeId, indicating the attribute that will receive the updates. The effect of adding the Select Many Shuttle is to also add a list binding called Employees to the page bindings, as shown in the following code snippet:

```
<bindings>
  <list IterBinding="EmployeesIterator"
    ListOperMode="multiSelect"ListIter="EmployeesIterator"
    id="Employees" SelectItemValueMode="ListObject">
    <AttrNames>
      <Item Value="EmployeeId"/>
    </AttrNames>
    <ListDisplayAttrNames>
      <Item Value="LastName"/>
      <Item Value="FirstName"/>
    </ListDisplayAttrNames>
  </list>
</bindings>
```

In steps 7 and 8, we have devised a way to initialize the shuttle's selections before the pop-up is shown. We have done this by adding a `PopupFetchListener` to the pop-up. A `PopupFetchListener` indicates a method that is executed when a pop-up fetch event is invoked during content delivery. For the listener method to be executed, the pop-up content delivery must be set to `lazyUnchached` or `lazy`. We set the pop-up content delivery to `lazyUnchached` in step 7. The `PopupFetchListener` method was called `onEmployeesShuttleInit()`. In it, we retrieve the `Employees` list binding by utilizing the `ADFUtils.findCtrlBinding()` helper method. We introduced the `ADFUtils` helper class in the *Using ADFUtils/JSFUtils* recipe in *Chapter 1, Pre-requisites to Success: ADF Project Setup and Foundations*. Once the list binding is retrieved as a `JUCtrlListBinding` object, we call `clearSelectedIndices()` on it to clear the selections. This will ensure that the selected list is empty once the pop-up is displayed.

To handle the list selections, we added a `DialogListener` to the dialog in steps 9 and 10. A `DialogListener` is a method that can be used to handle the outcome of a dialog event. In it, we first checked to see whether the **OK** button was clicked by checking for a `DialogEvent.Outcome.ok` outcome. If this is the case, we retrieve the list binding and call `getSelectedValues()` on it to retrieve a `java.lang.Object` array of the selections. In our case, since we have indicated in step 6 that the `EmployeeId` attribute will be used as the base attribute, this is an array of the selected employee identifiers. Once we have the list of selected employees (as employee identifiers), we can process it as needed.

Note in step 11 that we have added a command button with an embedded `af:showPopupBehavior` in order to show the pop-up.

To test the page, right-click on it in the **Application Navigator** and select **Run** or **Debug** from the context menu. Clicking on the command button will display the pop-up with a shuttle component displaying a list of available employees to select from, as shown in the following screenshot:

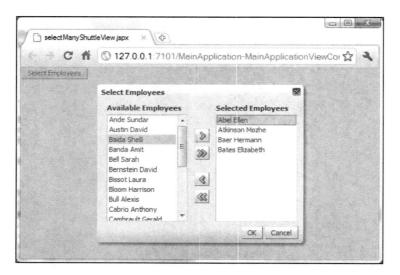

There's more...

Note that ADF Faces provides an additional shuttle component named `af:selectOrderShuttle` that includes additional buttons to allow for the reordering of the selected items.

For more information about the ADF Faces Select Many Shuttle component, take a look at the section *Using Shuttle Components* in the *Web User Interface Developer's Guide for Oracle Application Development Framework* which can be found at `http://docs.oracle.com/cd/E24382_01/web.1112/e16181/toc.htm`.

See also

▶ *Breaking up the application in multiple workspaces, Chapter 1, Pre-requisites to Success: ADF Project Setup and Foundations*

▶ *Overriding remove() to delete associated children entities, Chapter 2, Dealing with Basics: Entity Objects*

Using an af:carousel component

The ADF Faces Carousel component (`af:carousel`) is a model-driven databound user interface control that you can use on your pages as an alternate way to display collections of data. As the name suggests, the data is displayed in a revolving "carousel". The component comes with predefined controls that allow you to scroll through the carousel items. Moreover, images and textual descriptions can be associated and displayed for each carousel item.

In this recipe, we will demonstrate the usage of the `af:carousel` component by declaratively setting up a carousel to browse through the employees associated with each department.

Getting ready

You will need to create a skeleton **Fusion Web Application (ADF)** workspace before you proceed with this recipe. For this, we will use the `MainApplication` workspace that was developed in *Breaking up the application in multiple workspaces, Chapter 1, Pre-requisites to Success: ADF Project Setup and Foundations*.

The recipe also uses the `HRComponents` workspace, which was created in *Overriding remove() to delete associated children entities, Chapter 2, Dealing with Basics: Entity Objects*.

Both the `HRComponents` and `MainApplication` workspaces require database connections to the `HR` schema.

How to do it...

1. Ensure that the `HRComponents` and the `SharedComponents` ADF Library JARs are added to the ViewController project of your workspace.

2. Using the **Create JSF Page** wizard, create a **JSP XML** page called `carouselView.jspx`. Use any of the predefined quick start layouts.

3. Expand the **Data Controls** section in the **Application Navigator** and locate the `Departments` collection under the `HrComponentsAppModuleDataControl` data control. Drag-and-drop it on the `carouselView.jspx` page. From the **Create** menu, select **Table | ADF Read-only Table...**.

4. In the **Edit Table Columns** dialog, select the table columns and indicate **Single Row** for the **Row Selection**.

5. Drag-and-drop the `DepartmentEmployees` collection under the `Departments` collection on the `carouselView.jspx` page under the departments table. From the **Create** menu, select **Carousel**.

6. With the `af:carousel` selected in the **Structure** window, add a partial trigger to the departments table using the **Property Menu** next to the **PartialTriggers** attribute. Select **Edit...** from the property menu and in the **Edit Property: PartialTriggers** dialog add the table item to the selected items. Click **OK** to save your changes.

7. Expand the `af:carousel` component in the **Structure** window and locate the `af:carouselItem` underneath it. With the `af:carouselItem` selected in the **Structure** window, add the following to the **Text** attribute:

   `#{item.LastName} #{item.FirstName}, #{item.JobId}`

8. Using the **Component Palette**, locate an **Image** component and drag-and-drop it on the `af:carouselItem`. In the **Insert Image** dialog, specify `/images/#{item.JobId}.png` for the image **Source** and `#{item.LastName} #{item.FirstName}, #{item.JobId}` for the image **ShortDesc**.

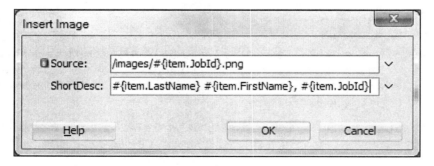

9. Under the `ViewController/public_html` directory create an `images` directory and add images for each employee job description. Ensure that the image filename conforms to the following naming standard: `#{item.JobId}.png`, where `#{item.JobId}` is the employee's job description. The employee's job descriptions are defined in `HR JOBS` and are identified by the `JOB_ID` column.

How it works...

Since we will be importing business components from the `HRComponents` workspace, in step 1, we ensured that the corresponding ADF Library JAR is added to our ViewController project. This can be done either through the **Project Properties | Libraries and Classpath** dialog or via the **Resource Palette**. The `HRComponents` library has dependencies to the `SharedComponents` workspace, so we make sure that the `SharedComponents` ADF Library JAR is also added to the project.

In step 2, we have created a JSF page that we will use to demonstrate the `af:carousel` component. In the top part of the page, we added a table bound to the `Departments` collection. In the bottom part of the page, we added the `af:carousel` component bound to the `DepartmentEmployees` collection. As you select a department in the table, the corresponding department employees can be browsed using the carousel.

The `Departments` table was added in steps 3 and 4. The carousel was added in step 5. We simply expanded the `HrComponentsAppModuleDataControl` data control in the **Data Controls** section of the **Application Navigator** and dropped the collections on the page, making the applicable selections from the menus each time. JDeveloper proceeded by adding the components to the page and creating the necessary bindings in the page definition file. If you take a closer look at the page's source, you will see that the `af:carousel` component is created, with an associated child `af:carouselItem` component inside a `nodeStamp` facet in it. The page source looks similar to the following code:

```
<af:carousel currentItemKey="#{bindings
  .DepartmentEmployees.treeModel.rootCurrencyRowKey}"
  value="#{bindings.DepartmentEmployees.treeModel}" var="item" ...
  <f:facet name="nodeStamp">
    <af:carouselItem ...
      <af:image ...
    </af:carouselItem>
  </f:facet>
</af:carousel>
```

The carousel value is set to the `treeModel` for the `DepartmentEmployees` tree binding. This binding is created when the `DepartmentEmployees` collection is dropped on the page as a carousel. The tree binding is used to iterate over `DepartmentEmployeesIterator`, which is also created when the `DepartmentEmployees` collection is dropped on the page. The iterator result set is wrapped in a `treeModel` object, which allows each item in the result set to be accessed within the carousel using the `var` attribute. The current data in the result set is then accessed by the `af:carouselItem` using the `item` variable indicated by the carousel `var` attribute.

In order to synchronize the department selection in the table with the department employees in the carousel, the necessary partial trigger was added in step 6.

In step 7, we have set the `af:carouselItem Text` attribute to the `#{item.LastName}` `#{item.FirstName}, #{item.JobId}` expression. This will display the employee's name and job description underneath each carousel item. Remember that the `item` variable indicates the current data object in the result set.

Finally, in steps 8 and 9, we have added an image component (`af:image`) to the carousel item to further enhance the look of the carousel. The image source filename is dynamically determined using the expression `/images/#{item.JobId}.png`. This will use a different image depending on the value of the employee's job identifier. In step 9, we added the images for each employee job identifier.

To see the carousel in action, right-click on `carouselView.jspx` in the **Application Navigator** and select **Run** or **Debug**. Navigate through the Departments table using the carousel component through the department's employees.

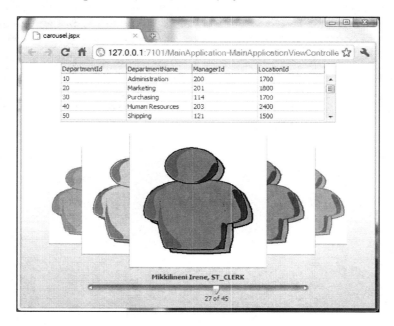

There's more...

For this recipe, the employee images were explicitly specified as filenames, each one indicating a specific employee job using the expression `/images/#{item.JobId}.png`. In a more realistic scenario, images for each collection item would be stored in the database in a `BLOB` column associated with the collection item (the employee in this example). To retrieve the image content from the database `BLOB` column, you will need to write a servlet and indicate your choice by passing a parameter to the servlet. For instance, this could be indicated in the `af:image source` attribute as `/yourservlet?imageId=#{item.EmployeeId}`. In this case, the image is identified using the employee identifier. A sample demonstrating the image servlet can be found in the FOD sample.

For more information about the ADF Faces Carousel component, take a look at the section *Using the ADF Faces Carousel Component* in the *Fusion Developer's Guide for Oracle Application Development Framework* which can be found at `http://docs.oracle.com/cd/E24382_01/web.1112/e16182/toc.htm`.

See also

▶ *Breaking up the application in multiple workspaces, Chapter 1, Pre-requisites to Success: ADF Project Setup and Foundations*

▶ *Overriding remove() to delete associated children entities, Chapter 2, Dealing with Basics: Entity Objects*

Using an af:poll component to periodically refresh a table

The ADF Faces Poll component (`af:poll`) can be used to deliver poll events to the server as a means to periodically update page components. Poll events are delivered to a poll listener—a managed bean method—by referencing the method using the `pollListener` attribute. These poll events are delivered to the poll listener based on the value specified by the `interval` attribute. The poll interval is indicated in milliseconds; polling can be disabled by setting the interval to a negative value. An `af:poll` can also be referenced from the `partialTriggers` property of a component to partially refresh the component. In this case, a `pollListener` is not needed.

In this recipe, we will implement polling in order to periodically refresh an employees table in the page. By periodically refreshing the table, it will reflect any database changes done to the corresponding `EMPLOYEES` schema table in the database.

Getting ready

You will need to create a skeleton **Fusion Web Application (ADF)** workspace before you proceed with this recipe. For this, we will use the `MainApplication` workspace that was developed in *Breaking up the application in multiple workspaces, Chapter 1, Pre-requisites to Success: ADF Project Setup and Foundations*.

The recipe also uses the `HRComponents` workspace, which was created in *Overriding remove() to delete associated children entities, Chapter 2, Dealing with Basics: Entity Objects*.

Both the `HRComponents` and `MainApplication` workspaces require database connections to the `HR` schema.

How to do it...

1. Ensure that the `HRComponents` and the `SharedComponents` ADF Library JARs are added to the ViewController project of your workspace.

2. Using the **Create JSF Page** wizard, create a **JSP XML** page called `pollView.jspx`. Use any of the predefined quick start layouts.

3. Expand the **Data Controls** section in the **Application Navigator** and locate the `Employees` collection under the `HrComponentsAppModuleDataControl` data control. Drag-and-drop it on the `pollView.jspx` page. Then, from the **Create** menu, select **Table | ADF Read-only Table...**.

4. In the **Edit Table Columns** dialog, select the table columns and choose **Single Row** for the **Row Selection**.

5. Switch to the **Page Data Binding Definition** by clicking on the **Bindings** tab at the bottom of the page editor.

6. Click on the **Create control binding** button (the green plus sign icon) in the **Bindings** section and select **Action** from the **Generic Bindings** category.

7. In the **Creation Action Binding** dialog, select the `Employees` collection under the `HrComponentsAppModuleDataControl` and then select **Execute** for the **Operation**.

8. With the **Execute** action selected in the **Structure** window, change the **Id** property from **Execute** to `RefreshEmployees` using the **Property Inspector**.

9. Return to the page **Design** or **Source** editor. Using the **Component Palette**, drag a **Poll** component from the **Operations** section and drop it on the page.

10. With the `af:poll` component selected in the **Structure** window, change the **Interval** property to **3000** and add a poll listener using the **Property Menu** next to the **PollListener** property in the **Property Inspector**. If needed, create a new managed bean.

11. Open the managed bean Java class in the Java editor and add the following code to the poll listener:

```
ADFUtils.findOperation("RefreshEmployees").execute();
```

12. Finally, add a partial trigger to the `af:table` component using the **Property Menu** next to the **PartialTriggers** property in the **Property Inspector**. In the **Edit Property: PartialTriggers** dialog, select the poll component in the **Available** list and add it to the **Selected** list.

How it works...

In step 1, we have added the `HRComponents` ADF Library JAR to our application's ViewController project. We have done this since we will be using the business components included in this library. The ADF Library JAR can be added to our project either via the **Resource Palette** or through the ViewController's **Project Properties | Libraries and Classpath**. The `HRComponents` library has dependencies to the `SharedComponents` workspace, so we make sure that the `SharedComponents` ADF Library JAR is also added to the project.

Then, in step 2, we created a JSF page called `pollView.jspx` that we used to demonstrate the `af:poll` component by periodically refreshing a table of employees. So, in steps 3 and 4, we dropped the `Employees` collection—available through the `HrComponentsAppModuleDataControl` data control—as a read-only table on the page.

In steps 5 through 8, we created an action binding called `RefreshEmployees`. The `RefreshEmployees` action binding will invoke the `Execute` operation on the `Employees` collection, which will query the underlying `Employees` view object. So, by executing the `RefreshEmployees` action binding, we will be able to update the employees table, which is bound to the same `Employees` collection.

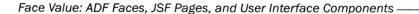

To accomplish a periodic update of the employees table, we dropped an `af:poll` component on the page (step 9) and adjusted the time interval in which a poll event will be dispatched (in step 10). This time interval is indicated by the `Interval` poll property in milliseconds, so we set it to 3 seconds (3000 milliseconds).

Then, in steps 10 and 11, we declared a poll listener using the `PollListener` property of the `af:poll` component. This is the method that will receive the poll event each time the poll is fired. In the process, we had to create a new managed bean (step 10). In the poll listener, we use the `ADFUtils findOperation()` helper method to retrieve the `RefreshEmployees` action binding from the bindings container. The `ADFUtils` helper class was introduced in *Using ADFUtils/JSFUtils, Chapter 1, Pre-requisites to Success: ADF Project Setup and Foundations*. The `findOperation()` helper method returns an `oracle. binding.OperationBinding` object, on which we call `execute()` to execute it. As stated earlier, this will have the effect of querying the `Employees` collection underlying view object, which in effect refreshes the table.

Finally, in step 12, we had to indicate in the employees table's partial triggers the ID of the poll component. This will cause a partial page rendering for the `af:table` component triggered from the `af:poll` component each time the poll listener is executed.

To test the recipe, right-click on the `pollView.jspx` page in the **Application Navigator** and select **Run** or **Debug** from the context menu. Notice how the employees table is refreshed every 3 seconds, reflecting any modifications done to the `Employees` table.

See also

- ▸ *Breaking up the application in multiple workspaces, Chapter 1, Pre-requisites to Success: ADF Project Setup and Foundations*
- ▸ *Overriding remove() to delete associated children entities, Chapter 2, Dealing with Basics: Entity Objects*

Using page templates for pop-up reuse

Back in *Chapter 1, Pre-requisites to Success: ADF Project Setup and Foundations* in the *Using a generic backing bean actions framework* recipe, we introduced a generic backing bean actions framework, called `CommonActions`, to handle common JSF page actions. In this recipe, we will enhance this generic actions framework by demonstrating how to add pop-up dialogs to a page template definition, that can then be reused by pages based on the template using this framework. The specific use case that we will implement in this recipe is to add a delete confirmation pop-up to the page template. This will provide a uniform delete behavior for all application pages based on this template.

Getting ready

You will need to have access to the `SharedComponents` workspace that was developed in _Breaking up the application in multiple workspaces, Chapter 1, Pre-requisites to Success: ADF Project Setup and Foundations_. The functionality will be added to both the `CommonActions` generic backing bean framework and the `TemplateDef1` page template definition that were created in the _Using a generic backing bean actions framework_ and _Using page templates_ recipes in _Chapter 1, Pre-requisites to Success: ADF Project Setup and Foundations_.

For testing purposes, you will need to create a skeleton **Fusion Web Application (ADF)** workspace. For this, we will use the `MainApplication` workspace that was developed in _Breaking up the application in multiple workspaces, Chapter 1, Pre-requisites to Success: ADF Project Setup and Foundations_.

The recipe also uses the `HRComponents` workspace, which was created in _Overriding remove() to delete associated children entities, Chapter 2, Dealing with Basics: Entity Objects_.

Both the `HRComponents` and `MainApplication` workspaces require database connections to the `HR` schema.

How to do it...

1. Open the `SharedComponents` workspace and locate the `TemplateDef1` page template definition using the **Application Navigator**. It can be found under the `WEB-INF/templates` package. Double-click on it so you can open it.

2. Using the **Component Palette**, drop a **Popup** component to the `top` facet. Modify the `af:popup` component's `id` property to `DeleteConfirmation`.

3. Drop a **Dialog** component inside the `af:popup` added in the previous step. Using the **Property Inspector**, update the dialog's **Title** to **Confirm Deletion**. Also change the **Type** property to **cancel**.

4. Drop an **Output Text** component from the **Component Palette** to the dialog. Change its **Value** property to **Continue with deleting this record?**

5. Using the **Component Palette**, drop a **Button** component to the dialog's `buttonBar` facet. Change the `af:commandButton text` property to `Continue`.

6. Using the **Property Inspector**, add the following **ActionListener** to the `af:commandButton`: `#{CommonActionsBean.onContinueDelete}`. The pop-up source should look similar to the following:

```
<af:popup id="DeleteConfirmation">
  <af:dialog id="pt_d1" title="Confirm Deletion" type="cancel">
  <af:outputText value="Continue with deleting this record?"
    id="pt_ot1"/>
```

```
    <f:facet name="buttonBar">
      <af:commandButton text="Continue"id="continueDeleteButton"
        actionListener="#{CommonActionsBean.onContinueDelete}"/>
    </f:facet>
  </af:dialog>
</af:popup>
```

7. Locate the ADFUTils helper class and open it in the Java editor. Add the following code to the showPopup() method:

```
FacesContext facesContext = FacesContext.getCurrentInstance();
ExtendedRenderKitService service =
  Service.getRenderKitService(facesContext,
  ExtendedRenderKitService.class);
service.addScript(facesContext,
  "AdfPage.PAGE.findComponentByAbsoluteId ('generic:"
  + popupId + "').show();");
```

8. Redeploy the SharedComponents workspace into an ADF Library JAR.

9. Open the MainApplication workspace or create a new **Fusion Web Application (ADF)** workspace. Ensure that you add both the SharedComponents and HRComponents ADF Library JARs to the ViewController project.

10. Open the adfc-config unbounded task flow, go to **Overview | Managed Beans** and add a managed bean called CommonActionsBean. For the managed bean class, use the CommonActions class in the com.packt.jdeveloper.cookbook. shared.view.actions package imported from the SharedComponents ADF Library JAR.

11. Create a new JSPX page called templatePopup.jspx based on the TemplateDef1 page template definition.

12. With the af:pageTemplate selected in the **Structure** window, change the template **Id** in the **Property Inspector** to generic.

13. Now, expand the HrComponentsAppModuleDataControl data control in the **Data Controls** section of the **Application Navigator** and drop the Employees collection on the **mainContent** facet of the page as an **ADF Read-only Form**. In the **Edit Form Fields** dialog, ensure that you select the **Include Navigation Controls** checkbox.

14. Using the **Component Palette**, drop a **Button** component to the form next to the **Last** button. With the button selected in the **Structure** window, change its **Text** property to **Delete**. Also set the ActionListener property to #{CommonActionsBean.delete}.

How it works...

In steps 1 through 6, we have expanded the `TemplateDef1` page template definition by adding a pop-up called `DeleteConfirmation`. We can raise this pop-up prior to deleting a record consistently for all of the application pages that are based on the `TemplateDef1` template. Notice that the name of the pop-up should match the name used in the `CommonActions.onConfirmDelete()` method to display the pop-up. This method looks similar to the following:

```
public void onConfirmDelete(final ActionEvent actionEvent) {
  ADFUtils.showPopup("DeleteConfirmation");
}
```

The necessary code to display the pop-up is added in the `ADFUtils.showPopup()` method in step 7. The `ADFUtils` helper class was introduced in *Using ADFUtils/JSFUtils, Chapter 1, Pre-requisites to Success: ADF Project Setup and Foundations*. The following is the `ADFUtils.showPopup()` method:

```
public static void showPopup(String popupId) {
  FacesContext facesContext =FacesContext.getCurrentInstance();
  ExtendedRenderKitService service =
    Service.getRenderKitService(facesContext,
    ExtendedRenderKitService.class);
  service.addScript(facesContext,"AdfPage.PAGE.
    findComponent('generic:"+ popupId + "').show();");
}
```

The code in `ADFUtils.showPopup()` has been explained in the *Using an af:pop-up component to edit a table row* recipe in this chapter. One important thing to notice is how the template ID (`generic`) is prepended to the pop-up ID.

The `onConfirmDelete()` method is called by the generic delete action listener `CommonActions.delete()`. The following is the code for the `CommonActions.delete()` method:

```
public void delete(final ActionEvent actionEvent) {
  onConfirmDelete(actionEvent);
}
```

Notice how in step 5 we have added a **Continue** button to the delete confirmation pop-up and in step 6 we explicitly specify the `CommonActions.onContinueDelete()` method as the continue button's action listener. The code for this method is shown as follows:

```
public void onContinueDelete(final ActionEvent actionEvent) {
  CommonActions actions = getCommonActions();
   actions.onBeforeDelete(actionEvent);
   actions.onDelete(actionEvent);
   actions.onAfterDelete(actionEvent);
}
```

First we call `getCommonActions()` to determine if the `CommonActions` bean has been subclassed and then we call the appropriate action framework methods `onBeforeDelete()`, `onDelete()` and `onAfterDelete()`. The following is the code of the `getCommonActions()` method:

```
private CommonActions getCommonActions() {
  CommonActions actions =
    (CommonActions)JSFUtils.getExpressionObjectReference("#{"
    + getManagedBeanName() + "}");
  if (actions == null) {
    actions = this;
  }
  return actions;
}
```

The subclassed `CommonActions` managed bean name is determined by calling `getManagedBeanName()`. If a subclassed managed bean is not found, then the generic `CommonActions` bean is used; otherwise, the subclassed managed bean class is loaded using the `JSFUtils.getExpressionObjectReference()` helper method, which resolves the expression based on the bean name and instantiates it. The code for the `getManagedBeanName()` method is shown as follows:

```
private String getManagedBeanName() {
  return getPageId().replace("/", "").replace(".jspx", "");
}
```

As you can see, the subclassed managed bean name is determined by calling the helper `getPageId()`, which is shown as follows:

```
public String getPageId() {
  ControllerContext ctx = ControllerContext.getInstance();
  return ctx.getCurrentViewPort().getViewId().substring(
  ctx.getCurrentViewPort().getViewId().lastIndexOf("/")); }
```

The `getPageId()` determines the subclassed `CommonActions` managed bean name from the associated page. The fact that the subclassed managed bean name must match the page name, makes it a requirement for the `CommonActions` framework.

We continue in step 8 by redeploying the SharedComponents workspace to an ADF Library JAR.

To test the generic template pop-up, in step 9, we created a **Fusion Web Application (ADF)** workspace and added the SharedComponents and HRComponents ADF Library JARs to its ViewController project.

In step 10, we added a managed bean, called CommonActionsBean, to our application based on the CommonActions class implemented in the SharedComponents workspace.

In steps 11 through 14, we created a page called templatePopup.jspx based on the TemplateDef1 template and drop the Employees collection imported from the HRComponents workspace, as a read-only form. Notice in step 12 how we ensured that the af:pageTemplate component's identifier value is set to the same identifier value as in the template definition, that is, generic. This is important for the code in step 7 that loads the pop-up to function properly.

Finally, notice in step 14, how we set the delete button action listener to #{CommonActionsBean.delete}. This will allow for generic processing of the delete action.

To test the recipe, right-click on the templatePopup.jspx page in the **Application Navigator** and select **Run** or **Debug** from the context menu. When you click on the **Delete** button, the **Confirm Deletion** pop-up defined in the page template will be displayed and the CommonActions framework will be used to handle the delete action.

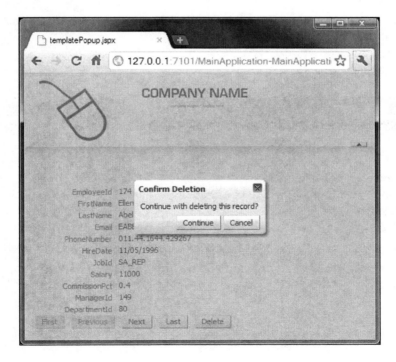

There's more...

For this recipe, we configured the delete button action processing so that it can be provided by the generic `CommonActions delete()` method. Assuming that you wanted to provide specialized handling of the delete action, you can do the following:

▸ Create a new managed bean with the same name as the page, that is, `templatePopup`

▸ Create the managed bean class and ensure that it extends the `CommonActions` class

▸ Provide specialized delete action functionality by overriding the following methods: `delete()`, `onBeforeDelete()`, `onDelete()`, `onAfterDelete()` and `onConfirmDelete()`

▸ Set the delete command button action listener to: `#{templatePopup.delete}`

See also

▸ *Using a generic backing bean actions framework, Chapter 1, Pre-requisites to Success: ADF Project Setup and Foundations*

▸ *Using page templates, Chapter 1, Pre-requisites to Success: ADF Project Setup and Foundations*

▸ *Breaking up the application in multiple workspaces, Chapter 1, Pre-requisites to Success: ADF Project Setup and Foundations*

▸ *Overriding remove() to delete associated children entities, Chapter 2, Dealing with Basics: Entity Objects*

Exporting data to a client file

You can export data from the server and download it to a file in the client by using the ADF Faces File Download Action Listener component, available in the **Operations** section of the **Component Palette**. Simply specify the default export filename and a managed bean method to handle the download. To actually export the data from the model using business components, you will have to iterate through the relevant view object and generate the exported string buffer.

In this recipe, we will use the File Download Action Listener component (`af:fileDownloadActionListener`) to demonstrate how to export all employees to a client file. The employees will be saved in the file in a comma-separated-values (CSV) format.

Getting ready

You will need to create a skeleton **Fusion Web Application (ADF)** workspace before you proceed with this recipe. For this, we will use the `MainApplication` workspace that was developed in *Breaking up the application in multiple workspaces, Chapter 1, Pre-requisites to Success: ADF Project Setup and Foundations*.

The recipe also uses the `HRComponents` workspace, which was created in *Overriding remove() to delete associated children entities, Chapter 2, Dealing with Basics: Entity Objects*.

Both the `HRComponents` and `MainApplication` workspaces require database connections to the `HR` schema.

How to do it...

1. Open the `HRComponents` workspace and locate the `HrComponentsAppModule` application module. Open the custom application module Java implementation file `HrComponentsAppModuleImpl.java` in the Java editor.

2. Add the following `exportEmployees()` method to it:
    ```java
    public String exportEmployees() {
      EmployeesImpl employees = this.getEmployees();
      employees.executeQuery();
      StringBuilder employeeStringBuilder = new StringBuilder();
      RowSetIterator iterator =
      employees.createRowSetIterator(null);
      iterator.reset();
      while (iterator.hasNext()) {
        EmployeesRowImpl employee = (EmployeesRowImpl)iterator.next();
        employeeStringBuilder.append(employee.getLastName()
          + " " + employee.getFirstName());
        if (iterator.hasNext()) {
          employeeStringBuilder.append(",");
        }
      }
      iterator.closeRowSetIterator();
      return employeeStringBuilder.toString();
    }
    ```

3. Double-click the `HrComponentsAppModule` application module in the **Application Module** and go to the **Java** section. Add the `exportEmployees()` method to the application module's client interface by clicking on the **Edit application module client interface** button (the pen icon).

4. Redeploy the `HRComponents` workspace as an ADF Library JAR.

5. Open the `MainApplication` workspace and add the `HRComponents` and the `SharedComponents` ADF Library JARs to its ViewController project.

6. Create a new JSPX page, called `exportEmployees.jspx`, using one of the quick start layouts.

7. Expand the `HrComponentsAppModuleDataControl` in the **Data Controls** section of the **Application Navigator** and locate the `exportEmployees()` method. Drop the `exportEmployees()` method on the page selecting **ADF Button** from the **Create** menu.

8. Right-click on the `af:commandButton` in the **Structure** window and select **Surround With...** from the context menu. In the **Surround With** dialog, select **Toolbar**.

9. With the `af:commandButton` selected in the **Structure** window, change the **Text** property to **Export Employees** and reset the **ActionListener** and **Disabled** properties to default (remove their expressions).

10. Switch to the **Bindings** tab and add a binding using the **Create control binding** button (the green plus sign icon). In the **Insert Item** dialog, select **methodAction** and click **OK**. In the **Create Action Binding** dialog, select the `HrComponentsAppModuleDataControl` in the **Data Collection** list and **exportEmployees()** for the **Operation**.

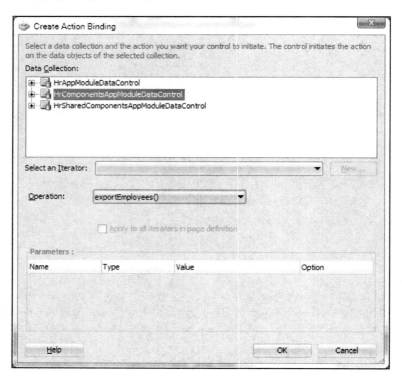

11. Return to the page **Design** or **Source**. Right-click on the `af:commandButton` in the **Structure** window and select **Insert Inside af:commandButton ADF Faces...** from the context menu. In the **Insert ADF Faces Item** dialog, select **File Download Action Listener** and click **OK**.

12. With the `af:fileDownloadActionListener` selected in the **Structure** window, set the **Filename** property to `employees.csv` in the **Property Inspector**. For the **Method** property, expand on the **Property Menu** and select **Edit....** In the **Edit Property: Menu** dialog, create a new managed bean called `ExportEmployeesBean` and a new method called `exportEmployees`. Click **OK** to dismiss the **Edit Property: Menu** dialog.

13. Now, open the managed bean and add the following code to the `exportEmployees()` method:

```
String employeesCSV = (String)ADFUtils.findOperation
   ("exportEmployees").execute();
try {
   OutputStreamWriter writer =
     new OutputStreamWriter(outputStream, "UTF-8");
   writer.write(employeesCSV);
   writer.close();
   outputStream.close();
} catch (IOException e) {
   // log the error
}
```

How it works...

In steps 1 through 4 we have updated the `HRComponents` ADF Library JAR by adding a method called `exportEmployees()` to the `HrComponentsAppModule` application module. In this method, we iterate over the `Employees` view object, and for each row we add the employee's last and first name to a string. We separate each employee name with a comma to create a string with all of the employee names in a comma-separated-values (CSV) format. In step 3, we have added the `exportEmployees()` method to the application module's client interface to make it available to the ViewController layer. Then, in step 4, we redeploy the `HRComponents` workspace into an ADF Library JAR.

Steps 5 through 13 cover working on the `MainApplication` workspace. You could instead create your own **Fusion Web Application (ADF)** workspace and apply them to that workspace instead. First, in step 5, we add the `HRComponents` ADF Library JAR to the ViewController project of the `MainApplication` workspace. You can do this either through the **Resource Palette** or through the **Project Properties | Libraries and Classpath** settings. The `HRComponents` library has dependencies to the `SharedComponents` workspace, so we make sure that the `SharedComponents` ADF Library JAR is also added to the project.

In step 6, we created a JSF page using one of the predefined quick start layouts. Then, in steps 7 through 10, we added a command button to the page with the underlying bindings. In step 7, note how we initially dropped the `exportEmployees()` method from the **Data Controls** window to the page as a button. We did this so that we can initialize the underlying page bindings. However, note how in step 10, we had to re-bind the `exportEmployees()` method as a `methodAction`. This is because in step 9 we removed the expressions from the `ActionListener` and `Disabled` properties, which as a result removed the `exportEmployees() methodAction` binding. Defining and using this `methodAction` binding will allow us to execute the `exportEmployees()` application module method that returns the employees in a CSV string buffer.

In steps 10 through 13, we added the File Download Action Listener component to the command button. Note in step 12, how we indicated a listener method, called `exportEmployees()`, that will be executed to perform the download action. The actual code for the listener was added in step 13. This code uses the `ADFUtils` helper class to programmatically execute the `exportEmployees methodAction` binding that we added in step 10. Executing the `exportEmployees methodAction` binding will result in returning the employees in a CSV formatted string. Then, using the `OutputStream` passed to the download action listener automatically by the ADF framework, we can write it to the stream. We introduced the `ADFUtils` helper class in *Using ADFUtils/JSFUtils, Chapter 1, Pre-requisites to Success: ADF Project Setup and Foundations*.

To test the recipe, right-click on the `exportEmployees.jspx` page in the **Application Navigator** and select **Run** or **Debug** from the context menu. Observe what happens when you click on the **Export Employees** button. A **Save As** dialog is displayed asking you for the name of the file to save the employee CSV data. The default filename in this dialog is the filename indicated in the `Filename` property of the `af:fileDownloadActionListener` component, that is, `employees.csv`.

There's more...

For more information on the `af:fileDownloadActionListener` component, consult the section *How to Use a Command Component to Download Files* in the *Web User Interface Developer's Guide for Oracle Application Development Framework* which can be found at `http://docs.oracle.com/cd/E24382_01/web.1112/e16181/toc.htm`.

See also

- ▸ *Breaking up the application in multiple workspaces, Chapter 1, Pre-requisites to Success: ADF Project Setup and Foundations*
- ▸ *Overriding remove() to delete associated children entities, Chapter 2, Dealing with Basics: Entity Objects*

8
Backing not Baking: Bean Recipes

In this chapter, we will cover:

- ▶ Determining whether the current transaction has pending changes
- ▶ Using a custom af:table selection listener
- ▶ Using a custom af:query listener to allow execution of a custom application module operation
- ▶ Using a custom af:query operation listener to clear both the query criteria and results
- ▶ Using a session scope bean to preserve session-wide information
- ▶ Using an af:popup during long-running tasks
- ▶ Using an af:popup to handle pending changes
- ▶ Using an af:iterator to add pagination support to a collection

Introduction

Backing (also referred to as managed) beans are Java beans referenced by JSF pages in an ADF Fusion web application through Expression Language (EL). They are usually dedicated to providing specific functionality to the corresponding page. They are part of the ViewController layer in the Model-View-Controller architecture. Depending on their persistence in memory throughout the lifetime of the application, managed beans are categorized based on their scope: from `request` (minimal persistence in memory for the specific user request only) to `application` (maximum persistence in memory for the duration of the application). They can also exist in any of the `session`, `view`, `pageFlow`, and `backingBean` scopes. Managed bean definitions can be added to any of the following ADF Fusion web application configuration files:

- ▶ `faces-config.xml`: The JSF configuration file. It is searched first by the ADF framework for managed bean definitions. All scopes can be defined, except for `view`, `backingBean`, and `pageFlow` scopes, which are ADF-specifc.

- ▶ `adfc-config.xml`: The unbounded task flow definition file. Managed beans of any scope may be defined in this file. It is searched after the `faces-config.xml` JSF configuration file.

- ▶ `Specific task flow definition file`: In this file, the managed bean definitions are accessed only by the specific task flow.

Additionally, if you are using Facelets, you can register a backing bean using annotations.

Determining whether the current transaction has pending changes

This recipe shows you how to determine whether there are unsaved changes to the current transaction. This may come in handy when, for instance, you want to raise a warning pop-up message each time you attempt to leave the current page. This is demonstrated in the recipe *Using an af:popup to handle pending changes* in this chapter. Furthermore, by adding this functionality in a generic way to your application, making it part of the `CommonActions` framework for example, you can provide a standard application-wide approach for dealing with pending uncommitted transaction changes. The `CommonActions` framework was introduced in the *Using a generic backing bean actions framework, Chapter 1, Pre-requisites to Success: ADF Project Setup and Foundations*.

Getting ready

The functionality implemented in this recipe will be added to the `ADFUtils` helper class introduced in *Using ADFUtils/JSFUtils, Chapter 1, Pre-requisites to Success: ADF Project Setup and Foundations*. This class is part of the `SharedComponents` workspace.

How to do it...

1. Open the `SharedComponents` workspace and locate the `ADFUtils.java` class in the **Application Navigator**.

2. Double-click on the `ADFUtils.java` to open it in the Java editor and add the following code to it:

```
public static boolean isBCTransactionDirty() {
    // get application module and check for dirty
    // transaction
    ApplicationModule am =
      ADFUtils.getDCBindingContainer().getDataControl()
      .getApplicationModule();
    return am.getTransaction().isDirty();
}
public static boolean isControllerTransactionDirty() {
    // get data control and check for dirty transaction
    BindingContext bc = BindingContext.getCurrent();
    String currentDataControlFrame =
      bc.getCurrentDataControlFrame();
    return bc.findDataControlFrame(
      currentDataControlFrame).isTransactionDirty();
}
```

3. Locate the `hasChanges()` method in the `ADFUtils` helper class. Add the following code to it:

```
// check for dirty transaction in both the model
// and the controller
return isBCTransactionDirty() ||
    isControllerTransactionDirty();
```

How it works...

In steps 1 and 2, we added two helper methods to the `ADFUtils` helper class, namely, `isBCTransactionDirty()` and `isControllerTransactionDirty()`.

The `isBCTransactionDirty()` method determines whether there are uncommitted transaction changes at the ADF-BC layer. This is done by first retrieving the application module from the data control `DCDataControl` class and then calling `getTransaction()` to get its `oracle.jbo.Transaction` transaction object. We call `isDirty()` on the `Transaction` object to determine if any application module data has been modified but not yet committed.

The `isControllerTransactionDirty()` method, on the other hand, checks for uncommitted changes at the controller layer. This is done by first calling `getCurrentDataControlFrame()` on the binding context to return the name of the current data control frame, and then calling `findDataControlFrame()` on the binding context to retrieve the `oracle.adf.model.DataControlFrame` object with the given name. Finally, we call `isTransactionDirty()` on the data control frame to determine whether unsaved data modifications exist within the current task flow context.

When checking for unsaved changes, we need to ensure that both the ADF-BC and the controller layers are checked. This is done by the `hasChanges()` method, which calls both `isBCTransactionDirty()` and `isControllerTransactionDirty()` and returns `true` if unsaved changes exist in any of the two layers.

There's more...

Note that for transient attributes used at the ADF-BC layer, `isDirty()` will return `true` only for entity object modified transient attributes. This is not the case for view object modified transient attributes, and `isDirty()` in this case returns `false`. In contrast, calling `isTransactionDirty()` at the ADFm layer will return `true` if any attributes have been modified.

See also

▸ *Using ADFUtils/JSFUtils, Chapter 1, Pre-requisites to Success: ADF Project Setup and Foundations*

▸ *Using an af:popup to handle pending changes*, in this chapter.

Using a custom af:table selection listener

The `selectionListener` attribute of the ADF Table (`af:table`) component synchronizes the currently selected table row with the underlying ADF table binding iterator. By default, upon dropping a collection to a JSF page as an ADF table, JDeveloper sets the value of the `selectionListener` attribute of the corresponding `af:table` component to an expression similar to `#{bindings.SomeCollection.collectionModel.makeCurrent}`. This expression indicates that the `makeCurrent` method of the collection's model is called in order to synchronize the table selection with the table iterator binding.

In this recipe, we will cover how to implement your own custom table selection listener. This will come in handy if your application requires any additional processing before or after a table selection is made.

Getting ready

You will need to create a skeleton **Fusion Web Application (ADF)** workspace before you proceed with this recipe. For this, we will use the `MainApplication` workspace that was developed in _Breaking up the application in multiple workspaces, Chapter 1, Pre-requisites to Success: ADF Project Setup and Foundations_.

The recipe also uses the `HRComponents` workspace, which was created in _Overriding remove() to delete associated children entities, Chapter 2, Dealing with Basics: Entity Objects_.

Both the `HRComponents` and `MainApplication` workspaces require database connections to the `HR` schema.

Moreover, this recipe enhances the `JSFUtils` helper class introduced in _Using ADFUtils/ JSFUtils, Chapter 1, Pre-requisites to Success: ADF Project Setup and Foundations_, which is part of the `SharedComponents` workspace.

How to do it...

1. Open the `SharedComponents` workspace and locate the `JSFUtils` helper class in the **Application Navigator**. Double-click on it to open it in the Java editor.

2. Add the following method to it, ensuring that you redeploy the `SharedComponents` workspace to an ADF Library JAR afterwards.

```
public static Object invokeMethodExpression(String expr,
  Class returnType, Class argType, Object argument) {
  FacesContext fc = FacesContext.getCurrentInstance();
  ELContext elctx = fc.getELContext();
  ExpressionFactory elFactory =
    fc.getApplication().getExpressionFactory();
  MethodExpression methodExpr =
    elFactory.createMethodExpression(elctx,
    expr, returnType, new Class[] { argType });
  return methodExpr.invoke(elctx, new Object[] { argument });
}
```

3. Now, open the `MainApplication` workspace and add the `SharedComponents` and the `HRComponents` ADF Library JARs to the ViewController project.

4. Create a JSP XML page based on any of the quick start layouts and drop the `Employees` collection, under the `HrComponentsAppModuleDataControl` in the **Data Controls** section of the **Application Navigator**, to the page.

5. With the **af:table** component selected in the **Structure** window, use the **SelectionListener** property menu **Edit...** in the **Property Inspector** and add a new selection listener, called `selectionListener`. Create a new managed bean when asked.

6. Open the managed bean and add the following code to the custom selection listener created previously:

```
// invoke makeCurrent via method expression
  JSFUtils.invokeMethodExpression(
"#{bindings.Employees.collectionModel.makeCurrent}",
  Object.class, SelectionEvent.class, selectionEvent);
// get selected data
RichTable table = (RichTable)selectionEvent.getSource();
JUCtrlHierNodeBinding selectedRowData =
  (JUCtrlHierNodeBinding)table.getSelectedRowData();
// process selected data
String[] attrbNames = selectedRowData.getAttributeNames();
for (String attrbName : attrbNames) {
  Object attrbValue =
    selectedRowData.getAttribute(attrbName);
  System.out.println("attrbName: " + attrbName +
    ", attrbValue: " + attrbValue);
```

How it works...

In steps 1 and 2, we updated the `JSFUtils` helper class by adding a method called `invokeMethodExpression()` used to invoke a JSF method expression. We also ensured that the `SharedComponents` workspace, where the `JSFUtils` helper class is defined, was redeployed into an ADF Library JAR. Then, in step 3, we added the newly deployed `SharedComponents` ADF Library JAR into the ViewController project of our application. We also added the `HRComponents` ADF Library JAR to the ViewController project, as we will be using the `Employees` collection in the steps that follow. You can add the ADF Library JARs either through the **Resource Palette** or through the ViewController **Project Properties | Libraries and Classpath** dialog settings.

In steps 4 and 5, we created a JSF page and dropped the `Employees` collection in it as an ADF Table (`af:table`) component. The `Employees` collection can be found in the `HrComponentsAppModule` application module which resides in the `HRComponents` ADF Library JAR. Then in step 6, we added a custom table `SelectionListener` by defining a method called `selectionListener()` in a managed bean. The code in the custom selection listener first invokes the default selection listener, by invoking the JSF method expression `#{bindings.Employees.collectionModel.makeCurrent}` using the helper method `invokeMethodExpression()` that we added in step 2.

The custom selection listener also demonstrates how to get the selected row data by first retrieving the ADF Table component as an `oracle.adf.view.rich.component.rich.data.RichTable` object. We call `getSource()` on the selection event and then call `getSelectedRowData()` on it. The call to `getSelectedRowData()` returns the ADF table binding as an `oracle.jbo.uicli.binding.JUCtrlHierNodeBinding` object, which can be used to subsequently retrieve the row data. This is done by calling `getAttributeNames()`, for instance, to retrieve the attribute names or by calling `getAttribute()` to retrieve the data value for a specific attribute. Once this information is known for the current table selection, additional business logic can be added to implement the specific application requirements.

There's more...

To do the analogous task with Java code, without invoking the default selection listener `makeCurrent`, involves getting the current row key from the node binding and setting the table `DCIteratorBinding` iterator binding (by calling `setCurrentRowWithKey()` on the iterator binding) to that key. For more information about this approach, take a look at Frank Nimphius' *ADF Corner* article *How-to build a generic Selection Listener for ADF bound ADF Faces Table*. It can be found currently in the following address: `http://www.oracle.com/technetwork/developer-tools/adf/learnmore/23-generic-table-selection-listener-169162.pdf`.

See also

- *Using ADFUtils/JSFUtils, Chapter 1, Pre-requisites to Success: ADF Project Setup and Foundations*
- *Breaking up the application in multiple workspaces, Chapter 1, Pre-requisites to Success: ADF Project Setup and Foundations*
- *Overriding remove() to delete associated children entities, Chapter 2, Dealing with Basics: Entity Objects*

Using a custom af:query listener to allow execution of a custom application module operation

The `queryListener` attribute of the ADF Faces Query (`af:query`) component indicates a method that is invoked to execute the query. By default, the framework executes the `processQuery()` method referenced by the `searchRegion` binding associated with the `af:query` component. This is indicated by the following expression: `#{bindings.SomeQuery.processQuery}`. By creating a custom query listener method, you can provide a custom implementation each time a search is performed by the `af:query` component.

In this recipe, we will demonstrate how to create a custom query listener. Our custom query listener will programmatically execute the query by invoking the default expression as indicated previously. Moreover, after the query execution, it will display a message with the number of rows returned by the specific query.

Getting ready

You will need to create a skeleton **Fusion Web Application (ADF)** workspace before you proceed with this recipe. For this, we will use the `MainApplication` workspace that was developed in the *Breaking up the application in multiple workspaces, Chapter 1, Pre-requisites to Success: ADF Project Setup and Foundations*.

The recipe also uses the `SharedComponents` and `HRComponents` workspaces, which were created in *Breaking up the application in multiple workspaces, Chapter 1, Pre-requisites to Success: ADF Project Setup and Foundations* and in *Overriding remove() to delete associated children entities, Chapter 2, Dealing with Basics: Entity Objects* respectively.

Both the `HRComponents` and `MainApplication` workspaces require database connections to the `HR` schema.

How to do it...

1. Open the `MainApplication` workspace and ensure that both the `SharedComponents` and the `HRComponents` workspaces are added to the ViewController project.

2. Create a JSP XML page called `queryListener.jspx` using one of the quick start layouts.

3. Locate the `EmployeesCriteria` named **criteria** under the **HrComponentsAppModuleDataControl | Employees** collection in the **Data Controls** section of the **Application Navigator**, and drop it on the page. Select **Query | ADF Query Panel with Table...** from the **Create** menu when asked.

4. With the **af:query** component selected in the **Structure** window, select **Edit...** from the **Property Menu** next to the **QueryListener** and create a new custom query listener method called `queryListener`. Create a new managed bean as well.

5. Open the managed bean that implements the custom query listener and add the following code it:

```
// handle the presence of certain query criterion data
List criteria =
  queryEvent.getDescriptor()
  .getConjunctionCriterion().getCriterionList();
for (int i = 0; i < criteria.size(); i++) {
  AttributeCriterion criterion =
    (AttributeCriterion)criteria.get(i);
```

```
    // do some special processing when a particular
    // criterion was used
    if ("SomeCriterionName".equals(
      criterion.getAttribute().getName()) &&
      criterion.getValues().get(0) != null) {
      // do something, for instance a rollback
      ADFUtils.findOperation("Rollback").execute();
      break;
    }
  }
  // invoke default processQuery query listener
  JSFUtils.invokeMethodExpression(
    "#{bindings.EmployeesCriteriaQuery.processQuery}",
    Object.class, QueryEvent.class, queryEvent);
  // display an information message indicating the
  // number of rows found
  long rowsFound = ADFUtils.findIterator("EmployeesIterator")
    .getEstimatedRowCount();
  FacesContext.getCurrentInstance().addMessage("",
    new FacesMessage(FacesMessage.SEVERITY_INFO,
    "Total Rows Found: " + rowsFound + "", null));
```

How it works...

In step 1, we added both the SharedComponents and HRComponents ADF Library JARs to the ViewController project of our application. This can be done either through the **Resource Palette** or via the **Project Properties | Libraries and Classpath** dialog settings.

In steps 2 and 3, we created a JSF page and dropped the EmployeesCriteria named criteria, defined in the Employees view object, as an **ADF Query Panel with Table** to the page. The Employees view object is part of the HrComponentsAppModule, that in turn is part of the HRComponents workspace imported as an ADF Library JAR in step 1. Once this JAR is imported to our project, the HrComponentsAppModule application module is available in the **Data Controls** section of the **Application Navigator**. Dropping the EmployeesCriteria named **criteria** on the page automatically creates the af:query and af:table components on the page, along with the underlying binding objects in the page definition file.

In steps 4 and 5, we created a custom query listener to be executed by the af:query component when performing the search. We did this declaratively through the **Property Inspector** that also allows us to create and configure a new managed bean, if needed. We simply called our custom query listener queryListener and added the necessary code to perform the search in step 4.

The code in the custom query listener `queryListener()` starts by demonstrating how to access the underlying `af:query` component's criteria. In the code, we iterate over the criteria looking for a specific criterion called `SomeCriterionName`. Once we find the specific criterion, we check whether a value is supplied for it and if so, we perform some action specific to our business domain. The criteria are obtained by calling `getCriterionList()` on the `oracle.adf.view.rich.model.ConjunctionCriterion` object, which is obtained by calling `getConjunctionCriterion()` on the `oracle.adf.view.rich.model.QueryDescriptor`. The `QueryDescriptor` is obtained from the event `QueryEvent` passed by the ADF framework to the query listener. The `getCriterionList()` method returns a `java.util.List` of `AttributeCriterion`, which we iterate over to check for the presence of the specific `SomeCriterionName` criterion. The `AttributeCriterion` indicates a query criterion. We can then call its `getValues()` method to retrieve the values supplied for the specific criterion.

To actually perform the search, we invoke the default `processQuery` method supplied by the framework via the expression `#{bindings.EmployeesCriteriaQuery.processQuery}`. This is done using the `JSFUtils` helper class method `invokeMethodExpression()`. The `JSFUtils` helper class was introduced in *Using ADFUtils/JSFUtils, Chapter 1, Pre-requisites to Success: ADF Project Setup and Foundations*. We added the `invokeMethodExpression()` method to the `JSFUtils` class in the *Using a custom af:table selection listener* recipe in this chapter.

Finally, we retrieved the rows obtained after performing the search by calling `getEstimatedRowCount()` on the `Employees` iterator and displayed a message indicating the number of records yielded by the search.

There's more...

The `ConjunctionCriterion` object represents the collection of the search fields for a `QueryDescriptor` object. It contains one or more `oracle.adf.view.rich.model.Criterion` objects, and possibly other `ConjunctionCriterion` objects, combined using a conjunction operator.

For more information regarding the `af:query` UI artifacts and the associated `af:query` model class operations and properties, consult the section *Creating the Query Data Model* in the *Web User Interface Developer's Guide for Oracle Application Development Framework*, which can be found at `http://docs.oracle.com/cd/E24382_01/web.1112/e16181/toc.htm`.

▸ *Using ADFUtils/JSFUtils, Chapter 1, Pre-requisites to Success: ADF Project Setup and Foundations*

▸ *Breaking up the application in multiple workspaces, Chapter 1, Pre-requisites to Success: ADF Project Setup and Foundations*

▸ *Overriding remove() to delete associated children entities, Chapter 2, Dealing with Basics: Entity Objects*

Using a custom af:query operation listener to clear both the query criteria and results

In the *Using a custom af:query listener to allow execution of a custom application module operation* recipe in this chapter, we demonstrated how to create your own custom query listener in order to handle the af:query component's search functionality yourself. In this recipe, we will show how to provide a custom reset operation functionality for the af:query component.

The default reset functionality implemented by the ADF framework resets the af:query component by clearing the criteria values, but does not clear the results of the associated af:table component that the framework creates when we drop some named criteria on the page. This reset functionality is indicated by the queryOperationListener attribute of the af:query component, and it is implemented by default by the framework processQueryOperation() method referenced by the searchRegion binding associated with the af:query component. It is indicated by the following expression: #{bindings. SomeQuery.processQueryOperation}. The processQueryOperation() method is used to handle all of the af:query component's operations such as RESET, CREATE, UPDATE, DELETE, MODE_CHANGE, and so on. These operations are defined by the ADF framework in the inner Operation class of the oracle.adf.view.rich.event. QueryOperationEvent class.

In this recipe, we will implement a custom queryOperationListener that will reset both the af:query and the af:table components used in conjunction in the same page to provide search functionality.

Getting ready

This recipe relies on having completed the *Using a custom af:query listener to allow execution of a custom application module operation* recipe in this chapter.

The recipe also uses the `SharedComponents` and `HRComponents` workspaces, which were created in *Breaking up the application in multiple workspaces, Chapter 1, Pre-requisites to Success: ADF Project Setup and Foundations* and in *Overriding remove() to delete associated children entities, Chapter 2, Dealing with Basics: Entity Objects* respectively.

Both the `HRComponents` and `MainApplication` workspaces require database connections to the `HR` schema.

How to do it...

1. Open the `SharedComponents` workspace and locate the `ExtApplicationModuleImpl.java` custom application module extension class. Add the following `resetCriteria()` method to it:

```java
public void resetCriteriaValues(ViewCriteria vc) {
  // reset automatic execution
  vc.setProperty(ViewCriteriaHints.CRITERIA_AUTO_EXECUTE,
    false);
  // reset view criteria variables
  VariableValueManager vvm = vc.ensureVariableManager();
  Variable[] variables = vvm.getVariables();
  for (Variable variable : variables) {
    vvm.setVariableValue(variable, null);
  }
  // reset view criteria
  vc.resetCriteria();
  vc.saveState();
}
```

2. Redeploy the `SharedComponents` workspace to an ADF Library JAR.

3. Open the `HRComponents` workspace and locate the `HrComponentsAppModuleImpl.java` application module implementation class. Add the following `resetEmployees()` method to it:

```java
public void resetEmployees() {
  EmployeesImpl employees = this.getEmployees();
  ViewCriteria vc = employees.getViewCriteria(
    "EmployeesCriteria");
  // reset view criteria
  super.resetCriteriaValues(vc);
```

```
employees.removeViewCriteria("EmployeesCriteria");
employees.applyViewCriteria(vc);
// reset Employees view object
employees.executeEmptyRowSet();
}
```

4. Add the `resetEmployees()` method to the application module client interface and redeploy the `HRComponents` workspace to an ADF Library JAR.

5. Open the `MainApplication` workspace. Double-click on the `queryListener.jspx` page in the **Application Navigator** to open the page in the page editor.

6. Click on the **Bindings** tab. Add a `methodAction` binding for the `resetEmployees()` operation under the `HrComponentsAppModuleDataControl` data control.

7. With the **af:query** component selected in the **Structure** window, select **Edit...** from the **Property Menu** next to the **QueryOperationListener** property in the **Property Inspector**.

8. In the **Edit Property: QueryOperationListener** dialog, select the `QueryListenerBean` and create a new method called `queryOperationListener`.

9. Open the `QueryListenerBean.java` in the Java editor and add the following code to the `queryOperationListener()` method:

```
// handle RESET operation only
if (QueryOperationEvent.Operation.RESET.name()
  .equalsIgnoreCase(queryOperationEvent.getOperation()
  .name())) {
  // execute custom reset
  ADFUtils.findOperation("resetEmployees").execute();
} else {
  // default framework handling for all other
  // af:query operations
  JSFUtils.invokeMethodExpression(
    "#{bindings.EmployeesCriteriaQuery.processQueryOperation}",
    Object.class, QueryOperationEvent.class,
    queryOperationEvent);
}
```

10. Finally, ensure that a partial trigger is added to the `af:table` component for the `af:query` component. You can do this using the **Property Menu** next to the **PartialTriggers** property in the `af:table` **Property Inspector**.

How it works...

In step 1, we added the `resetCriteriaValues()` method to the
`ExtApplicationModuleImpl` custom application module extension class. This method
becomes available to all derived application module classes, and is used to reset the
specific named criteria values. The method accepts the `ViewCriteria` to reset, and
iterates over the criteria variables obtained from the criteria `VariableValueManager`
by calling `getVariables()`. For each variable, we call `setVariableValue()` on
the `VariableValueManager` specifying the variable and a `null` value. We also call
`resetCriteria()` to restore the criteria to the latest saved state, and `saveState()` to
save the current state. We proceed to step 2 with redeploying the `SharedComponents`
workspace to an ADF Library JAR.

In step 3, we added a method called `resetEmployees()` to the `HrComponentsAppModule`
application module implementation class, which is used to reset the `EmployeesCriteria`
named criteria defined for the `Employees` view object. In this method, we obtain the
criteria by calling `getViewCriteria()` on the `Employees` view object and then call
the `resetCriteriaValues()` method implemented in step 1 to reset the criteria
variables. Then, we reapply the criteria to the `Employees` view object by first calling
`removeViewCriteria()` and subsequently calling `applyViewCriteria()`. We also call
`executeEmptyRowSet()` to empty the `Employees` view object result set. This will, in effect
reset the `af:table` component on the page to display no records. In step 4, we added the
`resetEmployees()` to the application module client interface, so that it can be bound to
and invoked by the ViewController layer. We also redeployed the `HRComponents` workspace to
an ADF Library JAR.

In steps 5 and 6, we added a method action binding for the `resetEmployees()` method
implemented in step 3. We will call this method to reset the criteria and the `Employees` view
object rowset in step 9 from a custom query operation listener.

In steps 7 and 8, we defined a custom query operation listener, called
`queryOperationListener()` for the `af:query` component defined in the
`queryListener.jspx` page. This page was created in the *Using a custom af:query listener
to allow execution of a custom application module operation* recipe in this chapter.

In step 9, we wrote the necessary Java code to implement the custom query operation
listener. First, we checked for the specific operation to ensure that we are dealing with a reset
operation. We did this by retrieving the query operation from the `QueryOperationEvent`
by calling `getOperation()` on it, and comparing it to the `QueryOperationEvent.
Operation.RESET` operation. For a reset operation, we proceeded with executing the
`resetEmployees` operation binding. Calling `resetEmployees` will reset both the
`af:query` and `af:table` components. For all other `af:query` operations, we executed
the default framework `processQueryOperation()` method by invoking the expression
`#{bindings.EmployeesCriteriaQuery.processQueryOperation}`. This is done by
calling the `JSFUtils` helper class `invokeMethodExpression()` method.

To ensure that the table will be visually updated by the custom reset operation, we added a partial trigger to the `af:table` component by indicating the `af:query` component identifier in its `partialTriggers` property.

There's more...

If you are writing a generic query operation listener and the presence of the `reset` operation binding cannot be guaranteed, use the `QueryModel.reset()` method to reset the `af:query` component only. The `reset()` method in this case is called for all system saved searches as it is shown in the code snippet:

```
try {
    // execute custom reset
    OperationBinding op = ADFUtils.findOperation("reset");
    op.execute();
} catch (RuntimeException e) {
    // just reset the af:query component only
    QueryModel queryModel = ((RichQuery)queryOperationEvent
                            .getSource()).getModel();
    for (int i = 0; i < queryModel.getSystemQueries().size();
                                    i++) {
        queryModel.reset(
            queryModel.getSystemQueries().get(i));
    }
}
```

See also

▸ *Breaking up the application in multiple workspaces, Chapter 1, Pre-requisites to Success: ADF Project Setup and Foundations*

▸ *Overriding remove() to delete associated children entities, Chapter 2, Dealing with Basics: Entity Objects*

▸ *Using a custom af:query listener to allow execution of a custom application module operation* recipe in this chapter

Using a session scope bean to preserve session-wide information

Information stored in the DBMS can be preserved for the duration of the user session by utilizing ADF business components to retrieve it, and a session scope managed bean to preserve it throughout the user session. Using this technique allows us to access session-wide information from any page in our application, without the need to create specific bindings for it in each page.

This recipe demonstrates how to access and preserve session-wide information by implementing the following use case. For each employee authenticated to access the application, its specific information will be maintained by a session-scoped managed bean.

Getting ready

You will need to create a skeleton **Fusion Web Application (ADF)** workspace before you proceed with this recipe. For this, we will use the `MainApplication` workspace that was developed in *Breaking up the application in multiple workspaces, Chapter 1, Pre-requisites to Success: ADF Project Setup and Foundations*.

The recipe also uses the `SharedComponents` and `HRComponents` workspaces, which were created in *Breaking up the application in multiple workspaces Chapter 1, Pre-requisites to Success: ADF Project Setup and Foundations* and in *Overriding remove() to delete associated children entities, Chapter 2, Dealing with Basics: Entity Objects* respectively.

Both the `HRComponents` and `MainApplication` workspaces require database connections to the `HR` schema.

The recipe assumes that ADF security has been enabled for the application and specific users matching the employee's last name have been added to the `jazn-data.xml` file. For information on how to enable ADF security take a look at *Enabling ADF security, Chapter 9, Handling Security, Session Timeouts, Exceptions, and Errors*.

How to do it...

1. Open the `HRComponents` workspace. Create a view object called `UserInfo` based on the `Employees` entity object.

2. Update the `UserInfo` view object query by adding the following `WHERE` clause to its query: `Employee.LAST_NAME = :inEmployeeName`.

3. Add a bind variable called `inEmployeeName`. Ensure that the **Value Type** is set to **Expression** and use the following Groovy expression in the **Value** field to initialize it: `adf.context.securityContext.userName`.

4. Ensure that you create both view object and view row Java classes.

5. Create an application module called `UserInfoAppModule` and add the `UserInfo` view object to its data model.

6. Generate an application module implementation class, and add the following methods to it. Also add these methods to the application module client interface.

```
public String getFirstName() {
   String firstName = null;
   UserInfoImpl usersInfo = (UserInfoImpl)getUserInfo();
   try {
     usersInfo.executeQuery();
     UserInfoRowImpl userInfo =
       (UserInfoRowImpl)usersInfo.first();
     if (userInfo != null) {
       firstName = userInfo.getFirstName ();
     }
   } catch (SQLStmtException sqlStmtException) {
     // handle exception
   }
   return firstName;
}
public String getLastName() {
   String lastName = null;
   UserInfoImpl usersInfo = (UserInfoImpl)getUserInfo();
   try {
     usersInfo.executeQuery();
     UserInfoRowImpl userInfo =
       (UserInfoRowImpl)usersInfo.first();
     if (userInfo != null) {
       lastName = userInfo.getLastName();
     }
   } catch (SQLStmtException sqlStmtException) {
     // handle exception
   }
   return lastName;
}
```

7. Redeploy the `HRComponents` workspace to an ADF Library JAR.

8. Open the `MainApplication` workspace and add both the `HRComponents` and the `SharedComponents` ADF Library JARs to the ViewController project.

9. Create a managed bean called `SessionInfoBean`. Make sure that the managed bean's scope is set to `session`. Also generate the managed bean class.

10. Open the `SessionInfoBean.java` class in the Java editor, and add the following code to it:

```java
private String.firstName;
private String lastName;
public SessionInfoBean() {
}
public String getFirstName() {
  if (firstName == null) {
    UserInfoAppModule userInfoAppModule =
      (UserInfoAppModule)ADFUtils
      .getApplicationModuleForDataControl(
      "UserInfoAppModuleDataControl");
    firstName = userInfoAppModule.getFirstName();
  }
  return firstName;
}
public String getLastName() {
  if (lastName == null) {
    UserInfoAppModule userInfoAppModule =
      (UserInfoAppModule)ADFUtils
      .getApplicationModuleForDataControl
      ("UserInfoAppModuleDataControl");
    lastName = userInfoAppModule.getLastName();
  }
  return lastName;
}
```

How it works...

In steps 1 through 4, we created a new view object called `UserInfo` based on the `Employees` entity object. Assuming that each employee will be authenticated to access our application using the employee's last name, we will use the information available in the `EMPLOYEES` database table to provide information specific to the employee currently authenticated. In order to retrieve information specific to the authenticated employee, we updated the `UserInfo` view object query by adding a `WHERE` clause to retrieve the specific employee based on a bind variable (in step 2). In step 3, we created the bind variable and used the Groovy expression `adf.context.securityContext.userName` to initialize it. This expression retrieves the authenticated user's name from the `SecurityContext` and uses it to query the specific employee.

In steps 5 and 6, we created an application module called `UserInfoAppModule`, and added the `UserInfo` view object to its data model and methods to retrieve the authenticated user's information. For this recipe, we added the methods `getFirstName()` and `getLastName()` to retrieve the user's first and last name respectively. These methods execute the `UserInfo` view object and retrieve the first row from the result set. In each case, the specific information is received by calling the corresponding `UserInfo` view row implementation class getter, that is, `getFirstName()` and `getLastName()`. Other methods can be added to retrieve additional user information based on your specific business requirements. In step 5, we also exposed these methods to the application module client interface, so that the methods can be bound and invoked from the ViewController layer.

In step 7, we redeployed the `HRComponents` workspace to an ADF Library JAR. Then, in step 8, we added the `HRComponents` along with the dependent `SharedComponents` ADF Library JARs to the `MainApplication`'s ViewController project.

Finally, in steps 9 and 10, we added a session-scoped managed bean, called `SessionInfoBean`, to the `MainApplication` ViewController project and implemented methods `getFirstName()` and `getLastName()` to retrieve the authenticated user's information. These methods call the corresponding `getFirstName()` and `getLastName()` implemented by the `UserInfoAppModule` application module in step 6. We got a reference to the `UserInfoAppModule` application module in the `SessionInfoBean` constructor by calling the `ADFUtils` helper class `getApplicationModuleForDataControl()` method. The `ADFUtils` helper class was introduced in *Using ADFUtils/JSFUtils, Chapter 1, Pre-requisites to Success: ADF Project Setup and Foundations*.

Now, we can use the following expressions on any page of our application to display the authenticated user's information:

Authenticated user's information	Expression
First Name	`#{SessionInfoBean.firstName}`
Last Name	`#{SessionInfoBean.lastName}`

See also

- *Breaking up the application in multiple workspaces, Chapter 1, Pre-requisites to Success: ADF Project Setup and Foundations*
- *Overriding remove() to delete associated children entities, Chapter 2, Handling Security, Session Timeouts, Exceptions and Errors*

Using an af:popup during long running tasks

For long-running tasks in your application, a pop-up message window can be raised to alert the users that the specific task may take a while. This can be accomplished using a combination of ADF Faces components (`af:popup` and `af:dialog`) and some JavaScript code.

In this recipe, we will initiate a long-running task in a managed bean, and raise a pop-up for the duration of the task to alert us to the fact that this operation may take awhile. We will hide the pop-up once the task completes.

Getting ready

You will need to create a skeleton **Fusion Web Application (ADF)** workspace before you proceed with this recipe. For this, we will use the `MainApplication` workspace that was developed in *Breaking up the application in multiple workspaces, Chapter 1, Pre-requisites to Success: ADF Project Setup and Foundations*.

How to do it...

1. Open the `MainApplication` workspace and create a new JSPX page called `longRunningTask.jspx` based on any of the quick start layouts.

2. Drop a **Button** (`af:commandButton`) component from the **Component Palette** to the page. You may need to surround the button with an `af:toolbar` component. Using the **Property Inspector**, change the button's **Text** property to **Long Running Task** and set its **PartialSubmit** property to **true**.

3. Create an action listener for the button by selecting **Edit...** from the **Property Menu** next to the **ActionListener** property in the **Property Inspector**. Create a new managed bean called `LongRunningTaskBean` and a new method called `longRunningTask`.

4. Edit the `LongRunningTaskBean` Java class and add the following code to the `longRunningTask()` method:

    ```
    try {
        // wait for 5 seconds
        Thread.currentThread().sleep(5000);
        } catch (InterruptedException e) {
    }
    ```

5. Return to the `longRunningTask.jspx` page editor. Right-click on the **af:commandButton** in the **Structure** window and select **Insert Inside af:commandButton | ADF Faces...**. From the **Insert ADF Faces Item** dialog, select **Client Listener**. In the **Insert Client Listener** dialog, enter `longRunningTask` for the **Method** field and select **action** for the **Type** field.

6. Add an `af:resource` to the `af:document` tag. Make sure that the `af:resource` `type` attribute is set to `javascript` and add the following JavaScript code inside it:

```
function longRunningTask(evt) {
    var popup = AdfPage.PAGE.findComponentByAbsoluteId(
      'longRunningPopup');
    if (popup != null) {
      AdfPage.PAGE.addBusyStateListener(popup,
        busyStateListener);
      evt.preventUserInput();
    }
}
function busyStateListener(evt) {
    var popup = AdfPage.PAGE.findComponentByAbsoluteId(
      'longRunningPopup');
    if (popup != null) {
      if (evt.isBusy()) {
        popup.show();
      }
      else if (popup.isPopupVisible()) {
        popup.hide();
        AdfPage.PAGE.removeBusyStateListener(popup,
          busyStateListener);
      }
    }
}
```

7. Finally, add a Popup (`af:popup`) ADF Faces component to the page with an embedded Dialog (`af:dialog`) component in it. Ensure that the pop-up identifier is set to `longRunningPopup` and that its `ContentDelivery` attribute is set to `immediate`. Also add an `af:outputText` component to the dialog with some text indicating a long running process. Your pop-up should look similar to the following:

```
<af:popup childCreation="deferred" autoCancel="disabled"
  id="longRunningPopup" contentDelivery="immediate">
<af:dialog id="d2" closeIconVisible="false" type="none"
  title="Information">
<af:outputText value="Long operation in progress... Please
  wait..." id="ot1"/>
</af:dialog>
</af:popup>
```

How it works...

In steps 1 and 2, we created a JSF page called `longRunningTask.jspx` and added a button component to it. When pressed, the button will initiate a long-running task through an action listener. The action listener is added to the button in steps 3 and 4. It is defined to a method called `longRunningTask()` in a managed bean. The implementation of `longRunningTask()` simply waits for 5 seconds (step 4). We have also ensured (in step 2) that the button component's `partialSubmit` property is set to `true`. This will enable us to call the `clientListener` method that is added in steps 5 and 6.

In steps 5 and 6, we defined a `clientListener` for the button component. The client listener is implemented by the `longRunningTask()` JavaScript method, added to the page in step 6. The `longRunningTask()` JavaScript method adds a busy state listener for the pop-up component (the pop-up itself is added to the page in step 7) by calling `addBusyStateListener()` and prevents any user input by calling `preventUserInput()` on the JavaScript event. The busy state listener is implemented by the JavaScript method `busyStateListener()`. In it, we hide the pop-up and remove the busy state listener once the event completes.

Finally, in step 7, we added the `longRunningPopup` pop-up to the page. The pop-up is raised by the `busyStateListener()` as long as the event is busy (for 5 seconds). We made sure that the pop-up's `contentDelivery` attribute was set to `immediate` to deliver the pop-up content immediately once the page is loaded.

To test the recipe, right-click on the `longRunningTask.jspx` page in the **Application Navigator** and select **Run** or **Debug** from the context menu. When you click on the button, the pop-up is raised for the duration of the long-running task (the action listener in the managed bean). The pop-up is hidden once the long-running task completes.

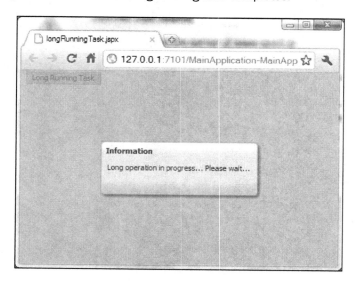

- ▸ *Breaking up the application in multiple workspaces, Chapter 1, Pre-requisites to Success: ADF Project Setup and Foundations*

Using an af:popup to handle pending changes

In the recipe *Determining whether the current transaction has pending changes* in this chapter, we showed how to establish whether there are uncommitted pending changes to the current transaction. In this recipe, we will use the functionality implemented in that recipe to provide a generic way to handle any pending uncommitted transaction changes. Specifically, we will update the CommonActions framework introduced in *Using a generic backing bean actions framework, Chapter 1, Pre-requisites to Success: ADF Project Setup and Foundations* to raise a pop-up message window asking you whether you want to commit the changes. We will add the pop-up window to the TemplateDef1 page template definition that we created in *Using page templates, Chapter 1, Pre-requisites to Success: ADF Project Setup and Foundations*.

Getting ready

We will modify the TemplateDef1 page template definition and the CommonActions actions framework. Both reside in the Sharedcomponents workspace, which is deployed as an ADF Library JAR and it was introduced in *Breaking up the application in multiple workspaces, Chapter 1, Pre-requisites to Success: ADF Project Setup and Foundations*.

Furthermore, we will utilize the HRComponents workspace, also deployed as an ADF Library JAR. This workspace was introduced in *Overriding remove() to delete associated children entities, Chapter 2, Dealing with Basics: Entity Objects*.

Finally, you will need to create a skeleton **Fusion Web Application (ADF)** workspace before you proceed with the recipe. For this, you can use the MainApplication workspace introduced in *Breaking up the application in multiple workspaces, Chapter 1, Pre-requisites to Success: ADF Project Setup and Foundations*.

Both the HRComponents and MainApplication workspaces require database connections to the HR schema.

How to do it...

1. Open the `SharedComponents` workspace, locate the `TemplateDef1` page template definition and open it in the page editor.

2. Add a Popup (`af:popup`) component to the page. Set the pop-up identifier to `CreatePendingChanges`. Add an embedded Dialog (`af:dialog`) component to the pop-up and set its **Title** attribute to **Confirm Pending Changes**.

3. Add an Output Text (`af:outputText`) component to the dialog and set its **Value** attribute to **Pending changes exist. Do you want to save changes?** Also add a Button (`af:commandButton`) component to the dialog and set its `ActionListener` property to `#{CommonActionsBean.onContinueCreate}`. The `CreatePendingChanges` dialog definition should look similar to the following:

```
<af:popup id="CreatePendingChanges">
<af:dialog id="pt_d2" title="Confirm Pending Changes"
  type="cancel">
<af:outputText value=
  "Pending changes exist. Do you want to save changes?"
  id="pt_ot2"/>
<f:facet name="buttonBar">
<af:commandButton id=
  "continuePendingChangesButton" text="Continue"
  binding=
  "#{CommonActionsBean.onContinueCreate}"/>
</f:facet>
</af:dialog>
</af:popup>
```

4. Open the `CommonActions` Java class in the Java editor and add the following methods to it:

```
public void create(final ActionEvent actionEvent) {
  if (ADFUtils.hasChanges()) {
    onCreatePendingChanges(actionEvent);
  } else {
    onContinueCreate(actionEvent);
  }
}
public void onCreatePendingChanges(
  final ActionEvent actionEvent) {
  ADFUtils.showPopup("CreatePendingChanges");
}
public void onContinueCreate(final ActionEvent actionEvent) {
  CommonActions actions = getCommonActions();
  actions.onBeforeCreate(actionEvent);
  actions.onCreate(actionEvent);
```

```
    actions.onAfterCreate(actionEvent);
  }
  protected void onBeforeCreate(final ActionEvent actionEvent) {
    // commit before creating a new record
    ADFUtils.execOperation(Operations.COMMIT);
  }
  public void onCreate(final ActionEvent actionEvent) {
    ADFUtils.execOperation(Operations.INSERT);
  }
  protected void onAfterCreate(final ActionEvent actionEvent) {
  }
```

5. Redeploy the `SharedComponents` workspace into an ADF Library JAR.

6. Open the main workspace application and ensure that both the `SharedComponents` and the `HRComponents` ADF Library JARs are added to the ViewController project.

7. Create a JSPX page called `pendingChanges.jspx` based on the `TemplatedDef1` template. Ensure that the `af:pageTemplate` component identifier in the page is set to `generic`.

8. Expand the **Data Controls** section of the **Application Navigator** and drop the `Employees` collection under the `HrComponentsAppModuleDataControl` to the page as an **ADF Form**.

9. Expand the **Operations** node under the `Employees` collection and drop a **CreateInsert** operation as an **ADF Button** to the page. Change the **CreateInsert** button's `ActionListener` property to the `CommonActions` framework `create()` method. The `ActionListener` expression should be `#{CommonActionsBean.create}`.

10. Switch to the page bindings and add an action binding for the `HrComponentsAppModuleDataControl` **Commit** operation.

How it works...

In steps 1 through 3, we added an `af:popup` component called `CreatePendingChanges` to the `TemplateDef1` page template definition. This is the popup that will be raised by the `CommonActions` framework if there are any unsaved transaction changes when we attempt to create a new record. This is done by the `CommonActions onCreatePendingChanges()` method (see step 4). Note that in step 3, we added a **Continue** button, which when pressed, saves the uncommitted changes. This is done through the button's action listener implemented by the `onContinueCreate()` method in the `CommonActions` framework (see step 4). If we press **Cancel**, the uncommitted changes are not saved (are still pending) and the creation of the new row is never initiated.

In step 4, we updated the `CommonActions` framework by adding the methods to handle the creation of a new row. Specifically, the following methods were added:

- ▶ `create()`: This method calls the `ADFUtils` helper class method `hasChanges()` to determine whether there are uncommitted transaction changes. If it finds any, it calls `onCreatePendingChanges()` to handle them. Otherwise, it calls `onContinueCreate()` to continue with the row creation action.

- ▶ `onCreatePendingChanges()`: The default implementation displays the `CreatePendingChanges` pop-up.

- ▶ `onContinueCreate()`: Called either directly from `create()`—if there are no pending changes—or from the `CreatePendingChanges` pop-up upon pressing the **Continue** button. Implements the actual row creation by calling the methods `onBeforeCreate()`, `onCreate()`, and `onAfterCreate()`.

- ▶ `onBeforeCreate()`: Called to handle any actions prior to the creation of the new row. The default implementation invokes the `Commit` action binding.

- ▶ `onCreate()`: Called to handle the creation of the new row. The default implementation invokes the `CreateInsert` action binding.

- ▶ `onAfterCreate()`: Called to handle any post creation actions. The default implementation does nothing.

In step 5, we redeploy the `SharedComponents` workspace to an ADF Library JAR. Then, in step 6, we add it along with the `HRComponents` ADF Library JAR to the `MainApplication`'s ViewController workspace.

In step 6, we created a JSPX page called `pendingChanges.jspx` based on the `TemplatedDef1` template. We made sure that the template identifier was set to `generic`, the same as the identifier of the `af:pageTemplateDef` component in the `TemplatedDef1` template definition. This is necessary because the code in the `ADFUtils.showPopup()` helper method, which is used to raise a pop-up, prepends the pop-up identifier with the template identifier.

In step 8, we created an ADF Form by dropping the `Employees` collection to the page. The `Employees` collection is part of the `HrComponentsAppModuleDataControl` data control, which is available once the `HRComponents` ADF Library JAR is added to the project.

Then, in step 9, we dropped the `CreateInsert` operation, available under the `Employees` collection, as an ADF Button to the page. Furthermore, we changed its `actionListener` property to the `CommonActions create()` method. This will handle the creation of the new row in a generic way and it will raise the pending changes pop-up, if there are any unsaved transaction changes.

Finally, in step 10, we added an action binding for the `Commit` operation. This is invoked by the `CommonActions onBeforeCreate()` method to commit any transaction pending changes.

The functionality to raise a pop-up message window indicating that there are pending unsaved transaction changes and committing the changes—as it is implemented in this recipe—applies specifically to the new row creation action. Similar functionality will need to be added for the other actions in your application, for instance, navigating to the next, previous, first, and last row in a collection.

See also

▶ _Determining whether the current transaction has pending changes_, in this chapter.

▶ _Using page templates, Chapter 1, Pre-requisites to Success: ADF Project Setup and Foundations_

▶ _Using a generic backing bean actions framework, Chapter 1, Pre-requisites to Success: ADF Project Setup and Foundations_

▶ _Breaking up the application in multiple workspaces, Chapter 1, Pre-requisites to Success: ADF Project Setup and Foundations_

Using an af:iterator to add pagination support to a collection

A collection in an ADF Fusion web application, when dropped from the **Data Controls** window to a JSF page as an ADF Table, may be iterated through using the `af:table` ADF Faces component. Alternatively, when dropped as an ADF Form, it may be iterated a row at a time using the accompanying form buttons which can optionally be created by JDeveloper.

In this recipe, we will show how to add pagination support to a collection by utilizing the iterator (`af:iterator`) ADF Faces component along with the necessary scrolling support provided by a managed bean.

Getting ready

You will need to create a skeleton **Fusion Web Application (ADF)** workspace before you proceed with this recipe. For this, we will use the `MainApplication` workspace that was developed in _Breaking up the application in multiple workspaces, Chapter 1, Pre-requisites to Success: ADF Project Setup and Foundations_.

The recipe also uses the `HRComponents` workspace, which was created in _Overriding remove() to delete associated children entities, Chapter 2, Dealing with Basics: Entity Objects_.

Both the `HRComponents` and `MainApplication` workspaces require database connections to the `HR` schema.

How to do it...

1. Open the main workspace application. Ensure that the HRComponents ADF Library JAR is added to its ViewController project.

2. Create a new JSP XML page called collectionPagination.jspx based on a quick start layout.

3. Expand the **Data Controls** window, locate the Employees collection under the HrComponentsAppModuleDataControl and drop it on the page as an ADF Read-only Table.

4. Switch to the page bindings editor, and with the EmployeesIterator iterator selected in the **Executables** list, change its **RangeSize** property to the desired page size. We will use 3 for this recipe.

5. Using the **Component Palette**, locate an Iterator component and drop it to the page. Using the **Property Inspector**, update the af:iterator component Value, Var, and Rows properties as shown in the following code fragment:

```
<af:iterator id="i1"
   value="#{bindings.Employees.collectionModel}" var="row"
   rows="#{bindings.Employees.rangeSize}"/>
```

6. Using the **Property Inspector,** bind the af:iterator component to a newly created managed bean, called CollectionPaginationBean. Now the af:iterator definition should look similar to the following:

```
<af:iterator id="i1"
   value="#{bindings.Employees.collectionModel}" var="row"
   rows="#{bindings.Employees.rangeSize}"
   binding="#{CollectionPaginationBean.employeesIterator}"/>
```

7. Move the af:table column contents (the af:outputText components) inside the af:iterator component. Remove the af:table component when done.

8. Surround the af:iterator with a Panel Box (af:panelBox) component. Drop a Toolbar component inside the panel box's toolbar facet. Add four buttons to the toolbar called First, Previous, Next, and Last.

9. For each of the buttons, add the action listeners and the disabled conditions shown in the following code fragment:

```
<af:panelBox
   text="Page # #{CollectionPaginationBean.pageNumber}"
   id="pb2">
<f:facet name="toolbar">
<af:toolbar id="t1">
<af:commandButton text="First" id="cb1"
   actionListener="#{CollectionPaginationBean.onFirst}"
   disabled="#{CollectionPaginationBean.previousRowAvailable
   eq false}"/>
```

```
  <af:commandButton text="Previous" id="cb2"
    actionListener="#{CollectionPaginationBean.onPrevious}"
    disabled="#{CollectionPaginationBean.previousRowAvailable
    eq false}"/>
  <af:commandButton text="Next" id="cb3"
    actionListener="#{CollectionPaginationBean.onNext}"
    disabled="#{CollectionPaginationBean.nextRowAvailable
    eq false}"/>
  <af:commandButton text="Last" id="cb4"
    actionListener="#{CollectionPaginationBean.onLast}"
    disabled="#{CollectionPaginationBean.nextRowAvailable
      eq false}"/>
</af:toolbar>
</f:facet>
<af:iterator id="i1"
  value="#{bindings.Employees.collectionModel}" var="row"
  rows="#{bindings.Employees.rangeSize}"
  binding="#{CollectionPaginationBean.employeesIterator}">
```

10. Open the `CollectionPaginationBean` managed bean in the Java editor and add the following code to it:

```java
public void onFirst(ActionEvent actionEvent) {
  this.employeesIterator.setFirst(0);
}
public void onPrevious(ActionEvent actionEvent) {
  this.employeesIterator.setFirst(
  this.employeesIterator.getFirst() - PAGE_SIZE);
}
public void onNext(ActionEvent actionEvent) {
  this.employeesIterator.setFirst(
  this.employeesIterator.getFirst() + PAGE_SIZE);
}
public void onLast(ActionEvent actionEvent) {
  this.employeesIterator.setFirst(
  employeesIterator.getRowCount() -
  employeesIterator.getRowCount() % PAGE_SIZE);
}
public boolean isPreviousRowAvailable() {
  return this.employeesIterator.getFirst() != 0;
}
public boolean isNextRowAvailable() {
  return (employeesIterator.getRowCount() >=
  employeesIterator.getFirst() + PAGE_SIZE);
}
public int getPageNumber() {
  return (this.employeesIterator.getFirst()/PAGE_SIZE) + 1;
}
```

How it works...

In step 1, we ensure that the `HRComponents` ADF Library JAR is added to the ViewController project of the `MainApplication` workspace. We will be using this library in order to access the `Employees` collection available through the `HrComponentsAppModule`. The library can be added to the project either through the **Resource Palette** or via the **Project Properties | Libraries and Classpath** options.

We created a new JSF page called `collectionPagination.jspx` in step 2, and in step 3, dropped the `Employees` collection on the page as an ADF Read-only Table component (`af:table`). When we did this JDeveloper created the underlying iterator and tree bindings. Then, in step 4, we switched to the page bindings and change the `EmployeesIterator` range size to our desired value. Note that this page size is indicated in the managed bean created in step 6 by the constant definition `PAGE_SIZE` and set to 3 for this recipe.

In steps 5 through 7, we setup an iterator (`af:iterator`) component. First, we dropped the iterator component on the page from the **Component Palette** and then we updated its `value` property (in step 5) to indicate the `CollectionModel` of the `Employees` tree binding, created earlier when we dropped the `Employees` collection to the page as a table. In addition, in step 5, we updated its `rows` and `var` attributes so that we will be able to copy over the table column contents to the `af:iterator` component. We did this in step 7. In step 6, we also bound the `af:iterator` component to a newly created managed bean called `CollectionPaginationBean` as a `UIXIterator` variable called `employeesIterator`.

In steps 8 and 9, we added a navigation toolbar to the page along with buttons for scrolling through the `Employees` collection namely buttons First, Previous, Next, and Last. For each button, we added the appropriate action listener and disabled the condition methods implemented by the `CollectionPaginationBean` managed bean (implemented in step 10). For the complete page source code, refer to the book's relevant source code.

Finally, in step 10, we implemented the action listener and disabled the condition methods for the navigation buttons. These methods are explained as follows:

- `onFirst()`: Action listener for the First button. Uses the bound iterator's `setFirst()` method with an argument of 0 (the index of the first row) to set the iterator to the beginning of the collection.
- `onPrevious()`: Action listener for the Previous button. Sets the first row to the current value decreased by the page size. This will scroll the collection to the previous page.
- `onNext()`: Action listener for the Next button. Sets the first row to the current value increased by the page size. This will scroll the collection to the next page.
- `onLast()`: Action listener for the Last button. Sets the first row to the first row of the last page. We call the `getRowCount()` iterator method to determine the iterator's row count and subtract the last page's rows from it. This will scroll the collection to the first row of the last page.

- ▶ isPreviousRowAvailable(): Disable condition for the First and Previous buttons. Returns `true` if the iterator's row index is not the first one.

- ▶ isNextRowAvailable(): Disable condition for the Last and Next buttons. Returns `true` if there are available rows beyond the current page.

- ▶ getPageNumber(): It is used in the page to display the current page number.

To test the recipe, right-click on the `collectionPagination.jspx` in the **Application Navigator** and select **Run** or **Debug** from the context menu.

See also

- ▶ *Breaking up the application in multiple workspaces, Chapter 1, Pre-requisites to Success: ADF Project Setup and Foundations*

- ▶ *Overriding remove() to delete associated children entities, Chapter 2, Dealing with Basics: Entity Objects*

9
Handling Security, Session Timeouts, Exceptions, and Errors

In this chapter, we will cover:

- ▶ Enabling ADF security
- ▶ Using a custom login page
- ▶ Accessing the application's security information
- ▶ Using OPSS to retrieve the authenticated user's profile from the identity store
- ▶ Detecting and handling session timeouts
- ▶ Using a custom error handler to customize how exceptions are reported to the ViewController
- ▶ Customizing the error message details
- ▶ Overriding attribute validation exceptions

Introduction

The ADF security framework provides authentication and authorization services for the ADF Fusion web application. To a certain degree, this security framework is supported in JDeveloper through a number of wizards and overview editors (available via the **Application | Secure** menu options) that allow interactive declarative configuration of certain parts of the application's security configuration. The security overview editors simplify the work needed to secure the application by authorizing ADF resources in a declarative manner. This resource authorization is achieved at the task flow, page definition and business components (entity objects and their attributes) levels. Authorization defined for task flows protects not only the task flow's entry point but all the pages included in the task flow as view activities.

Configuring the application's session timeout can be done through a number of options in the application's deployment descriptor file `web.xml`.

Customization of error and exception handling for an ADF Fusion web application can be achieved by overriding certain framework classes and by creating your own exception classes.

Enabling ADF security

Enabling security for an ADF Fusion web application involves enabling both user authentication and authorization. Authentication refers to enabling users to access your application using a credentials validation login facility. On the other hand, authorization refers to controlling access to the application resources by defining and configuring security policies on ADF application resources, such as task flows, page definitions, and business components (entity objects and their attributes). ADF security is enabled for the Fusion web application through the use of the **Configure ADF Security** wizard available under the **Application | Secure** menu option. Moreover, JDeveloper provides additional declarative support through the `jazn-data.xml` security configuration overview editor, and through declarative security support at the business components level using the entity object overview editor (**General** and **Attributes** tabs).

In this recipe, we will go over the process of enabling security for an ADF Fusion web application by creating and configuring the necessary artifacts, such as login, error and welcome pages, redirection, user and role creation, and configuration using the **Configure ADF Security** wizard.

Getting ready

You will need to create a skeleton **Fusion Web Application (ADF)** workspace before you proceed with this recipe. For this, we will use the `MainApplication` workspace that was developed in *Breaking up the application in multiple workspaces, Chapter 1, Pre-requisites to Success: ADF Project Setup and Foundations*.

How to do it...

1. Open the `MainApplication` workspace. From the **Application** menu select **Secure | Configure ADF Security...** to start the **Configure ADF Security** wizard.

2. In the **Enable ADF** Security page, select **ADF Authentication and Authorization** and click **Next**.

3. In the **Select authentication type** page, select the appropriate ViewController project from the **Web Project** combo box. Select **Form-Based Authentication** and click on the **Generate Default Pages** checkbox. Click **Next** to proceed.

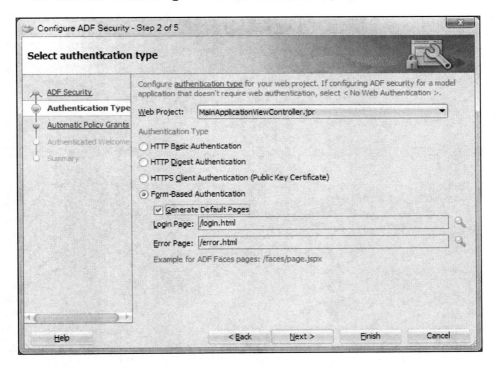

4. In the **Enable automatic policy grants** page, select **Grant to All Objects**. Click **Next** to proceed.

5. In the **Specify authenticated welcome** page, click on the **Redirect Upon Successful Authentication** checkbox and specify your main application page. You can click on the **Generate Default** checkbox to generate a default `welcome.jspx` page. Click **Next** to proceed. In the **Summary** page, review your selections and click **Finish** to complete the security configuration wizard.

6. Select **Users** from the **Application | Secure** menu to open the `jazn-data.xml` security configuration overview editor. With the **Users** tab selected, create a user called `user1` and assign to it the `test-all` role. Use `user1234` for the password.

7. Locate the `web.xml` deployment descriptor in the **Web Content | WEB-INF** folder in the **Application Navigator** and double-click on it to open it. Click on the **Source** tab. Change the `success_url` parameter value for the `adfAuthentication` servlet to `/faces/welcome.jspx`.

8. Add the following welcome file list to the `web.xml` deployment descriptor:

```
<welcome-file-list>
   <welcome-file>/faces/welcome.jspx</welcome-file>
</welcome-file-list>
```

9. Open the `welcome.jspx` page in the page editor and add a Button (`af:commandButton`) component. Change the button's `text` property to **Logout**. Using the property menu add an **Action** to a method called `logout` defined in a newly created managed bean called `AuthenticationBean`.

10. Open the `AuthenticationBean` managed bean in the Java editor and add the following code to the `logout()` method:

```
// create a dispatcher and forward to the login.html page
final String LOGOUT_URL =
   "/adfAuthentication?logout=true&end_url=login.html";
FacesContext ctx = FacesContext.getCurrentInstance();
HttpServletRequest request =
   (HttpServletRequest)ctx.getExternalContext().getRequest();
```

```
HttpServletResponse response =
  (HttpServletResponse)ctx.getExternalContext()
getResponse();
RequestDispatcher dispatcher =
  request.getRequestDispatcher(LOGOUT_URL);
try {
  dispatcher.forward(request, response);
} catch (Exception e) {
// log exception
}
ctx.responseComplete();
return null;
```

How it works...

To enable ADF security for our ADF Fusion web application, we have used the **Configure ADF Security** wizard, available in JDeveloper through the **Application | Secure | Configure ADF Security...** menu selection. Using the wizard will allow us to enable security in a declarative manner as it will create all related security artifacts, including a login page, an error page, redirection upon a successful authentication to a specific page (welcome.jspx in our case), a test-all application role assigned to all application task flows and securable pages, and configuration of the adfAuthentication servlet in web.xml. We started the ADF security configuration wizard in step 1.

In step 2, we choose to enable both ADF authentication and authorization. This option enables the ADF authentication servlet adfAuthentication to enforce access to the application through configured login and logout pages. The adfAuthentication servlet is added to web.xml deployment descriptor.

This also adds a security constraint for the adfAuthentication resource, a security role called valid-users to allow all users to access the adfAuthentication resource, and a filter mapping to web.xml.

The valid-users role is mapped in the weblogic.xml configuration file to an implicit group called users defined in WebLogic. WebLogic configures all authenticated users to be members of the users group. The following code snippet from weblogic.xml shows this role mapping:

```
<security-role-assignment>
  <role-name>valid-users</role-name>
  <principal-name>users</principal-name>
</security-role-assignment>
```

This step also configures authorization for the application, which is enforced through authorization checks on application resources based on configured application roles assigned to them and to authenticated users.

In step 3, we select the authentication type. In this case, we choose form-based authentication and let the wizard create default login and error pages. You could create your own login page using ADF Faces components and handle the authorization process yourself, as it is demonstrated in *Using a custom login page* in this chapter. The generated login page defines a form with the standard `j_security_check` action, which accepts the username and password as input and passes them to the `j_SecurityCheck` method within the container's security model. The wizard updates the `web.xml` file to indicate form-based authentication and identify the login and error pages as shown in the following code snippet:

```
<login-config>
  <auth-method>FORM</auth-method>
  <form-login-config>
    <form-login-page>/login.html</form-login-page>
    <form-error-page>/error.html</form-error-page>
  </form-login-config>
</login-config>
```

In step 4, by selecting **Enable automatic policy grants**, we allow the wizard to create a `test-all` application role and assign it to all application resources. This will allow us to create users with full access to the application resources once we assign the `test-all` role to them. At a later phase of the application development process, you should remove this role. Also, note that the `test-all` role is granted to anonymous users as well.

In step 5, we create a default welcome page that we will be redirected to upon a successful authentication. This option added the `success_url` initialization parameter to the `adfAuthentication` servlet. We have prepended the `welcome.jspx` page with `/faces/` (see step 7) since we will be adding ADF Faces components to it in step 9. Step 5 completes the security wizard. For a complete list of the files that are updated by the security wizard and their changes, consult the table *Files Updated for ADF Authentication and Authorization* in section *What Happens When You Enable ADF Security* of the *Fusion Developer's Guide for Oracle Application Development Framework*, which can be found at `http://docs.oracle.com/cd/E24382_01/web.1112/e16182/toc.htm`.

In step 6, we create a user called `user1`. We will use this user to test the recipe. We map the `test-all` application role to the user to allow access to all of the application resources.

We add a `welcome-file-list` configuration to the `web.xml` file indicating our `/faces/welcome.jspx` welcome page in step 8, so that we will be successfully redirected to the welcome page upon successful authentication. This will allow us to test the recipe by running the `login.html` page.

In step 9, we added a Button component to the welcome page to perform the application log out. Log out is done by defining an action called `logout` implemented by an `AuthenticationBean` managed bean. The `logout` action was implemented by the `logout()` method in step 10. The method creates a `RequestDispatcher` for the logout URL and calls its `forward()` method to redirect the request. The logout URL passes a `logout` parameter to the `adfAuthentication` servlet with the value `true` to indicate a logout action. It also specifies an `end_url` parameter to the `adfAuthentication` servlet with the `login.html` URL. This in effect logs us out of the application and redirects us back to the `login.html` page.

To test the recipe, right-click on the `login.html` page and go through the authorization process. You can log in using the `user1/user1234` credentials. Upon successful authorization, you will be forwarded to the `welcome.jspx` page. Click on the **Logout** button to log out from the application.

There's more...

Note that the Configure ADF Security wizard does not enable authorization for pages that are not associated with databound components, that is, they neither have associated page definition bindings and they are not associated with a specific task flow. In such cases, these pages appear in the **Resource Grants** section of the `jazn-data.xml` overview editor as unsecurable pages. The welcome page, `welcome.jspx` page in this recipe, is one such case. You can still enforce authorization checking in these cases by creating an empty page definition file for the page. This is done by right-clicking on the page and selecting **Go to Page Definition** from the context menu. In the **Confirm Create New Page Definition** dialog click on the **Yes** button to proceed with the creation of the page definition file.

For more information about enabling and configuring ADF security, consult chapter *Enabling ADF Security in a Fusion Web Application* in the *Fusion Developer's Guide for Oracle Application Development Framework*, which can be found at `http://docs.oracle.com/cd/E24382_01/web.1112/e16182/toc.htm`.

See also

- ▶ *Breaking up the application in multiple workspaces, Chapter 1, Pre-requisites to Success: ADF Project Setup and Foundations*
- ▶ *Using a custom login page, Chapter 9, Handling Security, Session Timeouts, Exceptions and Errors*

Using a custom login page

In the recipe *Enabling ADF security* in this chapter, we've seen how to enable ADF security for an ADF Fusion web application using the **Configure ADF Security** wizard (available in JDeveloper through the **Application | Secure** menu). In one of the steps, the wizard allows for the creation of a default login page that handles the user authorization process. For the specific step in that recipe, we have chosen to create a default login page.

In this recipe, we will create a custom login page utilizing ADF Faces components. Moreover, we will handle the user authentication ourselves using custom login authentication code implemented by the `AuthenticationBean` managed bean. This managed bean was introduced in the *Enabling ADF security* recipe in this chapter.

Getting ready

You need to complete the *Enabling ADF security* recipe in this chapter before you start working on this recipe. The *Enabling ADF security* recipe requires a skeleton **Fusion Web Application (ADF)** workspace. For this purpose, we will use the `MainApplication` workspace that was developed in *Breaking up the application in multiple workspaces, Chapter 1, Pre-requisites to Success: ADF Project Setup and Foundations*.

How to do it...

1. Open the `MainApplication` workspace in JDeveloper. Locate and open the `AuthenticationBean` managed bean in the Java editor. Add the following code to it:

```
private String username;
private String password;
public void setUsername(String username) {
  this.username = username.toLowerCase();
}
public String getUsername() {
  return this.username;
}
public void setPassword(String password) {
  this.password = password;
}
public String getPassword() {
  return this.password;
}
public String login() {
  final String WELCOME_URL =
    "/adfAuthentication?success_url=/faces/welcome.jspx";
```

```
      FacesContext ctx = FacesContext.getCurrentInstance();
      HttpServletRequest request =
        (HttpServletRequest)ctx.getExternalContext().getRequest();
      if (authenticate(request)) {
        HttpServletResponse response =
          (HttpServletResponse)ctx.getExternalContext().getResponse();
        RequestDispatcher dispatcher =
          request.getRequestDispatcher(WELCOME_URL);
        try {
          dispatcher.forward(request, response);
        } catch (Exception e) {
          reportLoginError(e.getMessage());
        }
        ctx.responseComplete();
      }
      return null;
    }
    private boolean authenticate(HttpServletRequest request) {
      String password = getPassword() == null ? "" : getPassword();
      CallbackHandler handler = new URLCallbackHandler(
        getUsername(), password.getBytes());
      boolean authenticated = false;
      try {
        Subject subject = Authentication.login(handler);
        ServletAuthentication.runAs(subject, request);
        ServletAuthentication.generateNewSessionID(request);
        authenticated = true;
      } catch (FailedLoginException failedLoginException) {
        reportLoginError("Wrong credentials specified.");
      } catch (LoginException loginException) {
        reportLoginError(loginException.getMessage());
      }
      return authenticated;
    }
    private void reportLoginError(String errorMessage) {
      FacesMessage fm = new FacesMessage(
      FacesMessage.SEVERITY_ERROR, null, errorMessage);
      FacesContext ctx = FacesContext.getCurrentInstance();
      ctx.addMessage(null, fm);
    }
```

2. Create a page called `login.jspx` based on a quick start layout.

3. Using the **Component Palette**, drop two Input Text (`af:inputText`) components on the page, one for the username and another for the password. Set the **Secret** property of the password input text to `true`. In addition, set the `value` attribute of the username and password input text components (you can use the **Expression Builder** dialog to do this) to the expressions `#{AuthenticationBean.username}` and `#{AuthenticationBean.username}` respectively.

4. Drop a Button (`af:commandButton`) component on the login page and change its `text` property to **Login**. Moreover, set the button's `action` property to the expression `#{AuthenticationBean.login}`.

5. Open the `web.xml` deployment descriptor located in the **Web Content | WEB-INF** folder in the **Application Navigator** and switch to the **Security** tab. Change the **Login Page** to `/faces/login.jspx`.

6. Finally, change the `LOGOUT_URL` constant definition in the `logout()` method of the `AuthenticationBean` managed bean to `/adfAuthentication?logout=true&end_url=/faces/login.jspx`.

How it works...

In step 1, we added a `login()` method to the `AuthenticationBean` managed bean (introduced in the *Enabling ADF security* recipe in this chapter to handle the logout functionality), to handle the user authentication process. The `login()` method is set to the `action` property of the **Login** button added to the login page in step 4. To authenticate the user, we call the `authenticate()` helper method from the `login()` method. The code in `authenticate()` retrieves the username and password values supplied by the user and calls the static `Authentication.login()` to create a `javax.security.auth.Subject`. It subsequently uses the `Subject` when calling `ServletAuthentication.runAs()` to authenticate the request. The authentication process completes by calling `ServletAuthentication.generateNewSessionID()` to generate a new session identifier. Once the user is authenticated, the request is forwarded to the welcome page. This is done by calling `forward()` on a `RequestDispatcher` object and specifying the welcome page URL. The welcome page URL is specified using the parameter `success_url` to the `adfAuthentication` servlet. It is identified by the constant definition `WELCOME_URL`, which is defined as: `/adfAuthentication?success_url=/faces/welcome.jspx`.

Furthermore, we have added setters and getters for the username and password. These are specified as `value` attributes to the corresponding username and password input text components that are added to the login page in step 3.

In steps 2 through 4, we created the custom login page. We added two input text fields that we will use to specify the login credentials (username and password), and a **Login** button, which when pressed will initiate the authentication process. The username and password input text `value` attributes are bound to the `username` and `password` attributes of the `AuthenticationBean` managed bean respectively. Moreover, the **Login** button `action` property is set to the `login()` method of the `AuthenticationBean` managed bean.

In step 5, we updated the login page configuration in `web.xml` to point to the custom login page. Note how we prepended the login page URL with `/faces/` to allow processing of the page by the faces servlet, since it contains ADF Faces components.

Finally, we updated the `LOGOUT_URL` constant used by the `logout()` method in the `AuthenticationBean` managed bean, so that we are redirected to our custom login page instead.

To test the recipe, right-click on the `login.jspx` page and go through the authorization process. You can use the `user1/user1234` credentials. Upon successful authorization, you should be forwarded to the `welcome.jspx` page.

There's more...

Note that the way we have explained programmatic authentication in this recipe is proprietary to the WebLogic Server. The recipe will have to be adapted using similar APIs offered by other application servers.

For more information about creating a custom login page, consult section *Creating a Login Page* in the *Fusion Developer's Guide for Oracle Application Development Framework*, which can be found at `http://docs.oracle.com/cd/E24382_01/web.1112/e16182/toc.htm`.

See also

- *Breaking up the application in multiple workspaces, Chapter 1, Pre-requisites to Success: ADF Project Setup and Foundations*
- *Enabling ADF security, Chapter 9, Handling Security, Session Timeouts, Exceptions and Errors*

Accessing the application's security information

You can access the application's security information at the ViewController layer either through Java code in a managed bean or through Expression Language (EL) in your JSF pages by utilizing the methods available via the `oracle.adf.share.security.SecurityContext` bean. These methods will allow you to determine whether authorization and/or authentication are enabled in your application, the roles assigned to the authenticated user, whether the user is assigned a specific role, and so on. At the ADF-BC level, security information can be accessed through the methods available in the `oracle.jbo.Session`.

In this recipe, we will see how to access the application's security information from a managed bean, a JSF page and at the ADF-BC level.

Getting ready

You will need to create a skeleton **Fusion Web Application (ADF)** workspace before you proceed with this recipe. For this purpose, we will use the `MainApplication` workspace that was developed in *Breaking up the application in multiple workspaces Chapter 1, Pre-requisites to Success: ADF Project Setup and Foundations*. The recipe assumes that you have enabled ADF security by completing recipes *Enabling ADF security* and *Using a custom login page* in this chapter.

The recipe also uses the `HRComponents` workspace, which was created in *Overriding remove() to delete associated children entities. Chapter 2, Dealing with Basics: Entity Objects.*

Both the `HRComponents` and `MainApplication` workspaces require database connections to the `HR` schema.

How to do it...

1. Open the `HRComponents` workspace and locate the `Employees` custom row implementation Java class `EmployeesRowImpl.java` in the **Application Navigator**. Double-click on it to open it in the Java editor.

2. Override the `isAttributeUpdateable()` method and add the following code to it:

```
// allow employee changes only if the user has the
// 'AllowEmployeeChanges' role
return ADFContext.getCurrent().getSecurityContext().isUserInRole(
   "AllowEmployeeChanges")
     ? super.isAttributeUpdateable(i) : false;
```

3. Redeploy the `HRComponents` workspace to an ADF Library JAR.

4. Open the `MainApplication` workspace. Add the `HRComponents` ADF Library JAR to the ViewController project.

5. Create a JSPX page called `applicationSecurity.jspx` and drop the `Employees` collection (available under the `HrComponentsAppModuleDataControl` data control in the **Data Controls** window) as an **ADF Form** on it.

6. Add a Button (`af:commandButton`) component to the page. Using the **Property Inspector,** change the button's **Disabled** property to `#{securityContext.userIn Role['AllowEmployeeChanges'] eq false}`.

7. Add an action listener to the button component by defining a new managed bean called `ApplicationSecurityBean` and a method called `onApplicationSecurity`.

8. Open the `ApplicationSecurityBean` managed bean and add the following code to the `onApplicationSecurity()` method:

```
// check for user having the 'AllowEmployeeChanges' role
if (ADFContext.getCurrent().getSecurityContext()
  .isUserInRole("AllowEmployeeChanges")) {
  FacesContext context =
    FacesContext.getCurrentInstance();
  context.addMessage(null,new FacesMessage
    (FacesMessage.SEVERITY_INFO, "User is allowed to
    edit the employee data.", null));
}
```

9. Select **Application Roles** from the **Application | Secure** menu. Create a new application role called `AllowEmployeeChanges`. Click on the **Add User or Role** button (the green plus sign icon) in the **Mappings** section, then **Add User** to map the `user1` user to the `AllowEmployeeChanges` role.

10. Select **Resource Grants** from the **Application | Secure** menu. Select **Web Page** for the **Resource Type** and locate the **applicationSecurity** page. Click on the **Add Grantee** button (the green plus sign icon) in the **Granted To** section, then select **Add Application Role** from the menu. Add the `AllowEmployeeChanges` role ensuring that the **view** action in the **Actions** section is selected.

How it works...

In steps 1 through 3, we have updated the `HRComponents` ADF Library JAR in order to demonstrate how to access the application security information at the business components level. Specifically, we have overridden the `ViewRowImpl isAttributeUpdateable()` method for the custom `EmployeesRowImpl` row implementation class, in order to control the `Employees` view object attributes that can be updated based on a specific role assigned to the currently authorized user. We did this by calling `isUserInRole()` on the `oracle.jbo.Session` and specifying the specific role, `AllowEmployeeChanges` in this case. We obtained the `Session` object from the application module by calling `getSession()`. The effect of adding this piece of code is that if the authorized user does not have the `AllowEmployeeChanges` role, none of the `Employees` attributes will be updatable. The `HRComponents` workspace is deployed to an ADF Library JAR in step 3.

In steps 4 through 6, we created a page called `applicationSecurity.jspx` for the main application and dropped in it the `Employees` collection as an ADF Form (step 5). The `Employees` collection is available under the `HrComponentsAppModuleDataControl` data control in the **Data Controls** window once we add the `HRComponents` ADF Library JAR to the ViewController project of the application (which we did in step 4). In step 6, we added an `af:commandButton` component to the page and set its `Disabled` property to the EL expression `#{securityContext.userInRole['AllowEmployeeChanges'] eq false}`. This expression uses the `SecurityContext` bean to check whether the currently authorized user has the `AllowEmployeeChanges` role assigned to it. If the user does not have the role assigned, the button will appear on the page disabled.

In steps 7 and 8, we added an action listener to the button, specifying the `onApplicationSecurity` method on a newly created bean. We have added code to the `onApplicationSecurity()` action listener to call the `SecurityContext` bean `isUserInRole()` method to determine whether the current user has been assigned the `AllowEmployeeChanges` role. For the purpose of this recipe, we display a message if the user is authorized to edit the employee data.

Finally, in steps 9 and 10, we added an application role called `AllowEmployeeChanges` and mapped it to the `user1` user. We also enabled view access to the `applicationSecurity.jspx` page by adding the `AllowEmployeeChanges` role to it.

Observe what happens when you run the main application: if you run the `applicationSecurity.jspx` page by right-clicking on it in the **Application Navigator**, the employee information and the button in the page are disabled. This is because we have not gone through the user authorization process and the current anonymous user does not have the `AllowEmployeeChanges` role. This is not the case if you access the `applicationSecurity.jspx` page after a successful authorization. For this purpose, we have updated the `welcome.jspx` page, the page that we are redirected to upon a successful log in, and added a link to the `applicationSecurity.jspx` page. Observe in this case that both the employee fields and the button in the page are enabled.

There's more...

Some of the other commonly used `SecurityContext` methods and/or expressions are listed in the following table:

Method/Expression	Description
`#{secrityContext.taskflowViewable['SomeTaskFlow']}`	Returns `true` if the user has access to the specific `SomeTaskFlow` task flow.
`#{secrityContext.regionViewable['SomePageDef']}`	Returns `true` if the user has access to the specific `SomePageDef` page definition file associated with a page.
`#{secrityContext.userName}`	Returns the authenticated user's username.

Method/Expression	Description
#{securityContext.authenticated}	Returns true if the user has been authenticated.
#{securityContext.userInAllRoles['roleList']}	Returns true if the user has all roles in the comma-separated roleList assigned.

For a comprehensive list of the SecurityContext EL expressions take a look at the section *Using Expression Language (EL) with ADF Security* in the *Fusion Developer's Guide for Oracle Application Development Framework*, which can be found at http://docs.oracle.com/cd/E24382_01/web.1112/e16182/toc.htm.

Note that you can access the SecurityContext bean at the business components layer using the adf.context.securityContext Groovy expression. For instance, to get the username of the currently authorized user, use the expression adf.context.securityContext.userName.

See also

▸ *Breaking up the application in multiple workspaces, Chapter 1, Pre-requisites to Success: ADF Project Setup and Foundations*

▸ *Overriding remove() to delete associated children entities, Chapter 2, Dealing with Basics: Entity Objects*

▸ *Enabling ADF security, Chapter 9, Handling Security, Session Timeouts, Exceptions and Errors*

▸ *Using a custom login page, Chapter 9, Handling Security, Session Timeouts, Exceptions and Errors*

Using OPSS to retrieve the authenticated user's profile from the identity store

Oracle Platform Security Services (OPSS) is a comprehensive standards-based security framework and the underlying security-providing platform for Oracle Fusion Middleware. It provides an abstract layer through the use of an Application Programming Interface (API) for accessing security provider and identity management details. It is through the use of the OPSS API that generic access is achieved to vendor-specific security providers.

In this recipe, we will introduce the OPSS framework by implementing the following use case: using the HR schema, for an authenticated employee-user, we will update the employee information in the EMPLOYEES table with information from the user's profile obtained from the identity store. For an authenticated employee-user who is not already in the EMPLOYEES table, we will create a new row in it.

Getting ready

This recipe adds a security utility helper class to the `SharedComponents` workspace. This workspace was introduced in *Breaking up the application in multiple workspaces, Chapter 1, Pre-requisites to Success: ADF Project Setup and Foundations*. It also updates the `UserInfo` application module introduced in *Using a session scope bean to preserve session-wide information, Chapter 8, Backing not Baking: Bean Recipes*. The `UserInfo` application module resides in the `HRComponents` workspace, which was also created in *Breaking up the application in multiple workspaces, Chapter 1, Pre-requisites to Success: ADF Project Setup and Foundations*

You will need to create a skeleton **Fusion Web Application (ADF)** workspace before you proceed with this recipe. For this purpose, we will use the `MainApplication` workspace that was developed in *Breaking up the application in multiple workspaces, Chapter 1, Pre-requisites to Success: ADF Project Setup and Foundations*.

The recipe also requires that ADF security is enabled for the main application (see additional recipes *Enabling ADF security* and *Using a custom login page* in this chapter) and the presence of a main application page (we will use the `welcome.jspx` page developed for the *Enabling ADF security* recipe).

Finally, you need a connection to the HR schema.

How to do it...

1. Open the `SharedComponents` workspace and add the following `SecurityUtils` helper class to it:

```
public class SecurityUtils {
  private static ADFLogger LOGGER =
    ADFLogger.createADFLogger(SecurityUtils.class);
  public static UserProfile getUserIdentityStoreProfile(
    String username) {
    UserProfile userProfile = null;
    try {
      // get the identity store
      IdentityStore idStore = getIdentityStore();
      // create a search filter based on the
      // specific username
      SimpleSearchFilter filter =
        idStore.getSimpleSearchFilter(UserProfile.NAME,
        SimpleSearchFilter.TYPE_EQUAL, username);
      SearchParameters sp = new SearchParameters(filter,
        SearchParameters.SEARCH_USERS_ONLY);
      // search identity store
      SearchResponse response = idStore.search(sp);
```

```
      // check for search results
      if (response.hasNext()) {
        User user = (User)response.next();
        if (user != null) {
          // retrieve the user profile
          userProfile = user.getUserProfile();
        }
      }
    } catch (Exception e) {
      LOGGER.severe(e);
    }
    // return the user profile
    return userProfile;
  }
  private static IdentityStore getIdentityStore()
    throws JpsException {
    // get the JPS context
    JpsContext jpsCtx = JpsContextFactory.getContextFactory()
      .getContext();
    // return the identity store
    IdentityStoreService service =
      jpsCtx.getServiceInstance(IdentityStoreService.class);
    return service.getIdmStore();
  }
}
```

2. Redeploy the SharedComponents workspace to an ADF Library JAR.

3. Open the HRComponents workspace and add the SharedComponents ADF Library JAR to the HRComponentsBC business components project.

4. Locate the UserInfoAppModuleImpl.java custom application module implementation class in the **Application Navigator**. Double-click on it to open it in the Java editor. Add the following methods to it:

```
public void synchronizeEmployee() {
  try {
    // get information for currently logged-in user
    // from identity store
    UserProfile userProfile = SecurityUtils
      .getUserIdentityStoreProfile(getUserPrincipalName());
    if (userProfile != null) {
      // get EMPLOYEES row from currently logged-in user
      UserInfoImpl employees = (UserInfoImpl)getUserInfo();
      employees.executeQuery();
      UserInfoRowImpl employee =
        (UserInfoRowImpl)employees.first();
```

```
          // if user is not in EMPLOYEES table, add it
          if (employee == null) {
            addEmployee(employees, userProfile);
          } else { // user in EMPLOYEES table
            String email = userProfile.getBusinessEmail();
            if (email != null &&
              !email.equals(employee.getEmail())) {
              employee.setEmail(email);
            }
          }
          // commit transaction
          this.getDBTransaction().commit();
          // requery users to fetch any calculated attributes
          employees.executeQuery();
        }
      } catch (Exception e) {
        // log exception
      }
    }
    private void addEmployee(UserInfoImpl employees,
      UserProfile userProfile) throws IMException {
      // create employee row
      UserInfoRowImpl employee =
        (UserInfoRowImpl)employees.createRow();
      // set required employee row data from
      // identity store profile
      employee.setLastName(getUserPrincipalName());
      employee.setEmail(userProfile.getBusinessEmail()== null ?
        "n/a" : userProfile.getBusinessEmail());
      employee.setHireDate(new Date(
        new Timestamp(System.currentTimeMillis())));
      employee.setJobId("IT_PROG");
      employee.setDepartmentId(new Number(60));
      // add employee row
      employees.insertRow(employee);
    }
```

5. Add the `synchronizeEmployee()` method to the `UserInfoAppModule` application module client interface and redeploy the `HRComponents` workspace to an ADF Library JAR.

6. Open the `MainApplication` workspace and add the `HRComponents` ADF Library JAR to the ViewController project.

7. Create a bounded task flow called `syncEmployeesTaskFlow`. Using the **Property Inspector** change the **URL Invoke** property to **url-invoke-allowed**.

8. Expand the `UserInfoAppModuleDataControl` in the **Data Controls** window and drop the `synchronizeEmployee()` method to the `syncEmployeesTaskFlow` task flow.

9. Create a managed bean called `SyncEmployeesBean`, and add the following methods to it:

```
public String getProgrammaticallyInvokeTaskFlow() {
  // setup task flow parameters
  Map<String, Object> parameters =
    new java.util.HashMap<String, Object>();
  // construct and return the task flow's URL
  return getTaskFlowURL("/WEB-INF/taskflows/chapter9/
syncEmployeesTaskFlow.xml#syncEmployeesTaskFlow", parameters);
}
private String getTaskFlowURL(String taskFlowSpecs,
  Map<String, Object> parameters) {
  // create a TaskFlowId from the task flow specification
  TaskFlowId tfid = TaskFlowId.parse(taskFlowSpecs);
  // construct the task flow URL
  String taskFlowURL =
    ControllerContext.getInstance().getTaskFlowURL(
    false, tfid, parameters);
  // remove the application context path from the URL
  FacesContext fc = FacesContext.getCurrentInstance();
  String taskFlowContextPath =
    fc.getExternalContext().getRequestContextPath();
  return taskFlowURL.replaceFirst(taskFlowContextPath, "");
}
```

10. Open the `welcome.jspx` page. Using the **Component Palette**, drop a **Link (Go)** (`af:goLink`) component to the page and set the link's **Destination** property to `#{SyncEmployeesBean.programmaticallyInvokeTaskFlow}`.

How it works...

In steps 1 and 2 we have added a helper class called `SecurityUtils` to the `SharedComponents` workspace. We will use this class to retrieve the user's profile from the identity store. For this purpose, we have implemented the method `getUserIdentityStoreProfile()`. To search for the specific username in the identity store, it calls the `IdentityStore search()` method. The username specified for the search is passed as an argument to the `getUserIdentityStoreProfile()`. The search yields an `oracle.security.idm.SearchResponse`, which is then iterated to retrieve an `oracle.security.idm.User` identity. We retrieve the user's identity store profile by calling `getUserProfile()` on the `User` object.

In step 2, we have redeployed the `SharedComponents` workspace to an ADF Library JAR.

In steps 3 through 5, we have made the necessary changes to the `UserInfoAppModule` application module to allow for the synchronization of employee-users. We have assumed that each employee in the `EMPLOYEES` HR schema table is also a user of the application. In step 3, we have added the `SharedComponents` ADF Library JAR to the `HRComponents` business components project so that we can make use of the `SecurityUtils` helper class. Then, in step 4, we implemented a method called `synchronizeEmployee()`, to allow for the synchronization of the `EMPLOYEES` table. This method is also exposed to the application module's client interface (in step 5), so that it can be invoked from the ViewController layer as an operation binding.

The synchronization of the `EMPLOYEES` table is based on the following logic: if the currently authorized user is not in the `EMPLOYEES` table, it is added. Information from the user's identity store profile is used to populate the `EMPLOYEES` table fields. If the user is already in the `EMPLOYEES` table, the user's information in the `EMPLOYEES` table is updated with the information from the user's identity store profile. The currently authorized user is searched in the database using the `UserInfo` view object. If the user is not found in the database, we call `addEmployee()` to add it. Otherwise, the user's information in the database is updated. Note that the query used by the `UserInfo` view object uses a `WHERE` clause that is based on the currently authorized user. This is done in a declarative manner by specifying the Groovy expression `adf.context.securityContext.userName` for the binding variable `inEmployeeName` used by the `UserInfo` view object query.

In steps 6 through 8, we have created a task flow called `syncEmployeesTaskFlow` and dropped in it the `synchronizeEmployee()` method as a method call activity. The `synchronizeEmployee()` method is available under the `UserInfoAppModuleDataControl` in the **Data Controls** window once the `HRComponents` ADF Library JAR is added to the project (this is done in step 6). Observe how in step 7 we set the task flow **URL Invoke** property to `url-invoke-allowed`. This will allow us to invoke the `syncEmployeesTaskFlow` task flow using its URL.

Steps 9 and 10 are added only so that we can test the recipe. For more information about the code in the `getProgrammaticallyInvokeTaskFlow()` and `getTaskFlowURL()` methods, take a look at *Calling a task flow as a URL programmatically*, *Chapter 6, Go with the flow: Task Flows*.

To test the recipe, right-click on the `login.jspx` page and go through the authorization process. You can use the `user1/user1234` credentials. Upon a successful authorization, you will be forwarded to the `welcome.jspx` page. Click on the `syncEmployeesTaskFlow.xml` link. Observe that for new employee-users, the user information is added to the `EMPLOYEES` HR table. For existing employee-users, the user information is updated in the table.

There's more...

One of the hurdles in getting the OPSS framework to work for your specific application security environment involves the proper configuration of the Identity Store Service. Configuration is done through the `jps-config.xml` file located in the `config/fmwconfig` folder under the domain directory in WebLogic. For example, in order to configure OPSS when multiple LDAP authenticators are used in WebLogic, you will need to set up the `virtualize` property in WebLogic. For a comprehensive reference on OPSS configuration, consult section *Configuring the Identity Store Service* in the *Fusion Middleware Application Security Guide*, which can be found at `http://docs.oracle.com/cd/E24382_01/web.1112/e16181/toc.htm`.

See also

- ▶ *Breaking up the application in multiple workspaces, Chapter 1, Pre-requisites to Success: ADF Project Setup and Foundations*

- ▶ *Calling a task flow as a URL programmatically, Chapter 6, Go with the flow: Task Flows*

- ▶ *Using a session scope bean to preserve session-wide information, Chapter 8, Backing not Baking: Bean Recipes*

- ▶ *Enabling ADF security, Chapter 9, Handling Security, Session Timeouts, Exceptions and Errors*

- ▶ *Using a custom login page, Chapter 9, Handling Security, Session Timeouts, Exceptions and Errors*

Detecting and handling session timeouts

Each time a client request is sent to the server a predefined, application-wide, configurable session timeout value is written to the page to determine when a session timeout should occur. A page is considered eligible to timeout if there is no keyboard, mouse or any other programmatic activity on the page. Moreover, an additional application configuration option exists to warn the user sometime prior to the session expiration that a timeout is imminent.

In this recipe, we will see how to gracefully handle a session timeout by redirecting the application to a specific page, the login page in this case, once a session timeout is detected.

Getting ready

You will need to create a skeleton **Fusion Web Application (ADF)** workspace before you proceed with this recipe. For this purpose, we will use the `MainApplication` workspace that was developed in *Breaking up the application in multiple workspaces, Chapter 1, Pre-requisites to Success: ADF Project Setup and Foundations*.

How to do it...

1. Open the `MainApplication` workspace in JDeveloper. Add the following `SessionTimeoutFilter` filter to the ViewController project:

```java
public class SessionTimeoutFilter implements Filter {
  private FilterConfig filterConfig = null;
  public SessionTimeoutFilter() {
    super();
  }
  @Override
  public void init(FilterConfig filterConfig) {
    this.filterConfig = filterConfig;
  }
  @Override
  public void destroy() {
    filterConfig = null;
  }
  @Override
  public void doFilter(ServletRequest servletRequest,
    ServletResponse servletResponse, FilterChain filterChain)
    throws IOException, ServletException {
    // get requested session
    String requestedSession =
      ((HttpServletRequest)servletRequest)
        .getRequestedSessionId();
    // get current session
    String currentSession =
      ((HttpServletRequest)servletRequest).getSession().getId();

    // check for invalid session
    if (currentSession.equalsIgnoreCase(requestedSession)
                  == false && requestedSession != null) {
      // the session has expired or renewed
      // redirect request to the page defined by the
      // SessionTimeoutRedirect parameter
      ((HttpServletResponse)servletResponse)
        .sendRedirect(((HttpServletRequest)
        servletRequest).getContextPath()
        + ((HttpServletRequest)servletRequest)
              .getServletPath()
            + "/" + filterConfig.getInitParameter(
                "SessionTimeoutRedirect"));
    } else {
      // current session is still valid
```

```
        filterChain.doFilter(servletRequest, servletResponse);
      }
    }
  }
```

2. Open the web.xml deployment descriptor and add the following filter and filter-mapping definitions to it. Make sure that you add these definitions at the end of any other filter and filter-mapping definitions.

```xml
<filter>
  <filter-name>SessionTimeoutFilter</filter-name>
  <filter-class>com.packt.jdeveloper.cookbook.
    hr.main.view.filters.SessionTimeoutFilter</filter-class>
  <init-param>
    <param-name>SessionTimeoutRedirect</param-name>
    <param-value>/faces/login.jspx</param-value>
  </init-param>
</filter>
<filter-mapping>
  <filter-name>SessionTimeoutFilter</filter-name>
  <servlet-name>Faces Servlet</servlet-name>
</filter-mapping>
```

3. For testing purposes add the following session-timeout configuration to web.xml:

```xml
<session-config>
  <session-timeout>4</session-timeout>
</session-config>
```

How it works...

In step 1, we have added a filter called SessionTimeoutFilter. In it, we obtain from the request both the session identifier of the current request and the identifier of the current session. We compare the session identifiers, and if they differ we redirect the user to the page identified by the SessionTimeoutRedirect filter initialization parameter. A difference in the session identifiers indicates that a session timeout has occurred. We have set the SessionTimeoutRedirect filter parameter to the login.jspx page in step 2. Also in step 2, we have added the SessionTimeoutFilter filter definition to the web.xml deployment descriptor.

Finally, for testing purposes only, we have set the application-wide session timeout to 4 minutes in step 3.

There's more...

In addition to the `session-timeout` configuration setting in `web.xml`, you can configure a session timeout warning interval by defining the context parameter `oracle.adf.view.rich.sessionHandling.WARNING_BEFORE_TIMEOUT`. This parameter is set to a number of seconds before the actual session timeout would occur and raises a warning dialog indicating that the session is about to expire. You then have the opportunity to extend the session by performing some activity on the page. Note that if its value is set to less than 120 seconds, this feature might be disabled under certain conditions.

See also

▶ *Breaking up the application in multiple workspaces, Chapter 1, Pre-requisites to Success: ADF Project Setup and Foundations*

Using a custom error handler to customize how exceptions are reported to the ViewController

You can alter the way error messages are reported to the ADF Controller by implementing a custom error handler class that extends the `oracle.adf.model.binding.DCErrorHandlerImpl` class. The custom error handler class can then provide custom implementations for the following methods:

▶ `reportException()`: This method is called by the ADF framework to report an exception. You can override this method to handle how each exception type is reported.

▶ `getDisplayMessage()`: Returns the exception error message. You can override this method in order to change the error message.

▶ `getDetailedDisplayMessage()`: Returns the exception error message details. You can override this method in order to change the error message details.

This recipe shows you how to extend the `DCErrorHandlerImpl` error handling class so that you can provide custom handling and reporting of the application exceptions to the ViewController layer.

Getting ready

We will add the custom error handler to the `SharedComponents` workspace. This workspace was created in *Breaking up the application in multiple workspaces, Chapter 1, Pre-requisites to Success: ADF Project Setup and Foundations*.

For testing purposes, you will need to create a skeleton **Fusion Web Application (ADF)** workspace. For this purpose, we will use the `MainApplication` workspace that was developed in *Breaking up the application in multiple workspaces, Chapter 1, Pre-requisites to Success: ADF Project Setup and Foundations.*

How to do it...

1. Open the `SharedComponents` workspace and add the following `CustomDCErrorHandlerImpl` class to its ViewController project:

```
public class CustomDCErrorHandlerImpl
  extends DCErrorHandlerImpl {
  public CustomDCErrorHandlerImpl() {
    super(true);
  }
  public void reportException(DCBindingContainer
    dCBindingContainer,Exception exception) {
    // report JboExceptions as errors
    if (exception instanceof ExtJboException
      || exception instanceof JboException) {
      FacesContext.getCurrentInstance().addMessage(
        null,new FacesMessage(FacesMessage.SEVERITY_ERROR,
        exception.getMessage(), null));
    } else { // report all others as information
      FacesContext.getCurrentInstance().addMessage(
        null,new FacesMessage(
        FacesMessage.SEVERITY_INFO,
        exception.getMessage(), null));
    }
  }
}
```

2. Redeploy the `SharedComponents` workspace to an ADF Library JAR.

3. Open the `MainApplication` workspace and add the `SharedComponents` ADF Library JAR to its ViewController project.

4. Open the `DataBindings.cpx` Data Binding Registry file and select the root **Databindings** node in the **Structure** window. Using the **Property Menu** next to the **ErrorHandlerClass** in the **Property Inspector**, specify the `CustomDCErrorHandlerImpl` class implemented previously.

How it works...

We have created a custom error handler called `CustomDCErrorHandlerImpl` in steps 1 and 2 as part of the `SharedComponents` workspace. The class extends the default error handling implementation provided by the `oracle.adf.model.binding.DCErrorHandlerImpl` class. We only need to override the `reportException()` method at this time to provide custom handling for the application-generated exceptions. For the purposes of this recipe, we are looking for `ExtJboException` and `JboException` types of exceptions, that is, exceptions generated by the business components layer, and we are displaying them as error Faces messages at the ViewController layer. `ExtJboException` is a custom application exception that was implemented in *Using a custom exception class, Chapter 1, Pre-requisites to Success: ADF Project Setup and Foundations*. All other exceptions are shown as informational messages to the user. We make sure that the `SharedComponents` workspace is redeployed as an ADF Library JAR and that is added to the main workspace ViewController project in step 3.

One last thing that we need to do is set the `ErrorHandlerClass` property of the `Databindings` node in the `DataBindings.cpx` bindings registry file to our custom `CustomDCErrorHandlerImpl` class. We do this in step 4.

There's more...

In this recipe, we customized the way the application exceptions are handled and reported to the ViewController layer by providing a custom implementation of the `reportException()` method. To customize the way the actual error message is formatted take a look at the *Customizing the error message details* recipe in this chapter.

For more information about custom error handling in your application, consult the *Customizing Error Handling* section of the *Fusion Developer's Guide for Oracle Application Development Framework*, which can be found at `http://docs.oracle.com/cd/E24382_01/web.1112/e16182/toc.htm`.

See also

- ▶ *Breaking up the application in multiple workspaces, Chapter 1, Pre-requisites to Success: ADF Project Setup and Foundations*
- ▶ *Customizing the error message details, Chapter 9, Handling Security, Session Timeouts, Exceptions and Errors*

Customizing the error message details

In the recipe *Using a custom error handler to customize how exceptions are reported to the ViewController* in this chapter, we've seen how to create a custom `DCErrorHandlerImpl` class and override its `reportException()` method in order to provide custom handling of the application's exceptions. In this recipe, we will go over the process of overriding the `DCErrorHandlerImpl` class `getDisplayMessage()` method, so that we can provide custom handling of specific application error messages. In particular, we will see how to reformat error messages generated by exceptions thrown from the database business logic code, using functionality provided by the ADF resource bundles. More specifically, we will assume that our application's database business logic source code throws exceptions using a user-defined database error number, with the actual resource error number and parameters bundled within the exception message. An example of the error message thrown by the database layer is: `ORA-20200: APPL-00007: Some Error $1parameter1$1 $2parameter2$2`. In this case, the business exception generated by the database is identified by the user-defined error number `-20200`. The actual error message is bundled within the message details and it is identified by the error number `00007`. The error message parameters are delimited by the parameter placeholders `$1` and `$2`.

Getting ready

You will need to complete *Using a custom error handler to customize how exceptions are reported to the ViewController* recipe in this chapter before delving into this recipe.

How to do it...

1. Open the `SharedComponents` workspace and locate the `CustomDCErrorHandlerImpl` class. Open the class in the Java editor and override the `getDisplayMessage()` method.

2. Add the following code to the `getDisplayMessage()` method:

```
// get the error message from the framework
String errorMessageRaw =
  super.getDisplayMessage(bindingContext,exception);
// handle messages generated by the database business logic
return handleDatabaseApplicationError(errorMessageRaw);
```

3. Add the following helper methods to the `CustomDCErrorHandlerImpl` class:

```
private String handleDatabaseApplicationError(
  String errorMessageRaw) {
  // the error code for application-specific messages
  // generated by the database application-specific
  // business code
  final String APPLICATION_ERROR_CODE = "20200";
```

```java
  // the application error messages bundle
  final ResourceBundle errorMessagesBundle =
    ResourceBundle.getBundle("com.packt.jdeveloper.cookbook.
    shared.bc.exceptions.messages.ErrorMessages");
  // check for null/empty error message
  if (errorMessageRaw == null||"".equals(errorMessageRaw)) {
    return errorMessageRaw;
  }
  // check for database error message
  if (errorMessageRaw.indexOf("ORA-") == -1) {
    return errorMessageRaw;
  }
  // check for end of database error code indicator
    int endIndex = errorMessageRaw.indexOf(":");
    if (endIndex == -1) {
      return errorMessageRaw;
    }
  // get the database error code
  String dbmsErrorMessageCode =
    errorMessageRaw.substring(4, endIndex);
  String errorMessageCode = "";
  if (APPLICATION_ERROR_CODE.equals(dbmsErrorMessageCode)) {
    int start = errorMessageRaw.indexOf("-", endIndex)+1;
    int end = errorMessageRaw.indexOf(":", start);
    errorMessageCode = errorMessageRaw.substring(
    start, end);
  } else {
    // not application-related error message
    return errorMessageRaw;
  }
  // get the application error message from the
  // application resource bundle using the specific
  // application error code
  String errorMessage = null;
  try {
    errorMessage = errorMessagesBundle.getString(
    "message." + errorMessageCode);
  } catch (MissingResourceException mre) {
    // application error code not found in the bundle,
    // use original message
    return errorMessageRaw;
  }
  // get the error message parameters
  ArrayList parameters =
    getErrorMessageParameters(errorMessageRaw);
```

```
      if (parameters != null && parameters.size() > 0) {
        // replace the message parameter placeholders with the
        // actual parameter values
      int counter = 1;
      for (Object parameter : parameters) {
        // parameter placeholders appear in the message
        // as {1}, {2}, and so on
        errorMessage = errorMessage.replace("{" +
          counter + "}", parameter.toString());
        counter++;
      }
    }
    // return the formated application error message
    return errorMessage;
  }
  private ArrayList getErrorMessageParameters(
    String errorMessageRaw) {
    // the parameter indicator in the database
    // application-specific error
    final String PARAMETER_INDICATOR = "$";
    ArrayList parameters = new ArrayList();
    // get parameters from the error message
    for (int i = 1; i <= 10; i++) {
      int start = errorMessageRaw.indexOf(PARAMETER_INDICATOR + i)
        + 2;
      int end = errorMessageRaw.indexOf(PARAMETER_INDICATOR
        + i, start);
      if (end == -1) {
        parameters.add(i - 1, "");
      } else {
        parameters.add(i - 1,errorMessageRaw.substring(start, end));
      }
    }
    // return the parameters
    return parameters;
  }
```

4. Redeploy the `SharedComponents` workspace into an ADF Library JAR.

How it works...

In steps 1 and 2, we have updated the `CustomDCErrorHandlerImpl` custom error handler class by overriding the `getDisplayMessage()` method. The `CustomDCErrorHandlerImpl` custom error handler class was added to the `SharedComponents` workspace in the recipe *Using a custom error handler to customize how exceptions are reported to the ViewController* in this chapter. By overriding the `getDisplayMessage()` method, we will get a chance to reformat the error message displayed by the application before it is displayed. In our case, we will reformat any messages related to exceptions thrown from the database business logic code. This is done by the helper method `handleDatabaseApplicationError()` added in step 3. This method checks for errors originating from database exceptions by looking for the "ORA-" substring in the error message. If this is found, the database business error message number is extracted. This is a user-defined application-specific error message number used in the database business logic code to throw application business logic exceptions. PL/SQL error numbers in the range of -20000 to -20999 are reserved for user-defined errors. For this recipe, it is defined by the constant `APPLICATION_ERROR_CODE` and it is equal to 20200 (we parse the error number after the -).

If this is indeed a business logic error message, the actual resource error number is bundled within it and it is extracted; the actual error number is saved in the `errorMessageCode` variable. We use this error number to look up the actual error message string in the application resource bundle, which is initialized by the call `ResourceBundle.getBundle()`. We have used the `ErrorMessages.properties` bundle, introduced in *Using a custom exception class, Chapter 1, Pre-requisites to Success: ADF Project Setup and Foundations*, to store the application error messages. Resources in this bundle are identified by error numbers prepended with the "message." string, for instance, `message.00007`. So, we called `getString()` on the resource bundle to locate the actual error message after we prepended the error code with "message.". This functionality is also implemented by the `BundleUtils` helper class introduced in *Using a generic backing bean actions framework, Chapter 1, Pre-requisites to Success: ADF Project Setup and Foundations*.

We retrieve the parameter values bundled in the database error message by calling the `getErrorMessageParameters()` helper method. This method identifies any parameters bundled in the raw database error message by looking for the parameter placeholder identifiers $1, $2, and so on. The parameters are added to an `ArrayList`, which is iterated when replacing the parameter placeholder identifiers {1}, {2}, and so on, in the actual message string.

This is an example error message thrown by the database business logic code: `ORA-20200: APPL-00007: Some Error $1parameter1$1 $2parameter2$2`. The error message defined in the resource bundle for error number 00007 is `message.00007=Message generated by the database business code. Parameters: {1}, {2}`. When we go through our custom `getDisplayMessage()` method, the actual message displayed by the application would be: **Message generated by the database business code. Parameters: parameter1, parameter2**.

The final step redeploys the `SharedComponents` workspace to an ADF Library JAR, so that it can be reused by other application workspaces.

See also

▸ *Using a custom exception class, Chapter 1, Pre-requisites to Success: ADF Project Setup and Foundations*

▸ *Using a custom error handler to customize how exceptions are reported to the ViewController, Chapter 9, Handling Security, Session Timeouts, Exceptions and Errors*

Overriding attribute validation exceptions

At the ADF-BC layer, built-in validators are stored in the XML metadata definition file with no ability to customize the exception message and/or centralize the application error messages in a single application-wide message bundle file. To overcome this you can extend the `oracle.jbo.ValidationException` and `oracle.jbo.AttrValException` classes. Then in your custom entity object implementation class you can override the `validateEntity()` and `setAttributeInternal()` methods to throw these custom exceptions instead. Even better, if you have gone through the process of creating framework extension classes (see *Setting up BC base classes, Chapter 1, Pre-requisites to Success: ADF Project Setup and Foundations*), this functionality can be added to the base entity object framework extension class and thereby used in a generic way throughout the application.

In this recipe, we will extend the `oracle.jbo.AttrValException` class in order to provide a custom attribute validation exception. We will then override the `setAttributeInternal()` method in the entity object framework extension class to throw the custom attribute validation exception.

Getting ready

We will add the custom attribute validation exception to the `SharedComponents` workspace. The `SharedComponents` workspace was created in *Breaking up the application in multiple workspaces, Chapter 1, Pre-requisites to Success: ADF Project Setup and Foundations*. Moreover, we will update the entity object framework extension class, which resides in the `SharedComponents` workspace. The entity object framework extension class was created in *Setting up BC base classes, Chapter 1, Pre-requisites to Success: ADF Project Setup and Foundations*.

How to do it...

1. Open the `SharedComponents` workspace in JDeveloper and add the following `ExtAttrValException` class to the `SharedBC` project:

```
public class ExtAttrValException extends AttrValException {
  public ExtAttrValException(String errorCode,
    Object[] errorParameters) {
  super(ResourceBundle.class, errorCode,
    errorParameters);
  }
  public ExtAttrValException(final String errorCode) {
    super(ResourceBundle.class, errorCode, null);
  }
  public String getMessage() {
    return BundleUtils.loadMessage(this.getErrorCode(),
    this.getErrorParameters());
  }
}
```

2. Open the `ExtEntityImpl` entity object framework extension class in the Java editor and override the `setAttributeInternal()` method.

3. Add the following code to the `setAttributeInternal()` method:

```
try {
  super.setAttributeInternal(attrib, value);
} catch (AttrValException e) {
  // throw custom attribute validation exception
  throw new ExtAttrValException(e.getErrorCode(),
    e.getErrorParameters());
}
```

4. Redeploy the `SharedComponents` workspace to an ADF Library JAR.

How it works...

In step 1, we have extended the `AttrValException` framework attribute validation exception by providing our custom implementation class called `ExtAttrValException`. This overrides the `getMessage()` method, which uses the helper class `BundleUtils` to load the error message from the application-wide message bundle file. Using the specific exception error code, the `BundleUtils` helper class was created in *Using a generic backing bean actions framework, Chapter 1, Pre-requisites to Success: ADF Project Setup and Foundations*.

In order to utilize the custom attribute validation exception in our application, we have overridden the `setAttributeInternal()` method of the `ExtEntityImpl` entity object framework extension class to throw `ExtAttrValException` instead of `AttrValException`. This was done in steps 2 and 3. The `setAttributeInternal()` method validates and sets the attribute value for the attribute identified by the `attrib` index.

Finally, in step 4, we redeploy the `SharedComponents` workspace to an ADF Library JAR.

There's more...

You can follow similar steps to customize the validation exceptions of your application's entity objects. In this case, you will need to extend the `oracle.jbo.ValidationException` class. Then you will need to override the `validateEntity()` method of the entity object framework extension class to throw your custom validation exception.

See also

- *Breaking up the application in multiple workspaces, Chapter 1, Pre-requisites to Success: ADF Project Setup and Foundations*
- *Setting up BC base classes, Chapter 1, Pre-requisites to Success: ADF Project Setup and Foundations*

10
Deploying ADF Applications

In this chapter, we will cover:

- ▶ Configuring and using the Standalone WebLogic Server
- ▶ Deploying on the Standalone WebLogic Server
- ▶ Using ojdeploy to automate the build process
- ▶ Using Hudson as a continuous integration framework

Introduction

The development and testing of ADF Fusion web applications in JDeveloper does not require any special deployment work by you, the developer. JDeveloper does a pretty good job setting up and configuring a WebLogic domain, namely the Integrated WebLogic Server, that is subsequently used to transparently deploy applications. This transparent deployment process takes place each time you choose to run or debug an application in JDeveloper.

To further test ADF Fusion web applications, using an environment that more closely resembles the actual production environment, you ought to consider configuring the Standalone WebLogic Server. This involves the creation of a WebLogic domain configured as closely as possible to the actual production environment (server instances, clusters, security realm configuration, services configuration, and so on) and deploying your ADF Fusion web application to it periodically.

There are a number of techniques used to deploy applications to the Standalone WebLogic Server. For instance, to deploy in a continuous integration production or testing environment, a script technique needs to be considered. On the other hand, for local development and testing purposes, deploying from JDeveloper will suffice.

Configuring and using the Standalone WebLogic Server

JDeveloper Studio Edition ships along with the WebLogic application server included. WebLogic Server is an essential part of the ADF Fusion web application development process, as it allows for the deployment, running, debugging, and testing of your application. It is installed on the development machine during the installation of JDeveloper.

When you choose to run or debug a Fusion web application from within the JDeveloper IDE, WebLogic is started and the application is deployed and run automatically on it. This configuration is called "Integrated WebLogic Server" as it is tightly integrated with the JDeveloper IDE. The very first time an ADF Fusion web application is run (or debugged) in JDeveloper, the necessary integrated WebLogic Server configuration takes place automatically. The configuration process creates the WebLogic domain and a server instance to deploy the application onto.

In addition to the Integrated WebLogic Server, the WebLogic configuration software allows for the creation and configuration of a "standalone" WebLogic domain. This domain that you configure separately according to your specific configuration requirements is known as the Standalone WebLogic Server. This is started independently of JDeveloper, and you deploy your applications on it using a separate deployment process. The Standalone WebLogic Server offers, among others, the following advantages: control over the specific configuration of the WebLogic domain; control over the deployment process; freeing up resources in JDeveloper when debugging and testing; freeing up resources on the development machine (when the WebLogic Server runs on another machine); and the ability to remotely debug the application.

In this recipe, we will go over the steps involved in configuring the Standalone WebLogic Server that we can use subsequently to deploy our ADF Fusion web application.

Getting ready

You will need WebLogic installed on your development environment. WebLogic is installed during the installation of JDeveloper Studio Edition based on your installation choices. For information on installing JDeveloper on a Linux distribution, take a look at the *Installation of JDeveloper on Linux* recipe in *Chapter 1, Pre-requisites to Success: ADF Project Setup and Foundations*.

How to do it...

1. Start the **Fusion Middleware Configuration Wizard**. You do this by running the `config` script located in the `common/bin` directory under the WebLogic installation directory. In the **Welcome** page, select **Create a new WebLogic domain** and click **Next**.

2. In the **Select Domain Source** page, select **Oracle JRF – 11.1.1.0 [oracle_common]** and click **Next**.

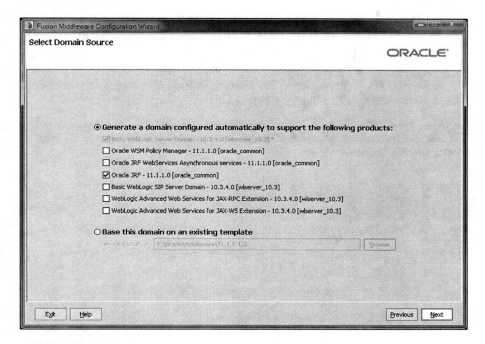

3. In the **Specify Domain Name and Location** page, enter the **Domain name** and the **Domain location** and click **Next**. You may keep the default values.

4. In the **Configure Administrator User Name and Password** page, enter the domain administrator **Name** and **User password**. Confirm the password and click **Next**.

5. In the **Configure Server Start Mode and JDK** page, select **Development Mode** for the **WebLogic Domain Startup Mode** and the **Sun SDK** from the list of **Available JDKs**. Click **Next** to continue.

6. In the **Select Optional Configuration** page, click on the **Administration Server, Managed Servers, Clusters and Machines**, and **Deployments and Services** checkboxes. Click **Next** to continue.

7. In the **Configure the Administration Server** page, enter the **Name, Listen address**, and **Listen port** of the administration server. You may keep the default values. Then click on the **Next** button.

8. In the **Configure Managed Servers** page, click on the **Add** button and specify the **Name**, **Listen address**, and **Listen port** of the managed server. You may choose the default values. Click **Next** to continue.

9. In the **Configure Clusters** page, click **Next**.

10. In the **Configure Machines** page, click on the **Add** button and specify the machine **Name**, **Node manager listen address**, and **Node manager listen port**. You may keep the default values. Click **Next** to continue.

11. In the **Assign Servers to Machines** page, shuttle the managed server from the **Server** list to the specific machine in the **Machine** list and click **Next**.

12. In the **Target Deployments to Clusters or Servers** page, make sure that all libraries are targeted to both administration and managed servers. You can do this by selecting the managed server in the **Target** list and selecting the **Library** node in the **Deployments** list. Click **Next** to continue.

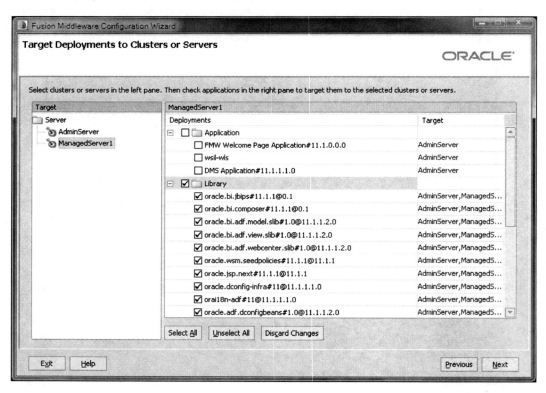

13. In the **Target Services to Clusters or Servers** page, make sure that all services are targeted to both the administration and managed server. You can do this by selecting the managed server in the **Target** list and clicking on the high level service nodes in the **Service** list. Click **Next** to continue.

14. In the **Configuration Summary** page, verify the domain configuration in the **Domain Summary** and **Details** sections. Click on the **Create** button to proceed with the creation of the domain.

15. Once the domain is created successfully, click on the **Done** button in the **Creating Domain** page to dismiss the configuration wizard.

How it works...

In Steps 1 through 15, we go through the process of creating and configuring a new WebLogic domain. A domain in WebLogic is the basic administrative unit, and it consists of associated resources such as one or more WebLogic server instances, machines, clusters, services, applications, libraries, and others. Creation and configuration of a new WebLogic domain is achieved using the **Fusion Middleware Configuration Wizard** utility. The configuration utility can be started by running the `config` script located in the `common/bin` directory under the WebLogic installation directory. WebLogic is installed in the `wlserver_xx.x` directory under the Middleware home directory, where `xx.x` is the WebLogic Server version. Note that for a Windows installation of JDeveloper, a shortcut is created for the configuration utility, called **Configuration Wizard**, under the **Oracle Fusion Middleware 11.1.2.x.x | WebLogic Server 11gR1 | Tools** group in the **Start** menu.

In step 1 of the domain configuration wizard, we have chosen to create a new domain. You can also choose to extend an existing domain by adding additional extension sources to the domain and/or reconfiguring the domain structure (servers, clusters, machines, and so on).

In step 2, we have selected the **Oracle JRF – 11.1.1.0** domain source. This will install the necessary libraries to the domain in order to support the deployment and execution of ADF Fusion web applications.

We proceed in step 3 to specify the domain name and location. By default, domains are created in the `user_projects/domains` directory under the Middleware home directory. Choosing this default location is acceptable for development purposes. For production installations, you should choose a top level directory independent of the specific WebLogic Server installation.

In step 4, we have specified the domain's administrator username and password. These credentials are necessary to access the domain for administrative purposes either using the `console` application or through any other administration utilities (`WLST`, `weblogic.Deployer`, and so on).

In step 5, we configured the server startup mode to be in development mode. This mode enables the WebLogic auto-deployment feature, which allows for the automatic deployments of applications that reside in the `autodeploy` domain directory. This will be fine for this recipe. In a production environment configuration, production mode should be selected along with the JRockit JDK. For a comprehensive list of differences between the development and production startup modes, take a look at the *Differences Between Development and Production Mode* table in the *Creating Domains Using the Configuration Wizard* documentation. This document is available through the Oracle WebLogic Server Documentation Library currently at `http://docs.oracle.com/cd/E14571_01/wls.htm`.

In step 6, we indicated which components we will be providing additional configuration for. In this case, we configured the administration server, a managed server and its machine, and the deployments and services. For each component, an additional wizard page will be presented to further configure the specific component.

In steps 7 through 11, we created and configured the domain's server instances. The administration server is used to manage the domain, and its creation is required. The managed server will be used to deploy ADF applications. In both cases, we specified the server's name, listen address, and listen port. Managed servers are assigned to WebLogic machines (this is done in step 11). This identifies a physical unit of hardware that is associated with a WebLogic Server instance. They are used in conjunction with the WebLogic node manager to start and shutdown remote servers. Furthermore, WebLogic uses a configured machine in order to delegate tasks, such as HTTP session replication, in a clustered configuration. A machine was created and configured in step 10.

In steps 12 and 13, we have made available all installed product libraries and services, to the managed server instance. This will allow us to deploy and run ADF Fusion web applications on the managed server.

After reviewing the configuration in step 14, we create the domain in step 15.

There's more...

Once the domain creation completes successfully, it can be started by separately starting the administration and managed server instances. To start the administration server, run the `startWebLogic` script located in the domain `bin` directory. When you do so, observe in the console window that the server is started successfully, as shown in the following screenshot:

The managed server can be started by running the `startManagedWebLogic` script, also located in the domain `bin` directory. Run the `startManagedWebLogic` script by specifying the name of the managed server instance and the URL of the administration server, for instance, `startManagedWebLogic.cmd ManagedServer1 http://localhost:7001`. In this case, it has been assumed that the managed server name is `ManagedServer1` and that the administration server runs locally and listens to port 7001.

Note that each time you start the managed server instance, you will be asked to enter the domain administrator username and password. To avoid having to specify these credentials each time, create a file called `boot.properties` and add the following information to it:

```
username=<adminusername>
password=<adminpassword>
```

Replace `<adminusername>` and `<adminpassword>` with the administrator username and password respectively, and place the `boot.properties` file in the `servers/ManagedServer1/security` directory under the domain directory. Note that the `ManagedServer1` directory under the domain `servers` directory will not exist until you start the managed server at least once. You may also need to create the `security` directory yourself. Observe that the administrator username and password specified in the `boot.properties` file will be encrypted after starting the WebLogic Server.

To start the WebLogic administration console, browse the following address: `http://localhost:7001/console`. Use the administrator credentials specified during domain creation to log in.

To avoid having to redeploy the console application each time the domain is restarted, uncheck the **Enable on-demand deployment of internal applications** checkbox in the **Configuration | General** tab and click **Save**.

☐ **Enable on-demand deployment of internal applications**	Specifies whether internal applications such as the console, uddi, wlstestclient, and uddiexplorer are deployed on demand (first access) instead of during server startup. More Info...

For more information on the Fusion Middleware Configuration Wizard, consult the *Creating Domains Using the Configuration Wizard* documentation.

See also

▶ *Installation of JDeveloper on Linux, Chapter 1, Pre-requisites to Success: ADF Project Setup and Foundations*

Deploying on the Standalone WebLogic Server

Once you have created and configured a WebLogic domain, ADF Fusion web applications can be deployed onto it. During development, deployment can take place from the JDeveloper IDE. The process involves the creation of an Application Server connection in the **Resource Palette** and the creation of deployment profiles for the ViewController project and the application workspace. The application can then be deployed onto the standalone WebLogic domain using the **Application | Deploy** menu.

In this recipe, we will go through the process of manually deploying a Fusion web application to a WebLogic domain using the JDeveloper IDE.

Getting ready

You need to complete the *Configuring and using the Standalone WebLogic Server* recipe in this chapter before delving in this recipe. Furthermore, a skeleton **Fusion Web Application (ADF)** workspace is required for this recipe. For this purpose, we will use the MainApplication workspace that was developed in the *Breaking up the application in multiple workspaces* recipe in *Chapter 1, Pre-requisites to Success: ADF Project Setup and Foundations*. The MainApplication workspace requires a connection to the HR schema.

How to do it...

1. Open the MainApplication workspace. Double-click on the ViewController project in the **Application Navigator** to open the **Project Properties** dialog.

2. Click on **Deployment** and then click on the **New...** button to create a new deployment profile.

3. On the **Create Deployment Profile** dialog, select **WAR File** for the **Profile Type** and enter the name of the **Deployment Profile Name**.

4. On the **Edit WAR Deployment Profile Properties** dialog in the **General** section, enter the name and location of the **WAR File** and specify the **Java EE Web Context Root**. When done, click **OK** to dismiss all dialogs.

5. Select **Application Properties...** from the **Application** menu. On the **Application Properties** dialog, select **Deployment** and click on the **New...** button to create a new application deployment profile.

6. On the **Create Deployment Profile** dialog, select **EAR File** for the **Profile Type** and enter the **Deployment Profile Name**.

7. On the **Edit EAR Deployment Profile Properties** dialog, select the **General** section. Enter the name and location of the **EAR file** and specify the **Application name**.

8. Select **Application Assembly** and ensure that the **Java EE Modules** to be included in the EAR are selected. In this case, include both the Model and ViewController projects. When done, dismiss all dialogs by clicking **OK**.

9. Select **View | Resource Palette** to display the **Resource Palette** window. In the **Resource Palette**, expand the **IDE Connections** node. Right-click on the **Application Server** node and select **New Application Server Connection....**

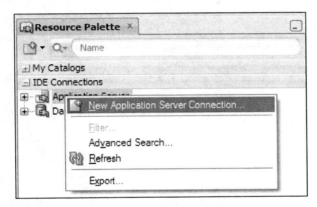

10. In the **Name and Type** page of the **Create Application Server Connection** wizard, enter the **Connection Name**. Select **WebLogic 10.3** for the **Connection Type** and click **Next**.

11. In the **Authentication** page, enter the WebLogic administrator credentials and click **Next**.

12. In the **Configuration** page, enter the WebLogic domain configuration and click **Next**.

13. In the **Test** page, click on the **Test Connection** button and ensure that **Status** is successful for all tests. Make sure that the WebLogic administration server instance is started before commencing with the tests. Click on the **Finish** button to complete the definition of the connection.

14. From the **Application** menu, select **Deploy** and then the deployment profile name.

15. In the **Deployment Action** page of the **Deploy** wizard, select **Deploy to Application Server** and click **Next**.

16. In the **Select Server** page, select the application server connection created earlier from the list of **Application Servers**. You can leave the **Overwrite modules of the same name** checkbox selected. Click **Next** to continue.

17. In the **Weblogic Options** page, click on the **Deploy to selected instances** radio button, and select the managed server instance to deploy onto, from the list of WebLogic Server instances. Click **Next** to continue.

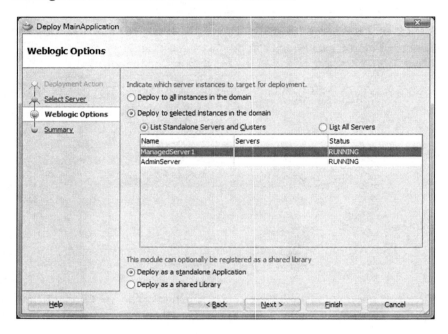

18. In the **Summary** page, verify the **Deployment Summary** and click **Finish** to proceed with the deployment. Observe in the **Deployment Log** window that the application is deployed successfully.

How it works...

In steps 1 through 4, we have defined a deployment profile for the ViewController project of the `Mainapplication` workspace. This project will be deployed as a Web Archive (WAR) file. In step 4, we have set the location and name of the WAR file that will be generated during deployment and specified the application context root. The context root is combined with the servlet mapping defined in `web.xml` to form the complete application URL. It is the base address for the application and all its associated resources.

In steps 5 through 8, we have defined the application's Enterprise Archive (EAR) deployment profile. Observe how in step 7, we specify the name and location of the EAR file along with the application name. This is the name of the Java EE application as it will appear in the **Deployments** table in WebLogic. Moreover, note that in step 8, we specify the EE modules to be included in the EAR. In this case, we have included both the Model and ViewController projects. Failure to include both of these projects will result in a failed deployment.

In steps 9 through 13, we have created a new application server connection. We use the **Resource Palette** facility and the **Create Application Server Connection** wizard to go through the steps required to define a connection for a standalone WebLogic domain. Ensure that the WebLogic domain has been started before going through this process.

With the deployment profiles in place, and with the connection to the standalone WebLogic Server properly configured and successfully tested, we use the **Application | Deploy** menu to deploy the application. This is done in steps 14 through 18. The available application server connections were presented in step 16 based on the application server connections defined in JDeveloper. In step 17, we choose to deploy the application to the managed server instance.

There's more...

You can check the application deployment status using the WebLogic administrator console. To do this, go to the **Summary of Deployments** available by selecting **Deployments** from the **Domain Structure** tree. The following screenshot shows our test application's deployment status:

	MainApplication	Active	✅ OK	Enterprise Application	100
	Modules				
	HR			JDBC Configuration	
	mainApplication			Web Application	

Observe that the **Health** status of the application is **OK**. Also, note that the HR data source is bundled in the deployed application. Whether the data source is bundled in the enterprise archive (EAR) produced by the deployment process, or not, is configured in the **Application Properties** dialog in JDeveloper. In the **Deployment | WebLogic** page, check or uncheck the **Auto Generate and Synchronize WebLogic JDBC Descriptors During Deployment** option to include or exclude the data source in the EAR file.

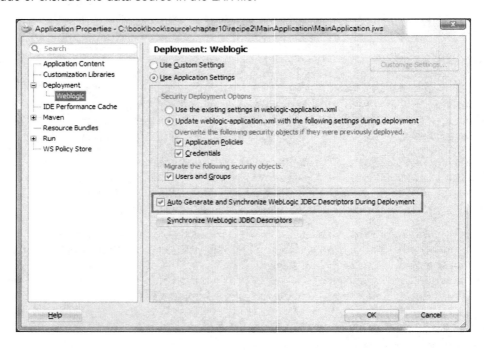

Note that this recipe presents a method to deploy applications directly to a WebLogic domain using JDeveloper. This technique is typically used to deploy the application to a test environment during the development process, as it allows testing of features such as OPSS security configuration, LDAP configuration, and so on, that are not otherwise available when running the application directly in JDeveloper. An alternative technique involves deploying the application to an EAR file, which can be deployed in turn by a separate process using a variety of other tools. The EAR file can be produced using JDeveloper or with tools such as ojdeploy (see recipe *Using ojdeploy to automate the build process* in this chapter). In production environments, continuous integration tools such as Hudson (see recipe *Using Hudson as a continuous integration framework* in this chapter), can be combined with ojdeploy, ant, and WLST scripts to automatically deploy the application to its application server. For more information on deploying ADF applications, take a look at the section *Deploying the Application* in the *Fusion Developer's Guide for Oracle Application Development Framework*, which can be found at http://docs. oracle.com/cd/E24382_01/web.1112/e16182/toc.htm.

▶ *Breaking up the application in multiple workspaces, Chapter 1, Pre-requisites to Success: ADF Project Setup and Foundations*

▶ *Configuring and using the Standalone WebLogic Server,* in this chapter

Using ojdeploy to automate the build process

ojdeploy is a command-line utility that can be used to automate the build and deployment process of ADF Fusion web applications. It is part of the JDeveloper installation package, and is installed alongside JDeveloper in the `jdeveloper/jdev/bin` directory (under the Middleware home directory). The utility can be run directly from the command line or it can be called from an ant script.

In this recipe, we demonstrate how to use ojdeploy to build an ADF Fusion web application comprised of three different workspaces. The final output of the build process is the application's Enterprise Archive file (EAR) file, which can be deployed to the Application Server using one of several possible techniques outlined in the *Deploying on the Standalone WebLogic Server* recipe in this chapter.

Getting ready

You need to have access to the `SharedComponents`, `HRComponents` and `MainApplication` workspaces. These workspaces were created in the *Breaking up the application in multiple workspaces* recipe in *Chapter 1, Pre-requisites to Success: ADF Project Setup and Foundations*. You also need to complete the recipe *Deploying on the Standalone WebLogic Server* in this chapter, to ensure that you have created the necessary deployment profiles for the `MainApplication` workspace. Finally, ensure that the `jdeveloper/jdev/bin` directory (under the Middleware home directory) is added to the `PATH` environment variable before running ojdeploy.

How to do it...

1. Using a text editor create the following ojdeploy build file `ojbuild.xml` as follows:

```
<?xml version="1.0" encoding="UTF-8" ?>
<ojdeploy-build basedir=".">
<!-- shared components workspace -->
<!-- This will build the SharedComponents.jar ADF Library JAR in
the ReUsableJARs directory -->
<deploy>
```

```
    <parameter name="workspace"
      value="${application.root}
      \SharedComponents\SharedComponents.jws"/>
    <parameter name="project" value="SharedViewController"/>
    <parameter name="profile" value="SharedComponents"/>
    </deploy>
    <!-- HRComponents workspace -->
    <!-- This will build the HRComponents.jar ADF Library JAR in the
      ReUsableJARs directory -->
    <deploy>
    <parameter name="workspace"
      value="${application.root}\HRComponents\HRComponents.jws"/>
    <parameter name="project" value="HRComponentsViewController"/>
    <parameter name="profile" value="HRComponents"/>
    </deploy>
    <!-- main application workspace -->
    <!-- This will build both of the MainApplication.war and
      MainApplication.ear archives in the
      MainApplication\MainApplicationViewController\deploy and
      MainApplication\deploydirectories respectively -->
    <deploy>
    <parameter name="workspace"
      value="${application.root}
      \MainApplication\MainApplication.jws"/>
    <parameter name="profile" value="MainApplication"/>
    </deploy>
    </ojdeploy-build>
```

2. Open a command shell and start the ojdeploy process by running the following command. Change `<application_root_directory>` to the appropriate directory under which your workspaces are located, as follows:

```
ojdeploy -buildfile ojbuild.xml -define
    application.root=<application_root_directory>
```

How it works...

In step 1, we have created an ojdeploy build file called `ojbuild.xml`. This is an XML file that comprises `ojdeploy-build` nodes along with embedded `deploy` nodes. Each `deploy` node defines a deployment process for the specific workspace, the project within the workspace, and the named deployment profile defined for the project. This information is specified by the `workspace`, `project`, and `profile` parameters respectively. If you do not specify a project name, then the workspace deployment profile is used, as in the case of the `MainApplication` workspace `deploy` configuration.

In step 2, we have initiated the deployment process by running ojdeploy with the `-buildfile` command-line argument. This parameter is used to specify the ojdeploy build file defined in step 1. Moreover, observe the usage of the `-define` argument to define a value for the macro `application.root`. This macro is used in the `ojbuild.xml` build file to reference the root application directory under which all application workspaces are located.

The result of running the ojdeploy deployment process for this recipe is the creation of the `SharedComponents.jar` and `HRComponents.jar` ADF Library JARs in the `ReUsableJARs` directory, the `MainApplication.war` archive in the `MainApplication\MainApplicationViewController\deploy` directory and the `MainApplication.ear` archive in the `MainApplication\deploy` directory.

There's more...

Note that the ojdeploy process performs a full business components validation. This involves the validation of all referenced business components throughout the ADF-BC projects involved in the build process. The validation process cross-references the component metadata XML files with the corresponding custom Java implementation classes.

For additional help on ojdeploy command-line arguments, built-in macros, and usage examples, run `ojdeploy -help` in the command line. A sample output is as listed:

```
Oracle JDeveloper Deploy 11.1.2.1.0.6081
Copyright (c) 2003, 2010, Oracle and/or its affiliates. All rights
reserved.
```

Usage:

```
ojdeploy -profile <name> -workspace <jws> [ -project <name> ] [
  <options> ]
ojdeploy -buildfile <ojbuild.xml> [ <options> ]
ojdeploy -buildfileschema
```

Arguments:

Name	Description
profile	The name of the profile to be deployed
workspace	Full path to the JDeveloper Workspace file(.jws)
project	Name of the JDeveloper Project within the .jws where the Profile can be found. If omitted, the Profile is assumed to be in the workspace
buildfile	Full path to a build file for batch deploy
buildfileschema	Print XML Schema for the build file

Options:

Name	Description
basedir	Interpret path for workspace relative to a base directory
outputfile	Substitute for the output file specified in the profile
nocompile	Skip compilation of Project or Workspace
nodependents	Do not deploy dependent profiles
clean	Clean output directories before compiling
nodatasources	Not include datasources from IDE
forcerewrite	Rewrite output file even if it is identical to existing file
updatewebxmlejbrefs	Update EJB references in web.xml
define	Define variables as comma separated name-value pairs
statuslogfile	Full path to an output file for status summary - no macros allowed
failonwarning	Stop deployment on warnings
timeout	Time in seconds allowed for each deployment task
stdout	Redirect stdout to file
stderr	Redirect stderr to file
ojserver	Run deployment using ojserver
address	Listen address for ojserver

Built-in macros:

Name	Description
workspace.name	name of the workspace (without the .jws extension)
workspace.dir	directory of the workspace.jws file
project.name	name of the project (without the .jpr extension)
project.dir	directory of the project.jpr file
profile.name	name of the profile being deployed
deploy.dir	default deploy directory for the profile
base.dir	current ojdeploy directory unless overridden by the -basedir parameter or by the "basedir" attribute in the build script

Note: project.name and project.dir are only available when project-level profile is being deployed.

Examples:

Deploy a Project-level profile
```
ojdeploy -profile webapp1 -workspace
  /usr/jdoe/Application1/Application1.jws -project Project1
ojdeploy -profile webapp1 -workspace Application1/Application1.jws -
  basedir /usr/jdoe -project Project1
```

Deploy a Workspace-level profile
```
ojdeploy -profile earprofile1 -workspace
  /usr/jdoe/Application1/Application1.jws
```

Deploy all Profiles from all Projects of a Workspace
```
ojdeploy -workspace /usr/jdoe/Application1/Application1.jws -project
  \* -profile \*
```

Build in batch mode from a ojbuild file
```
ojdeploy -buildfile /usr/jdoe/ojbuild.xml
```

Build using ojbuild file, pass into, or override default variables in, the build file.
```
ojdeploy -buildfile /usr/jdoe/ojbuild.xml -define
  myhome=/usr/jdoe,mytmp=/tmp
ojdeploy -buildfile /usr/jdoe/ojbuild.xml -basedir /usr/jdoe
```

Build using ojbuild file, set or override parameters in the default section
```
ojdeploy -buildfile /usr/jdoe/ojbuild.xml -nocompile
ojdeploy -buildfile /usr/jdoe/ojbuild.xml -outputfile
  '${workspace.dir}/${profile.name}.jar'
ojdeploy -buildfile /usr/jdoe/ojbuild.xml -define mydir=/tmp -
  outputfile  '${mydir}/${workspace.name}-${profile.name}'
```

More examples:
```
ojdeploy -workspace
  Application1/Application1.jws,Application2/Application2.jws -
  basedir /home/jdoe -profile app*
ojdeploy -buildfile /usr/jdoe/ojbuild.xml -define
  outdir=/tmp,rel=11.1.1
-outputfile
  '${outdir}/built/${workspace.name}/${rel}/${profile.name}.jar'
ojdeploy -workspace Application1/Application1.jws -basedir /home/jdoe
  -nocompile
-outputfile '${base.dir}/${workspace.name}-${profile.name}'
ojdeploy -workspace /usr/jdoe/Application1.jws -project \* -profile
  \* -stdout /home/jdoe/stdout/${project.name}.log
```

See also

▶ *Breaking up the application in multiple workspaces, Chapter 1, Pre-requisites to Success: ADF Project Setup and Foundations*

▶ *Deploying on the Standalone WebLogic Server,* in this chapter

Using Hudson as a continuous integration framework

Hudson is an open source continuous integration server that can be used to execute and monitor the execution of repeated jobs, such as building a software project. In the context of developing ADF Fusion web applications, Hudson can be used to build an ADF application directly from the version control sources and to deploy the built enterprise archive onto the application server. This is done automatically and continuously based on how Hudson is configured for each job.

In this recipe, we will go through the steps of defining a Hudson job that will build and deploy a sample ADF Fusion web application. We will check out the latest version of the application from the version control (Subversion) repository, build the application using ojdeploy, and finally deploy the application on the Standalone WebLogic Server using the weblogic.Deployer deployment tool.

Getting ready

For the sample ADF Fusion web application, we will use the `SharedComponents`, `HRComponents`, and `MainApplication` workspaces that were created in the *Breaking up the application in multiple workspaces* recipe in *Chapter 1, Pre-requisites to Success: ADF Project Setup and Foundations*. It is assumed that the application components reside in a Subversion repository. In addition, we will utilize the ojdeploy build file developed in the *Using ojdeploy to automate the build process* recipe in this chapter.

How to do it...

1. Download the latest version of Hudson. At the time of this writing, Hudson can be downloaded from `http://hudson-ci.org/`.

2. Install Hudson according to the documentation instructions. For the purpose of this recipe, we will run Hudson directly by executing `java -jar hudson-x.x.x.war` from the command line. `hudson-x.x.x.war` is the specific version of Hudson that was downloaded.

3. Access the Hudson dashboard using your browser. If you are running Hudson locally as stated previously, the URL would be `http://localhost:8080`.

4. Create a new job by clicking on the **New Job** link in the main page.

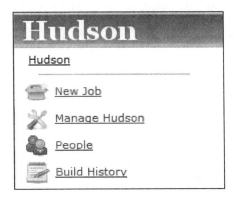

5. Provide the **Job Name** and select **Build a free-style software project**. Click **OK** to proceed.

6. In the job configuration page, select **Discard Old Builds**.

7. In the **Source Code Management** section, select **Subversion** and provide the **Repository URL**.

8. In the **Build Triggers** section, select **Build periodically** and enter 10 minutes for the **Schedule** value. Use the following cron syntax **10 * * * ***.

9. In the **Build** section, click on the **Add build step** button. Select **Execute Windows batch command** (**Execute shell** if Hudson is running on Linux) and enter build.cmd in the **Command** field.

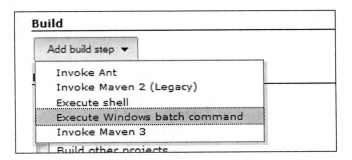

10. Click on the **Save** button to save the job definition.

11. With the job selected, click on the **Configure** link. In the **Source Code Management** section, click on the **Update credentials** link under the **Subversion Repository URL**.

12. In the **Subversion Authorization** screen, select **User name/password authentication** and enter the Subversion credentials.

13. From the main dashboard page, click on **Manage Hudson | Configure System**. In the **Global properties** section, click on **Environment variables** and then the **Add** button. Create new environment variables OJDEPLOY_PATH, WLS_DOMAIN_HOME, WLS_ADMIN_URL, WLS_ADMIN_USERNAME, WLS_ADMIN_PASSWORD, WLS_APPLICATION_NAME, and WLS_TARGETS and set their values appropriately.

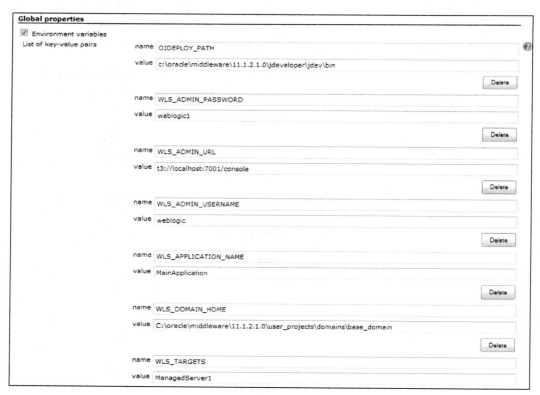

14. Create the `build.cmd` script file at the application root folder with the the following code as its contents. Ensure that the `build.cmd` file is added to Subversion.

```
REM Build application using ojdeploy
"%OJDEPLOY_PATH%\ojdeploy" -buildfile ojbuild.xml -define
   application.root="%WORKSPACE%"  REM Deploy EAR
call "%WLS_DOMAIN_HOME%\bin\setDomainEnv.cmd" %*
java weblogic.Deployer -adminurl %WLS_ADMIN_URL% -username
   %WLS_ADMIN_USERNAME% -password %WLS_ADMIN_PASSWORD% -name
   %WLS_APPLICATION_NAME% -undeploy
java weblogic.Deployer -adminurl %WLS_ADMIN_URL% -username
   %WLS_ADMIN_USERNAME% -password %WLS_ADMIN_PASSWORD% -name
   %WLS_APPLICATION_NAME% -deploy -upload
   "%WORKSPACE%\MainApplication\deploy\
   %WLS_APPLICATION_NAME%.ear" -
   targets "%WLS_TARGETS%"
```

How it works...

In steps 1 through 3, we have downloaded Hudson from the Hudson website and started it using the `java -jar hudson-x.x.x.war` command. This is not the recommended way to run Hudson in a production environment, but it will do for this recipe. It is recommended that the Hudson Web Archive (WAR) file is deployed onto one of the supported Web containers, as outlined in the Hudson installation documentation currently available in the Hudson wiki page `http://wiki.hudson-ci.org/display/HUDSON/Installing+Hudson`. Once started, Hudson can be accessed through a Web browser using the IP address or hostname of the server it is running on. We have executed it locally using the default startup configuration, so in this case, it is accessible through `http://localhost:8080`. The main Hudson page is called the Hudson Dashboard.

Steps 4 through 10 detail the definition of a Hudson job that will be used to build an ADF Fusion web application. The job uses ojdeploy to build the application Enterprise Archive (EAR) file and weblogic.Deployer to deploy the EAR file to the Standalone WebLogic Server. Both ojdeploy and weblogic.Deployer are accessed via an operating system script file. As we will be running Hudson on a Windows operating system, a cmd script file is used.

A Hudson job is defined by clicking on the **New Job** link in the Hudson Dashboard. This eventually takes you to the job definition page, a page with a rather long list of configuration parameters. However, the basic configuration parameters needed to get a simple job up and running are outlined in steps 6 through 10. First you need to specify the name of the Hudson job and select its type. Note that the job name also becomes part of the workspace directory, the directory used by Hudson to check out and stage the build, so be careful if you specify a job name with spaces in it. In this case, ensure that you access the workspace directory (when referenced) within double quotes, as in `"%WORKSPACE%"`. The Hudson workspace is accessible via the system-defined environment variable `WORKSPACE`.

In step 5, we have also chosen a `free-style software project` job type, which is a general job type.

In step 6, we have indicated what to do with previous builds. The option **Discard Old Builds** will allow you to define how many days to keep your builds and the maximum number of builds to keep.

In step 7, we specified the source control management system that we are using and entered the source control repository information. For this recipe, we are using Subversion as our source control management system. The credentials for accessing Subversion are specified at a later stage (see steps 11 and 12).

In step 8, we specified the job triggers. These are the possible ways that you can trigger the execution of the job. You can define multiple triggers. We have indicated that this job will run every 10 minutes. Observe that we have specified the time value using cron syntax. The cron syntax time value consists of 5 fields separated with white space: MINUTE HOUR DOM MONTH DOW, where DOM is the day of the month and DOW is the day of the week. For further details and examples on the cron time value syntax, see the Hudson online help.

We have concluded the definition of the job by indicating in step 9 the execution of a Windows batch command. As indicated earlier, this is fine for the purposes of this recipe since we are running Hudson on a Windows operating system. You will adapt this step depending on your specific configuration. The Windows batch file that we will execute is called `build.cmd` and is implemented in step 14. We saved the job definition in step 10.

In steps 11 through 13, we provide additional configuration information. Note the definition of the environment variables in step 13. We will be using these environment variables in the `build.cmd` script.

The `build.cmd` script file is implemented in step 14. We have used ojdeploy and the `ojbuild.xml` build file that we created in recipe *Using ojdeploy to automate the build process* in this chapter. Note that the `application.root` parameter has been set to the job workspace directory. Hudson will check out the application from Subversion into this directory. The script file shows how to deploy the resulted EAR file to a Standalone WebLogic Server target. This is done using the weblogic.Deployer tool, a Java-based command-line tool that allows for the deployment (and undeployment) of applications to and from WebLogic. To ensure the proper configuration of the WebLogic domain environment, we have run the `setDomainEnv.cmd` script prior to the deployment process. Also, note that we have chosen to undeploy the application before its deployment. Finally, observe the usage of the environment variables defined in step 13.

There's more...

To manually start the job, return to the Hudson Dashboard and click on the **Schedule a build** icon (the icon with the green arrow to the right).

You can monitor the job status using the **Console Output** page. The status of the job is indicated at the bottom of the **Console Output**.

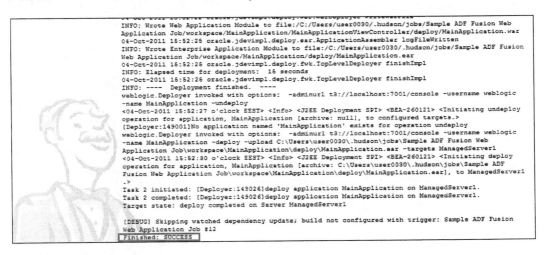

See also

▶ *Breaking up the application in multiple workspaces, Chapter 1, Pre-requisites to Success: ADF Project Setup and Foundations*

▶ *Using ojdeploy to automate the build process, in this chapter*

11
Refactoring, Debugging, Profiling, and Testing

In this chapter, we will cover:

- ▸ Synchronizing business components with database changes
- ▸ Refactoring ADF components
- ▸ Configuring and using remote debugging
- ▸ Logging Groovy expressions
- ▸ Dynamically configuring logging in WebLogic Server
- ▸ Performing log analysis
- ▸ Using CPU profiler for an application running on a Standalone WebLogic Server
- ▸ Configuring and using JUnit for unit testing

Introduction

Refactoring support in JDeveloper allows you to modify the structure of an ADF Fusion web application without altering the overall behavior of the application. Each time you refactor an application component, JDeveloper transparently transforms the application structure by taking care of any references to the component. Refactoring at the ADF Fusion web application level allows renaming, modifying, and deleting application components. More options exist when refactoring Java code.

JDeveloper includes a comprehensive list of debugging features to allow you to debug ADF Fusion web applications deployed and running both locally on the Integrated WebLogic Server and remotely on the Standalone WebLogic Server. Similarly, profiling support in JDeveloper allows you to gather CPU and memory profiling statistics for applications deployed and running both locally and remotely.

You test your ADF Fusion web application by debugging it and profiling it in the JDeveloper IDE. When it comes to unit testing, JUnit can be integrated in JDeveloper through the installation of separate JDeveloper JUnit extensions. Once installed, these extensions make available a number of wizards in JDeveloper that make adding JUnit unit tests to ADF Fusion web applications quite easy.

Synchronizing business components with database changes

During the development process of an ADF Fusion web application, as the database schema evolves, there will be a need to synchronize the corresponding business components used in order to reflect these changes in the database schema. The process of synchronizing the business components is inherently supported in JDeveloper via the **Synchronize with Database** feature. Other capabilities also exist, such as making an attribute transient for a database table column that has been removed, and adding new entity attributes to view objects via the **Add Attribute from Entity** feature.

In this recipe, we will demonstrate a business components synchronization scenario that involves the addition, deletion, and modification of database table columns.

Getting ready

Before engaging in this recipe, you need to create a sample table in your database schema called SYNCHRONIZATION. We will use this table to demonstrate the business objects synchronization features. Use the following SQL code to accomplish this:

```
CREATE TABLE SYNCHRONIZATION (DELETED_COLUMN    VARCHAR2(30),
    MODIFIED_COLUMN   VARCHAR2(30));
```

How to do it...

1. Create a **Fusion Web Application (ADF)** workspace. Using the **New Entity Object...** wizard, create an entity object for the SYNCHRONIZATION table. Also, generate a default view object called SynchronizationView.

2. Use the following SQL to modify the `SYNCHRONIZATION` table in the database:

```
ALTER TABLE SYNCHRONIZATION MODIFY(MODIFIED_COLUMN VARCHAR2(20
   BYTE));
ALTER TABLE SYNCHRONIZATION ADD (NEW_COLUMN  VARCHAR2(30));
ALTER TABLE SYNCHRONIZATION DROP
  COLUMN DELETED_COLUMN;
```

3. Right-click on the **Synchronization** entity object in the **Application Navigator** and select **Synchronize with Database...**.

4. In the **Synchronize with Database** dialog, click on the **Synchronize All** button and click **OK** on the verification dialog.

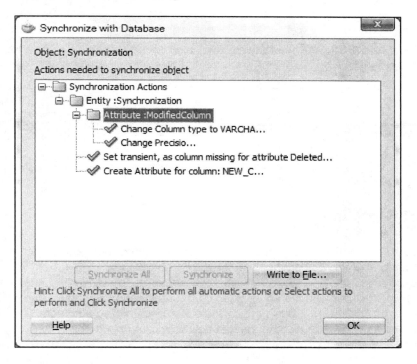

5. Open the `Synchronize` entity object in the **Overview** editor and click on the **Attributes** tab. Select the `DeletedColumn` attribute and click on the **Delete selected attribute(s)** button (the red X icon).

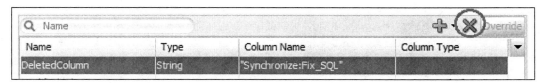

6. In the **Delete Attribute** dialog, click on the **View Usages** button. Repeat step 5, this time clicking on the **Ignore** button.

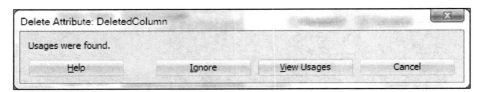

7. Double-click on the `SynchronizationView` view object in the **Application Navigator** and click on the **Attributes** tab in the **Overview** editor. Select the `DeletedColumn` attribute and click on the **Delete selected attribute(s)** button (the red X icon).

8. Select **Add Attribute from Entity...** by clicking on the green plus sign on top of the attributes list.

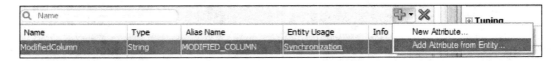

9. In the **Attributes** dialog, select the `NewColumn` attribute in the **Available** tree and shuttle it to the **Selected** list.

How it works...

To demonstrate the business components database synchronization feature in JDeveloper, we have created an entity object based on the `SYNCHRONIZATION` table. Then we altered the table by adding, removing, and modifying table columns. The synchronization feature is accessible by right-clicking on the entity object in the **Application Navigator** and selecting **Synchronize with Database....** Only entity objects are synchronized automatically. You will have to manually synchronize all other related business component objects, including any bindings that were made for the affected attributes and any references to these bindings and attributes in pages and in Java code (managed beans, business components custom implementation classes).

Observe in step 5 that the removal of a table column does not automatically remove the corresponding entity object attribute, but makes the attribute transient instead. As the attribute referring to a deleted column may be referenced by entity-based view objects, you will have to delete the corresponding view object attribute manually. We did this in step 7. Furthermore, observe that any new entity object attributes that were generated for the newly added table columns are not automatically added to the view object. You will have to do this manually. We do did this in steps 8 and 9.

There's more...

Note that adding new columns to a table does not affect the behaviour of the application, if the corresponding entity object is not synchronized. However, to use the new columns in your application, synchronization is required.

Refactoring ADF components

JDeveloper offers extensive support for refactoring ADF Fusion web application components, available through the **Refactor** main menu selections or via context menus for selected ADF components. The refactoring of ADF application components in most cases includes renaming, moving, and deleting these components. Refactoring of ADF components is supported throughout the Model-View-Controller architecture of the application including business components and their attributes, task flows, bindings, JSF files, and managed beans. Refactoring transparently takes care of updating any references to the refactored object, without affecting the overall functionality of the application.

In this recipe, we will demonstrate the refactoring facilities in JDeveloper by refactoring business components, business components attributes, task flows, JSF pages, associated page definition files and their bindings, and managed beans.

Getting ready

This recipe requires that you already have a **Fusion Web Application (ADF)** workspace that comprises business components, task flows, JSF pages, associated page definition files, and managed beans. For this purpose, we will use the `MainApplication` and `HRComponents` workspaces. These workspaces were developed in *Breaking up the application in multiple workspaces, Chapter 1, Pre-requisites to Success: ADF Project Setup and Foundations* and in *Overriding remove() to delete associated children entities, Chapter 2, Dealing with Basics: Entity Objects* respectively.

How to do it...

1. To refactor a business component, right-click on it in the **Application Navigator**, select **Refactor** from the context menu and a refactoring option (**Rename...** or **Move...**). To delete a business component, select **Delete** from the context menu. Alternatively, select **Rename...**, **Move...**, or **Delete** from the **Refactor** main menu.

2. To refactor a business component attribute, double-click on the business component in the **Application Navigator** to open the **Overview** editor and select the **Attributes** tab. Right-click on the attribute to refactor and select any of the **Rename...**, **Delete**, or **Change Type...** option.

3. To refactor a task flow, right-click on it in the **Application Navigator** and select any of the **Rename...**, **Move...**, **Delete** under the **Refactor** selection in the context menu.

4. To refactor a JSF page, right-click on the page in the **Application Navigator** and select any of the refactoring options available under the **Refactor** menu.

5. To refactor a page definition file, select any of the refactoring options under the **Refactor** main menu.

6. To refactor a page definition binding object, open the page data binding definition **Overview** editor and right-click on the binding object to refactor in the **Bindings** or **Executables** lists. Use the options available under the **Refactor** menu.

7. To refactor a managed bean, right-click on the managed bean in the **Application Navigator** and select any of the refactoring options available under the **Refactor** menu.

8. To refactor a plain file, select the file in the **Application Navigator** and use any of the available refactor options under the **Refactor** main menu.

How it works...

In steps 1 through 8, we have shown how to refactor almost any ADF Fusion web application component. In most cases, the refactoring options are available in both the main menu and context menu **Refactor** selections. In certain cases, such as when refactoring a page definition filename, the refactoring options are available only in the main menu **Refactor** selection. In other cases, as in the case of refactoring managed beans, additional options exist. Finally, observe what happens when you try to delete a component that is referenced by another component. A **Confirm Delete** dialog is displayed giving you the ability to discover the component's usages. The **Find Usages** feature is also separately available and can be used to determine the component's references prior to refactoring it.

There's more...

To refactor (rename) a deployment profile defined for a project, open the project configuration file (`.jpr`) in a text editor and locate the `oracle.jdeveloper.deploy.dt.DeploymentProfiles` node. Rename the profile identified by the `profileName` value. Similarly, you can rename a deployment profile defined for the workspace. Open the workspace configuration file (`.jws`) and locate the `oracle.jdeveloper.deploy.dt.DeploymentProfiles` node. Rename the profile identified by the `ProfileName` value. Alternatively, you can create a new deployment profile.

For information on how to manually refactor (move) the ADF business components project configuration file (`.jpx`), refer to the *Moving the ADF Business Components Project Configuration File (.jpx)* section in the *Fusion Developer's Guide for Oracle Application Development Framework*, which can be found at `http://docs.oracle.com/cd/E24382_01/web.1112/e16181/toc.htm`.

For information on how to refactor the data bindings registry file `DataBindings.cpx`, refer to section *Refactoring the DataBindings.cpx File* in the *Fusion Developer's Guide for Oracle Application Development Framework*, which can be found at `http://docs.oracle.com/cd/E24382_01/web.1112/e16181/toc.htm`.

Finally, to rename a workspace project, you can use the **File | Rename** menu.

For a comprehensive reference to refactoring ADF components in JDeveloper, refer to the chapter *Refactoring a Fusion Web Application* in the *Fusion Developer's Guide for Oracle Application Development Framework*, which can be found at `http://docs.oracle.com/cd/E24382_01/web.1112/e16181/toc.htm`.

See also

- *Breaking up the application in multiple workspaces, Chapter 1, Pre-requisites to Success: ADF Project Setup and Foundations*
- *Overriding remove() to delete associated children entities, Chapter 2, Dealing with Basics: Entity Objects*

Configuring and using remote debugging

Remote debugging allows you to debug an ADF Fusion web application deployed and running remotely on a Standalone WebLogic Server directly from JDeveloper. Once both the remote WebLogic Server and the ADF project(s) in JDeveloper are configured to support it, a remote debugging session can be started in JDeveloper through the **Debug** menu selection. The session does not differ from a local debugging session for an application running on the Integrated WebLogic Server, but offers a number of advantages when compared to it. Some of these advantages are the ability to easily break inside any of the application's ADF Library JARs, the separation of the development process from the debugging of the application, freeing resources in JDeveloper, and using a Standalone WebLogic Server that closely matches the production environment configuration. When WebLogic is running on a separate machine, also consider the resources that are saved in the developer's machine.

In this recipe, we will see how to configure a managed WebLogic Server instance and JDeveloper to support remote debugging. We will also see how to initiate a remote debugging session in JDeveloper.

Getting ready

You will need a Standalone WebLogic Server, configured and started as explained in *Configuring and using the Standalone WebLogic Server, Chapter 10, Deploying ADF Applications*. You will also need an ADF Fusion web application deployed to the Standalone WebLogic Server. For this, you can consult *Deploying on the Standalone WebLogic Server, Chapter 10, Deploying ADF Applications*.

How to do it...

1. Open the `startManagedWebLogic` script in a text editor located in the `bin` directory under the domain directory. Add the following definitions to it before calling the `startWebLogic` script:

```
@REM Configuring and using remote debugging
if "%SERVER_NAME%"=="ManagedServer1" (
  set debugFlag=true
  set DEBUG_PORT=4001
)
```

2. While in the `startManagedWebLogic` script, remove the `nodebug` argument when calling the `startWebLogic` script.

3. Restart the WebLogic domain and log in to the WebLogic administrator console. Go to the **Summary of Servers** page by clicking **Environment | Servers** in the **Domain Structure** tree.

4. Click on the `ManagedServer1` managed server instance and then on the **Protocols | General** tabs. Click on the **Enable Tunneling** checkbox and then on the **Save** button. Log out from the WebLogic administrator console and restart the WebLogic domain.

5. In JDeveloper, double-click on the project that you want to configure for remote debugging to open the **Project Properties** dialog. In the **Project Properties** dialog, select **Run/Debug/Profile**.

6. Click on the **Edit...** button to edit the **Default** run configuration. Alternatively, you can create a new run configuration specifically for remote debugging. In the **Edit Run Configuration** dialog, Launch **Settings** page to ensure that the **Remote Debugging** checkbox is selected.

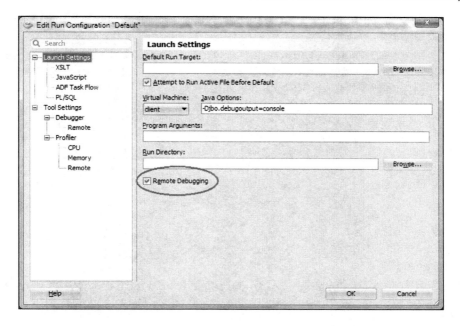

7.   While at the **Edit Run Configuration** dialog, select **Tool Settings | Debugger |
     Remote**. Ensure that the **Protocol** is set to **Attach to JPDA** and enter the information
     for the **Host**, **Port**, and **Timeout** fields. Make sure that you enter the debug port
     specified in step 1, that is, 4001 for this recipe.

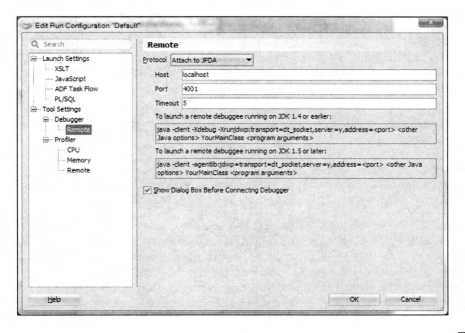

8. Dismiss the **Edit Run Configuration** and **Project Settings** dialogs by clicking **OK** to save the configuration changes.

9. To start a remote debugging session, right-click on the specific project that was configured in the **Application Navigator** and select **Debug**. Verify the connection settings in the **Attach to JPDA Debuggee** dialog and click **OK**.

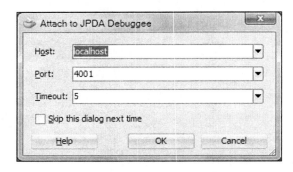

10. Observe in the **Debugging Log** that the connection to the remote WebLogic Server was successful. Set the necessary breakpoints in your code and start the application in the web browser.

How it works...

In steps 1 through 4, we configured the WebLogic managed server instance that we want to enable for remote debugging. This was done by editing the startManagedWebLogic script and setting the debugFlag environment variable to true. This is the script that we use to start a managed WebLogic server instance. By setting the debugFlag to true, the managed server will start to support remote debugging. This is actually done in the setDomainEnv script where the JAVA_DEBUG environment variable is set. Following are the debug configuration parameters specified in setDomainEnv:

```
set JAVA_DEBUG=-Xdebug -Xnoagent -
  Xrunjdwp:transport=dt_socket,address=%DEBUG_PORT%,server=y,
  suspend=n -Djava.compiler=NONE
```

The remote connection debug port is specified with the DEBUG_PORT environment variable, which was also set in step 1. The changes in step 1 were specified for the Windows operating system.

Note in step 1 how we check for the specific ManagedServer1 managed server instance in order to set the remote debugging configuration parameters. Following this strategy, you will be able to enable remote debugging only for the specific server instances that you are interested. This will also allow you to specify different remote debugging ports for each managed server. Also, note in step 2 that we had to remove the nodebug argument when calling the startWebLogic script from within the startManagedWebLogic script.

In step 3, we restarted the WebLogic domain with the new configuration. Then, using the administration console, we enabled HTTP tunnelling for the `ManagedServer1` instance (step 4). This will enable WebLogic to simulate a T3 protocol connection using an HTTP connection and allow remote debugging to commence via a stateful connection between JDeveloper and WebLogic.

In steps 5 through 8, we configure the specific ADF project to allow for remote debugging. This configuration is done by configuring a project **Run Configuration**. A **Run Configuration** is available in the **Project Properties** dialog. Part of the configuration is to specify the host and remote connection port (4001) used in step 1.

To start a remote debugging session, ensure that the WebLogic domain is up and running. Right-click on the project configured for remote debugging in the **Application Navigator** and select **Debug**. Debugging is done as usual.

There's more...

To break inside an ADF Library JAR that is part of the application, you will need to enable remote debugging for the specific ADF Library JAR project as it is outlined in steps 5 through 8. In this case, if a remote debugging session is currently in progress, you need to first detach from it by clicking on the **Terminate** debug button and selecting **Detach** in the **Terminate Debuggee Process** dialog.

See also

- *Configuring and using the Standalone WebLogic Server, Chapter 10, Deploying ADF Applications*
- *Deploying on the Standalone WebLogic Server, Chapter 10, Deploying ADF Applications*

Logging Groovy expressions

Groovy is a Java-like scripting language that is integrated in the context of ADF business components, and is used in a declarative manner in expressions ranging from attribute and bind variable initializations to entity object validation rules and error messages. It runs in the same JVM as the application, is interpreted at runtime and is stored as metadata in the corresponding business component definitions. JDeveloper does not currently offer a debugging facility for Groovy expressions. In this recipe, we will implement a Groovy helper class that will allow us to log and debug Groovy expressions throughout the application.

Getting ready

We will add the Groovy logger class to the `SharedComponents` workspace. This workspace was created in *Breaking up the application in multiple workspaces, Chapter 1, Pre-requisites to Success: ADF Project Setup and Foundations.*

How to do it...

1. Open the `SharedComponents` workspace and create a new Java class called `GroovyLogger` for the business components project.

2. Open the `GroovyLogger` Java class in the Java editor and add the following code to it:

```
private static ADFLogger LOGGER =
  ADFLogger.createADFLogger(GroovyLogger.class);
public GroovyLogger() {
  super();
}
public static <T> T log(String groovyExpression, T data) {
  LOGGER.info("GroovyLogger ==> Expression: " +
    groovyExpression + ", Data: " + data);
  return data;
}
```

3. Redeploy the shared components workspace to an ADF Library JAR.

How it works...

We have added a `GroovyLogger` class to the `SharedComponents` workspace to allow for the logging and debugging of Groovy expression. The class implements a `log()` method, which accepts the Groovy expression to log, along with the expression data. It uses an `ADFLogger` to log the Groovy expression. The expression data is then returned to be used by the ADF framework.

Following is an example of how the `GroovyLogger` helper class can be used in your ADF business components Groovy expressions:

```
com.packt.jdeveloper.cookbook.shared.bc.logging.GroovyLogger
.log("adf.context.securityContext.userName",
  adf.context.securityContext.userName)
```

To debug your Groovy expressions, use the `GroovyLogger` class in your expressions as shown in the previous example and set a breakpoint anywhere in the `log()` method. Then inspect or watch the Groovy expressions using the available debug tools in JDeveloper.

▶ *Breaking up the application in multiple workspaces, Chapter 1, Pre-requisites to Success: ADF Project Setup and Foundations*

Dynamically configuring logging in WebLogic Server

In the recipe *Setting up logging* in *Chapter 1, Pre-requisites to Success: ADF Project Setup and Foundations,* we introduced the Oracle Diagnostics Logging (ODL) framework and how it could be utilized in an ADF Fusion web application through the `ADFLogger` class. In this recipe, we will demonstrate how to dynamically configure the ODL log level for a WebLogic Server instance at runtime. Specifically, we will configure the `oracle.jbo` business components logger for the `ManagedServer1` WebLogic Server instance to use the `NOTIFICATION` log level. `ManagedServer1` was created in *Configuring and using the Standalone WebLogic Server, Chapter 10, Deploying ADF Applications.* Dynamic log configuration is done via the **WLST** WebLogic administration utility. This program allows for the execution of custom scripts written in jython (an implementation of Python written in Java) to configure ODL.

Getting ready

You will need a Standalone WebLogic Server domain configured and started. This was explained in *Configuring and using the Standalone WebLogic Server, Chapter 10, Deploying ADF Applications.*

How to do it...

1. With the WebLogic Standalone Server started, run the WLST program located in the `oracle_common/common/bin` directory under the Middleware home. You do this by typing `wlst` in the shell command line.

2. Connect to the WebLogic administration server instance by issuing the following WLST command:

   ```
   connect('weblogic','weblogic1','t3://localhost:7001')
   ```

3. Change the log level of the `oracle.jbo` logger to `NOTIFICATION` by issuing the following WLST command:

   ```
   setLogLevel(target="ManagedServer1", logger="oracle.jbo",
     level="NOTIFICATION")
   ```

4. Verify that the `oracle.jbo` logger's log level was changed successfully by entering the following command:

   `getLogLevel(target="ManagedServer1",logger='oracle.jbo')`

5. Exit from WLST by typing `exit()`.

How it works...

In step 1, we started the WLST WebLogic script tool located in the Oracle home directory. This is the directory `oracle_common/common/bin` under the Middleware home. It is important that you run WLST in the specific directory because it supports custom commands to manage WebLogic logging.

In step 2, we connected to the WebLogic administration server instance using the `connect()` command. To do so, we have specified the administrator's authentication credentials and the administration server instance URL using the T3 protocol.

We changed the log level of the `oracle.jbo` logger to `NOTIFICATION` in step 3. The `oracle.jbo` logger is defined in the `logging.xml` logging configuration file located in the `config/fmwconfig/servers/ManagedServer1` directory under the domain directory, and it is utilized by the ADF Business Components framework. The log level was changed by issuing the command `setLogLevel()` and specifying the target server instance, the logger, and the new log level. The log level can be specified either as an ODL or as a Java log level. Valid Java levels are any of the following: `SEVERE`, `WARNING`, `INFO`, `CONFIG`, `FINE`, `FINER`, or `FINEST`. On the other hand valid ODL levels include a message type followed by a colon and a message level. The valid ODL message types are: `INCIDENT_ERROR`, `ERROR`, `WARNING`, `NOTIFICATION`, and `TRACE`. The message level is represented by an integer value that qualifies the message type. Possible values are from 1 (highest severity) through 32 (lowest severity).

To verify that the log level has been successfully changed, we issued the command `getLogLevel()` (in step 4) specifying the WebLogic Server instance target and the logger. We exited from WLST by typing `exit()` in step 5.

There's more...

WLST includes additional commands for dynamically configuring logging in WebLogic, which allow you to configure log handlers and to list loggers and log handlers. For a comprehensive reference of the custom logging commands supported by WLST, refer to the *Logging Custom WLST Commands* chapter in the *WebLogic Scripting Tool Command Reference* document. This document is part of the WebLogic Server Documentation Library available online currently at the address `http://docs.oracle.com/cd/E14571_01/wls.htm`.

▶ *Configuring and using the Standalone WebLogic Server, Chapter 10, Deploying ADF Applications*

Performing log analysis

A possibly lesser known feature of JDeveloper is its ability to perform ODL log analysis, known as the Oracle Diagnostic Log Analyzer. This feature allows you to open a diagnostics log file (or use the log file currently in the **Log** window in JDeveloper) and do a limited yet useful log analysis. For the Standalone WebLogic Server, diagnostics log files are produced by applications running on the specific WebLogic Server instance. The log files are produced and saved by WebLogic in a directory configured by the WebLogic administrator. This directory defaults to the `logs` directory under the `servers` directory for the specific server instance; that is, for a server instance called `ManagedServer1` they can be found in `servers/ManagedServer1/logs`. The `servers` directory is located under the specific domain directory.

In this recipe, we will see how to analyze a diagnostics log produced when running an ADF Fusion web application on a Standalone WebLogic Server. Alternatively, you can run the application in JDeveloper and analyze the log produced in the **Log** window.

Getting ready

You will need a Standalone WebLogic Server domain configured and started. You will also need your Fusion web application deployed to the Standalone WebLogic Server. For more information on these topics, refer to *Configuring and using the Standalone WebLogic Server* and *Deploying on the Standalone WebLogic Server, Chapter 10, Deploying ADF Applications*.

How to do it...

1. Run the application deployed on the Standalone WebLogic Server, so that a diagnostics log file is generated. Alternatively, if you already have a diagnostics log file to analyze, you can ignore this step.

2. In JDeveloper, select **Tools | Oracle Diagnostic Log Analyzer** from the main menu.

3. Click on the **Browse Log Files** button (the search icon) to locate the diagnostics file and open it.

4. Click on the **By Log Message** tab and specify the search criteria in the **Search** section. Press the **Search** button to commence with the search.

5. In the **Results** table, click on a value inside the **Related** column for a log entry of interest and select **Related By Request** from the context menu.

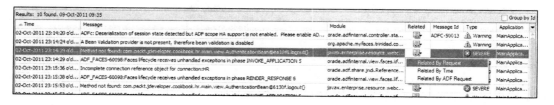

How it works...

Steps 1 through 5 give the details of the process of analyzing a diagnostics log file using the Oracle Diagnostics Log Analyzer feature in JDeveloper. The Oracle Diagnostics Analyzer is accessible via the **Tools | Oracle Diagnostic Log Analyzer** menu selection. Once started, you will need to load the specific diagnostics log file to analyze. We have done this in step 3. You can search the diagnostics log entries using either the **By ADF Request** or the **By Log Message** tab and specifying the search criteria. The **By ADF Request** tab will display only the log entries related to ADF requests made when a page is submitted. On the other hand the **By Log Message** tab will search all log entries in the log file by their log level. Moreover, the search criteria in both tabs allow you to search for diagnostic log entries based on their **Log Time** and based on the message content (**Message Id, User, Application, Module,** and so on).

The results of the search are displayed in the **Results** table. The results data are sortable by clicking on the column headers. To display all related log entries, click inside the **Related** column for a log entry of interest and select any of the choices available in the context menu. These choices are:

Related By	Results
Time	Filter diagnostic log entries to view all log entries leading up to the specific entry. You can refine the time before the entry using the dropdown.
Request	Filter diagnostic log entries to view all log entries for the same web request.
ADF Request	Switches to the **By ADF Request** tab to display the diagnostic log entries in a hierarchical arrangement to show their execution dependencies.

See also

- ▸ *Configuring and using the Standalone WebLogic Server, Chapter 10, Deploying ADF Applications*

- ▸ *Deploying on the Standalone WebLogic Server, Chapter 10, Deploying ADF Applications*

Using CPU profiler for an application running on a standalone WebLogic server

Profiling allows you to connect to a Standalone WebLogic Server instance and gather profiling statistics for your application. Profiling statistics can be subsequently used to identify and correct performance issues. JDeveloper supports both a CPU and a memory profiler. The CPU profiler gathers statistics related to CPU usage by the application. The memory profiler identifies how the application utilizes memory and can be used to diagnose memory leaks.

In this recipe, we will demonstrate how to use the CPU profiler to profile an ADF Fusion web application deployed to a Standalone WebLogic managed server instance running on the local machine.

Getting ready

You will need a Standalone WebLogic Server configured and started as explained in *Configuring and using the Standalone WebLogic Server, Chapter 10, Deploying ADF Applications*. You will also need an ADF Fusion web application deployed to the Standalone WebLogic Server. For this, you can consult *Deploying on the Standalone WebLogic Server, Chapter 10, Deploying ADF Applications*.

How to do it...

1. In JDeveloper, double-click on the project that you want to profile in the **Application Navigator** to bring up its **Project Properties** dialog.

2. Select **Run/Debug/Profile** and click on the **Edit...** button to edit the **Default Run Configuration**.

3. In the **Tool Settings | Profiler** page, enter `com.packt.jdeveloper.cookbook.*` in the **Start Filter**. Click **OK** a couple of times to dismiss the **Project Settings** dialog, saving the changes.

4. Select **Run | Attach to | CPU Profilee** from the main menu. On the **Attach to CPU Profilee** dialog, select the **WebLogic profiler agent** process and click **OK**. The profiler agent process is started along with the Standalone WebLogic Server.

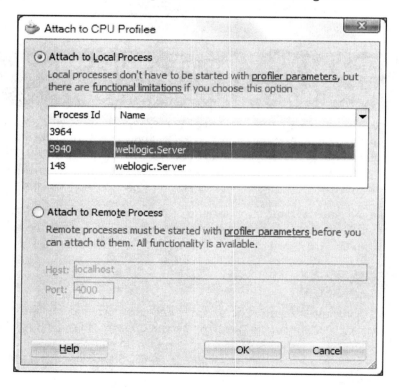

5. Once attached to the profiler agent, the **Profiling <project_name>** tab is displayed, where `<project_name>` is the name of project you are profiling. Click on the **Begin Use Case** button (the first icon in the toolbar) to initiate a new profiling use case.

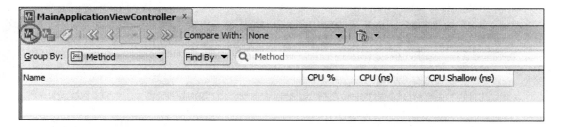

6. To generate profiler statistics, run the application in the web browser. To terminate the profiling session, click on the **Terminate Profiling** button (the red box icon) in the main toolbar.

How it works...

Steps 1 through 3 demonstrate how to configure a project for profiling. Observe in step 3, how we have indicated the specific package filter based on which we would like to filter the profiler results. Profiler data will be collected only for those stack levels whose class name satisfies the **Stack Filter** entry. Multiple filters can be entered, separated with spaces. You can also click on the **Advanced** button in the **Profiler** page to select the classes you want to profile.

Steps 4 through 6 show how to start a profiling session and how to create a new use case to collect profiling statistics. Observe in step 4, our choice for connecting to the profiler agent. As we are running the Standalone WebLogic Server locally, we have chosen the profiler agent from the **Attach to Local Process** list.

There's more...

To profile an ADF Fusion web application running on a WebLogic Server on a remote machine, the profiler agent must also be started on the remote machine as part of the WebLogic start-up configuration. To determine the profiler agent start-up configuration parameters, select **Tool Settings | Profiler | Remote** in the **Edit Run Configuration** dialog and then the **Remote Process Parameters** tab. Adjust the remote process port as needed in the **Default Settings** tab.

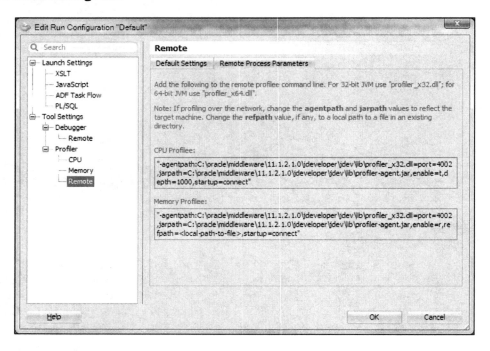

See also

- ▶ *Configuring and using the Standalone WebLogic Server, Chapter 10, Deploying ADF Applications*

- ▶ *Deploying on the Standalone WebLogic Server, Chapter 10, Deploying ADF Applications*

Configuring and using JUnit for unit testing

JUnit is a unit testing framework for Java code. Unit testing refers to programmatically testing individual pieces of code and it is actually part of the software development and construction process. In JDeveloper, JUnit is supported via the **BC4J JUnit Integration** and **JUnit Integration** extensions available through the **Official Oracle Extensions and Updates** update center. The BC4J JUnit Integration extension makes available wizards for constructing JUnit unit test cases, suites, and fixtures specifically for business components projects. On the other hand, the JUnit Integration extension includes wizards to help you setup generic JUnit artifacts. Upon installation, these extensions make available the **Unit Tests** category under the **General** category in the **New Gallery** dialog.

A unit test class is a class that contains unit test methods. Unit test classes are grouped in a test suite that runs all of the test cases together when executed. A unit test fixture is a special class used to configure the unit tests.

In this recipe, we will implement a JUnit test suite that will test the functionality of an application module and the view objects that are part of its data model.

Getting ready

You will need access to the HRComponents workspace created in *Overriding remove() to delete associated children entities, Chapter 2, Dealing with Basics: Entity Objects.*

How to do it...

1. In JDeveloper, select **Help | Check for Updates...** from the main menu. This will start the **Check for Updates** wizard.

2. In the **Source** page, select **Official Oracle Extensions and Updates** and click **Next**.

3. In the **Updates** page, select the **BC4J JUnit Integration** and **JUnit Integration** extensions and click **Next**.

4. Accept the JUnit license agreement and click **Next**. This will initiate the download of the JUnit extensions. Once the download is complete, in the **Summary** page, click on the **Finish** button. On the **Confirm Exit** dialog, click on the **Yes** button to restart JDeveloper.

5. Open the HRComponents workspace and create a project by selecting **Custom Project** from the **General | Projects** category in the **New Gallery** dialog.

6. In the **Name your project** page of the **Create Custom Project** wizard, enter HRComponentsUnitTests for the **Project Name** and click on the **Finish** button.

7. Right-click on the HRComponentsUnitTests project in the **Application Navigator** and select **New....** From the **General | Unit Tests** category, select **ADF Business Components Test Suite** and click **OK**.

8. In the **Configure Tests** page of the **JUnit ADF Business Components Test Suite Wizard**, make sure that the appropriate **Business Components Project, Application Module**, and **Configuration** are selected. For this recipe, we will select `HRComponentsBC.jpr`, `HrComponentsAppModule`, and `HrComponentsAppModuleLocal` respectively. Then click **Next**.

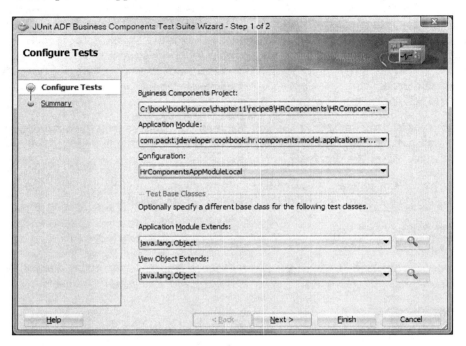

9. In the **Summary** page, review the JUnit classes that will be generated and click **Finish** to proceed.

10. Edit the `HrComponentsAppModuleAMTest` class and add the following code to the `setup()` method:

```
// get the application module from the JUnit test fixture
HrComponentsAppModuleAMFixture fixture =
  HrComponentsAppModuleAMFixture.getInstance();
_amImpl = (HrComponentsAppModule)fixture
  .getApplicationModule();
```

11. Add the following code to the `testExportEmployees()` method:

```
String employees = _amImpl.exportEmployees();
```

12. To run the unit tests, right-click on the `AllHrComponentsAppModuleTests.java` file in the **Application Navigator** and select **Run**. Observe the status of the unit tests in the **JUnit Test Runner Log** window.

How it works...

In steps 1 through 4, we downloaded the JUnit JDeveloper extensions using the **Check for Updates...** facility. As stated earlier, there are two separate extensions for JUnit one being specific to ADF business components projects.

In steps 5 and 6, we created a custom project to house the JUnit unit tests. Then (in steps 7 through 9), we created a JUnit business components test suite using the **ADF Business Components Test Suite Wizard**. We have indicated the HRComponentsBC business components project, and selected the HrComponentsAppModule application module and its HrComponentsAppModuleLocal configuration. Upon completion, the wizard creates the JUnit test suite, a test fixture class for the application module and unit test case classes for the application module and all view object instances in the application module data model. The unit tests that are included in the test suite are indicated by the @Suite.SuiteClasses annotation in the test suite, as shown in the following code snippet:

```
@Suite.SuiteClasses( { EmployeeCountVOTest.class,
    ApplicationModulePoolStatisticsVOTest.class,
    CascadingLovsVOTest.class,
    DepartmentEmployeesVOTest.class,
    EmployeesManagedVOTest.class,
    DepartmentsManagedVOTest.class, DepartmentsVOTest.class,
    EmployeesVOTest.class,
    HrComponentsAppModuleAMTest.class })
```

Furthermore, observe the code in the constructor of the HrComponentsAppModuleAMFixture fixture class. It uses the oracle.jbo. client.Configuration createRootApplicationModule() method to create the HrComponentsAppModule application module based on the configuration indicated in step 8. The HrComponentsAppModule application module is then available via the getApplicationModule() getter method.

The JUnit test cases created by the wizard are empty in most cases. In step 11, we have added test code to the testExportEmployees() application module test case to actually call the exportEmployees() HrComponentsAppModule application module method. To do this, we used the application module class variable _amImpl. This variable was initialized with a reference to the HrComponentsAppModule by calling the HrComponentsAppModuleAMFixture getApplicationModule() method in step 10.

Finally, we run the `AllHrComponentsAppModuleTests.java` file in the **Application Navigator** in step 11 to execute the JUnit test suite.

There's more...

Note the `@Test` annotation to indicate a test method in the test case class. You can add additional test methods to the unit test class by simply preceding them with this annotation. Also, observe the `@Before` and `@After` annotations on methods `setup()` and `teardown()` to indicate methods that are executing before and after the unit test case.

To include additional test cases to the test suite, implement the JUnit test case class and add it to the `@Suite.SuiteClasses` annotation in the test suite class.

JUnit unit test suites can be integrated with ant and be part of a continuous integration framework that runs your unit tests each time a new build of your application is being made. For a continuous integration example using Hudson, take a look at *Using Hudson as a continuous integration framework, Chapter 10, Deploying ADF Applications.*

See also

▶ *Overriding remove() to delete associated children entities, Chapter 2, Dealing with Basics: Entity Objects*

12
Optimizing, Fine-tuning, and Monitoring

In this chapter, we will cover:

- ▶ Using Update Batching for entity objects
- ▶ Limiting the rows fetched by a view object
- ▶ Limiting large view object query result sets
- ▶ Limiting large view object query result sets by using required view criteria
- ▶ Using a Work Manager for processing of long running tasks
- ▶ Monitoring the application using JRockit Mission Control

Introduction

The ADF framework offers a number of optimization and tuning settings related to entity objects, view objects, and application modules. Many of these settings are accessible in JDeveloper in the **General** tab **Tuning** section of the corresponding **Overview** editor. Others are programmatic techniques that optimize the performance of the application, such as limiting the result set produced by a view object query, or providing query optimizer hints for the underlying view object query. Yet more are implemented by utilizing facilities offered by the application server, such as the use of work managers in the WebLogic Server.

When it comes to monitoring, profiling, and stress testing an ADF Fusion web application, in addition to the tools offered by JDeveloper (that is, the CPU and Memory Profiler) other external tools can be useful. Such tools include the JRockit Mission Control, Enterprise Manager Fusion Middleware Control, and Apache JMeter.

Using Update Batching for entity objects

When multiple entity objects of the same type are modified, the number of DML (INSERT, UPDATE, and DELETE) statements that are issued against the database corresponds to one for each entity object that was modified. This can be optimized by using entity object update batching optimization. When update batching is used, the DML statements are grouped per DML statement type (INSERT, UPDATE, and DELETE) and bulk-posted based on a configured threshold value. This threshold value indicates the number of entity objects of the same type that would have to be modified before update batching can be triggered.

In this recipe, we will see how to enable update batching for an entity object.

Getting ready

We will enable update batching for the Department entity object. This entity object is part of the HRComponents workspace, which was created in *Overriding remove() to delete associated children entities, Chapter 2, Dealing with Basics: Entity Objects*.

The HRComponents workspace requires a database connection to the HR schema.

How to do it...

1. Open the HRComponents workspace. In the **Application Navigator** expand the HRComponentsBC components project and locate the Department entity object. Double-click on it to open the **Overview** editor.

2. In the **General** tab, expand the **Tuning** section and check the **Use Update Batching** checkbox.

3. Enter 1 for the **When Number of Entities to Modify Exceeds**.

⊟ **Tuning**

Select Use Update Batching to have this entity object perform inserts, updates, and deletes in batches at runtime, instead of one at a time.

☑ Use Update Batching

 When Number of Entities to Modify Exceeds: | 1 |
---

4. Redeploy the `HRComponents` workspace to an ADF Library JAR.

How it works...

We have enabled update batching for the `Department` entity object by opening the entity object **Overview** editor and clicking on the **Use Update Batching** checkbox in the **Tuning** section of the **General** tab. We have also indicated the update batching threshold by entering a number in the **When Number of Entities to Modify Exceeds**. This threshold indicates the number of `Department` entity objects that would have to be modified in order for update batching to be triggered by the ADF framework. If the threshold is satisfied, then the framework will use a cursor to bulk-post the DML operations (one post per DML operation type). Otherwise, separate DML statements will be posted for each modified entity object.

There's more...

Using update batching will not affect the number of times an overridden `doDML()` will be called by the framework. This method will be called consistently for each modified entity object, regardless of whether the entity object uses update batching or not.

Furthermore, note that update batching cannot be used for entity objects that fall in any of the following categories (in these cases, update batching is disabled in JDeveloper).

 ▸ An entity object that defines attributes that are refreshed on inserts and/or updates (**Refresh on Insert**, **Refresh on Update** properties).

 ▸ An entity object that defines `BLOB` attributes.

 ▸ An entity object that defines a ROWID-type attribute as a primary key. This attribute is also refreshed on inserts.

See also

 ▸ *Overriding remove() to delete associated children entities, Chapter 2, Dealing with Basics: Entity Objects*

Limiting the rows fetched by a view object

The ADF Business Components framework allows you to declaratively and/or programmatically set an upper limit for the number of rows that can fetched from the database layer by a view object. Declaratively, this can be accomplished through the view object **Tuning** section in the **General** page of the view object **Overview** editor. You can do this by selecting **Only up to row number** in the **Retrieve from the Database** section and providing a row count.

⊟ Tuning

Enter tuning parameters for this View, to control SQL execution and how data is fetched from the database.

┌─Retrieve from the Database──

   ◯ All Rows   ◉ Only up to row number | 10 |

      in Batches of: | 1 |

     ◉ As Needed   ◯ All at Once

This can also be accomplished programmatically by calling a view object's `setMaxFetchSize()` method and specifying an upper row limit.

To globally set an upper limit for the number of rows that can be fetched by all view objects in an ADF Fusion web application, the global configuration setting `rowLimit` in the `adf-config.xml` configuration file can be used instead. Then, by overriding the framework `getRowLimit()` method, you can adjust this upper limit for individual view objects as needed. When an attempt is made to fetch rows beyond this upper limit, the framework will generate an `oracle.jbo.RowLimitExceededWarning` exception. This exception can then be caught by your custom `DCErrorHandlerImpl` implementation and presented as a Faces warning message box (see *Using a custom error handler to customize how exceptions are reported to the ViewController, Chapter 9, Handling Security, Session Timeouts, Exceptions and Errors*).

In this recipe, we will see how to globally limit the number of rows fetched by all view objects and how to override this global setting for specific view objects.

Getting ready

We will set an upper limit for the number of rows fetched by all view objects used in the `MainApplication` workspace. This workspace was created in *Breaking up the application in multiple workspaces Chapter 1, Pre-requisites to Success: ADF Project Setup and Foundations*. We will also update the `Employees` view object to override this upper limit. This view object is part of the `HRComponents` workspace developed in *Overriding remove() to delete associated children entities, Chapter 2, Dealing with Basics: Entity Objects*.

The `HRComponents` workspace requires a database connection to the `HR` schema.

How to do it...

1. Open the `MainApplication` workspace and locate the `adf-config.xml` file. The file is located in the **Application Resources** section of the **Application Navigator** under the **Descriptors | ADF META-INF** node. Double-click on the file to open it.

2. In the **Overview** page, click on the **Business Components** tab.

3. Click on the **Row Fetch Limit** checkbox and specify `1000` for the upper rows fetched limit.

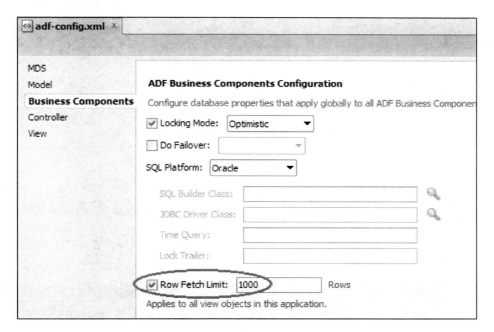

4. Now, open the `HRComponents` workspace and edit the `EmployeesImpl.java` view object custom implementation class.

5. Override the `getRowLimit()` method and replace the call to `super.getRowLimit()` with the following:

```
// return -1 to indicate no row fetch limit for the
// Employees View object
return -1;
```

6. Redeploy the `HRComponents` workspace to an ADF Library JAR.

How it works...

In steps 1 through 3, we have used the overview editor for the `adf-config.xml` ADF application configuration file to specify a global threshold value for the number of rows fetched by all view objects. For this recipe, we have indicated that up to 1000 rows can be fetched by all view objects throughout the application. Then, in steps 4 and 5, we have overridden the `getRowLimit()` method of the `Employees` view object to set a different fetch limit specifically for the `Employees` view object. In this case, by returning -1 we have indicated that there would be no fetch limit and that all rows should be fetched for this specific view object.

There's more...

Note that the maximum fetch limit of a view object is specified by -1, which indicates that all rows can be fetched from the database. This does not mean that all rows will be fetched by the view object at once, but that if you iterate over the view object result set, you will eventually fetch all of them. As stated earlier, when a fetched row limit is set, an attempt to iterate over the view object result set past this limit will produce an `oracle.jbo.RowLimitExceededWarning` exception.

See also

- ▸ *Breaking up the application in multiple workspaces, Chapter 1, Pre-requisites to Success: ADF Project Setup and Foundations*
- ▸ *Overriding remove() to delete associated children entities, Chapter 2, Dealing with Basics: Entity Objects*

Limiting large view object query result sets

In the recipe *Limiting the rows fetched by a view object* in this chapter, we have seen how to limit the number of rows that can be fetched from the database by a view object. While this technique limits the number of rows fetched from the database to the middle layer, it will not limit the view object query that runs in the database. In this case, a query that produces a result set in the thousands of records will still be executed, which would be detrimental to the application's performance. This recipe takes a different approach - actually limiting the view object query to a predefined row count defined by the specific view object using a custom property.

Getting ready

The recipe uses the `SharedComponents` and `HRComponents` workspaces. These workspaces were created in *Breaking up the application in multiple workspaces, Chapter 1, Pre-requisites to Success: ADF Project Setup and Foundations* and *Overriding remove() to delete associated children entities, Chapter 2, Dealing with Basics: Entity Objects* recipes respectively.

The `HRComponents` workspace requires a database connection to the `HR` schema.

How to do it...

1. Open the `SharedComponents` workspace. Locate and open the `ExtViewObjectImpl.java` view object framework extension class in the Java editor. Add the following helper methods to it. Also ensure that you add a constant definition for `QUERY_LIMIT` to "QueryLimit".

    ```java
    private boolean hasQueryLimit() {
      // return true if the View object query has a limit
      return this.getProperty(QUERY_LIMIT) != null;
    }
    private long getQueryLimit() {
      long queryLimit = -1;
      // check for query limit
      if (hasQueryLimit()) {
        // retrieve the query limit
        queryLimit = new Long((String)this.getProperty(QUERY_LIMIT));
      }
      // return the query limit
      return queryLimit;
    }
    ```

2. Override the `buildQuery(int, boolean)` method. Replace the call to `return super.buildQuery(i, b)` generated by JDeveloper with the following code:

    ```java
    // get the View object query from the framework
    String qryString = super.buildQuery(i, b);
    // check for query limit
    if (hasQueryLimit()) {
      // limit the View object query based on the
      // query limit defined
      String qryStringLimited = "SELECT * FROM (" + qryString
        + " ) WHERE ROWNUM <= " + getQueryLimit();
      qryString = qryStringLimited;
    }
    return qryString;
    ```

3. Redeploy the `SharedComponents` workspace to an ADF Library JAR.

4. Open the `HRComponents` workspace. Locate and open the `Employees` view object in the **Overview** editor.

5. In the **Custom Properties** section of the **General** tab, add a custom property called `QueryLimit`. Set its **Value** to the number of rows that view object query will be limited to.

6. Redeploy the `HRComponents` workspace to an ADF Library JAR.

How it works...

In step 1, we have added two helper methods called `hasQueryLimit()` and `getQueryLimit()` which respectively determine the presence and retrieve the value of a view object custom property called `QueryLimit`. The `QueryLimit` custom property, when added to a view object, specifies a maximum number of rows threshold that the specific query is allowed to produce.

In step 2, we have overridden the view object `buildQuery()` method in order to check for the definition of the `QueryLimit` custom property by the view object and, if this is indeed the case, to construct a wrapper query that will limit the rows returned by the original view object query. The ADF Business Components framework calls the `buildQuery()` method when it needs to construct the view object query prior to its execution. The view object query is limited by adding a `WHERE` clause for a `ROWNUM` upto the value specified by the `QueryLimit` custom property. Note that these methods were added to the `ExtViewObjectImpl` framework extension class, part of the `SharedComponents` workspace, making this functionality generic and available to all view objects throughout the ADF application. We redeployed the `SharedComponents` workspace to ensure that this functionality is part of the ADF Library JAR.

In steps 4 through 6, we have updated the `Employees` view object, part of the `HRComponents` workspace, by adding to it the `QueryLimit` custom property and setting its value to the number of rows that the query is limited to.

There's more...

You can present a message informing the user that the query results for a particular search were limited, by adding this additional functionality to the application:

1. Add the following code to the `ExtViewObjectImpl` view object framework extension class:

```
private void setQueryLimitApplied(Boolean queryLimitApplied) {
  this.queryLimitApplied = queryLimitApplied;
}
private Boolean isQueryLimitApplied() {
  return this.queryLimitApplied;
}
```

```
public String queryLimitedResultsMessage() {
  String limitedResultsError = null;
  // check for query limit having been applied
  if (isQueryLimitApplied()) {
  // return a message indicating that the
  // query was limited
  limitedResultsError =
    BundleUtils.loadMessage("00008", new String[] {
    String.valueOf(this.getQueryLimit()) });
  }
  return limitedResultsError;
}
```

2. While editing the `ExtViewObjectImpl` framework extension class, override the `executeQueryForCollection()` method and add the following code after the `super.executeQueryForCollection()` line generated by JDeveloper:

```
// set the queryLimitApplied indicator appropriately
if (hasQueryLimit()
    && this.getEstimatedRowCount() > getQueryLimit()) {
  this.queryLimitApplied = true;
} else {
  this.queryLimitApplied = false;
}
```

3. Add the `queryLimitedResultsMessage()` method to the client interface for the specific view object that its query is limited (`Employees` in this example).

4. Create a method binding for the `queryLimitedResultsMessage` method for the specific JSF page where the query is used.

5. Add to a managed bean with the necessary code to programmatically invoke the method binding, as shown in the following sample code:

```
public String getQueryLimitedResultsMessage() {
  return (String)ADFUtils.findOperation(
    "queryLimitedResultsMessage").execute();
}
```

6. Use an `af:outputText` on the JSF to display the message, as shown in the following sample code:

```
<af:outputText id="ot1" value="#{SomeManagedBean.
  queryLimitedResultsMessage}"
  partialTriggers="qry1" visible="#{bindings.
  EmployeesIterator.currentRow != null}"/>
```

See also

▸ *Breaking up the application in multiple workspaces, Chapter 1, Pre-requisites to Success: ADF Project Setup and Foundations*

▸ *Overriding remove() to delete associated children entities, Chapter 2, Dealing with Basics: Entity Objects*

Limiting large view object query result sets by using required view criteria

In the recipe *Limiting large view object query result sets* in this chapter, we presented a programmatic technique to limit the result set produced by a view object query. A simpler way to accomplish this in a declarative manner is to add named view criteria to the view object ensuring that some of the criteria items are required. This will force the user at runtime to enter values for those required criteria, thus limiting the size of the query result set.

In this recipe, we will add named view criteria to a view object and make the criteria items required.

Getting ready

We will add named view criteria to the `Employees` view object. It is part of the `HRComponents` workspace, which was created in *Overriding remove() to delete associated children entities, Chapter 2, Dealing with Basics: Entity Objects*.

The `HRComponents` workspace requires a database connection to the HR schema.

How to do it...

1. Open the `HRComponents` workspace and locate the `Employees` view object.

2. Open the `Employees` **Overview** editor and go to the **Query** tab.

3. Click on the **Create new view criteria** button (the green plus sign icon) in the **View Criteria** section.

4. In the **Create View Criteria** dialog, add criteria items by clicking on the **Add Item** button. To ensure that a specific criteria item is required, select **Required** from the **Validation** drop-down list.

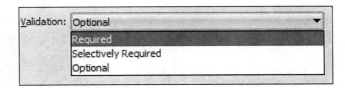

5. Redeploy the `HRComponents` workspace to an ADF Library JAR.

How it works...

Steps 1 through 4 show you how to add named view criteria to the `Employees` view object with required criteria items. View criteria are added to the view object by navigating to the **Query** tab of the view object **Overview** editor and clicking on the **Create new view criteria** button. You add criteria items to the view criteria by clicking on the **Add Item** button in the **Create View Criteria** dialog. To make a criteria item required for the query to be executed, ensure that you set the criterion **Validation** to **Required**.

At runtime, required criteria will appear with an asterisk (*) in front of them. If you attempt to execute the query without specifying values for any of the required criteria, a validation error message will be shown. To proceed with the query execution, you will need to provide values for all required criteria.

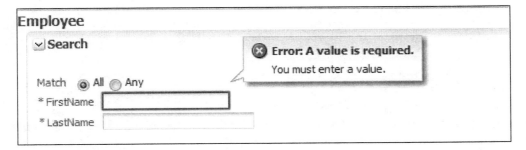

There's more...

The **Selectively Required** option for the view criteria item **Validation** indicates that the specific criteria item will be required only as long as no other values have been supplied for any of the other criteria items. In this case, a validation exception will be raised indicating that the criterion is required. If a value has been supplied for any of the other criteria items, then specifying a value for the specific criterion is not required.

See also

▶ *Overriding remove() to delete associated children entities, Chapter 2, Dealing with Basics: Entity Objects*

Using a work manager for processing of long running tasks

Work managers allow for the concurrent execution of multiple threads within the WebLogic Server. They provide an alternative to the `java.lang.Thread` API (this API should not be utilized by Java EE applications) for running a work, that is an isolated piece of Java code, concurrently (or serially) as separate WebLogic-managed threads.

Work managers in the WebLogic Server fall in three categories: default, global and application-specific work managers. The default work manager is used for applications that do not specify a work manager. This may be sufficient for most applications. Global work managers are WebLogic Server domain-specific and are defined explicitly in WebLogic. Applications utilizing the same global work manager create their own instance of the work manager to handle the threads associated with each application. Application-specific work managers are defined for specific applications only, making them available for use by the specific applications only.

Programmatically, work managers are supported through the interfaces defined in the work manager API. The API is defined in the `commonj.work` package in the `weblogic.jar` library.

In this recipe, we will define a global work manager in WebLogic and implement a wrapper framework around the work manager API. Then we will demonstrate how to utilize the wrapper framework to run part of an ADF Fusion web application on the global work manager.

Getting ready

You will need access to the `SharedComponents`, `HRComponents` and `MainApplication` workspaces before delving into this recipe. These workspaces were created in *Breaking up the application in multiple workspaces, Chapter 1, Pre-requisites to Success: ADF Project Setup and Foundations* and *Overriding remove() to delete associated children entities, Chapter 2, Dealing with Basics: Entity Objects*.

The `HRComponents` workspace requires a database connection to the `HR` schema.

You will also need access to a configured standalone WebLogic server domain and your application deployed on it. For information on these topics, take a look at *Configuring and using the Standalone WebLogic Server* and *Deploying on the Standalone WebLogic Server, Chapter 10, Deploying ADF Applications*.

How to do it...

1. Open the `SharedComponents` workspace. Add the following `ExtWorkManager`,
   `ExtWork` and `ExtWorkListener` classes to the `SharedBC` business components
   project. When done, redeploy the workspace to an ADF Library JAR.

```java
public class ExtWorkManager {
  private final static ADFLogger LOGGER =
    ADFLogger.createADFLogger(ExtWorkManager.class);
  private static final String DEFAULT_MANAGER_NAME =
    "MyWorkManager";
  private String managerName = DEFAULT_MANAGER_NAME;
  private WorkManager workManager;
  private WorkListener workListener;
  private List<ExtWork> works = new ArrayList<ExtWork>();
  List<WorkItem> workList = new ArrayList<WorkItem>();
  // run the Work Manager serially by default
  private long waitType = WorkManager.INDEFINITE;
  public ExtWorkManager() {
  }
  public ExtWorkManager(String managerName) {
    // check for valid name; used default name otherwise
    if (managerName == null || !"".equals(managerName)) {
      this.managerName = DEFAULT_MANAGER_NAME;
    }
  }
  public void addWork(ExtWork work) {
    works.add(work);
  }
  public void run() {
    LOGGER.info("WorkManager.run()");
    try {
      // get the Work Manager from the context
      InitialContext ctx = new InitialContext();
      workManager = (WorkManager)ctx.lookup("java:comp/env/"
        + managerName);
      // create a listener
      if (workListener == null) {
      workListener = new ExtWorkListener(this);
    }
    // schedule work items in a work list
    workList = new ArrayList<WorkItem>();
    for (ExtWork work : works) {
      WorkItem workItem = workManager.schedule(work,
        workListener);
```

```
        workList.add(workItem);
      }
      // run the Work Manager work list
      workManager.waitForAll(workList, waitType);
    } catch (Exception e) {
    LOGGER.severe(e);
    throw new ExtJboException(e);
    }
  }
  public List<ExtWork> getResult() {
    List<ExtWork> resultList = new ArrayList<ExtWork>();
    try {
    // iterate all work items and add their results
    // to the results list
    for (WorkItem workItem : workList) {
      resultList.add((ExtWork)workItem.getResult());
    }
  } catch (Exception e) {
    throw new ExtJboException(e);
  }
  // return the results list
  return resultList;
  }
  // see book's source code for complete listing
  }
  public abstract class ExtWork implements Work {
    private final static ADFLogger LOGGER =
      ADFLogger.createADFLogger(ExtWork.class);
    // parameters list
    protected List<Object> parameters =
      new ArrayList<Object>();
      public ExtWork(Object... parameters) {
        super();
        // add parameters to the parameter list
        for (Object parameter : parameters) {
          this.parameters.add(parameter);
      }
    }
    public abstract Object getResult();
    // see book's source code for complete listing
  }
  public class ExtWorkListener implements WorkListener {
    private final static ADFLogger LOGGER =
      ADFLogger.createADFLogger(ExtWorkListener.class);
```

```
    private ExtWorkManager manager;
    public ExtWorkListener(ExtWorkManager manager) {
      super();
      this.manager = manager;
    }
    public void workAccepted(WorkEvent workEvent) {
      LOGGER.info("Work accepted for work manager '" +
        manager.getManagerName() + "' at " + getTime());
    }
    private String getTime() {
      Calendar cal = Calendar.getInstance();
      SimpleDateFormat sdf =
        new SimpleDateFormat("HH:mm:ss");
      return sdf.format(cal.getTime());
    }
    // see book's source code for complete listing
  }
```

2. Open the `HRComponents` workspace and add the following `ExportEmployeesWork` class to it:

```
public class ExportEmployeesWork extends ExtWork {
  private final static ADFLogger LOGGER =
    ADFLogger.createADFLogger(ExportEmployeesWork.class);
  private StringBuilder employeeStringBuilder;
  public ExportEmployeesWork() {
    super();
  }
  public ExportEmployeesWork(Object... parameters) {
    super(parameters);
  }
  @Override
  public Object getResult() {
    // return the employees CSV string buffer
    return employeeStringBuilder;
  }
  @Override
  public void run() {
    LOGGER.info("ExportEmployeesWork.run()");
    // the Employees rowset iterator was passed as a
    // parameter when we created this work
    RowSetIterator iterator = (RowSetIterator)parameters.get(0);
    // get additional parameters as needed
    // Object param1 = parameters.get(1);
    // build the employees CSV string buffer
    employeeStringBuilder = new StringBuilder();
```

```
        iterator.reset();
        while (iterator.hasNext()) {
          EmployeesRowImpl employee =
            (EmployeesRowImpl)iterator.next();
          employeeStringBuilder.append(
          employee.getLastName() + " "
            + employee.getFirstName());
          if (iterator.hasNext()) {
            employeeStringBuilder.append(",");
          }
        }
        // done with the rowset iterator
        iterator.closeRowSetIterator();
      }
    }
```

3. Add the following `exportEmployeesOnWorkManager()` method to the `HrComponentsAppModuleImpl` custom implementation class.

```
public String exportEmployeesOnWorkManager() {
  // create a Work Manager
  ExtWorkManager mngr = new ExtWorkManager("MyWorkManager");
  // add the export employees work to the Work Manager
  mngr.addWork(new ExportEmployeesWork(
    getEmployees().createRowSetIterator(null)));
  // run the Work Manager
  mngr.run();
  // get the result from the Work Manager
  List<ExtWork> works = mngr.getResult();
  StringBuilder employeeStringBuilder = new StringBuilder();
  for (ExtWork work : works) {
    ExportEmployeesWork exportWork = (ExportEmployeesWork)work;
    employeeStringBuilder.append(exportWork.getResult());
  }
  // return the employees CSV string buffer
  return employeeStringBuilder.toString();
}
```

4. Ensure that the `exportEmployeesOnWorkManager()` method is added to the `HrComponentsAppModule` application module client interface. Then, redeploy the `HRComponents` workspace to an ADF Library JAR.

5. Open the main application workspace. Create a new JSPX page called
`exportEmployeesUsingWorkManager.jspx` and add the following code to it:

```
<?xml version='1.0' encoding='UTF-8'?>
<jsp:root xmlns:jsp="http://java.sun.com/JSP/Page" version="2.1"
xmlns:f="http://java.sun.com/jsf/core"
  xmlns:af="http://xmlns.oracle.com/adf/faces/rich">
  <jsp:directive.page contentType="text/html;charset=UTF-8"/>
  <f:view>
    <af:document title="exportEmployees
      UsingWorkManager.jspx" id="d1">
    <af:messages id="m1"/>
      <af:form id="f1">
        <af:panelStretchLayout id="psl1">
          <f:facet name="top"/>
          <f:facet name="center">
            <af:toolbar id="t1">
              <af:commandButton text="Export Employees" id="cb1">
                <af:fileDownloadActionListener filename=
                  "employees.csv"method="#{ExportEmployees
                  UsingWorkManagerBean.exportEmployees}"/>
              </af:commandButton>
            </af:toolbar>
          </f:facet>
          <f:facet name="bottom"/>
        </af:panelStretchLayout>
      </af:form>
    </af:document>
  </f:view>
</jsp:root>
```

6. Create a page definition file for the `exportEmployeesUsingWorkManager.jspx` page and add a method action binding for the `exportEmployeesOnWorkManager()` method. It is available under the `HrComponentsAppModuleDataControl` data control.

7. Create a managed bean called `ExportEmployeesUsingWorkManagerBean` and add the following `exportEmployees()` method to it:

```java
public void exportEmployees(FacesContext facesContext,
  OutputStream outputStream) {
  // get the employees CSV data
  String employeesCSV = (String)ADFUtils.findOperation(
    "exportEmployeesOnWorkManager").execute();
  try {
    // write the data to the output stream
    OutputStreamWriter writer = new
      OutputStreamWriter(outputStream, "UTF-8");
    writer.write(employeesCSV);
    writer.close();
    outputStream.close();
```

```
  } catch (IOException e) {
    // log exception
  }
}
```

8. Open the `web.xml` deployment descriptor in the **Source** editor and add the following resource reference to it:

```
<resource-ref>
  <res-ref-name>MyWorkManager</res-ref-name>
  <res-type>commonj.work.WorkManager</res-type>
  <res-auth>Container</res-auth>
  <res-sharing-scope>Shareable</res-sharing-scope>
</resource-ref>
```

9. Ensure that the standalone WebLogic server domain is started, then log in into the administration console using the following URL: `http://serverHost:serverPort/console`, where `serverHost` is the hostname or IP of the WebLogic Server machine and `serverPort` is the administration server's port.

10. Select **Environment | Work Managers** from the **Domain Structure** tree.

11. In the **Summary of Work Managers** page, click on the **New** button under the **Global Work Managers, Request Classes and Constraints** table.

12. In the **Select Work Manager Definition type** page, select **Work Manager** and click **Next**.

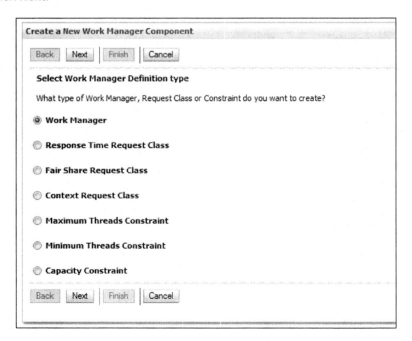

13. In the **Work Manager Properties** page, enter `MyWorkManager` for the work manager **Name** and click **Next**.

14. In the **Select deployment targets** page, select your managed server instance from the list of **Available targets** and click **Finish**. The work manager should now be visible in the **Global Work Managers, Request Classes and Constraints** table in the **Summary of Work Managers** page.

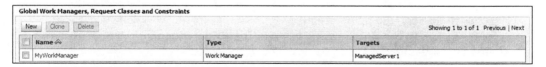

15. Click on `MyWorkManager` in the **Global Work Managers, Request Classes and Constraints** table in the **Summary of Work Managers** page. In the **Settings for MyWorkManager** page, select **Ignore Stuck Threads** and click on the **Save** button.

16. Restart the standalone WebLogic server domain and deploy to it the main application.

How it works...

To ease the task of dealing with work managers, we have introduced the following three classes (in step 1):

▶ `ExtWorkManager`: A wrapper around the functionality provided by the `commonj.work` work manager API. The following methods implemented by this class make it easy to get going with using work managers in our application:

   ❑ `ExtWorkManager(String managerName)`: Constructs a work manager identified by its name

   ❑ `addWork(ExtWork work)`: Adds `ExtWork` works to the work manager

   ❑ `run()`: Executes the work manager

   ❑ `getResult()`: Returns the work manager result(s)

▶ `ExtWork`: An abstract class built on top of the `commonj.work.Work` interface. It accepts generic parameters during construction, which it stores in the `parameters` class variable. Concrete classes must implement its `run()` and `getResult()` methods. Class `ExportEmployeesWork` in step 2 is an example of a concrete implementation of this class.

▶ `ExtWorkListener`: Implements the `commonj.work.WorkListener` interface.

In this recipe, we have identified the functionality of exporting data from a database table, which was originally implemented in *Exporting data to a file, Chapter 7, Face Value: ADF Faces, JSPX Pages and Components*, that can run on the work manager. It is implemented by the method `exportEmployees()` in the `HrComponentsAppModuleImpl` custom application module implementation class, part of the `HRComponents` workspace. Steps 2 and 3 illustrate how it is done:

- Create a class that extends the `ExtWork` class. This class identifies a piece of code that can run on a work manager. In our case, this was done with the `ExportEmployeesWork` class in step 2. The actual code that will be executed is then implemented by the `run()` method of the class.

- Create an `ExtWorkManager` class and call its `addWork()` method to add specific pieces of "work" to be executed by it. These are classes that extend `ExtWork`. In our case, this was done in step 3 when we called `addWork()` specifying `ExportEmployeesWork` as the specific `ExtWork` class:

```
mngr.addWork(new ExportEmployeesWork(getEmployees().
   createRowSetIterator(null)));
```

- Call the `ExtWorkManager` class `run()` method to commence with the execution of the works added to the work manager.

Observe the constructor of the `ExtWork` derived classes. It accepts a variable number of parameters that are stored in the `parameters` class variable. For instance, in our example, the `ExportEmployeesWork` was constructed specifying the `Employees RowSetIterator`, as shown in the following line of code:

```
new ExportEmployeesWork(getEmployees().createRowSetIterator(null))
```

These parameters can then be accessed as shown in the `ExportEmployeesWork run()` method, as follows:

```
RowSetIterator iterator = (RowSetIterator)parameters.get(0);
```

To retrieve the results produced by the work manager, you iterate over the `ExtWork` works and you call `getResult()` for each one. The works managed by the work manager are retrieved by calling `getResult()` on it. This is implemented in step 3 and is shown as follows:

```
List<ExtWork> works = mngr.getResult();
StringBuilder employeeStringBuilder = new StringBuilder();
for (ExtWork work : works) {
  ExportEmployeesWork exportWork = ExportEmployeesWork)work;
  employeeStringBuilder.append(exportWork.getResult());
}
```

As you can see in step 2, the `ExportEmployeesWork getResult()` method returns the CSV string buffer `employeeStringBuilder` that was built in the `run()` method when iterating over the `Employees` view object:

```
public Object getResult() {
  // return the employees CSV string buffer
  return employeeStringBuilder;
}
```

Work manager export functionality is added in a separate `HrComponentsAppModule` method called `exportEmployeesOnWorkManager` which is then added to the application module's client interface and once bound, (step 6) it is invoked from a backing bean (step 7).

Steps 8 through 15 show how to create, configure, and reference a work manager. In step 8, we reference the work manager in our application by adding a resource reference to it in the `web.xml` deployment descriptor. The work manager that we will be creating in steps 9 through 15 is called `MyWorkManager`. We use this reference to get hold of the work manager via JNDI lookup in our code. This is done in the `ExtWorkManager run()` method in step 1 as shown in the following code snippet:

```
InitialContext ctx = new InitialContext();
workManager = (WorkManager)ctx.lookup
("java:comp/env/" + managerName);
```

In this case, `managerName` is specified during the construction of the `ExtWorkManager`. This can be seen in step 3 when the work manager is constructed:

```
ExtWorkManager mngr = new ExtWorkManager("MyWorkManager");
```

Steps 9 through 15 detail the steps of creating and configuring a global work manager in WebLogic Server. Observe how in step 15 we have enabled the **Ignore Stuck Threads** setting. This will enable us to run long-running works on the work manager without getting an indication of a stuck thread by WebLogic. A WebLogic thread that executes for more than a specified-preconfigured amount of time is considered by WebLogic to be "stuck". If the number of the stuck threads in an application grow, the application might crash.

Finally, observe how the work manager is started in the `ExtWorkManager run()` method in step 1. The list of works added to the work manager (by calling its `addWork()` method) is iterated and each work is scheduled for execution by calling its `schedule()` method.

```
workList = new ArrayList<WorkItem>();
for (ExtWork work : works) {
  WorkItem workItem =
    workManager.schedule(work, workListener);
  workList.add(workItem);
}
```

The `schedule()` method returns a `commonj.work.WorkItem`, which is added to a `java.util.List`. We use this list to commence the execution of the work manager by calling its `waitForAll()` method:

```
workManager.waitForAll(workList, waitType);
```

One important thing to notice here is the `waitType` argument passed to the `waitForAll()` method. It can take either of the following two values:

- `WorkManager.INDEFINITE`: Calling code pauses, waiting until the execution of all works scheduled on the work manager completes.

- `WorkManager.IMMEDIATE`: Return is passed immediately to the calling code running the works scheduled on the work manager concurrently.

Furthermore, observe that the `WorkItem` list is iterated in the `getResult()` method to retrieve the result for each `WorkItem`, as shown in the following code snippet:

```
for (WorkItem workItem : workList) {
  resultList.add((ExtWork)workItem.getResult());
}
```

There's more...

For more information on work managers, consult sections *Description of the Work Manager API* and *Work Manager Example* in the *Timer and Work Manager API (CommonJ) Programmer's Guide for Oracle WebLogic Server* documentation manual. This can be found in the *WebLogic Server Documentation Library* currently at `http://docs.oracle.com/cd/E14571_01/wls.htm`.

See also

- *Breaking up the application in multiple workspaces, Chapter 1, Pre-requisites to Success: ADF Project Setup and Foundations*

- *Overriding remove() to delete associated children entities, Chapter 2, Dealing with Basics: Entity Objects*

- *Exporting data to a file, Chapter 7, Face Value: ADF Faces, JSPX Pages and Components*

- *Configuring and using the Standalone WebLogic Server, Chapter 10, Deploying ADF Applications*

- *Deploying on the Standalone WebLogic Server, Chapter 10, Deploying ADF Applications*

Monitoring the application using JRockit Mission Control

JRockit Mission Control is a suite of tools that can be used to monitor, profile, and manage applications deployed on the WebLogic Server running on the JRockit JVM. Moreover, the JRockit Mission Control tools allow you to record and replay sessions, perform garbage collection on demand, and eliminate memory leaks.

In this recipe, we will go over the installation of JRockit Mission Control Client and the steps necessary to configure the WebLogic Server to run it. Then we will look into a monitor session of a standalone WebLogic server instance.

Getting ready

You will need a standalone WebLogic server domain configured and your ADF application deployed on it. For information about these topics, take a look at *Configuring and using the Standalone WebLogic Server* and *Deploying on the Standalone WebLogic Server, Chapter 10, Deploying ADF Applications*.

How to do it...

1. Download the appropriate JRockit version for your client operating system by going to the **Oracle JRockit Downloads** page. This page is currently accessible via the following URL: `http://www.oracle.com/technetwork/middleware/jrockit/downloads/index.html`.

2. Start the installation by executing the file downloaded. Make sure that during the installation, you choose to install the JRockit JRE as well.

3. Once the installation completes, ensure that you can run the JRockit Mission Control Client by running the `jrmc` program in the target installation directory.

4. Edit the `setDomainEnv` script in the WebLogic Server domain `bin` directory and ensure that the `JAVA_VENDOR` variable is set to `Oracle`. Also, verify that the `BEA_JAVA_HOME` is set correctly to JRockit JDK home directory on the WebLogic server machine. Finally, update the `JAVA_OPTIONS` environment variable to:

   ```
   set JAVA_OPTIONS=%JAVA_OPTIONS% %MNGMNT_CONCOLE_OPTIONS%
   ```

5. Edit the `startManagedWebLogic` script (in the same directory) and add the following lines:

   ```
   if "%SERVER_NAME%"=="ManagedServer1" (set MNGMNT_CONCOLE_OPTIONS=-
     Xmanagement:ssl=false, authenticate=false -
     Dcom.sun.management.jmxremote.port=7092)
   ```

6. Restart the WebLogic Server domain and ensure that when starting the server instance configured for the management console, the JMX connectors are started.

7. Start the JRockit Mission Control as indicated earlier. Right-click anywhere in the **JVM Browser** and select **New Connection**.

8. In the **New Connection** dialog, specify the standalone WebLogic server **Host** name or IP and the management connection **Port**. Enter a **Connection name** and click on the **Test connection** button to test the connection. Once successful, click on the **Finish** button.

9. The connection should appear under the **Connectors** node in the **JVM Browser** tree. Now, right-click on the connection and select **Start Console**. The JRockit management console **Overview** tab will be displayed, monitoring the WebLogic standalone managed server instance.

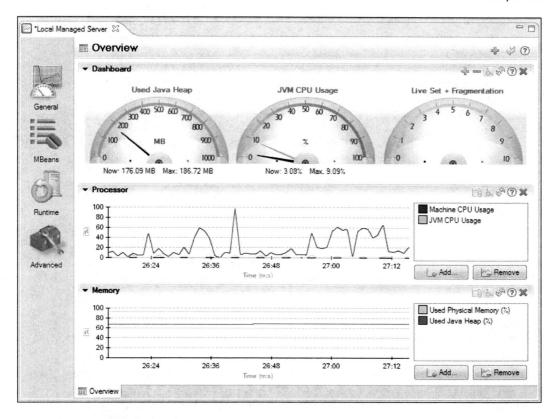

How it works...

Steps 1 through 3 go through the process of downloading and installing JRockit Mission Control. The installation process is straightforward; simply run the downloaded executable file and follow the installation wizard. As noted in step 2, ensure that the JRockit JRE is also installed.

Steps 4 through 6 demonstrate how to start a WebLogic managed server instance with management console options enabled. This will allow us to connect to it using the JRockit Mission Control Client (steps 7 through 9). First we need to ensure that the WebLogic Server is started with the JRockit JVM. This can be done by specifying `Oracle` for the `JAVA_VENDOR` environment variable in the `setDomainEnv` script (see step 4). You will also need to specify the location of the JRockit JDK path on the WebLogic Server machine using the `BEA_JAVA_HOME` environment variable (also in step 4).

In the same script file, we have also updated the `JAVA_OPTIONS` environment variable to include additional options related to the management console. These options are defined using a new environment variable called `MNGMNT_CONCOLE_OPTIONS` (step 4). Then, in step 5, we have defined the management console options specifically for our managed server instance (it is called `ManagedServer1` for this recipe). We have used the `-Xmanagement:ssl=false,aut henticate=false` JVM argument to indicate that no authentication (and no SSL connection) will be required for the management console. This will allow us in step 8, when we define the JVM connection, to specify that no authentication credentials are required to access the JVM. We have also indicated the management connection port (it was set to 7092 for this recipe). In step 6, we restarted the WebLogic Server with the new management connection options.

In steps 7 through 9, we started the JRockit Mission Control Client and created a connection to the WebLogic managed server instance configured earlier (in step 8). In step 9, we started the management console to monitor the JRockit JVM instance configured. By default, the management console **Overview** tab includes a **Dashboard** with predefined Java Heap and JVM CPU dials, and monitors for the **Processor** (machine and JVM CPU usage) and **Memory** (used machine and Java heap memory). Additional JVM run-time metrics can be added to the management console by clicking on the **Add Dial** (the green plus sign icon) and the **Add...** buttons.

There's more...

In addition to the management console, the JRockit Mission Control Client includes the **flight recorder** and **memory leak detector** tools. These tools are available by right-clicking in the **JVM Browser** and selecting **Start Flight Recording...** and **Start Memleak** from the context menu respectively. For more information on these tools, consult the *JRockit JDK Tools Guide* and *JRockit Flight Recorder Run Time Guide*. These documents can be found in the *JRockit Documentation Library* currently at `http://docs.oracle.com/cd/E15289_01/index.htm`.

See also

▶ *Configuring and using the Standalone WebLogic Server, Chapter 10, Deploying ADF Applications*

▶ *Deploying on the Standalone WebLogic Server, Chapter 10, Deploying ADF Applications*

Index

B

backing beans 84, 234
backingBean scope 234
bAppend Boolean parameter 125
BC4J JUnit Integration extension 343
BC base classes
  setting up 19-21
BEA_JAVA_HOME environment variable 371
beforeCommit() method 53
beforeRollback() method 96, 97
binding container
  getting 34
bindParametersForCollection()
  about 121
  overriding, for setting up view object bind
    variable 118, 120
bindParametersForCollection() method 118-
  120
bind variables
  about 66, 106
  values associated with view criteria, clearing
    126, 127
bind variables values, associated with view
  criteria
  clearing 126-128
build.cmd script file 319, 320
buildfile command-line 313
buildFromClause() 99
buildOrderByClause() 99
buildQuery(int, boolean) method 353
buildQuery() method 99, 354
buildSelectClause() 99
buildWhereClause()
  about 99
  overriding 100
built-in macros, ojdeploy. *See* ojdeploy, built-
  in macros
bundled exceptions 31
BundleUtils class 296
BundleUtils helper class 296
business component
  refactoring 327
  synchronizing, with database changes 324-
    326

business component attribute
  refactoring 327
Business Component Browser 53
business components framework extension
  classes
  adding, to SharedComponents project 19-21
  configuring 22
  configuring, at component level 22
  configuring, at project level 22
busyStateListener() method 254
buttonBar facet 223

C

cascading LOVs
  about 110
  setting up 110-114
CascadingLovs entity object 111
CASCADING_LOVS table 110
CascadingLovs view object 112
case-insensitive
  handling, view criteria used 128, 129
case-insensitively
  searching, view criteria used 128, 129
circular dependencies
  eliminating 18
clearSelectedIndices() 214
client file
  data, exporting to 228-232
clientListener method 254
CollectionPaginationBean 260
collectionPagination.jspx 260
ColorDesc attribute 116, 117
commit() method 44
COMMITSEQ_PROPERTY constant 52
CommitSequenceDepartmentDepartmentId
  property 57
CommitSequence property 52
CommonActions 222
CommonActions base class 98
CommonActions bean 224, 226
CommonActions create() method 258
CommonActions delete() method 228
CommonActions.delete() method 225
CommonActions framework
  create() method 258

H

I

passivateState(Document, Element) method
144
passivateState() method 143
passivation 143
passivation framework
for custom session-specific data 143-150
passivation store 143
pending changes
determining, in current transation 234-236
handling, af:popup used 255-258
plain file
refactoring 328
pollListener attribute 219
pollView.jspx page 221, 222
populateAttributeAsChanged() method 49, 52
pop-up
reusing, page templates used 222-224
PopupFetchListener attribute 212, 214
posted attribute's value
determining, getPostedAttribute() method
used 58, 59
prepare() method 164, 167, 168, 170
prepare() method call activity 166, 168, 190
prepareRowSetForQuery() 121
prepareSession() method 97, 147
prepareSession(Session) method 95
preventUserInput() 254
PrintWriter object 155
processQuery() method 239, 242
processQueryOperation() method 243, 246
profile parameter 312
project parameter 312
property sets
about 54
applying 54-57
creating 54-57

Q

query
clearing, custom af:query operation listener
used 243-247
Queryable flag 87
Queryable property, view object attributes
setting 86, 87

Queryable status
determining 86
QueryDescriptor object 242
QueryLimit 354
queryLimitedResultsMessage() method 355
queryListener attribute 239, 240
QueryListenerBean.java 245
queryListener.jspx page 240, 246
QueryModel.reset() method 247
QueryOperationEvent 246
queryOperationListener attribute 243
queryOperationListener() method 245, 246
queryView.jspx 195

R

Range Paging access mode
configuring, for view object 92
Range Paging optimization 94
Range Size option setting 94
read-only view object 76
refactoring support 323
RefreshEmployees 221
refreshView() method 93, 94
remote debugging
configuring 329-332
using 329
working 332
remote debugging session
starting 333
removeEmployeeFromCollection() method
102
removeFromCollection() 101, 103
remove() method 44, 48
overriding, for deleting associated children
entities 60-62
overriding, for deleting parent entity in
association 63, 65
removeViewCriteria() 246
reportException() method 288-291
RequestDispatcher object 274
resetCriteria() method 244
resetCriteriaValues() method 246
resetEmployees() method 244, 246
reset() method 79, 247

ResourceBundle.getBundle() 294
Resource Palette 213
Retrieve from the Database section 350
RIA 194
Rich Internet Applications. *See* RIA
rollback() method 44
root view
  component, locating 34
RowCountLimit 101
Row.remove() method 101
rows
  inserting, at beginning of rowset 92
  inserting, at the end of rowset 90, 91
  removing, from rowset without deleting from
    database 101, 102
rowset 95
rowsets, iterating
  drawbacks 81
rows, fetched by view object
  limiting, 350, 351
RowValException objects 31
run() method 365, 366

S

saveState() 246
schedule() method 368
Scrollable 80
scrollToRangePage() 80
searchEmployeesUsingAdditionalCriteria()
  method 124
search page
  constructing, af:query component used 194-
    196
searchRegion 243
searchUsingAdditionalCriteria() method 122,
  124
secondary rowset iterator
  used, for iterating view object 76-80
SecurityContext methods
  #{secrityContext.authenticated} 279
  #{securityContext.
    regionViewable['SomePageDef']} 278
  #{securityContext.taskflowViewable['SomeTask
    Flow']} 278

#{secrityContext.userName} 278
#{securityContext.userInAllRoles['roleList']}
  279
security, for ADF Fusion Web Application
  enabling 266-269
security information
  accessing 275-279
SecurityUtils helper class 280, 284
selectionListener() 205, 238
selectionListener attribute 236
Selectively Required option 357
SelectManyShuttleBean 212
selectManyShuttleView.jspx 211, 213
sequence attribute
  populating, custom property used 48, 49
SequenceImpl object 49
service data object (SDO) component 132
service interface method
  accessing, from another application module
    139-142
ServletAuthentication.
    generateNewSessionID() 274
ServletAuthentication.runAs() 274
SessionInfoBean 249
SessionInfoBean.java class 250
session scope bean
  using, for preserving session-wide information
    248, 250
SessionTimeoutFilter filter 286, 287
SessionTimeoutRedirect filter 287
session timeouts
  detecting 285, 287
  handling 285, 287
session-wide information
  preserving, session scope bean used 248-
    251
setApplyViewCriteriaNames() method 125
setAttribute() 125
setAttributeInternal() method 295-297
setBindVariableValue() method 120
setBundledExceptionMode() method 31
setClearCacheOnRollback() 97
setConjunction() 124
setCurrentRowWithKey() 239
setDepartmentId() method 83

Thank you for buying
Oracle JDeveloper 11gR2 Cookbook

About Packt Publishing

Packt, pronounced 'packed', published its first book "*Mastering phpMyAdmin for Effective MySQL Management*" in April 2004 and subsequently continued to specialize in publishing highly focused books on specific technologies and solutions.

Our books and publications share the experiences of your fellow IT professionals in adapting and customizing today's systems, applications, and frameworks. Our solution-based books give you the knowledge and power to customize the software and technologies you're using to get the job done. Packt books are more specific and less general than the IT books you have seen in the past. Our unique business model allows us to bring you more focused information, giving you more of what you need to know, and less of what you don't.

Packt is a modern, yet unique publishing company, which focuses on producing quality, cutting-edge books for communities of developers, administrators, and newbies alike. For more information, please visit our website: www.PacktPub.com.

About Packt Enterprise

In 2010, Packt launched two new brands, Packt Enterprise and Packt Open Source, in order to continue its focus on specialization. This book is part of the Packt Enterprise brand, home to books published on enterprise software – software created by major vendors, including (but not limited to) IBM, Microsoft and Oracle, often for use in other corporations. Its titles will offer information relevant to a range of users of this software, including administrators, developers, architects, and end users.

Writing for Packt

We welcome all inquiries from people who are interested in authoring. Book proposals should be sent to author@packtpub.com. If your book idea is still at an early stage and you would like to discuss it first before writing a formal book proposal, contact us; one of our commissioning editors will get in touch with you.

We're not just looking for published authors; if you have strong technical skills but no writing experience, our experienced editors can help you develop a writing career, or simply get some additional reward for your expertise.

Oracle Database 11g – Underground Advice for Database Administrators

ISBN: 978-1-84968-000-4   Paperback: 348 pages

A real-world DBA survival guide for Oracle 11g database implementations

1. A comprehensive handbook aimed at reducing the day-to-day struggle of Oracle 11g Database newcomers

2. Real-world reflections from an experienced DBA— what novice DBAs should really know

3. Implement Oracle's Maximum Availability Architecture with expert guidance

4. Extensive information on providing high availability for Grid Control

EJB 3.0 Database Persistence with Oracle Fusion Middleware 11*g*

ISBN: 978-1-849681-56-8   Paperback: 448 pages

A complete guide to building EJB 3.0 database persistence applications with Oracle Fusion Middleware 11*g*

1. Integrate EJB 3.0 database persistence with Oracle Fusion Middleware tools: WebLogic Server, JDeveloper, and Enterprise Pack for Eclipse

2. Automatically create EJB 3.0 entity beans from database tables

3. Learn to wrap entity beans with session beans and create EJB 3.0 relationships

Oracle Fusion Middleware Patterns

ISBN: 978-1-847198-32-7   Paperback: 224 pages

10 unique architecture patterns enabled by Oracle Fusion Middleware

1. First-hand technical solutions utilizing the complete and integrated Oracle Fusion Middleware Suite in hardcopy and ebook formats

2. From-the-trenches experience of leading IT Professionals

3. Learn about application integration and how to combine the integrated tools of the Oracle Fusion Middleware Suite - and do away with thousands of lines of code

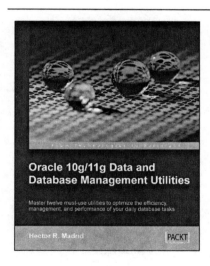

Oracle 10g/11g Data and Database Management Utilities

ISBN: 978-1-847196-28-6   Paperback: 432 pages

Master twelve must-use utilities to optimize the efficiency, management, and performance of your daily database tasks

1. Optimize time-consuming tasks efficiently using the Oracle database utilities

2. Perform data loads on the fly and replace the functionality of the old export and import utilities using Data Pump or SQL*Loader

3. Boost database defenses with Oracle Wallet Manager and Security

Please check **www.PacktPub.com** for information on our titles

CPSIA information can be obtained at www.ICGtesting.com
Printed in the USA
LVOW052102220312

274351LV00010B/67/P